The Politics of Greed

WORLD SOCIAL CHANGE

Series Editor: Mark Selden

The Politics of Greed

How Privatization Structured Politics in Central and Eastern Europe

Andrew Harrison Schwartz

Prologue by John Zysman

Foreword by David Ellerman

With the assistance of Jordan Gans-Morse

ROWMAN & LITTLEFIELD PUBLISHERS, INC.
Lanham • Boulder • New York • Toronto • Plymouth, UK

ROWMAN & LITTLEFIELD PUBLISHERS, INC.

Published in the United States of America
by Rowman & Littlefield Publishers, Inc.
A wholly owned subsidary of The Rowman & Littlefield Publishing Group, Inc.
4501 Forbes Boulevard, Suite 200, Lanham, Maryland 20706
www.rowmanlittlefield.com

Estover Road
Plymouth PL6 7PY
United Kingdom

British Library Cataloguing in Publication Information Available

Library of Congress Cataloging-in-Publication Data

Schwartz, Andrew, 1957–
    The politics of greed : how privatization structured politics in Central and Eastern
Europe / Andrew Harrison Schwartz ; prologue by John Zysman ; foreword by David
Ellerman with the assistance of Jordan Gans-Morse.
        p. cm. — (World social change)
    Includes bibliographical references and index.
    ISBN-13: 978-0-7425-5307-1 (cloth : alk. paper)
    ISBN-10: 0-7425-5307-8 (cloth : alk. paper)
    ISBN-13: 978-0-7425-5308-8 (pbk. : alk. paper)
    ISBN-10: 0-7425-5308-6 (pbk. : alk. paper)
    1. Privatization—Europe, Eastern.   2. Privatization—Europe, Central.   3.
Privatization—Former Soviet republics.   I. Title.   II. Series.
    HD4140.7.S39 2006
    338.947'05—dc22

                                                                      2006010114

Printed in the United States of America

♾™ The paper used in this publication meets the minimum requirements of American
National Standard for Information Sciences—Permanence of Paper for Printed
Library Materials, ANSI/NISO Z39.48–1992.

Contents

Figures

Notes and Abbreviations

FINANCIAL

CZK Czech (prior to January 1, 1993, Czechoslovakian) crowns
$ United States dollars
DM   Deutschmarks

For most of 1989 to 1992, CZK = 20 to 25 US$.
For most of 1992 to 1997, CZK = 25 to 30 US$.

bn   billion
mn   million

FDI   Foreign direct investment
MNC   Multinational corporation
IPF   Investment privatization fund

INSTITUTIONS AND ORGANIZATIONS

Banks
KB   Komerční banka (Commercial Bank)
IPB   Investiční and poštovní banka (Investment and Postal Bank)
ČSOB Československá obchodní banka (Czechoslovak Trading Bank)
ČS   Česká spořitelna (Czech Savings Bank)

State
FNP   Czech Fund of National Property
MIT   Czech Ministry of Industry and Trade
MoP   Czech Ministry of Privatization
MoF   Czech Ministry of Finance

CZECH AND SLOVAK POLITICAL PARTIES AND POLITICAL MOVEMENTS

ODA	Civic Democratic Alliance
ODS	Civic Democratic Party
OF	Civic Forum
VPN	Public Against Violence (Slovak)
KDU-ČSL	Christian Democratic Union–Czech People's Party
KDS	Christian Democratic Party
ČSSD	Czech Social Democratic Party
KSČ	Czech Communist Party

Prologue

John Zysman

In *The Politics of Greed*, Andrew Schwartz provides a unique perspective on the creation of a market economy from the remnants of the Soviet-style command economies. The book combines the theoretical power of a fine young scholar with the insight of an accomplished businessman experienced in the chaotic workings of commodity markets. Making sense of the creation of market economies and of property in Central and Eastern Europe really required both the understanding of a scholar as well as the instincts that come from firsthand experience in the marketplace. Academic training and theory could provide the frameworks within which to situate the transition, but too often the real logic and motivations of the actors were simply misunderstood. The journalistic literature of the day often captured the greed and confusion that characterized these times but found itself mired in the detail without a means to make sense of the whole story.

Schwartz was able to integrate a theory of transition politics with a practical understanding of the confused emergence of markets and property. He saw the market strategies for what they were—efforts to capture the resources of the old system—and understood the political strategies to build property rights as an extension of that objective. Before Schwartz entered graduate school, he was an accomplished commodities trader. There are many commodities traders, operating from seats on the exchanges owned by their employers and trading with the money of their clients. Schwartz was different, a real entrepreneur and businessman. The seats on the exchanges were his, and he traded principally on his own behalf. The chaos of the exchanges prepared him well to see deeply into the transitions he studied as a scholar. *The Politics of Greed* embeds analysis of the process by which property was seized in a story of and about politics.

This book, published posthumously, is the legacy of an excellent young scholar and a testament to the enormous talent of a remarkable man. Andy was straightforward and blunt—straightforward with a depth of insight and feeling expressed with humor and consistent decency that set him apart. He had an enthusiasm and generosity of spirit that were truly unique. At the Berkeley

Roundtable on the International Economy (BRIE), the research institute where Andy found a home over the years, all spoke not only of his ability and capacity, but of the endless small kindnesses and gentle gestures that made so many people's lives better. His passionate engagement with life, with those around him, was expressed in all ways, but not least as a student and scholar. Andy had an inquisitive, intuitive, brilliant mind; he never fooled himself and was reluctant to allow others to fool themselves. This capacity was fundamental to all aspects of Andy's life and was evident not only in his scholarship but also in frequent conversations about everything from politics to friends, events, and, of course, continuously and endlessly, sports. He was never willing to accept authority as the basis for a conclusion but had to shake a problem and pursue it, until it released some inner truth. With remarkable quickness and agility he could leap to a conclusion, and then he would battle until he could be shown why or in what way he must think that question through again.

Andrew Schwartz had the potential to shape how we all would see and understand market economies and political democracies; had he had the time to settle into a life of scholarship, his contribution would have been great and unique. From the beginning Andy was more than a student; he was a peer and became a friend. I learned so much from him both about life and about the intellectual pursuits we shared. It was an honor and privilege to know him and to work with him.

Berkeley, May 2006

Foreword

David Ellerman

It was an unprecedented event—the transition during the 1990s from socialism/communism to a private property market economy in Central and Eastern Europe, in the Soviet Union, and even in China. There were no blueprints or prior case studies. Hence there was a "Great Debate" about how best to do it. Over a decade has passed since those transition debates, so it is time for some calm stock taking of what happened in fact, as well as intellectually evaluating the arguments made then and now. One of the biggest opportunities now is to review the self-knowledge of the West and its understanding of economics and politics. The historically new challenge of the transition put great strain on the West's know-how. The self-confident advisors from the West were, in effect, "born on third base and thought they knew how to hit a triple." But their advice on "how to hit a triple" usually turned out to be ineffective, if not institutionally naïve, and often only made matters worse.

In the transition, the case of Czechoslovakia and later the Czech Republic was perhaps the most important at least from the viewpoint of the neoliberal approach often known as the "Washington consensus." The Czechs under Václav Klaus were the pioneers. Where others hesitated and searched for solid ground, the Klaus-led Czech revolutionaries charged off into the unknown. It was their seeming success that induced other countries and the major Western advisory institutions such as the World Bank and the IMF to make the "Czech way"—voucher privatization and institutional shock therapy—into the One Best Way to make the transition. The adoption of these methods in Russia and in many of the former Soviet countries (with even more disastrous results) was based on the seeming success of the Czech privatization program.

This is why Andrew Schwartz's case study focusing on the Czech transition is so important. A similar study of Poland, Hungary, or even Russia would not have such an importance for historical understanding. The "Czech miracle" was the model for nearly a decade of policy advice to transition countries from the major institutions—advice that went on long after the bottom fell out of the Czech miracle. For instance, long after the hollowness of the "Czech success story" was clear and even after the 1998 meltdown in Russia, the World Bank in 1999 foisted a voucher privatization program on war-torn Bosnia—with, by then, quite predictable results.

Andy Schwartz had direct knowledge and involvement in the Czech events. Much of what is conveyed in the description of the "selling" of the voucher program could only have been felt by someone personally present. That sort of knowledge is a strength that goes well beyond the usual citations by a historian later picking over the remains of those intense times. I also lived in Eastern Europe during those times (in Ljubljana, 1990–1992). I incorporated in Prague a Czech affiliate of my Slovene consulting company, and so I was often present in Prague and participated in the same debates (e.g., through interviews in the Czech press), although I didn't know Andy at the time. In 1992, I joined the World Bank but continued to work in Eastern Europe as bank staff. Schwartz's sense of what was going on rings absolutely true to me from my own experiences with the debates in Prague as well as in Slovenia.

The transition functioned as an optic or a mirror to reflect back to the West its own understanding of what was important in a market economy and in a democratic polity. The inadequacies of the Western-supported programs of voucher privatization and institutional shock therapy were reflections of inadequacies in the West's self-understanding of what is important in a market economy and of how basic institutions change. Schwartz's analysis contributes to a new understanding based on the tragedies of the Czech voucher privatization program and the attempts to mimic it elsewhere.

What were those Western presuppositions about a market economy? Voucher privatization grew out of an understanding of a market economy that sees Wall Street—the stock market—as *the* key institution—not simply as a quasi-religious symbol or totem but as the central feature of a proper market economy. Not an entrepreneurial class with a long-term commitment to business development, not agile closely held small- and medium-sized businesses to adapt quickly to the new environment, and not a banking sector that can finance such businesses—but a stock market! Since voucher privatization would in a sense "jump-start" the stock market by putting almost all medium-to-large firms on the market, it was thus seen as the quickest transition to a market economy.

The scheme failed in many ways; it even failed to jump-start the stock market. Hungary and Poland developed their stock markets in a more gradual and better regulated way so that today they have stronger stock markets than the Czechs. It is the old tortoise and hare story all over again. Schwartz brought out this story well—the fastest runner out of the blocks is not necessarily the first across the finish line.

Perhaps Schwartz's telling of this story is particularly powerful because he partly shared the view of the importance of the stock market. Andy's earlier formation was as a successful commodity trader in New York (before returning to graduate school to get his PhD) so he viewed the economy through a "market" lens rather than an "enterprise" lens. Hence, his critique is all the more telling, coming from one who shared some of the presuppositions. In hindsight, not only was voucher privatization the wrong way to build a stock market but it was also even more wrong in focusing the transitional reforms on "financial engineering" rather than on reanimating the previously strong Czechoslovakian industrial tradition.

As emphasized by some economists such as Herbert Simon, a modern industrialized economy is characterized not just by successful markets but by successful organizations. Indeed, the "economies of modern industrialized society can more appropriately be labeled organizational economies than market economies" (Simon 1991, 42). From this perspective, the greatest damage done by voucher privatization was not the overlisting and underregulation of the stock market, but the whole shift of perspective away from the organizations that needed the long-term commitment of the participants (managers and workers) to be modernized—a shift of perspective to making money through sharp trading with shares and eventually through the tunneling of assets out of the enterprises.

In a time of massive systemic change, people need some stable ground upon which they can rebuild their lives. The two most important places are one's living place (house or flat) and one's workplace. By far the most successful transition was in China where the most remarkable increases in production took place in the so-called township village enterprises or TVEs. There was little labor mobility in China during the 1980s and 1990s. And there was a hard-budget constraint; unlike the state-owned enterprises, there were no government bailouts for failing TVEs. This combination of circumstances generated a strong commitment on the part of the managers and workers in each TVE; it was their stable ground, if they could make it work. Like the captain and crew on a ship without lifeboats, the managers and workers knew that it was their one chance to make it through the storms of transition and to be successful.

In the decades before the 1990s, there were liberalizing and decentralizing experiments that had started in Yugoslavia with self-management, in Hungary with goulash communism, in Poland with Solidarity, and in the Soviet Union with the Gorbachev reforms. These reforms had given managers and workers a larger role in their enterprises so that the workplace was potentially a stable ground where people could rebuild their lives during the transition without getting "blown off their feet" by the winds of change. If further reforms had

created a hard-budget constraint, then the circumstances would have been created (such as in the TVEs) for the managers and workers to see that restructuring
their enterprises was their one best chance for any success.

But voucher privatization was designed to have precisely the opposite effect. Like city planners who see home ownership as just another impediment to
their grand redevelopment schemes, any stable grounds in the workplace upon
which people could rebuild their lives were seen by the academic economists
and neoliberal advisors as "rigidities" and "impediments" to their dreams of institutional shock therapy. The previous decentralizing reforms that empowered
managers and workers needed to be reversed to remove those "impediments
to restructuring." The trick was to sell people on trading off their influence
in their own workplace for a packet of shares (in companies or in investment
funds) that they could buy on the stock market with their vouchers.

Isn't Wall Street how people do well in the West? And don't the people in the
postsocialist countries want to have the good life "like in the West"? And isn't
the whole idea of people having direct influence and control in their workplace
some kind of "socialist" thing anyway? Don't these people need to give up
these socialist things to benefit from the magic of the market? Aren't those
who oppose voucher privatization either some sort of crypto-communists or
simply those managers and workers who are trying to protect their "rents" and
special privileges acquired under the old system? Those were the arguments
of the "*voucheristas*" and their advisors.

But if all companies of any size were floated on the stock market and people were given vouchers to buy shares, then how would the enterprises get
restructured? In the neoliberal perspective, "restructuring" was seen as something that suddenly takes place once "assets" on the stock market gravitate into
the right hands, such as the hands of foreign owners who would bring capital
and expertise. In a caricature of the most simplistic theory of organizational
change, experts come in to tell people what to do, people follow the instructions
(otherwise they are fired), and, voilà, companies are restructured to function
in a market economy.

Alas, it didn't work that way. In the first place, the stock market was not
how a Western industrial company would want to invest. Once the individual
shareholders or investment funds knew a foreign company was buying shares,
they would hold out to get an excellent price from the deep-pocketed buyer or
they would hang on to the shares to get in on the capital gains as the Western
owner would restructure the target company. Since the foreign companies knew
this obvious fact, they preferred either direct asset deals (not share deals) or they
preferred buying all the shares directly from a privatization agency, not trying
to corral shares on a public stock market. Even though the "magic of markets"
was a quasi-religious belief for the "experts" in "private sector development"

in the World Bank and other development agencies, the whole theory about restructuring coming out of shares going on the public stock market to the best owner was a nonstarter—even for a perfectly regulated market. Foreign investment didn't come through the Czech stock market not simply because it was so poorly regulated; for the reasons just mentioned, the deep-pocketed foreign companies were not coming to that market anyway. If the powerful voucher investment funds could not, for the most part, cash in by selling shares to well-heeled foreign buyers, then the funds had to find—and did find—other ways to milk value out of their accumulated share holdings—the fraudulent asset-stripping schemes now known as "tunneling."

Hence, the voucher privatization scheme managed to disenfranchise the managers and workers from being in a position to have to learn and change in order to survive—and the scheme even created conditions that would ward off investment by Western industrial companies. Instead, it created a "feeding frenzy" of frauds and schemes devised by the voucher investment funds to liquidate productive assets and tunnel out the wealth—rather than to restructure the firms.

Luckily the neoliberal theory about any stable ground being an impediment to change was not extended to people's living places. The housing stock was not voucherized to jump-start the housing market. Instead of renationalizing the housing stock, people were generally allowed to turn the stable occupancy arrangements that had evolved in socialist times into private ownership.

The "born-on-third-base" experts—who see the stock market as "obviously" the central part of a private property market economy—are not the only ones who might profit from rethinking the transition. There were also lessons about institutional change. From Edmund Burke's critique of the Jacobins (as they were later called) in the French Revolution to Friedrich Hayek's critique of the Bolshevik or, more generally, socialist attempts at social engineering, there is a strong classical-liberal (in the European sense) tradition of conservative principles of social change. On principle, they opposed grand schemes to engineer social change in favor of pragmatism and decentralized experimentation. Social engineering schemes would uproot people from traditions and cultures where they could find the stability to make their own plans, and would tend to create a disembedded and atomized population that could be better manipulated "for their own good" by government planners.

But with pitifully few exceptions, this classical-liberal tradition of opposing socially engineered change forgot its principles as it toasted the "market Bolsheviks" such as Klaus in the Czech Republic and Anatoly Chubais in Russia, who used voucher privatization and institutional shock therapy to try to engineer change in the opposite direction from socialism to a market economy. One exemplary exception was Ralf Dahrendorf (1990) who wrote a book[1] deliberately echoing Burke's epistle and that called for open experimentation and a methodology of trial and error in making the transition. But unlike the "scientific socialists" of the past, the scientific economists of today have the Truth and know the One Best Way, so experimentation is only a detour and waste of time. The best representative of scientific economics in the transition debates was Jeffrey Sachs, who not only sponsored voucher privatization and institutional shock therapy but who specifically chided Dahrendorf for not appreciating those Truths: "If instead the philosophy were one of open experimentation, I doubt that the transformation would be possible at all, at least without costly and dangerous wrong turns" (Sachs 1993, 5).

Why did the neoliberal experiment unfold in such a pure and relatively extreme manner in Czechoslovakia? Schwartz gets it right. It was precisely because Czechoslovakia was such a conservative communist state that there were little or none of the decentralizing reforms that had been carried out in other countries. This lesson also matches up with another fact—that the most radical experiments were sponsored by those who had been in external or internal exile and had not been involved in the previous political struggles and reforms. Again and again across the transition economies, there was the phenomenon of the people being elected in the new democratic elections of 1989–1991 being not those embedded reformers who had worked within the old system for democratic and decentralizing change but those who had been in splendid external or internal exile and who thus were "clean" of any such past compromises. Klaus had been in an economics research institute and Dušan Tříska was a mathematically trained computer geek. Tomáš Ježek was a little more worldly (his brother Miroslav was a company manager) and, accordingly, he was a moderating influence among the radicals and one of the first to later see what had gone wrong. Real politics is based on compromise, experimentation, and pragmatism, not on a theoretical scheme such as voucher privatization that can be rammed through Parliament during the "window of opportunity" offered by the "fog of transition."

Schwartz is right that voucher privatization (where it was used) was primarily a political strategy to empower and enrich a new political class that had arisen in the elections of the early 1990s. It involved pulling economic power back to the state and undoing all the decentralized experiments where those had taken place. When the Berlin Wall fell and the socialist idea collapsed, the earlier embedded reformers who had already wrestled some power away from the state wanted to continue in the same direction toward the market. They did not want to recentralize power in the state's hands particularly when the state was being run by untested ideologues who had not been involved in the earlier reforms and by economics professors steeped in Western textbooks but with little practical experience.

This was nowhere more apparent than in Poland. When the Polish government tried to pass a version of voucher privatization that started by "corporatizing" all enterprises of any size as state-owned joint stock companies, Solidarity did not accept their hard-won decentralized power being taken away and everything turned into a crapshoot on the stock market. There were self-management councils dominated by Solidarity in the larger state-owned enterprises and they were not about to be cast aside by neoliberals wanting to recentralize power "in the right hands" so that it could be "properly" distributed. Similar battles took place in the other countries that had some history of decentralizing reforms under socialism.

But not in Czechoslovakia. The earlier Dubček reforms had failed and not enough time had passed to try again. Hence, Klaus virtually had carte blanche to try radical changes. There was little or no decentralized power in the enterprises that was legitimated by previous reforms to give opposition—only the delegitimated managers from the old regime. Hence, the most radical versions of neoliberal ideas met little resistance and were implemented in a relatively short period of time. And they became the model for the major development agencies (World Bank, IMF, and USAID) to promote in many of the other transition economies. History will eventually record what we—for better or worse—learn from the experience with the "Czech model" for the transition. But this book tells the story of how it all started.

NOTE

1. Ralf Dahrendorf, *Reflections on the Revolution in Europe: In a Letter Intended to Have Been Sent to a Gentleman in Warsaw* (New York: Random House, 1990). Burke's book two centuries earlier (1790) was titled *Reflections on the French Revolution: In a Letter Intended to Have Been Sent to a Gentleman in Paris*.

Acknowledgments

It gives me great pleasure to acknowledge and to thank the people who have made this book possible. First, I owe a special debt to those Czechs who took time out from busy schedules to educate me about their country, their nation, and Central Europe. I hope that I will not embarrass them with my errors and misjudgment. A limited list includes Vladimír Benáček, Petra Buzková, Vladislav Flek, Petr Havlík, Věra Havlíková, Jan Kavan, Josef Kotrba, František Mach, Jitka Machová, Milan Matěka, Jan Mládek, Helena Opolecka, Jana Reschová, Alice Sandersová, Jan Sokol, Jindřích Soukup, Jana Soupková, Vlasta Šafaříková, Jan Vrba, and Václav Žák.

A substantial part of my education about the Czech Republic also came from a very supportive community of foreigners living and working in Prague. We debated Czech politics and economics for countless hours, typically over beers at a local pub. These included Tom Bridle, Colum Garrity, Howard Golden, Amy Newman, Mitchell Orenstein, Mark Sanders, Jonathan Stein, Susan Storey, Petr Škla, Jonathan Terra, and Jonathan Zimmerman. I owe a special debt to Quentin Reed, who was at various times a partner in crime in digging up materials and information on Czech corruption.

I also benefited greatly from those who read and commented on different portions of the manuscript. For this chore, I must thank Dan Adler, John Connelly, Eureka Endo, Patricia Johnson, Quentin Reed, Petr Škla, and Jonathan Terra. Jonathan Stein and Jonathan Zimmerman deserve special acknowledgment for their efforts in bringing the book to publication. Jordan Gans-Morse worked as a research assistant for this volume, and at various times as a co-collaborator. Jiří Havel was a full co-collaborator, especially regarding chapter 10 and the updating of the manuscript; errors in these sections are mine alone, though. The book would have turned out far worse had these people not been involved.

I was incredibly lucky to have had a dissertation committee so committed and patient. Each member of the committee toiled over several drafts of my prose. Ken Jowitt inspired me to think creatively about why, and with what consequence, Central and East Europeans might approach problems from an unfamiliar cultural lens. Bob Kagan taught me about the importance of market regulation to functioning markets and democracies. Jonah Levy's kind and

xxi

painstaking analysis of the dissertation arguments challenged me to improve my logic; I am still not certain as to whether I have approached his high standards. Stephen Cohen taught me not to be afraid to try to write with innovation. I also owe and can't adequately repay Steve for his many years as a wonderful collaborator and close friend.

My overwhelming gratitude goes to my committee chair and mentor, John Zysman. Over the years, John has taught me about political science, about academics, and about life. He prodded me to do my best work, which was not always an easy and pain-free task. The book might have been incoherent and might not have existed without his generous and kind input. I will always be in his debt.

Financial resources were provided, at various times, by the John L. Simpson Memorial Research Fellowship, Institute for the Study of World Politics, International Research and Exchanges Board (IREX), the Institute of International Education (IIE), and the Berkeley Roundtable on the International Economy (BRIE).

Finally, my greatest debt is to my wife, Dagmar Machová Schwartz, who taught me firsthand what it meant to be Czech, patiently listened to my crazy ideas, and comforted me while I struggled with illness to finish this book. I dedicate it with the greatest love to her.

Introduction—Politics and Privatization

The program of liberalism ... if condensed into a single word, would have to read: *property*, that is, private ownership of the means of production.

—Ludwig von Mises

The liberty of a democracy is not safe if the people tolerate the growth of private power to a point where it becomes stronger than their democratic state itself.

—Franklin Delano Roosevelt

The privatization of entire economies following the collapse of communism in Central and Eastern Europe countries (CEECs) challenged Western thinking about politics and economics. Western policymakers and advisors pressured reformers to implement a free-market orthodoxy that prioritized market-determined prices, open trade, and especially private ownership, while diminishing any activity associated with the state. They believed that economic liberalization was the foundation for political freedom, a prescription proven by the waves of democratic development sweeping the Third World, the end of communism, and the ascendancy of the United States. The prominent voices advocating what came to be known as the Washington consensus were economists in the World Bank, International Monetary Fund (IMF), Organization for Economic Development (OECD), and from American universities, especially Harvard and MIT. Striving to create liberal democracy, reformers in Central and Eastern Europe initiated the largest transfer of wealth in human history, privatizing whole economies to what would truly be a first, private-owners class.

The first decade of liberalization in the postcommunist countries revealed a rich diversity of political and economic outcomes, several of which cannot be labeled capitalist and democratic. Countries that were fortunate enough to border on the European Union (EU) and NATO countries appeared to be building economies and political systems bounded by the entry requirements of the new, enlarged European political economy. Others, notably the former Soviet Union republics (FSU), were creating the trappings of free markets and democracies, such as private ownership and elections. Nonetheless these regimes now

1

resemble the corrupt and oppressive regimes along the lines of 1990s Latin America or Africa. A third set of countries, such as Romania, Bulgaria, the former Yugoslavia, and Slovakia, seem to have had chances to evolve in either direction, following the Central European or the FSU path. These postcommunist countries have generated market and political systems that vary widely in their institutions, economic performance, policy outcomes, and adherence to the rule of law. A regional convergence to free markets and democracy seems remote, and would be motivated by external factors rather than by an intrinsic causal connection between political and economic liberalism. How can we explain the surprising cross-national variation in the evolution of the postcommunist societies?

This book contends that national privatization strategies were often decisive for the future of political and economic development in the formerly state-owned economies. Privatization established the ownership structure, legal infrastructure, state institutions, ethical and legal precedents, and government-business relationships that are at the core of politics and economics, particularly in Central Europe. State officials, business leaders, factory managers, workers, the public, and foreign investors and organizations were consumed by privatization during the transition period. Corporate restructuring, macroeconomic policy, public political discourse, and political party development were of secondary importance to local players as state ownership stakes became available for transfer to private hands. Privatization generated an elite, a new capitalist class that would determine political and economic development, often without regard to the public interest. Privatization politics ultimately generated distinct forms of politics and markets in the postcommunist countries that belied the expectations of the Washington consensus that privately owned economies would produce liberal democracy and prosperity.

Conventional, usually economically grounded, analysts haven't valued the on-the-ground struggles for property as enduring events in CEECs. According to the Washington consensus, privatization is a means to an end, a characterless ramp from state to market. The reform process—and the criminality that has come to accompany it—is irrelevant over the long term, so long as it produces private owners. New private owners will build the regulatory institutions and write and enforce the laws that protect their property from the natural economic rent-seeking and political tyranny of the state. The tactics, organization, and orientation of the competing interests for state property recede as the incentives of private ownership take hold. According to the Washington consensus, the production of private owners—privatization—is the central imperative of state-dominated economies, no matter how it is achieved.

The Washington consensus assumed special meaning in the postcommunist societies of CEECs. The state owner of entire economies bore obvious responsibility for decades of economic stagnation and political alienation. The evident contrast to communism was the prosperous and free capitalist West, and especially the United States, where private owners were the dominant and visible actors in economics and politics. Reformers and their Western supporters pronounced "No bourgeois, no democracy," as did Schumpeter, Moore, and others (Schumpeter 1942/1975; Moore 1966). Drawing on what they perceived as the hard experience of communism, CEEC reformers supported policies intended to deprive the state of economic and political resources, such as privatization.

The thorny privatization issues for reformers centered on *how*—not *whether*—to privatize transition economies. The main challenge lay in overcoming the anticipated opposition of entrenched interests whose authority was based on control of assets in the state-owned economy and of populations bound to suffer from unemployment precipitated by privatization. Fortunately, the abrupt fall of communism had opened a historic chance, a "window of opportunity" for reformers. Reformers could privatize while threatened interests were in disarray and while popular enthusiasm for markets and democracy was robust, but only if they acted quickly. Rapid privatization's new owners, though they might resemble criminal mafias, would serve as a temporary coalition for reform, to be replaced in time by a democratically inclined middle class. Rapid privatization, the recommended policy choice for reformers, was at its core an opportunistic, top-down political strategy.

We can begin to evaluate only now, more than ten years after the fall of communism in the Eastern Bloc, the Washington consensus's best practice of rapid privatization. Our assessment hinges on the behavior and influence of the first private owners. Have the first private owners in countries that privatized rapidly restructured companies or transferred them to owners who would? Have the first private owners (or their immediate successors) pressed for secure private property rights, such as initiatives to increase transparency and honesty in government? Did the nondemocratic political tactics that enabled rapid privatization impact the character of politics after the state completed privatization? Did privatization shrink the role of the state? Did rapid privatization produce free markets and democratic politics?

Core values and basic principles governing capitalist political economics are at stake in the answers to those questions. Development models will need to account for the composition, structure, and political influence of privatization's first private owners if these empowered interests disappoint reformers by stripping enterprise assets or by creating institutions that subvert democracy. Recent refinements to the Washington consensus that stress a competent and honest state—the so-called post–Washington consensus—represent institutional attempts to eliminate the extreme immoral tendencies of new owners.

The new consensus may yet prove insufficient if the postcommunist political economies in twenty years' time resemble 1990s Africa or Latin America or even a political economy of a new type, rather than the Western Europe or the United States of today. Finally, we must ask whether any attempt to regulate the first markets, especially capital markets, was bound to fail given conditions in CEECs just after the fall of communism. We may then conclude that theories of market creation (and regulation) need to integrate the state–interest group politics that lie beneath the writing and enforcement of laws and the creation and functioning of market institutions. Either way, the privatization debates in the former communist states in the 1990s rank among the critical political and economic discourses of the modern era.

FUNDAMENTAL CONCEPTS

To frame the discussion, we define privatization as well as capitalism and democracy, the alleged objectives of privatization. *Privatization* as used here refers to "the process that *formally* transfers state-owned assets to private owners." Unless otherwise noted, *privatization* refers to "large privatization," which concerns the ownership transfer of large- and medium-sized enterprises. Privatization does not address directly corporate governance.[1] In addition, privatization does not refer to the transfer of government services (such as education, police, defense, post, or health) to the private sector—a common use of the term in American discourse.[2] Note that privatization in CEECs concerns thousands of enterprises and most of the nation's economic output. Outside the region, privatization normally involves a small number of major enterprises, such as utilities and telecommunications companies. Western and developing-country analysts thus conventionally refer to the privatization of enterprises, while CEEC analysts refer to the privatization of enterprises *and* to the privatization of entire economies.

 Capitalism is "an economic system dominated by the activities of private enterprises." Most developed economies and most CEECs now are "capitalisms" under this formulation (Shonfield 1969).[3] Here we differentiate capitalisms, compatible with contemporary economic liberalism, according to the market environment. High-quality capitalisms are distinguished by open competition among firms and free prices; low-quality capitalisms are distinguished by relatively closed competition among firms and state-controlled prices. The level and character of foreign direct investment, corporate restructuring, government intervention in the economy, and capital and product markets may indicate the quality of capitalism.

Democracy, following Schumpeter's classic institutional formulation, is "a series of electoral competitions for popular leadership."[4] Or, in Przeworski's succinct formulation, "Democracy is a system in which parties lose elections" (Przeworski 1991, 10). Most contemporary political systems and most CEECs fulfill the election requirement and thereby qualify as "democracies." We differentiate democracies, compatible with contemporary notions of political liberalism, according to citizen participation in government. High-quality democracies are marked by active citizen participation in government; low-quality democracies are marked by limited citizen participation in government (Collier and Mahoney 1995, 2; Dahl 1971). Weber's idea of democracy expresses the spirit of a "high quality of democracy" or "participatory democracy": "the *leveling of the governed* in the face of the governing and bureaucratically articulated group" (Weber 1978, 986; italics added). The level of corruption in the government and in the economy, and the openness and equality of access to policymakers and to information, may indicate the quality of democracy.[5]

Variations in privatization policy generate multiple paths of development, admixtures of capitalism and democracy, which are determined by internal politics, economic fundamentals, ideology, nationalism, and location in the emerging global political economy. Moreover, the new class of private owners in CEECs is most likely to be a guardian of its privilege and power and enemy of free-market and open dissent, contrary to the Washington consensus. The danger is that the new private owners generate a version of "pseudodemocracy," "competitive authoritarianism," "delegated democracy," or crony capitalism.[6] Privatization, above all, concerns the transfer of political power from the former communist elite to another elite, who may be called the "first owners."

POLITICS AND PRIVATIZATION

Privatization establishes trajectories of economic (and political) development by establishing the first owners as well as institutional incentive structures. State officials are under domestic pressure to choose privatization strategies that reflect the political and financial influence of disparate interests. Some of those interests grew out of established industrial or bureaucratic bases, while the privatization process itself fostered new interests, seemingly out of thin air. In the Czech Republic, for instance, the two men of transition who allegedly amassed the largest fortunes, V. Kožený and P. Kellner, were under thirty years of age in 1989. State decision-makers had the greatest latitude to choose privatization strategies without the influence of economic interests earlier rather than later in the process, though the (often corrupt) input of those interests was inevitable, whatever the privatization approach.[7]

Privatization decisions are not only about who gets what but also about how markets and politics operate. In particular, privatization establishes four essential characteristics of what we will call an ownership regime (see chapter 3): the resources and skills of the new private owners; the first-ownership structure; the financial institutions; and the autonomy and capacity of the state market regulator. The last item is crucial, because the state is the primary check on the actions of private owners in efficient markets and participatory democracies. A rapid privatization strategy that undervalues the importance of a regulatory framework, especially a regulatory framework for financial markets, may work perversely, nurturing groups whose interests are inimical to the development of capitalism and democracy. The postprivatization development hinges on the motives and behavior of the winners of privatization conflicts, the first owners. The political, legal, and institutional environment that is an artifact of privatization helps determine incentives and penalties for first owners and other actors. Privatization's first owners (or their successors) may or may not restructure enterprises, may or may not sell at the highest prices, may or may not promote laws that protect private property equally, and may or may not practice a high quality of democracy. Privatization generates more than just private owners; it generates private interests as well.

The argument presented here about the enduring importance of privatization and its political and historic roots supports the following hypotheses:

1. Privatization Context

Privatization in Central Europe may further the quality of capitalism and democracy; privatization in the FSU may have relatively little impact on the quality of capitalism and democracy.

Countries with better possibilities to integrate economically and politically into the West and with relatively antagonistic public attitudes toward the communist regimes have better chances to implement privatization programs with democratic and capitalist outcomes (see table I.1). Those initial conditions—geography, communist past, and economic fundamentals—tend to dominate the outcomes of subsequent market-oriented reforms, contrary to Washington-consensus evaluations (EBRD 1999; Åslund 2002). Indeed, the grouping of Category 1 countries with high privatization scores at the top of table I.2 illustrates that the possibilities for market reforms depend first on initial conditions and only secondarily on the determination and will of policymakers.

Table I.1. Privatization Environments

Category 1: West European Norms and Institutions	Category 2: Domestic and Russian Norms and Institutions	Category 3: Intermediate Cases
Czech Republic	Russia	Slovakia
Hungary	Ukraine	Serbia
Poland	Moldova	Croatia
Slovenia	Armenia	Bosnia
Estonia	Azerbaijan	Latvia
	Georgia	Lithuania
	Kazakhstan	Romania
	Kyrgyz Republic	Bulgaria
	Turkmenistan	Albania
	Uzbekistan	Macedonia
	Tajikistan	
	Belarus	

Category 1 Countries—West European Norms and Institutions Likely to Shape Country Evolution: Central Europe

Typical first owners were likely to restructure enterprises and protect property rights, thanks to optimistic prospects for Western investment and the potential for creating competitive companies. Governments were likely to foster a Western-style rule of law to facilitate inclusion into European alliances, including the European Union and NATO. Popular opinion tended to discredit interest groups likely to block economic reform—bureaucrats and enterprise interest groups (managers and workers). Those groups suffered from perceived close association with the prior regime, whom many people blamed for political, economic, and sometimes even cultural (read: Russian) backwardness. "Returning to Europe" was a theme common to nearly every new government in the region in 1989. That environment offered possibilities that privatization would generate high measures of capitalism and democracy, with key questions likely to involve the institutional mix, the speed of change, and the national place in the European political economy.

Category 2 Countries—Russian Influence and Domestic Factors Likely to Shape Country Evolution: FSU

Typical first owners in the FSU might milk the state for subsidies and favors (all the while blocking enforcement of property rights), since the carrot of significant Western investment is not usually available (save for raw material extraction, refinement, and distribution) and companies may not be competitive on world markets. Moreover, government officials lack the outside stimulus to

Table I.2. Privatization Diversity in Postcommunist Countries, 1999

Country	Score	Primary Method	Secondary Method
Czech Republic (1)	4.0	Voucher	Direct
Hungary (1)	4.0	Direct	MEBO
Slovakia (3)	4.0	Direct	Voucher
Estonia (1)	4.0	Direct	Voucher
Poland (1)	3.3	Direct	MEBO
Slovenia (1)	3.3	MEBO	Voucher
Russia (2)	3.3	Voucher	Direct
Georgia (2)	3.3	Voucher	Direct
Kyrgyz Republic (2)	3.0	Voucher	MEBO
Lithuania (3)	3.0	Voucher	Direct
Bulgaria (3)	3.0	Direct	Voucher
Croatia (3)	3.0	MEBO	Voucher
Kazakhstan (2)	3.0	Voucher	Direct
Latvia (3)	3.0	Direct	Voucher
Macedonia (3)	3.0	MEBO	Direct
Moldova (2)	3.0	Voucher	Direct
Armenia (2)	3.0	Voucher	MEBO
Romania (3)	2.7	MEBO	Voucher
Uzbekistan (2)	2.7	MEBO	Direct
Ukraine (2)	2.3	MEBO	Direct
Azerbaijan (2)	2.0	MEBO	Voucher
Albania (2)	2.0	MEBO	Voucher
Tajikistan (2)	2.0	Direct	Voucher
Turkmenistan (2)	1.7	MEBO	Direct
Belarus (2)	1.0	MEBO	Voucher
Bosnia (2)	–	Voucher	Direct

Notes:

a. *Source:* EBRD, "Transition Report," Washington, DC, 1999 (transcribed from *Transition,* World Bank, January–February 2002, 10).

b. MEBO, Management-Employee Buyout; Direct, Direct Sale; Voucher, Voucher Privatization.

c. Classification: 1 = Minimal Progress; 2 = Scheme Ready for Implementation, Some Firms Divested; 3 = More Than 25% Assets Privatized; 4 = More Than 50% Assets Privatized and Substantial Progress on Corporate Governance.

d. Figures in parentheses () represent categories in table I.1.

institute a Western-style rule of law, since the prospect of incorporation into European institutions is distant and the greatest influence emanates from the corrupt power elite in Russia. Elite alliances comprised of bureaucrats, first owners, and enterprise interest groups cow and intimidate the media and popular opinion to maintain power. The objective of elites is to dominate political parties, unions, and other manifestations of civil society, cutting off all incipient populism. A closed system of ruling elites in the FSU also conforms to the apparent popular comfort with authoritarian government and the traditional distrust of Western values (including individual freedom). Contrary to Central Europe, politics and history may limit the possibility of a capitalist and especially democratic future in the FSU. Privatization in Category 2 countries does not translate easily into progress toward capitalism and the market. Rather, privatization signifies the consolidation of economic power into the hands of a political elite that already exists.

Category 3 Countries—Intermediate Cases: The Baltics and Southeastern Europe

In these countries, the influence of initial conditions was indeterminate. Some intermediate cases could thus be expected to follow a reform path similar to the countries in Category 1, while other cases were likely to go the route of countries in Category 2.

2. Privatization Method

Rapid privatization strategies may generate first owners who delay capitalist and democratic development.

Cross-national variations of political and economic privatization outcomes indicate that there is diversity in the national privatization strategies that have actually been implemented (see table I.2). In particular, Washington consensus's best privatization practice—rapid privatization via the mass distribution of vouchers may:

a. Generate Private Owners Who Seek to Prevent the State from Regulating Markets

Rapid privatization with vouchers led to ownership consolidation in entities (privatization funds) whose managers were exempted from state monitoring. CEEC financial managers took advantage of the lack of effective regulation and engaged in self-dealing, including personal asset accumulation and theft. These managers and their allies blocked legal reforms in order to maintain asset control—invariably in collusion with state officials. The public stock markets that accompanied mass privatization with vouchers invariably became vehicles for self-dealing. This result was wholly unexpected by the Washington consensus, which held that privatization—irrespective of method—would generate an ownership class with a natural interest in open markets and participatory democracy.

b. Discredit Reformers, Prompting Popular Backlash or Apathy

Rapid privatization with vouchers tapped into three dominant strains of the popular mood in the early transition period: extreme anticommunism, pro-Western orientation, and suspicion of foreign (especially German, in Central Europe) ownership. It simultaneously promised to shatter the old system of power, return the newly postcommunist societies to the West, and ensure that assets would remain in native hands. Reformers rode the popularity of voucher privatization to electoral success throughout the region during the 1990s. As local populations increasingly regarded these schemes as cynical tricks to shift power to a new elite at their expense, reformers either lost elections to former communists (Czech Republic, Bulgaria) or allied with the new owners, often against democrats (Russia, Ukraine). Public apathy and revulsion with politics resulted in each case, thereby weakening future democratic prospects.

3. Privatization and Globalization

Privatization strategies that encourage foreign direct investment (FDI) are likely to accelerate the progress of capitalism and democracy.

Privatization was the major conduit for FDI during the transition period, not economic growth, as conventional accounts had mechanically asserted (UNCTAD 1996). It followed that the methods and schedule of privatization determined the timing, character, and extent of foreign involvement in domestic economies (Schwartz and Haggard 1997); FDI, and especially Western FDI, tended to improve company performance dramatically, and it tended to mitigate domestic corruption by inserting corporate ethics and monitoring procedures into domestic companies. Western FDI proved to be especially vital to encouraging professionalism and mitigating corruption in banks, which, in turn, hardened budget constraints and reduced corrupt lending practices throughout the economy. Consequently, countries that encouraged foreign or external ownership of privatized assets (Hungary, Estonia, East Germany) benefited from early and dramatic corporate restructuring and investment. These countries' industries inserted themselves into high value-added segments of the international division of labor, which might have been unattainable later (Schwartz and Haggard 1997). Likewise, countries that pursued voucher privatization strategies (Czech Republic, Bulgaria) delayed or prevented the infusion of FDI, and this led to a bureaucratic structure starved of capital, market access, technology, and experienced and honest management teams—which foreign firms typically injected as part of privatization. The state (or the native first owners) often sold the ones that did survive privatization, but at bargain prices relative to what they might have fetched at the outset of privatization. The first owners sometimes stripped assets prior to selling to foreigners or leaving the company and its debts to banks. Many FSU first owners chose to keep companies rather than sell to foreigners, partly to collect subsidies and favors from the state, but also to build economic empires. Companies in countries that have barely privatized (Romania, Belarus) appear to have hardly restructured as compared with foreign-purchased companies.

Not all FDI benefits development. For instance, Russian FDI throughout the region and Western FDI in Central Asia may have a counterproductive impact on corporate restructuring and on the development of democratic politics. Russian oligarchs, in cooperation with local clans, appear to be establishing linkages across the FSU that may hold the eventual potential for corporate restructuring but deter Western investors in the interim. Nor are these particular sources of FDI liable to allies of democratic change. Moreover, Western investors in raw materials industries, such as oil in Central Asia, appear to support authoritarian regimes in order to counter possible instability.

4. Market Regulation

Competent and independent market regulators are central to capitalism and democracies; financial market regulators are especially important.

Privatization experience and consequences in CEECs demonstrate general arguments about the dangers of unleashed market forces to capitalism and democracy. Figures in positions of asset control will attempt to seize assets for themselves, if penalties are minimal. Moreover, these figures logically will safeguard their position by seeking to co-opt state officials, which presumably have the coercive potential and popular mandate to act in the "public interest." Neoliberals oddly refer to asset stripping as "corruption," when this behavior is in fact economically rational. State officials have no monopoly on "rent seeking." It is Adam Smith's "fellow feeling" and trust that putatively allow for the existence of free markets that is irrational. These deductions imply that functioning markets, including the regulation that sustains them, invariably are political institutions as well as moral and economic institutions. As political institutions, interests may manipulate markets (whatever the written and enforced regulations) in the face of a docile and uninformed population and malleable state regulatory apparatus. This lesson, ironically, is on display in the United States and other developed countries, where the most intricate financial regulatory system failed to prevent corporate CEOs from bilking investors out of trillions of dollars. The post–Washington consensus on advocating bullet-proof regulation in CEECs, while a constructive step, will prove insufficient if it blithely presumes that the politics of markets will resolve in a capitalist and democratic direction.

The mixed privatization experience of CEECs does not imply an argument against private property per se. The communist experience elucidated quite clearly the perils of long-term state domination of the economy. Privatization may set a healthy template for future prosperity and democracy, so long as the state creates an impartial and enforceable market regulatory system at the outset of the transition period. Rather, the argument and evidence presented here address the roots, variations, and consequences of the ways in which states generate private owners. Rapid privatization schemes, in particular, may provoke capital flight, corruption, and economic and political instability, because they neglect the development of state regulatory institutions. In selected circumstances, such as in the FSU, privatization itself may prove counterproductive when the first owners represent interests determined and able to dictate state policy. Surprisingly, capitalism and the pluralism that is fundamental to democracy may prove incompatible goals in the postcommunist states, especially if the new governments pursue at-all-costs policies of private ownership.

Finally, the political and economic takeover of the new class of private owners in many CEECs demonstrates that democracy is not simply a matter of civil society winning over the state. Even if one accepts the conventional logic that recent authoritarian regimes of the Right (Franco Spain, apartheid South Africa) and the Left (European communist countries) voluntarily left the scene due to domestic legitimacy crises (Fukuyama 1992), it does not follow that the ensuing civil society–based governments will be democratic. They may well seek to manipulate government and political organizations to their own ends, ruling by corrupting and intimidating state officials and the population. Part of the story of transition in CEECs is that free-market reformers excluded democrats in the policymaking process in order to implement liberalization, as in Russia and the Czech Republic. And in several countries with authoritarian pasts—Colombia, several African states, and the FSU—the civil society groups in power are neither legitimate nor inherently democratic, despite the state's holding of free elections. An honest analysis of this category of political economy requires a detailed rendering of power relations within civil society and between civil society and the state. The diametric opposite of the authoritarian state therefore is not democratic civil society, and private ownership without restriction may be inimical to political freedom and popular participation in government.

COUNTRY CASES

By analyzing the Washington consensus "success case," rapid privatization in the Czech Republic, this book argues that privatization may set up unique and possibly nondemocratic national trajectories of development.

Czech Privatization: Delayed Development in the Free Market's "Success Case"

At first glance, Czech privatization appears an improbable case to demonstrate the premise that privatization may yield less than ideal economic and political outcomes.[8] The country's radical and novel voucher privatization approach, which distributed shares in the majority of state-owned enterprises to citizens in just a few years and achieved the highest privatization score in the region, appears to be responsible for the Czech Republic's successful emergence from communism. Although the country's macroeconomic performance lagged behind Hungary and Poland until the late 1990s, the Czech Republic is now a member of NATO; has recently joined the EU; has one of the strongest economies in Central and Eastern Europe; and has an economy that is nearly in private hands. Poland and Hungary may well be burdened in the future by substantial state sectors that survived privatization. The Czech Republic boasts free elections, competitive political parties, and a vibrant free press. Czech privatization outcomes evidently validate the conventional wisdom that a rapid and pervasive privatization approach yields a decent quality of capitalism and democracy. It's little wonder that the Czech Republic's novel voucher privatization strategy became the model for postcommunist countries, including Russia.

On the other hand, large-scale corruption characterized Czech privatization. The stress on speed undermined the state's ability to regulate markets; Czech privatization discouraged FDI; and the perceived incquities and scandals stemming from voucher privatization undermined popular support among Czech market reformers. In this contrarian view, the Czech Republic moved to the top of the Visegrád countries (an alliance of Poland, Hungary, Slovakia, and the Czech Republic) primarily due to its natural economic and political advantages—proximity to Germany and West Europe, magnetism as a tourist destination, and entry into the European Union—which cushioned the negative economic and political ramifications of rapid privatization. Shock privatization therapy, no matter how misguided, could not kill the Czech Republic.

The Czech privatization strategy attracted intense international scrutiny. Probably more was written about Czech privatization than that of any other country, with the possible exception of Russia. Ardent reformers were steadfast that the country's voucher privatization approach remain the model for postcommunist countries (Pohl et al. 1997). Discriminating reformers, including some World Bank economists, conceded that Czech privatization could have been implemented with more state attention to controlling corruption and establishing the institutional bases for constructive corporate governance (Nellis 1999; Spicer, McDermott, and Kogut 2000). Others acknowledged that other privatization strategies, such as leasing, were available to Czech reformers (Black, Kraakman, and Tarassova 2000). These views, which came to be incorporated into the post–Washington consensus, usually contended that rapid privatization, if implemented with attention to corporate governance and regulation, would result in a high measure of capitalism and democracy.

J. Stiglitz, as World Bank chief economist, built on the Czech voucher privatization case to offer a more penetrating critique of the Washington consensus and post–Washington consensus views (Stiglitz 1999; Ellerman 2003).[9] He argued that resolving problems of Czech privatization and privatization in other postcommunist countries went beyond regulating privatization better. According to Stiglitz, neoclassical models underestimated informational problems, "including those arising from problems of corporate governance, of social and organizational capital, and of the legal and institutional capital required to make an effective market economy" (Stiglitz 1999). Successful reform strategies, including the process of establishing market institutions, must emanate from a bottom-up analysis of the political economy to adduce current and potential informational asymmetries, rather than from a top-down, Washington-consensus, one-size-fits-all reform strategy.

While sharing Stiglitz's insight that privatization can best be analyzed from the bottom up, the argument presented here takes Stiglitz's argument a step further by emphasizing the politics behind privatization. In the Czech case, the voucher strategy that grew out of privatization politics consciously declined to regulate the privatization process, and it failed to create the regulatory bases for a financial market in privatized shares. Immediate outcomes of Czech asset redistribution were economic—slow economic growth, low FDI, and minimal corporate restructuring—and political—widespread corruption (including the neologism *tunneling*), political apathy, and the fall of the reform government of Václav Klaus. These outcomes reflected the asset management approach and political lobbying of the first Czech ownership class, who often chose to drain assets and co-opt government (and bank) officials rather than invest in enterprises. The asset manipulation games of the first owners only came to a close when foreigners entered the political economy—specifically, when the state sold its domestic bank shares to foreign banks and when the close of privatization finally enabled foreign companies to buy domestic assets. Only at that point did Czech economic indicators begin to turn upward. At the very least, the timing of the Czech comeback forces one to reconsider the Washington and post–Washington consensus.

Methodologically, the bottom-up creation of a political model of privatization demands a detailed "who did, what, when, why?" historical log. Despite all the attention analysts have devoted to Czech privatization, that empirical record has not existed until this book, not even in Czech. Years of painstaking research, including hundreds of conversations and interviews with Czech decision-makers and examination of official privatization documents, personal notes, and newspaper articles, were required to re-create Czech privatization history during the transition period. Building on the understanding and hypothesis derived from the Czech case, this book then considers other country cases in relief, relying primarily on interviews with local policymakers and businessmen and the secondary literature.

Regional Referents: Hungary's Foreign Privatization and Poland's (Hidden) Spontaneous Privatization

Hungary and Poland implemented privatization strategies that differed radically from the Czech approach, under different political regimes and pressures. The key differentiators were in the character and extent of FDI.

The Hungarian government aimed to sell enterprises to foreigners right from the start of transition. The overwhelming justifications were to raise revenues to pay for the accumulated foreign debt and to relieve the cash shortages of individual enterprises.[10] "Other issues, such as corporate governance, long-term marketability of residual shares were hardly considered, if at all" (Mihályi 1996, 4). Due to its privatization policy, Hungarian FDI illustrates a much earlier start—the GE-Tungsram joint venture, for instance, began in 1989—and a much higher and earlier volume of FDI than in either the Czech Republic or in Poland. The result of the Hungary privatization strategy was a dramatic increase in revenues to the budget, the creation of credible financial markets, and support for its FDI green-field investments (FDI that might otherwise have migrated to the country with the region's best-trained labor force, most established industries, and traditional networks instead went elsewhere, given an approach negative to foreign investors, as in the Czech Republic).

Polish privatization relies primarily on insider (both manager and worker types) privatization, institutional privatization (the use of quasi-state investment funds), and no privatization. Polish-style insider privatization (officially termed "liquidation") commonly takes the form of asset auctions (typical in bankruptcy liquidation cases) or leasing arrangements (typical in the liquidation of healthy companies). Neither form is open to foreign participation. The only avenues of foreign participation via liquidation are joint ventures or initial public offerings (IPOs)[11] (Jermakowicz 1995). Institutional privatization also allows no access for FDI, though the new national investment funds subsequently may sell privatized assets to foreign companies.[12] The results in Poland were delays in FDI (though not to the same extent as in the Czech case) while the state privatized many large enterprises gradually or not at all.

Each of the Visegrád countries (except Slovakia) began with different initial positions. However, these are emerging with important similarities in their financial markets, prove to be attractive destinations for FDI, and demonstrate a reasonably high and comparable quality of democracy. Nonetheless, though the three countries adopted radically different approaches, privatization apparently has laid unique legacies for capitalist and democratic growth, captured primarily in the character and extent of FDI.

Failed Privatization in Russia and Ukraine

Further east, in the FSU, privatization has an altogether different meaning than in Central Europe. Privatization in the EU border countries is a process that created an elite class from new and established interests. Privatization in the East, however, marked the consolidation of economic power in the hands of an already existing political plutocracy in combination with the development of unusually well-positioned interests such as sports teams, state ministries, youth organizations, and the like. It is now obvious to scholars of the region—to say nothing of the populations who live in these plutocracies—that privatization helped to corrupt political and economic life, though it might not bear the dominant responsibility.

Russian voucher privatization put industries in the hands of managers and their plutocratic partners. The soon-to-follow "Loans for Shares" privatization approach was an obvious gambit by the new plutocrats to seize state property. Economically, privatization did not seem to lead to comprehensive corporate restructuring, domestic investment, or FDI. Politically, privatization helped transform popular idealism into the deep cynicism that traditionally stereotypes Russians.

Ukrainian voucher privatization also put industries in the hands of managers and plutocratic partners, but if anything, the process was more orchestrated than in Russia. Whereas the Russian voucher privatization program attracted millions of participants, the Ukrainian public practically avoided it entirely, seeing it—accurately—for the sham that it was. Subsequent privatizations were allegedly corrupt and have been designed specifically to land with favored political interests. In many eyes, privatization in the Ukraine has led to even greater capture by the new plutocrats (often, communist clans) than in Russia.

Today's FSU reality suggests that privatization is not an automatic fix for countries emerging from communism. Corrupt plutocracies have appeared throughout the FSU, with the new owners conducting business in ways that mock ideal notions of private enterprise. Left without European options, privatization in the FSU appears to create private owners who find it easier to capture government than to build prosperous, competitive businesses, as the Czech example implied.

ANALYTIC ORGANIZATION OF THE CHAPTERS

Part I reviews the neoliberal case for rapid privatization, first from a theoretical basis (chapter 1) and next from a "best-case" (Czech Republic) analysis. While the theoretical basis appears well founded, unexpected outcomes in the Czech case call into question the entire common sense of the neoliberal idea. The institutionally derived post–Washington consensus is addressed at this point in the discussion, though this book contends that it too runs into serious "best-case" analysis issues. In particular, institutionalists might contend that decisions the state makes at the outset of transition are decisive for financial markets. While the Czech case validates that assertion to some degree, it is remarkable that in significant ways (the size of the equity markets, for instance), the markets of the Visegrád countries come to resemble one another. Indeed, radical institutional change during the transition period is common. The dissonance between conventional wisdom and reality forces one to reevaluate first theory and the "best-case" Czech experience.

Part II introduces the ownership regime concept to improve upon the prevailing consensus. Chapter 2 contends that privatization and the first owners that it generates behave according to:

1. *Attributes of the new owners*—skills, resources, and morals;
2. *Institutional framework*—laws, corporate governance, cross-holding arrangements;
3. *Financial markets*—role, efficiency, transparency;
4. *State financial market regulator*—capacity, autonomy.

Chapter 3 contends that state decisions ultimately determine the privatization ownership regime; the critical decisions are the speed of privatization and the role and organization of the state administration in privatization. Ideology and nationalism (in turn influenced by historical legacies, such as the nature of the prior communist regime) largely drive state choices. Once a privatization strategy reaches a particular momentum, usually when the elite formally approve a privatization approach, privatization may adhere to a path-dependent logic. That process yields the key outcome of privatization, an ownership regime. Chapter 4 considers the evolution of ownership regimes, arguing that privatization ends only with the institutionalization of stable ownership regimes. The remainder of this book structures the Czech case according to this new privatization logic as well as a set of comparative country cases in the final chapter.

Part III analyzes Czech privatization according to the model developed in part II and presented in the chronology and privatization tree introduced there. Chapter 5 shows that the conservative communist Czech regime was a likely cause of weak interests and strong proprivatization public opinion. Those factors were pivotal in the Czech government's decision to support a rapid privatization strategy.

Chapters 6 through 9 present privatization history in the Czech Republic. They test the hypotheses and tentative conclusions introduced in this prefatory chapter and theoretically developed in part II.

Chapter 6 shows that the government legitimized the rapid privatization strategy first in the June 1990 general elections and again in the Federal Parliament. During the public legitimization process, neoliberal economists led by Klaus seized the economic policymaking agenda. Nonetheless, the neoliberal economists compromised with ideological opponents so that a rapid privatization policy would be accepted. That compromise set Czech privatization on a path that was partly decentralized and partly centralized.

Chapter 7 shows that the supply-side component of Czech privatization was a rapid, but decentralized, process. The Czech neoliberals intentionally imposed time pressure on state bureaucracies in the matching of enterprise assets and privatization methods. That decision undermined the capacity and autonomy of state officials.

Chapter 8 shows that the implementation of Czech privatization was a largely centralized process that created conditions for corruption after privatization. To the extent that the implementation process was decentralized, state officials proved vulnerable to the entreaties of claimants. The most important outputs of implementation were large stock markets, unprepared financial market regulators, and a cumbersome ownership structure characterized by cross-holding.

Chapter 9 shows that the ownership regime produced by Czech rapid privatization evolved into plutocratic capitalism, that is, a government that operates for the benefit of a single wealthy class. It also shows that plutocratic capitalism in the Czech Republic translated into poor economic performance.

Chapter 10 discusses the political and economic implications of rapid privatization in the Czech Republic, given the country's comeback from 1998 through the present. Were the neoliberals proven right after all? This chapter argues that the neoliberal privatization strategy generated "delayed development," according to which enterprises were eventually sold at bargain-basement prices (to foreigners) and the public displayed contempt for Klaus's government and market reforms, contrary to optimistic expectations (although consistent with an ownership regime logic).

Chapter 11 then places the Czech privatization experience in comparative perspective, drawing on the insights of ownership regime theory as it applies to a broader range of cases—Hungary, Poland, Russia, and Ukraine.

The study concludes that a multimethod, gradual strategy, sensitive to state capacity and autonomy, is a sensible privatization approach. A sensible approach would also incorporate a prominent role for FDI. The broad policy lesson is that modern capitalism comprises more than financial markets and also includes the regulation of state institutions. The historic risk of economic reform is a permanent state of collusion between private competitors for economic resources and state officials. The roots of contemporary markets and democracy are varied: They include historically derived prejudices, skills, happenstance, politics, self-interested economic rationality, and economic planning. Local actors may behave contrary to Western expectations, and the relationships between capitalism and democracy may be more complex than the Washington consensus and the post–Washington consensus presume.

NOTES

1. Mládek (1996) and Chvojka (1997), for instance, incorporate these variables in a formulation of privatization.

2. In the United States, privatization usually refers to "enlisting private energies to improve the performance of tasks that would remain in some sense public" (Donahue 1989, 7).

3. Capitalisms may be differentiated also by, for example, the orientation and institutions of governments, by the function of primary interest groups, by the role of financial institutions, by the size of the social safety net, and by the arrangement of capital market institutions.

4. In Schumpeter's words, "the democratic method is that institutional arrangement for arriving at political decisions in which individuals acquire the power to decide by means of a competitive struggle for the people's vote" (Schumpeter 1942/1975, 269).

5. This view, which considers that democratic political regimes require both competitive elections and citizen participation, is sufficiently broad to allow for many varieties. Democracies are differentiated by the frequency and character of elections, the role and capability of the bureaucracy, the powers of elected officials over traditionally judicial, legislative, and administrative matters, the role of economic interest groups and political parties, the duties and obligations of the chief executive, rights of freedom of expression, and the chances to join and organize political organizations freely (Dahl 1971).

6. See Diamond (2002), O'Donnell (1994), and Levitsky and Way (2002).

7. The prevalence of nationalist or ethnic elements tends to be associated with delayed implementation of privatization (Estonia, Latvia, Ukraine, the former

Yugoslavia). Lithuania, which privatized quickly to assert national separation from Russia, is an exception.

8. The main impetus and ideas for privatization emanated from ethnic Czechs, though privatization began when Czechoslovakia was a united country and thus involved Slovak enterprises and citizens. Consequently, I refer to Czech privatization rather than to Czechoslovak privatization. The Czech Republic was founded on January 1, 1993, upon the split of the former Czechoslovakia into two parts, the Czech Republic and Slovakia.

9. Also see "Interview with Joseph Stiglitz" in *Transition: The Newsletter about Reforming Economies* (December 1997).

10. Hungarian foreign debt reached 65 percent of GDP with a service ratio of 57 percent of exports by 1990 (Henderson et al. 1995, 88).

11. Foreign participation was possible, though, in so-called capital privatization, a program that included provisions for foreign direct sales. The Polish state privatized 160 enterprises via capital privatization as of the end of 1995 (Kolodko and Nuti 1997, 37).

12. In fact, the national investment funds sold seven cement company stakes in a single month (July 1996) to foreign buyers (*Business Eastern Europe*, August 12, 1996, 1–2). The willingness of Polish national privatization funds to sell assets to foreign companies suggests that Polish institutional privatization may prove less resistant to foreign ownership than Czech voucher privatization in the postprivatization term.

Part I

MARKETS, DEMOCRACY, AND PRIVATIZATION—THE THEORETICAL ARGUMENT

Neoliberal Privatization—The Dream That if You Create Private Owners, Democracy and the Market Economy Will Follow

> History suggests that capitalism is a necessary condition for political freedom.
>
> —Milton Friedman (*Capitalism and Freedom*, 1962/1982)

Free-market theory presented a call to action to reformers throughout many of the underdeveloped and emerging market countries, and indeed in the more advanced countries as well. It also presented a set of propositions about the relationships between markets and politics, the main one being that free markets and democracy are complementary. CEEC reformers argued that private owners create free markets and free markets, in turn, create democracy. As a comprehensive analytic, free-market thinking represents an internally consistent argument that needs to be critiqued before evaluating its impact in the context of the transformation of CEECs.

The first half of this chapter develops two propositions from neoliberal privatization theory: (1) the speed of privatization determined the extent of privatization; and (2) a relatively more extensive privatization translates into a relatively higher quality of capitalism and a higher quality of democracy. The second half of the chapter tests these propositions against the Czech privatization experience, the neoliberals' "best practice" case. The apparent failure of neoliberalism to explain the antidemocratic and anticapitalist behavior of Czech first owners begs the need for a nuanced theory of privatization. Such a theory would explain why first owners restructure companies, lobby for secure property rights, and push for an open government. This alternative theory is presented in chapter 2.

NEOLIBERALISM: THE RECEIVED WISDOM

The analysis of neoliberalism in the transition period starts with the objectives of economic liberalization in CEECs. Reformers designed economic liberalization—price liberalization, price stabilization, free trade, and privatization—to produce an efficient economy. Removing the state from economic life was the overriding goal. Reformers styled economic liberalization after the main institutional features of the U.S.-British economic system: private ownership, stock markets, a noninterventionist state, and weak trade unions. That economic system best conformed to the sophisticated and mathematical free-market literature. More important, it offered reformers a proven working model, as epitomized in the revival of the United States under Ronald Reagan and of Great Britain under Margaret Thatcher.

The U.S.-British model advocated by neoliberals was generally more appealing to Eastern European reformers than ideological competitors such as Swedish-style corporatism or German-style social market economy. Reformers normally resisted moving in those directions because traditionally strong communist organizations, such as trade unions and state bureaucracies, were active political and economic participants in the continental European systems. That fact alone was sufficient for many reformers to regard certain models as unsuitable bases for the next regime. Reproducing the U.S.-British economic system emerged naturally as the goal of economic liberalization. The conviction that capitalism is the necessary condition for political freedom distinguishes what may be labeled *radical neoliberalism* or, in this study, *neoliberalism*. By contrast, some classic conceptions of liberalism (such as Madison's concerns, in the *Federalist Papers*, about the machinations of factions) presume only that economic and political freedom may be compatible, given appropriate checks and balances. Hayek was an important inspiration to neoliberalism in CEECs. He argued that the state's attempt to regulate the market and squelch individual economic freedom had led to communism and, in another context, to fascism.[1] Milton Friedman, who was vested with tremendous authority among Central and Eastern reformers due to his monetarist theories, asserted that "there is an intimate connection between economics and politics, that only certain combinations of political and economic arrangements are possible, and that in particular, a society which is socialist cannot be democratic, in the sense of guaranteeing individual freedom" (Friedman 1962/1982, 8).

The logic that placed democracy in a dependent position relative to capitalism precipitated the conviction that any potentially negative side effects from the politics of liberalization—compromises, alliances, and tactics—would be swept aside by the success of economic reforms. If economic reform implants market institutions, then efficient markets would naturally follow. Efficient markets, in turn, must produce democracy. Efficient markets and democracy would never happen if economic reform failed. Neoliberalism is more than an economic theory; it is also a political theory.

Eastern European adherents of neoliberalism and their Western advisors pushed that logic still further. They took a short and extreme analytic step, going from the view that the liberalization of politics is subordinate to the completion of economic liberalization policy, to the inference that political freedoms could be violated at rare times in order to align economic incentive structures. Once in place, market structures would deliver the capitalist class and political popularity necessary to implant democracy permanently (Schumpeter 1942/1975). Supporters of economic liberalism were justified in using "illiberal" political tactics against opposition politicians who blocked economic reform in the meantime.

The leading CEEC neoliberals were drawn disproportionately from the pool of technocrats—scientists, engineers, but especially economists—who worked in state ministries and state enterprises during the communist era. They passionately supported the creation of a market economy with minimal state intervention, a so-called market without adjectives, even at the cost of selected violations of political freedoms or compromises with political factions thought to be antagonistic to democracy. Neoliberals outlined their worldview in scholarly articles and in the popular press, and they actively pursued their ideas when they were in government. Well-known CEEC neoliberals included Klaus, Tříska, and Ježek of the Czech Republic; L. Balcerowicz, S. Kawalec, and J. Lewandowski of Poland; and Y. Gaidar and A. Chubais of the former Soviet Union.[2] Drawn together by historic chance and fortified by populations eager to (re)join Western civilization, neoliberals emerged as key policymakers in the first postcommunist leaderships.

Some readers will contend that the view of neoliberalism used here is simplistic, that it misleadingly reduces the wide diversity of reform opinion throughout CEECs on a number of complicated issues. However, this objection misunderstands the transition debates that actually occurred on the ground. First, although the reform debates did vary throughout much of the region, the viewpoints expressed by most reformers (freely using the name neoliberal) were couched in dogmatic language, as for instance, in the former Czechoslovakia, in Poland, and in Russia. Second, although it is true that neoliberals proved to be neoliberals on some issues only and not on others, it was not for lack of trying. For instance, although the Balcerowicz Plan liberalizing prices in Poland was a graphic case of "neoliberalism," the Polish government's privatization approach was gradual—the opposite of what neoliberals would have preferred. Yet, Polish neoliberalism's failure to implement privatization quickly does not necessarily make Polish neoliberals less neoliberal. Balcerowicz himself has lamented the fact that he did not have the same political latitude to impose privatization that another neoliberal, Klaus, had in

Prague.[3] Eastern neoliberalism was an extreme and readily understandable view of politics and economics not always evident in policy outcomes.

Other critics will cite those who argued for impartial legal frameworks in support of markets as evidence for a multifaceted and nuanced view of neoliberalism. Most of those citations, which evolved into the post–Washington consensus, however, followed the initial market reforms and were a response to market failures (especially corruption) that were fast becoming evident throughout CEECs in the early 1990s (Gray et al. 1993; Frydman and Rapaczynski 1994; World Bank 1996).

Neoliberal policy prescriptions and advice tell a different story prior to 1992. For instance, the frequently cited 1991 piece by neoliberals Blanchard, Dornbusch, Krugman, Layard, and Summers downplays the regulatory role of the state while emphasizing price stabilization, privatization, and market-led restructuring (Blanchard et al. 1991).[4] Western efforts to help remake the Eastern European economies similarly stressed the implementation of the reform agenda—price and trade liberalization, stabilization, and privatization.

The construction of a regulatory infrastructure and the state building that it implied was clearly a secondary consideration for neoliberals. Thus it was not surprising to see unregulated financial institutions (including banks and capital markets) spring up throughout the region. In the Czech Republic, for example, the neoliberal Klaus government repeatedly rejected attempts by Western experts to develop a regulatory framework for the Czech capital markets, even after privatization. Notable exceptions were the relatively (by regional standards) sophisticated and determined state regulation of capital markets in Hungary and Poland, where neoliberals were less successful than in the Czech Republic in privatizing large enterprises rapidly. Neoliberals acknowledged the role of the state only reluctantly and then in response to a reality that had in just a few years overwhelmed the original wisdom.

Transition

The transition period in Central and Eastern Europe offered economic challenges and political opportunities conducive to a drastic move to the market (economic liberalization), while retaining tactical political flexibility—in short, neoliberalism. Economically, the command economies' embarrassing comparisons with the advanced capitalist economies illustrated the need for markets in the former communist countries. Politically, transition offered reformers a historic chance to remake their countries. The leadership vacuum emanating from the sudden fall of communism vaulted reformers to the top posts in government. It also precipitated disarray in the groups expected to oppose economic liberalization as well as public enthusiasm for dramatic change.

The neoliberal solution therefore was appealing, *first* because economic liberalization would initiate the necessary economic restructuring process, and *second* because reformers could justifiably use the government in politically "illiberal" ways. The free market, the inevitable end of economic liberalization, would purge all political sins. Neoliberalism offered reformers the right philosophy at the right time.

Economic Challenges of Transition Countries

The central challenge of economic reform in Central and Eastern Europe was to redeploy productive assets. Oversized, vertically integrated monopolies that were both uncompetitive and overly concentrated in heavy industry dominated the communist command economy.[5] These factories had produced the wrong products at the wrong prices for decades. The well-known results were a "shortage economy" (Kornai 1980) that generated long waits for consumer goods—cars, dishwashers, and televisions—alongside a surfeit of arms and steel. These traits suggested that the former communist economy was misdeveloped, rather than underdeveloped.

Neoliberals distinguished the distorted economies of the former Second World from the underdevelopment in developing countries. The backward industrial base, few skilled workers, little or no modern infrastructure, and a shortage of cultural affinity with Western businessmen implied the need for whole new systems of production. CEECs, by contrast, needed to redirect existing economic assets toward more efficient and consumer-friendly uses. Government failure, not market failure, was the evident problem.

Western and Eastern European analysts alike attributed the misdevelopment of the Eastern Bloc economies to the Communist Party's monopoly of power over the state administration. Communists used the state apparatus to allocate goods and services, labor, and capital to suit their ideological or personal preferences. Prices and finance counted for little in this political-economic system; state planners distributed costs and benefits, and they dictated how and where productive assets would be used. The state, as had become evident, was patently incapable of running an economy that could produce goods efficiently—or even goods that consumers wanted. The main goal of economic reform, according to many reformers, was to "depoliticize" the economy by eliminating the state (Boycko, Shleifer, and Vishny 1995, 9–10).

Political Opportunities for Transition Countries

Transition offered neoliberals a historic chance to liberalize the closed economies of Central and Eastern Europe. First, the long-time communist leadership simply withdrew from power in many countries, thus leaving a power

vacuum at the elite level that reformers would fill. Second, the most likely economic liberalization opponents—managers, workers, bureaucrats, and old-line
communists—were in disarray and in retreat from angry populations. Third,
the Eastern European populations were willing to sacrifice materially so that
economic liberalization might move forward. Transition's "striking good luck"
(Szacki 1994, 147) brought neoliberals the political window of opportunity to
liberalize the command economies.

Transition's good luck facilitated economic liberalization, but it did not
guarantee it. Economic liberalization was widely expected to entail real costs to
most of society. It was likely to precipitate unemployment and, probably, a drop
in social policy expenditures. In addition, no existing social group appeared
to benefit from economic liberalization.[6] How could economic liberalization
move forward if there were losers, yet no winners (in the short run) from its
policy reforms?

Neoliberals responded that reformers must seize control of the state. Only
state-initiated reforms could relieve state control over the economy. Who else
would do it? No domestic authority existed outside of the state, and national
feelings of pride, hardened by past experience with Soviet colonialism, precluded foreigners from taking the lead. And, as noted above, economic liberalization lacked a popular constituency. Only the national state remained as
a vehicle of economic liberalization. Fortunately, transition had thrust believers in the market economy into leading positions in government throughout
Central and Eastern Europe.

What constituted appropriate political tactics for reformers who stood astride
the state but who professed disdain for state intervention in the economy?
Neoliberalism's schizophrenic solution was to forgo democratic procedure in
exchange for the long-term benefits of economic liberalization. Reformers
should "grab people by the throat and introduce liberalism" (Szacki 1994,
153). They should, if necessary, compromise with ideological enemies so that
economic liberalization could move forward. Russian privatizers consciously
followed this advice when they offered privatization preferences to enterprise
managers and workers, local officials, and powerful bureaucrats in exchange
for political support for privatization (Boycko, Shleifer, and Vishny 1995). In
some situations, they should even break the law or violate standard ethical
codes of conduct. The Czech reformer Ježek expressed the neoliberal position
in this defense of his government's cavalier attitude toward existing laws:
"The application of normal laws to the privatization process is inadmissible.
Privatization is here so that normal laws can be valid after it is finished" (*ČD*,
October 15, 1993, 26).[7]

Neoliberals thus adopted a "no-stick" or "Teflon" political strategy for
economic liberalization. They justified "illiberal" politics by the presumably

transitory impact of "necessary evil" compromises and alliances and immoral tactics. The familiar neoliberal logic was that market incentives would soon overwhelm the legacies of liberalization politics by providing a constituency for market changes and for democratic politics. If neoliberalism could produce capitalism and democracy in the United States, it could do the same in Central and Eastern Europe; neoliberals tactfully omitted mentioning any experience that implied a different conclusion, as in southern Italy or Africa. Thankfully, according to neoliberals, the impact of liberalization politics wouldn't stick.

First Private Owners and Privatization

Privatization is at the core of economic liberalization. According to neoliberals, private owners are at once the basis for a market economy and democracy and the main instrument to break the economic and political power of the state. Private owners deploy assets efficiently and support democratic policies owing to market incentives. Absent private owners, as before, enterprise managers rely on the largesse of the state and support policies that centralize political power. Privatization is the bridge from communism to capitalism.[8] Two prominent neoliberals, G. Allison and G. Yavlinsky, wrote,

> In economics, the core value of freedom is exercised in a *market economy* based on private ownership in which market forces of supply and demand answer the question of who produces what for whom. . . . Ownership means the freedom to use or dispose of property as an individual chooses. Basic laws of economics tolerate no equivocation on this point, none whatsoever. (Allison and Yavlinsky 1991, 3–4)

Privatization Objectives: First Private Owners

The immediate neoliberal objective of privatization is to create "first" private owners. Neoliberals pay no attention to the market experience, skills, or attitudes of the first owners. They argue that postcommunism's first owners would be "economic men," though those first owners had lived under a state socialist system for decades (Boycko, Shleifer, and Vishny 1995).

Neoliberals only disdain first owners, particularly workers, who would have "obvious" nonmarket incentives after privatization was complete. The policy recommendation of the neoliberal Institute for EastWest Studies is typical: "If concessions to managers and workers must be given in order to move privatization ahead, policy makers should ensure that . . . *workers get as little as possible*" (Institute for EastWest Studies 1994, 20; italics added).

Neoliberals argue that once (proper) first owners are in place, market logic automatically creates "active owners." *Active owners* are owners who seek to restructure companies for market activity. In order to cash in on what are generally privatized assets obtained cheaply, first private owners sell to active private owners (sometimes via intermediate private owners). Neoliberals deduce that "last" owners will be active owners. Active owners presumably will pay the highest prices for assets because they will put them to their most profitable use. According to what is known as the Coase Theorem, the first-ownership structure is an artifact of privatization, but little more (Coase 1960).

The Coase Theorem was underpinned by the political logic of reform. In what came to be known as the Political Coase Theorem (Hoff and Stiglitz 2002), neoliberals argued that first owners would advocate policies that regulate the market fairly and transparently. In theory, first owners could only sell assets at maximum prices to active owners if the active owners knew that property rights were secure, that is, that rules of exchange, production, and taxation were predictable and sensible. Stated somewhat differently, first owners would support the creation of transparent and honest regulatory institutions to minimize transaction costs and maximize profit from selling assets. As the European Bank for Reconstruction and Development (EBRD) put this position, "A basic and powerful way to accelerate institution-building in transition economies is to create private sector demand for it by privatization and other policies to reduce the role of the state in economic life" (EBRD 1997, 56).

Political and economic incentives impel first private owners in the neoliberal construct to establish a fairly regulated market economy and a participatory democracy. Privatization's clear logic and clarity of purpose focused reformers on the task at hand: how to privatize.

Privatization Best Practice: Rapid Privatization

Neoliberal best practice grew out of the recognition that privatization would jeopardize the positions of two groups: (1) entrenched interest groups—the state bureaucracy, managers, workers, and local politicians who would presumably lose control to the new private owners; and (2) workers, who would be fired when the new private owners restructured their companies.

Luckily, transition's political opportunities had offered the new reform leaderships of Central and Eastern Europe a historic chance. Reformers might be able to act before privatization's likely opponents, who were momentarily disoriented by the communist system's collapse, could respond. Quick action would also take advantage of the popular enthusiasm for markets and democracy. Popular support for privatization might dissipate if economic conditions worsened or if threatened interests became more active. Neoliberals argued that reformers risked a return to the communist past or an unthinkable move backward to the Third World if they delayed privatization or, worse, failed to privatize altogether. The neoliberal solution was then obvious—not just privatization, but *rapid* privatization.

Neoliberal Privatization Propositions

Neoliberal best practice can be distilled into two propositions. Each one can be evaluated against the privatization experience in CEECs, including the Czech Republic.

The *first* neoliberal proposition was that the speed of privatization determined the extent of privatization. Neoliberals assumed that the speed of privatization correlated inversely with the involvement of state officials. They regarded what may be referred to as administrative privatization approaches as "time-consuming" or "gradual," and saw nonadministrative privatization approaches as "rapid."

Voucher privatization was the rapid privatization method of choice. Voucher privatization schemes distribute enterprise shares (or shares in funds that own enterprises) to the population either for free or at nominal cost. By giving citizens "something for nothing" in privatization, neoliberals assumed that voucher privatization would buy popularity for rapid privatization and, ultimately, for economic reform. Privatization would pay off local populations vulnerable to the dislocation inevitable during economic liberalization.

The alternatives to rapid privatization were gradual methods of privatization, which included public sales, public tenders, and auctions. Most analysts use the term "standard" synonymously with "gradual" to refer to privatization methods that states outside Central and Eastern Europe—particularly Great Britain—had previously implemented. Neoliberals generally frowned upon standard privatization approaches because they tended to be case by case, and therefore required the time and input of state officials.[9]

Neoliberals typically measured the extent of privatization by the percentage of gross domestic product (GDP) produced by the private sector. Neoliberals expected that a fast privatization approach would lead to an extensive privatization, whereas a gradual privatization approach would lead to minimal privatization.

The *second* neoliberal proposition was that a relatively more extensive privatization translates into a relatively higher quality of capitalism and a higher quality of democracy. Indications that first owners were selling to active owners would constitute evidence that privatization was working economically. As this ownership transfer takes place, neoliberals expected an initial decline in economic performance followed by rapid improvement in GDP growth, inflation, unemployment rate, and the trade balance (Hellman 1998).

The formation of a new ownership class that endorsed the rule of law, transparency in government, and open and fair elections would be evidence that privatization was working politically. Neoliberals expected that reformers and market reform policies should become increasingly popular relative to the leftist opposition as the benefits attached to free markets became apparent to the public. In combination with the first proposition, this proposition implied that a rapid privatization strategy would produce efficient markets and participatory democracy in CEECs.

THE NEOLIBERAL SUCCESS CASE:
CZECH RAPID PRIVATIZATION

The Czech Republic's rapid privatization strategy became the prototype for neoliberal best practice.[10] It featured an innovative method, voucher privatization, which had been copied in one form or another by over a dozen former communist countries by 1995 (see table 1.1). One Western advisor to Russia wrote that "the Russian decision-makers looked at privatization in Poland

Table 1.1.   Countries That Privatized by Vouchers, 1991–1995

Country	Year Voucher Distribution Began
Czech Republic	**1992**
Slovakia	1992
Romania*	1992
Russia	1992
Estonia	1993
Lithuania	1993
Armenia	1994
Kazakhstan	1994
Kyrgyz Republic	1994
Latvia	1994
Moldova	1994
Slovenia	1994
Albania	1995
Belarus	1995
Bulgaria	1995
Georgia	1995
Poland	1995
Romania	1995
Ukraine	1995

Source: Estrin and Stone 1997, 174.
*Romania has had two mass privatization plans. In the 1992 version, Romania *encouraged* participating citizens to invest in intermediary organizations. In the 1995 version, Romania *required* participating citizens to invest in intermediary organizations.

primarily to learn what pitfalls to avoid and at that of Czechoslovakia to learn how to do it" (Åslund 1995, 229).

Czech rapid privatization produced a side effect unexpected by neoliberals: first owners who undermined the quality of Czech capitalism and democracy. This unexpected outcome suggested that neoliberal reformers had miscalculated the incentives of first owners. The neoliberals paid for their hubris with Klaus's resignation in 1997 and the sweeping leftist victory by the Social Democrats in 1998. The pathologies of Czech privatization were duplicated throughout the region, as the comparative privatization chapter at the end of the book will demonstrate.

Economic Challenges in the Czech Republic

At the demise of Czechoslovakian communism in November 1989, the Czech Republic appeared to be a prime candidate for privatization; it clearly needed private owners. Despite half-hearted attempts at economic reform in the late 1980s, the 1989 Czech economy exhibited classic features of the Soviet-style command economy: administrative planning, reliance on heavy industry, a dearth of light industry and consumer services, politically controlled foreign trade, and a passive financial sector. Most important, the 1989 Czech economy functioned with an extraordinarily high percentage of state ownership, even by the standards of the former Eastern Bloc countries (see table 1.2). The Czech Republic, much like a mismanaged industrial company with valuable productive assets, needed a turnaround and new ownership.

The Czech Republic also was well prepared economically for privatization, at least from a macroeconomic viewpoint. Czech macroeconomic fundamentals—foreign debt levels, government budget, price pressure—were unusually favorable by postcommunist standards; the country's geographical place next to Germany suggested good prospects for a quick recovery; and Czechoslovakia had the highest level of development in the Communist Bloc (see table 1.3). In addition, the Czech Republic proved far less susceptible to unemployment pressures than other CEECs, though no one realized it in 1989 (see tables 1.2 and 1.4). This consideration was of vital concern to Eastern European reformers—and to their Western advisors. They presumed that privatization, like the restructuring of that mismanaged industrial firm, would inevitably precipitate an initial drop in output and job layoffs. Neoliberals didn't emphasize that Czechoslovakia was far less experienced with the market than local referents Hungary and Poland.

The radical economic differences within Czechoslovakia—between the Czech Republic and Slovakia—accentuated positive Czech fundamentals. The Czech industrial sector relative to the Slovak sector was more diversified, less reliant on trade with the former Soviet Union, and could better benefit from

**Table 1.2.   Private Sector Output in Selected
Countries, Pre-1989**

Country	Private Sector Output (%)
Socialist Countries	
Bulgaria, *1970*	0.3
Czechoslovakia, *1988*	**0.7**
GDR, *1988*	3.6
USSR, *1985*	4.0
Romania, *1980*	4.4
Hungary, *1988*	7.1
Yugoslavia, *1987*	13.5
Poland, *1988*	18.8
OECD Countries	
France, *1982*	83.5
Austria, *1978–1979*	85.5
Italy, *1982*	86.0
West Germany, *1982*	89.3
United Kingdom, *1983*	89.3
Portugal, *1976*	90.3
Netherlands, *1971–1973*	96.4
United States, *1983*	98.7

Source: Kornai (1992, 72) for all socialist states except USSR;
Milanovic (1989, 20) for USSR; Milanovic (1989, 15) for OECD
countries.

Table 1.3.   Basic Indicators, Selected Transition Countries, 1994

Country	Population (mn)	GDP (bn $)	PPP per capita ($)*	Annual Inflation (1990–1995 %)	Annual Unemployment (%)	FDI stock per capita**
Czech Rep.	**10.3**	**36.0**	**9,791**	**19.8**	**3.2**	**243**
Slovakia	5.3	12.4	6,771	21.5	14.8	47
Hungary	10.3	41.4	6,361	26.1	11.4	346
Poland	38.5	92.6	5,040	132.4	16.0	65
Slovenia	2.0	14.0	10,014	156.9	14.2	67
Romania	22.7	30.1	3,959	135.2	10.9	16
Bulgaria	8.4	10.2	4,404	110.2	12.8	15
Russia	148.3	376.6	4,500	473.4	2.2	14
Ukraine	51.9	91.3	2,633	1,209.5	0.3	9

Sources: UNCTAD (1996); World Bank (1996, 1997); Schwartz and Haggard (1997); WIIW (1997).
*PPP per capita refers to Purchasing Power Parity in international $s of GNP per capita.
**Foreign Direct Investment (FDI) stock per capita refers to inflows from 1988 to 1994, with the exception
of Ukraine, which refers to inflows 1989–1996.

Table 1.4. Selected Transition Countries at the Cusp of Revolution

Country	Economic Development Level*	Cars per 1,000 Inhabitants**	Main Telephone Lines per 1,000 Inhabitants***	Ratio of Net Debt to Market Economy Exports (%)****
Czechoslovakia	**59.2**	**174**	**12.5**	**62**
Hungary	46.0	157	7.8	349
Poland	39.2	111	7.0	458
Yugoslavia	40.4	129	11.6	–
Romania	34.1	12	6.7	33
Bulgaria	40.8	127	15.1	–
Soviet Union	50.0	44	9.0	–

*US = 100, figures are from 1985 (Kornai 1992, 6–7).
**Figures are from 1986 (304).
***Figures are from 1987 (305).
****Figures are from 1988 (556).

tourism and from future demand for service industries. Consider the situation in military equipment, a sector certain to suffer when the free market came. Prior to 1989, 70 percent of Czechoslovakia's arms industry was located in Slovakia. Nearly all arms production was directed to the USSR or to other Eastern Bloc countries. After 1989, the collapse of the Eastern economies and the sudden cut in military priorities throughout the region caused the new Czechoslovakian leadership to slice the military budget by a factor of nine, from 18.8 bn CZK in 1988 to 2.1 bn CZK in 1991 (Kirschbaum 1995, 261).[11] On the other hand, more favorable Czech fundamentals translated into relatively high demand for labor in the new market economy. In the fourth quarter of 1992, for instance, there were nearly 10 times as many job vacancies in Slovakia as in the Czech Republic, and 140 times more than in Prague, the Czech capital city (Švejnar et al. 1995, 293). (See table 1.5 for unemployment figures.)

Table 1.5. Unemployment in Selected Transition Countries, 1992

Country	Unemployment Rate (%)
Czech Republic	**2.6**
Slovakia	10.4
Hungary	13.2
Poland	13.6
Slovenia	13.4
Former East Germany	14.8
Romania	8.2
Bulgaria	15.3

Source: WIIW (1997).

Czech favorable economic fundamentals implied that privatization could be quick and sweeping, since the potential disruption stemming from economic hardship might be minimal. The Czech Republic, especially if considered apart from Slovakia, appeared that much more attractive to neoliberals as a site to instigate a rapid privatization approach.

Political Opportunities for Neoliberal Reformers

The internal political situation in then-Czechoslovakia fit the neoliberal view that the transition state would have a good chance to complete privatization successfully. The collapse of the Czechoslovakian communist regime left chaos. Old-line communists were retiring from the top state posts and from government bureaucracies in droves; enterprise managers were abandoning companies (or else trying to make off with the assets); the trade unions were engaged in a nasty split between the communists and a dissident faction; and political parties, the democratic mediators of civil struggle, still were embryonic. Moreover, the Czech population (and, to a large extent, the Slovak population) was desperate to embrace neoliberal ideologies—free markets and democracy. In Czechoslovakia, confusion had created a power vacuum and an opportunity for neoliberal reformers to privatize assets quickly and completely.

Rapid Privatization in the Czech Republic

Czech neoliberals took advantage of Czechoslovakia's political turmoil to rapidly privatize the economy. The first step was to seize state economic decision-making control. The Klaus-led team of neoliberals accomplished this by gaining the economic ministerial posts immediately upon the official accession to power of the new Czechoslovak government in 1990. In 1992, Klaus and the neoliberals completed the power play when Klaus was elected Czech prime minister.

From a position of power, the Czech reformers conceived and implemented the most far-reaching privatization agenda in Central and Eastern Europe. The Czechoslovakian state restituted assets to former owners, privatized small enterprises, divested agricultural holdings, privatized large- and medium-sized enterprises, and liquidated thousands of worthless state assets.

The crux of the Czech privatization was the voucher privatization method through which the state distributed enterprise stakes to citizens. In voucher privatization, the state first distributed (at very low cost) vouchers to citizens. Next, citizens used these vouchers to bid on enterprise shares through the state's auction procedure. This procedure offered each Czechoslovakian citizen

Table 1.6. Czech Voucher Privatization at a Glance

Two Privatization Waves	1992 to 1995
Participating Enterprises*	1,749
Enterprise Book Value**	355
Participants (mn)***	5.95
Participants as a Percentage of Eligible Citizens***	78.0%
Voucher Privatization as a Percentage of Large Privatization by Book Value (Joint Stock Companies)****	48.5%

*Stakes in 124 enterprises were privatized in both waves
**Bn CZK
***First-wave figures
****The breakdown of other privatization methods was "State residual shareholding," 32.6%; "Other methods," 9.1%; "Market privatization," 4.9%; "Reprivatization," 3.0%; "Tender privatization," 1.4%; and "Insider privatization," 0.3%. (See chapter 2 for a full description of these privatization methods.)

equal and excellent chances to become a shareholder in the country's most valuable enterprises.

Voucher privatization energized the Czechoslovakian population, drawing millions of people into the new markets and driving up the popularity of Klaus's neoliberal government. By the time it was over, voucher privatization had created about six million new Czech shareholders (and over two million Slovak shareholders) (see table 1.6). After enduring decades without financial markets, the Czech Republic had the largest number of shareholders per capita in the world. Neoliberals expected that these new private owners would become the vanguard of the future capitalist economy and democratic political system.

The Czech reformers set up stock markets so that first private owners could transfer ownership stakes to active private owners after voucher privatization. The Czech reformers also wrote a Western-style commercial code to defend the new private ownership rights. Consistent with its new market institutions, the Czech Republic ranked among the world's "freest" economies—eighth out of 150 in the 1996 Heritage Foundation and *Wall Street Journal* lists (*HN*, December 16, 1996, 15). On its face, the Czech Republic had created the most dynamic and comprehensive free market in Central and Eastern Europe. Within a few years, the Czech Republic went from having an economy that was over 99 percent state-owned to one that was 80 percent privately owned (see tables 1.7 and 1.8). The Czech privatization experience seemingly validated a core neoliberal belief: fast privatization led to extensive privatization while building a solid foundation for market and democratic development.

Unexplained Outcomes, 1996 through 1998

The neoliberals' propositions were not satisfied empirically in the Czech Republic just after the completion of rapid privatization. The behavior of the

Table 1.7.   Private Sector Output in Selected Countries, 1996

Country	Private Sector Output (%)
Former Socialist States	
Czech Republic	**80**
Slovakia	72
Hungary	72
Estonia	72
Lithuania	65
Latvia	60
Russia	60
Romania	60
Poland	60
Croatia	50
Bulgaria	45
Slovenia	45
Ukraine	40

Source: Estimated from Lieberman 1997, 5.

first owners and their agents after privatization belied neoliberal expectations. Immediate personal enrichment in violation of the law or of ethical business practice, rather than enterprise restructuring, became standard operating procedure. The new owners commonly stripped enterprise assets. Sometimes they transferred the proceeds into personal overseas bank accounts.

The biggest, though by no means only, scoundrels were the Czech investment privatization funds (IPFs). IPFs emerged during voucher privatization from the state's decision to encourage citizens to pool their vouchers; it had feared that too many small shareholders would leave corporate governance in the hands of managers, as during the communist regime. Thanks to the incentive structure embedded in voucher privatization, most Czech citizens

Table 1.8.   Czech Republic: Selected Macroeconomic Indicators, 1996–2002

		1996	1997	1998	1999	2000	2001	2002
GDP growth	%, real	4.3	−0.8	−1.2	0.5*	3.3*	3.3*	3.0**
Industrial production	%, real	2.0	4.5	1.6	−3.1	5.8	6.8	4.0**
Construction output	%, real	4.8	−3.9	−7.0	−6.5	5.6	9.6	7.0**
Retail sales	%, real	11.4	1.9	−7.2	2.1	4.6	4.3	4.5**
Inflation	%, average	8.8	8.5	10.7	2.1	3.9	4.7	4.4**
Unemployment rate	%, e. o. p.	3.5	5.2	7.5	9.4	8.8	8.9	8.5**

Source: CNB (Czech National Bank), ČSÚ (Czech Statistical Bureau).
*Last revised numbers of ČSÚ from June 18, 2002.
**Forecast of Komerční banka, in Kamil Janáček and Eva Zamrazilová, "Czech Economy at the Beginning of 2002," *Prague Economic Papers* 9, no 2 (2002): 10.

Table 1.9.   GDP Growth Rates (%) in CEECs, 1994–1998

	1994	*1995*	*1996*	*1997*	*1998*
Czech Republic	**2.6**	**4.8**	**4.4**	**0.9**	**−2.6**
Hungary	2.9	1.5	1.0	3.0	5.2
Poland	5.2	7.0	6.1	5.6	4.8
Slovakia	4.9	7.4	7.0	5.0	5.2
Slovenia	4.9	3.5	3.5	3.5	4.0

Source: OECD survey, cited in *Transition* (December 1997, 24); various national sources.

entrusted their vouchers to IPFs.[12] They considered that IPFs would be wise investors because of good access to investment information and expertise. IPFs also sweetened the rewards for people who entrusted them with vouchers by guaranteeing citizens huge rates of return on their investment. Events did not justify investors' faith in IPFs. IPF managers instead found it more lucrative to hold on to ownership rights and siphon off enterprise assets to their own accounts, rather than sell ownership stakes to the active owners, which would have delivered the sale proceeds to the citizens. Unfortunately, the Czech stock market offered no exit for citizen IPF shareholders. IPFs often traded at over a 50 percent discount to net asset value, because it was well known that IPF managers were abusing their fiduciary responsibility. Other owners or agents of owners played variations of the same game.

The asset-milking process, locally coined "to tunnel" (*vytunelovat*) or "to dejuice" (*vydžusovat*)—the Western terms are "to defraud" or "to steal"— deprived companies of the chance to obtain restructuring funds. Consequently, quantitative economic performance indicators such as GDP growth, exchange rate, balance of trade, unemployment rate, and productivity have deteriorated since the second (and last) privatization wave in December 1994. The Czech Republic recorded a negative GDP growth rate for 1998 while other CEECs continued to grow rapidly (see tables 1.8 and 1.9).

From the standpoint of a comparative regional economy, delays in the economic restructuring of Czech enterprises threatened long-term growth prospects (Zysman and Schwartz 1998a). Research on East Asian development suggests that how and where an enterprise becomes inserted into international production networks largely explains its future development trajectory. Delay in restructuring of Czech enterprises implies that Czech companies would enter the production networks of foreign multinational corporations at a relatively low technological level, if at all. By contrast, Hungary, Poland, and Slovenia appear to be aggressively inserting themselves into the production networks of multinational corporations (Zysman and Schwartz 1998a). The Czech Republic has moved from CEEC pacesetter to the middle of the Visegrád pack.

Chapter 1

Table 1.10. Share Price Changes of Select Czech-Owned Companies in 1998

	December 30, 1997	December 21, 1998	Percentage Change
Banks			
KB	1305	357	−72.6
ČS	229	101	−55.8
IPB	195	97	−50.2
Energy/Power Companies			
Unipetrol	99	54	−45.7
ČEZ	1135	674	−40.6
Industrial Holding Companies			
ČKD	1150	128	−88.9
Škoda Plzeň	612	178	−70.9

Source: HN, December 23, 1998, 7.

In addition, delayed development potentially threatened the Czech Republic's entry into the European Union (EU). That concern, which turned out to be unfounded, could have conceivably depended on the achievement of a development level commensurate with the less-developed EU countries. That will require an acceleration in Czech economic growth—the 1997 GDP growth rate was 0.9 percent and the 1998 GDP growth rate was −2.6 percent (versus the 2.6 percent EU GDP 1997 growth rate). (See table 1.10.)

From a political perspective, the Czech private owners do not yet resemble the vibrant capitalist class that should, according to neoliberal theory, support domestic initiatives for transparency and the rule of law. They instead collude with state officials to manipulate market rules. In particular, private owners work with state officials in open defiance of public opinion to block the enactment or enforcement of clear ownership rights—exactly the opposite of the neoliberal hypotheses. The results are political practices that most people call corruption, rules that often lack meaning, influence peddling, and illicit campaign contributions. These practices mock the meaning of democracy—a political system characterized by effective citizen participation in government. Indeed, it is the perversion of democracy epitomized in the close relationships between rich private owners and state officials that enables the asset-milking game.

Furthermore, rapid privatization in the end bolstered support neither for market reforms nor for the politicians who advocated them. Market cynicism replaced market enthusiasm in the Czech Republic. In December 1997, two years after voucher privatization, Klaus's government resigned in disgrace over a campaign financing scandal. To be sure, to say that Czech privatization destroyed democracy is too strong—the Czech Republic holds regular and honest competitive elections. And after all, as Czechs are eager to point out, "the Czech Republic is not Russia." Still, rapid privatization undermined the quality of Czech democracy.

The unanticipated Czech outcomes illustrate that rapid privatization may precipitate an economic and political system antagonistic to a high quality of capitalism and of democracy. The Czech private owners found that collusion was a viable alternative to competition, and so they helped found a system conventionally labeled "crony capitalism," "racket economy," and "kleptocracy," or what might best be called a "plutocracy." The failure of neoliberalism to foster high-quality capitalism and democracy in the Czech Republic demands an explanation. How did rapid privatization produce such perverse results?

Starting (approximately) with the inauguration of the first leftist government since the fall of communism and the end of most privatization, Czech macroeconomic statistics showed a remarkable turnabout, and Czech equity markets began both to function and to resemble their regional counterparts. FDI surged to extraordinary levels, and foreigners bought each of the major banks. Politically, the party of the reformers (ODS) and its star, Klaus, had made an amazing surge in the polls by 2002. Klaus replaced Havel as Czech president in 2003, and ODS blew past the leftist Social Democrats in the elections. Although we will contend in the chapters that follow that the Czech comeback did not salvage neoliberalism, it does cause us to reconsider its theoretical foundation as well as that of its institutional refinements, especially the post–Washington consensus. This book argues that neither version best represents the reality of privatization. Rather, we have developed an *ownership regime theory* to explain the behavior and configuration of private owners in a recently privatized society.

NOTES

1. Hayek wrote, "it was the prevalence of socialist views and not Prussianism that Germany had in common with Italy and Russia" (Hayek 1944/1994, 12). Hayek believed that it was folly to conceive of a separate economic sphere that could be ruled by a "dictator in the economic field" with the trade-off of "greater freedom in the pursuit of higher values" (97).

2. Some economists who emerged as neoliberals after 1989 adopted other positions during communism. For instance, several Polish economists had supported worker self-management ideas (Orenstein 1996, 126).

3. Balcerowicz's remarks came at the Workshop on Regulatory and Institutional Reform in the Transitional Economies, Warsaw, Poland, November 7–9, 1995.

4. To be fair, Blanchard et al. acknowledge the problems of stock markets in the absence of a developed infrastructure. "Experience in Hong Kong, Taiwan, and a number of other countries suggests that in the absence of an appropriate regulatory

framework and well-audited, reliable information about corporate prospects, stock markets are likely to be subjected to manipulation and other forms of fraud" (Blanchard et al. 1991, 40).

5. Annual industrial investment in the Soviet Bloc socialist countries from 1973 to 1983 ranged from 34.2 percent in Hungary to 49.3 percent in Romania (Czechoslovakia's rate was 38.0 percent). Annual industrial investment in selected European capitalist countries ranged from a low of 16.7 percent in Denmark to a high of 34.2 percent in the United Kingdom from 1973 to 1980 (Kornai 1992, 175). Average firm size by number of employees in manufacturing was 197 in the Soviet Bloc countries versus 80 in the West. In some heavy industries the East-West discrepancy was much higher. For instance, it was 325 to 104 in chemicals and 2,542 to 350 in ferrous metals (Kornai 1992, 400). Finally, Hughes and Hare calculated that manufacturing in Czechoslovakia produced a negative value added share of 34 percent, in Hungary of 35.5 percent, and Poland of 38.9 percent in 1991 (figures cited in Dhar 1992, 6–8).

6. A. Smolar observed (regarding Poland), "[N]either the major industry workers who formed the core of the Solidarity movement, nor the state-protected individual farmers, nor the few private entrepreneurs thriving on inanities of clumsy central planning wanted a change that would go significantly beyond essentially redistributive action" (cited in Bauman 1988).

7. Ježek has protested that this quotation has been used out of context, though I believe it accurately reflected his views at that time (personal communication).

8. Scholars who stress institutional variables (Elster, Offe, and Preuss 1998) also commonly share this view.

9. The exceptions to this rule are *insider privatization approaches*, "privatization methods that granted privatization preferences to managers and/or workers." Depending on how the state administers them, insider privatization approaches fall into the rapid or gradual privatization category. If the state granted workers or managers preferences automatically (that is, without state administrative input), then we might call these rapid privatization methods. If, on the other hand, insiders were merely given advantages (for example, the rights to buy enterprise shares cheaper than others) in a standard privatization procedure, then insider privatization may be considered a gradual approach. In either case, neoliberals usually discouraged transition governments from implementing standard privatization approaches due to their perceptions of managers and workers as inherently "antimarket" (see chapter 2).

10. Before the Eastern European governments instituted rapid privatization policies (starting in 1992), most neoliberals recommended that the state issue citizens shares in holding companies rather than in individual enterprises (what later became the dominant Czech privatization method). Neoliberals accepted both methods, since each promised to distribute state assets rapidly (Blanchard et al. 1991; Frydman and Rapaczynski 1994).

11. The average commercial rate for 1988 was 14.36 CZK per $; for 1991 the exchange rate was approximately 28 CZK per $.

12. IPFs accumulated about two-thirds of total share value during voucher privatization.

Part II

INSTITUTIONALISM AND BEYOND—INTRODUCING OWNERSHIP REGIME THEORY

2

Institutional Policy Design, Politics, and the Creation of Capitalism

What's the Constitution among friends?

—Tammany Hall motto[1]

How can states create stable and honest market institutions—the capital markets, financial intermediaries, banks, regulatory organs, courts, and tax systems that underlie all successful capitalist economies? This is the critical political economic question facing developing countries today, whether we are discussing the Czech Republic, Russia, or Iraq. Privatization experience in CEECs suggests that a state's capitalist institutions will tend to be unstable and corrupt so long as the competition for ownership of assets remains unresolved among major interest groups. International efforts to foster domestic capitalist institutions at the outset of a transition period may prove disappointing or even counterproductive, despite the underlying importance of regulation and the rule of law to Western capitalism.

The rapid privatization experience of CEECs demonstrated to most analysts that the first successes of a neoliberal privatization approach were illusory. Massive corruption accompanied the state's rapid enterprise divestment nearly everywhere. The theoretical and policy response, commonly referred to as the post–Washington consensus, argued that the state needed to institute firm bases of market regulation and the rule of law prior to privatizing whole economies. This institutional critique of markets was accompanied by another institutional version, which stressed that varieties in the initial regulatory regimes in combination with the country-specific communist industrial structures created multipath trajectories for country development. According to this (second) institutional logic, policymakers needed to create reform programs tailored to specific countries.

The alternative institutional interpretation of privatization presented in this chapter lies in the logic of asset competition. Privatization may be viewed as a competition between politically connected actors seeking assets from the state under a state-designed set of incentives and constraints. In this view, the means of privatization and the subsequent tactics and behavior of the claimants for assets[2] determine the efficacy of markets. Institutions (rules, organizations, routines) may be fleeting during this period. Only after the key battles over the ownership of state enterprises are settled can one speak of permanent institutional progress in the CEECs. Czech transition, for instance, became economically rational when the domestic competition for the valuable enterprise assets ended. Functional and honest capital markets, financial intermediaries, and banks became possible only at that point. Ironically, it was the political enemies of the neoliberal reformers, including the Social Democrats, who instigated stability and economic rationality in Czech finance. Contrary to the two institutional schools of thought that predict a unique national trajectory for the Czech Republic, Czech capital markets now resemble Poland and Hungary, both in scale and regulatory scrutiny. These more recent trends are clear after 1998.

The picture of transition presented here is messier than normal politics and economics. Asset competition is a contingent process in which institutions may have limited relevance and a short life. Why may transition be indeterminate from an institution-building perspective? The reasons lie in fragile state structures, unpredictable politics, inexperienced and sometimes incompetent leaders, unresolved ethnic legacies, and divergent national histories. Institutions that appear familiar to Western eyes may function perversely depending on circumstances. Eventually, institutions may emerge consistent with conventional economic fundamentals, so long as winners of the national asset competition are comfortable with the outcome.

INSTITUTIONALISM (IN TWO FLAVORS) AND PRIVATIZATION

Chapter 1 addressed the neoliberal approach to privatization and the unexplained outcomes that occurred when reformers implemented it. A second school of thought—we will label it the *institutionalist* school—argues that market institutions emerge as a consequence of state policies (Polanyi 1944; Hirschman 1977). State privatization policies automatically establish not only an ownership distribution but also the *first* ownership institutions.[3] Those first-ownership institutions serve as an incentive template for the new private owners to buy, sell, and restructure assets. Ultimately, the activities of the new ownership class will stimulate state officials to adapt those first institutions to renewed state policy objectives.

Institutionalists proposed two privatization scenarios. The corruption that accompanied voucher privatization in the Czech Republic inspired what may be called the *unipath* variant. Unipath institutionalists, in the post–Washington consensus, argued that privatization couldn't create functioning and honest markets by itself.[4] Sequencing was the critical problem. The state needed to create the institutional market framework, especially a capital market regulatory system prior to privatization. Some unipath institutionalists went further, questioning the appropriateness of voucher privatization for the former communist economies. The weak states of the region were unlikely to quickly create a capital market system that could regulate hundreds of publicly traded enterprises (Stiglitz 2002).

Many former advocates of the Washington consensus joined the critique of the neoliberal wisdom, issuing mea culpas (World Bank 2002b, 79;[5] Nellis 1999; Black, Kraakman, and Tarassova 2000; Dabrowski, Gomulka, and Rostowski 2000, 14, note 24[6]). Western bastions of neoliberalism, such as the World Bank, shifted advice and emphasis from the simple transfer of ownership of state assets to the creation of state capacity, the effectiveness of state institutions, and problems of corruption (World Bank 1996). The subsequent collapse of Russian financial markets in 1998, which resembled the earlier experience in the Czech Republic, apparently demonstrated the validity and urgency of the new critique. Only a few true believers, who maintained that the neoliberal orthodoxy of rapid privatization had been successful despite the rampant corruption, remained Washington consensus advocates (Åslund 2002).

In what may be called the *multipath* variant, variations in state privatization strategies created distinct national institutional trajectories, a precursor to distinct national capitalisms. Supporters of this variant predicted that differences in CEEC capitalisms could be traced in large part to the original privatization strategy (Stark and Bruszt 1998; McDermott 2002). Multipath institutionalists tend to be sociologists, political scientists, and other social scientists who emphasized the importance of the social and political networks of the prior regime. They belong, broadly speaking, to the "varieties of capitalism" school of political economy (Shonfield 1969; Sabel 1982; Hall and Soskice 2001). Advocates of these views tended to support privatization policies that emphasized close working relationships between states (especially local governments) and enterprises. Although policymakers mostly have overlooked these institutionalists to this point, their theoretical position has attracted scholarly attention.[7]

According to the unipath and multipath institutional variants, the creation of capitalism is a path-dependent process in which the method of privatization has enduring consequences. Institutional changes in a path-dependent model emanate from the extant institutional setting, tracing a continuous if not always predictable trajectory. More generally, path-dependent institutionalism is emerging as a major organizing theme in political science (Collier and Collier 1991; Pierson 2000). From a policy standpoint, institutionalists argued that states should adopt privatization strategies that would prioritize developing market institutions at the outset of transition, especially market regulatory bodies, over the simple creation of private owners, as neoliberals advocated.

The neoliberal and institutional schools underplay the impact of the competition for asset ownership unleashed by privatization on institution building. Rivals for asset ownership may overwhelm state institutions through bribery and intimidation during a transition period, when the laws that govern state officials are poorly defined and enforced. The institutions that emerge from privatization to channel the capital of the new private owners, especially capital markets, financial intermediaries, and banks, are significant centers of asset redistribution. Though enterprise (and economy) restructuring is the critical variable for nearly all students of transition, many new and prospective owners tend to focus more on the immediate goal of asset ownership and control during transition. Local populations who lost in the asset competition often came to resent Western voices, which misunderstood that transition countries' capital markets, financial intermediaries, and banks may be "capitalist" in name only.

From the perspective that asset competition is the dominant driver of institution building during transition, we conclude that:

- Contrary to neoliberals
  - Assets may change hands via corruption and intimidation during and after privatization, not via *business valuation and rationality*.
  - Privatization insensitive to characteristics of the first new owners may result in delayed development (as measured in foreign direct investment [FDI]).
  - Privatization insensitive to the role of state market regulation may embed state corruption, compromising the neutral regulatory (and developmental) potential of the state.
- Contrary to institutionalists (*unipath and multipath*)
  - National privatization strategies may create the opportunity and incentive structures that influence the process of institution building, but this institution-building path may be jagged and unpredictable, *not path dependent*.
  - The eventual appearance of stable institutions may be unrelated to the state-policy-generated institutional configuration after privatization.

TRANSITION AS ASSET COMPETITION

Some of the more recent work emerging from the post–Washington consensus school emphasizes that transition is an inherently unstable period, in which the fight for state assets is paramount and issues of restructuring, economic development, and political development are secondary, at least for local interests. The "winner take all" perspective (Hellman 1998) is an important acknowledgment that economic reform efforts can go wrong if the winners have no interest in imposing a Western-style capitalist system. The corruption engendered can persist past the transition period (see also Cohen and Schwartz 1993). Moreover, Acemoglu (2003) and Hoff and Stiglitz (2002) demonstrate theoretically that the notion of a Political Coase Theorem (government leaders will choose the most efficient economic policies in order to become reelected) may flounder on the inability of the state to provide a credible commitment for investors to invest rationally for the long term. In this vein, the thrust of efforts emanating from the World Bank and other international organizations increasingly seeks to understand the roots and pathologies of corruption.

The post–Washington consensus school is correct to draw attention to corruption as a major problem during transition periods, just as the recognition that "winners write the rules" is a major step beyond early neoliberal theory. However, the post–Washington consensus viewpoint, in contrast to the institutional approach presented here, still fails to adequately confront and analyze the instability that is inherent in periods of transition. Supposed institutional progress toward capitalism may mask what is in essence a colossal power struggle. Transition as asset competition refers to the idea that much of an economy is, as Wall Street analysts might say, "in play," but unlike the rules of the markets in developed economies, the lack of rules and regulations is the distinguishing characteristic of transition. The Czech case, for instance, demonstrates that institutions may perform an entirely different function than the classic textbooks might indicate, as evidenced by the massive asset stripping carried out by managers of investment privatization funds. Apparent institutional progress may, for instance, mask the delay of more permanent institution building.

In addition, transition viewed as ownership competition takes an unusual perspective on the character of transition institutions. Most institutionalists who analyze Central and Eastern Europe implicitly assume transition institutions are *consolidated*, that is, they constrain most actors most of the time.[8] They ascribe reform policies' outcomes to newly created constitutions (Elster, Offe, and Preuss 1998), the number of decision-making veto points (Keefer and Shirley 1997), political party structure (Haggard, Kaufman, and Shugart 1998), or the first-ownership structure (Stark and Bruszt 1998). In transition, however, the reality is that sometimes structure matters and sometimes it doesn't. Reform politics may take place outside of an institutional setting, and may emphasize such traditionally noninstitutional variables such as ideology, nationalism, education, or personal connections. For instance, the Tammany Hall motto, "What's the Constitution among friends?" is as alive in CEECs today as it was in New York City a century ago. Institutionalists sometimes mistakenly presume that transition institutions are consolidated and thus attribute them causal power when none may exist.

It is invariably very tricky, then, to gauge where national institutions will "end up." In the Czech case, for instance, a Czech plutocracy analogous to that of Russia never developed, thanks to a variety of factors: the opportunity of Czech first owners to sell assets to foreign interests; the possibilities for managers to build profitable businesses after privatization; and the government's inability and unwillingness to subsidize the new owners.[9] And in Russia, the plutocrats remained precisely because, on the one hand, they had longer lasting opportunities to reap subsidies from the state and, on the other hand, relatively poor chances to sell assets to foreigners (see chapter 11).[10]

This chapter and the one that follows demonstrate a causal connection, *first*, between privatization strategies and first-ownership regimes (privatization outcomes), and *second* between first-ownership regimes and subsequent political and economic development. This second part pays particular attention to the nexus between privatization strategies and the capacity and autonomy of the state regulator of financial markets due to the importance that the reigning post–Washington consensus assigns to regulatory institutions. The discussion proceeds in four sections.

The first section introduces an institutional concept of ownership, called here an ownership regime. Privatization generates first-ownership regimes, which establish a template for future development. Ownership regimes are comprised of four characteristics: (1) owner attributes, (2) institutional framework, (3) financial markets, and (4) characteristics of the state market regulator.

The second section refines the concept of regulation. It shows how an effective system of financial regulations is essential to a functioning market economy and to a participatory democracy. While detailing the role of the state in the regulation of most market economies, it also illustrates the key role that nonstate actors may play in a modern regulatory system, as in the United States. Finally, the section contends that variations in ownership regimes may pressure the newly constituted CEEC state regulators to the breaking point, thereby undermining the relevance of the post–Washington consensus school.

The third section (beginning in chapter 3) offers a privatization decision-making model that illustrates how state choices at the outset of privatization (and, typically, during transition) create ownership regimes, including regulators who may vary in autonomy and capacity. The key state decisions revolve around the speed and extent of privatization as well as the character of the state administration that implements and monitors the privatization process. Initial conditions and historical legacies such as ideology, nationalism, and the bargaining power of interest groups help determine state privatization decisions.

This section employs a path-dependent framework to situate the variables influencing state privatization decisions.

The fourth section (beginning in chapter 4) considers how first-ownership regimes may evolve. The point of departure is that the first-ownership regimes of Central European countries—Group 1 countries—may tend to evolve according to a neo-Coasian or neoliberal logic, while the first-ownership regimes of the former Soviet Union—Group 2 countries—may tend to evolve according to a non-Coasian or political logic. This section derives two main hypotheses from this insight. First, privatization strategies may have greatly impacted the developmental trajectory of Group 1 countries, but may have had relatively little lasting impact on Group 2 countries. Second, plutocracies are likely to disappear in Group 1 countries, but to remain embedded in Group 2 countries for the foreseeable future.[11]

THE FIRST-OWNERSHIP REGIME: PRIVATIZATION'S OUTCOME

Privatization outcomes are predicated on a broad and complex conception of ownership—an *ownership regime*—in which the privatization process institutionally determines the interests and behavior of private owners. First private owners are critical precisely because they may establish a template for the future development of CEEC societies. Given circumstances, the first private owners may serve as positive impetuses for economic and political development, as neoliberals expect, or they may work against the development of capitalism and democracy, especially if markets lack safeguards.

Four parameters characterize an ownership regime:[12]

1. *Attributes of Owners* described by the owners' skills, resources, morals, cultural background, business experience, and contact with the West.
2. *Systems of Corporate Governance*
   a. *Ownership network structures* described by the links between ownership entities and by the network of cross-holding among private owners (illustrated by a flowchart of who owns whom).
   b. *Internal corporate governance patterns* described by the distribution of ownership stakes within enterprises.
   c. *Encompassing laws and rules* described by the tax system, bankruptcy, intellectual property, auditing, foreign trade, and so forth.
3. *Financial Markets* described by the role, efficiency, and transparency of stock exchanges, debt markets, banks, investment funds, and brokerage firms.

4. *The State Financial Market Regulator*
   a. *Autonomy* described by the regulators' willingness to maintain an identity independent of private interests and politicians.
   b. *Capacity* described by the state's ability to enforce financial regulations.

The advocates of the post–Washington consensus regard the state financial market regulator as a critical, perhaps *the* critical component of an ownership regime. Its capacity and autonomy are crucial because they impact the openness of markets (the quality of capitalism) and the equality of government (the quality of democracy).

Ownership regimes characterized by states that enact and enforce impartial ownership rules are *regulated ownership regimes*. Ownership regimes characterized by states unable or unwilling to enact and to enforce impartial ownership rules are *unregulated ownership regimes*. Regulated and unregulated ownership regimes may be best conceived of as representing points at extreme ends of a "regulation continuum," rather than as pairs of a dichotomy. Unregulated ownership regimes may be associated with the political and economic dominance of a plutocracy.

The importance of a state regulator with capacity and autonomy is heightened in CEECs, where many private owners, enterprise managers, financial organizations, and government officials lack the market experience and savvy to restructure enterprises for competition. A lack of market understanding, combined with high political and economic uncertainty, backward technology, overcapacity, and ineffective regulation, pressured economic actors to plan only for the short term. Unclear prospects persuaded many economic actors— particularly those who controlled (but may not have owned) enterprise assets— to extract cash from operating companies. The obvious tactic was some form of market manipulation in which actors could seize and then liquidate enterprise assets for their own account. Market manipulation, in turn, invariably involved the state; the state must be a co-conspirator in market manipulation, owing either to its incompetence as market regulator or its complicity.

Societal costs associated with market manipulation by private owners with state participation may be steep. The economic threat is that rent seeking and capital flight will displace enterprise investment and restructuring and thus jeopardize future growth. The political threat is that private owners will co-opt or capture state officials, and thus create a government dominated by a privileged minority. These political and economic threats differentiated Central and Eastern Europe from other places that sought to restructure entire economies, such as post–World War II Japan and Germany and perhaps East Asia, where many private owners were entrepreneurs (in Schumpeter's sense). In those societies, one can imagine a logic by which a little corruption could be a good thing. From an economic vantage, corruption might offer entrepreneurs a conduit to circumvent otherwise harmful (to business) state intervention (Huntington 1968). From a political vantage, it could give entrepreneurs and state bureaucrats—groups that otherwise might be losers—incentives to join a reform coalition (Huntington 1968). In CEECs, however, where the institutional configurations of postcommunism created significant opportunities to steal and asset strip, the incentive structures that elsewhere may have ameliorated some of the nasty effects of corruption did not exist.

FINANCIAL MARKET REGULATION

Contemporary states influence business activity in meaningful and diverse ways. They subsidize and tax companies and citizens (the customers of companies); restrict and open market access to companies; control certain input and output prices; design, maintain, and monitor a legal framework for enforcing agreements between economic parties; and impose penalties on economic parties for noncompliance with state statutes. States also operate a fiscal policy and monetary policy, as well as a foreign trade policy, that broadly influence the economy and regulate markets (Kagan 1978, 8).

Regulation, as used here, is the set of state activities that directly control the access and rights of actors to markets, through monitoring and compliance procedures. Regulation in this sense mainly (though not exclusively) limits or constrains the freedom of market actors. For instance, the term "regulation" as used here applies to state efforts to license would-be market participants such as doctors, lawyers, craftsmen, or stockbrokers, though not to automobile operators (unless they drive for commercial purposes). The term "regulation" also applies to state efforts to fix prices; to control the quantity, safety, and quality of firm products; and to regulate the environment, though this sense of the term is not emphasized here. The tools of regulators are regulations or laws, or what Kagan refers to as "direct *legal orders*" (Kagan 1978, 8; italics added).

Two key elements of regulation are the autonomy and capacity of the state regulatory administration. *Autonomy*, as used here, refers to the separation of the state regulatory administration from the parochial concerns of politicians and from the economic concerns of special interest groups. Autonomous "[regulatory] laws are expected to address broadly defined categories of individuals and acts and to be applied without personal or class favoritism" (Unger 1976, 53). From a practical standpoint, autonomous laws are transparent, freely accessible (with a minimum of effort and expense), and consistent in application over time (Hendley 1993, 31).

Capacity as used here refers to the state's ability to enforce regulations. Enforcement includes both the state's ability to monitor the regulated economic activity, to adjudicate in cases of suspected violations, and to act forcefully when the state considers that a regulation has been violated. Effective monitoring requires state officials who have expertise and competence in the regulated business sector and who have good access to information flows (Vickers and Yarrow 1988, 347). Effective adjudication requires comprehensive and clear laws, an efficient and independent court (or arbitration) system, and judges with expertise. The basis of enforcement—indeed, the basis of a legal order— is the comparative advantage of the state to use violence to punish violators of regulations. A legal order is, to cite Weber, "externally guaranteed by the probability that physical or psychological coercion will be applied by a *staff* of people in order to bring about compliance or avenge violation" (Weber 1978, 34; italics added).

Regulatory capacity also depends on reciprocity between the regulator and the regulated or, more broadly, between the governor and the governed. The authority of the state regulator goes beyond the state's ability to impose social control in top-down fashion; it acknowledges the existence of both state and society as participants in creating and maintaining a regulatory regime. The notion of law as reciprocity is a new concept to CEECs. Under communism, "law was always associated with the state and its own self-perpetuation.... The legal system was considered an appendage of the regime to be avoided whenever possible" (Hendley 1993, 38–39).

The acknowledgment of regulatory reciprocity between the state and society suggests the narrowness of the regulation concept developed thus far. Regulation may occur without the intervention of state regulators, as, for example, when a private party sues another private party for the breach of an agreement, or when a (privately owned) stock exchange imposes penalties on a rule-breaking member. Indeed, regulation involves more than just the state regulatory administration, but also courts and policemen as well as private actors. These additional factors force one to think about regulation broadly, not just in terms of state regulation but also of a *regulatory system*.

FINANCIAL MARKET REGULATION AND PRIVATE RENT SEEKING

The post–Washington Consensus is founded on the acknowledgment that regimes of corporate ownership and control are essential components of markets and politics. They depend on the regulations or regulatory systems that apply to financial assets and markets. Regulatory systems, in turn, depend on the integrity of principal-agent relationships that underlie the financial assets concept.

Financial assets are commonly accepted rights on physical assets, including corporate shares. When physical assets are rights or obligations on company assets, financial assets tend to come in permutations of equity and debt. Many financial assets are contracts that allow holders to "delegate" the inherent rights to another party to manage and safeguard (Spencer 2000, 1).

The worth of financial assets depends on the power balance of a network of principals' and agents' relationships. This very long list includes, and is not limited to, shareholder-broker; shareholder–fund manager; shareholder–company manager; fund manager–company manager; company manager–company employee; company manager–banker; and taxman–company manager. We can only appraise financial assets from a rendering of appropriate actors, incentive and penalty structures, and the character of information asymmetries (Akerlof 1970; Stiglitz 1994). The myriad scandals at many of the world's biggest (and once most reputable) companies (Enron, WorldCom, Tyco) demonstrate the difficulty of resolving principal-agent systems in the best of conditions. The challenge is that much greater in emerging economies.

Financial markets are arenas of exchange or marketplaces where financial actors lend, borrow, buy, sell, or barter financial assets. Financial actors come in innumerable organizational forms and sizes, and include banks, insurance companies, investors, speculators, traders, industrial companies, mutual funds, pension funds, and sometimes governments. Financial markets may be public, as in stock exchanges, futures pits, options, or bond markets, or they may be proprietary, as for example, investment banks that design derivative contracts for specific investors. *Stock markets* are public financial markets.

Financial market regulation is regulation of financial marketplaces and the actors who exchange financial assets. Financial market regulation is necessary to a high level of capitalism because it prevents agents from violating the financial asset rights of shareholders (principals). As we shall argue below, state privatization decisions establish the organization and set the effectiveness of financial market regulatory systems in CEECs.

Financial market regulations standard in the West include:[13]

- *Stock market regulations*, including company financial disclosure requirements, minority shareholder protection, mechanisms for investigating and penalizing fraud, procedures for registering market participants, rules and compliance procedures to guard against insider trading, front-running, and other abuses by stock market participants, and establishment and enforcement of capital requirements.
- *Laws constraining financial intermediaries* (*mutual funds, pension funds, insurance companies, banks*), including bank safety and soundness criteria, financial reporting requirements, rights of financial intermediary

investors, rules and mechanisms regulating the size of the portfolio, the percentage of ownership intermediaries may acquire in operating companies, the holding period, and the fee structure.

- *Antitrust or competition law,* including restrictions on ownership structures, restrictions on collusive pricing, and restrictions on coercive methods of competition.
- *Corporation law*, including regulations defining and restricting the rights and obligations of managers and shareholders, procedures for establishing managers (company directors) and fiduciary responsibilities (including restrictions on self-dealing, especially asset movements to the detriment of shareholders), and mechanisms for punishing directors who abuse their trust.

The interconnectedness of those financial market laws with other institutions (such as banks) reaffirms the analytic significance of distinguishing a regulatory system from a state regulatory administration. Consider the financial regulatory system of the United States, which "depends less on the affirmative action of particular agencies, such as the Federal Securities and Exchange Commission (SEC) and the Anti-Trust Division, as on private litigation and the courts." Class actions under the securities laws and private enforcement of the antitrust laws, with their promise of treble damages, are as important as enforcement by U.S. regulatory authorities (Kagan memorandum 1999).

The salience of a complex and integrated regulatory system of financial markets in Western capitalism shows that effective financial market regulation demands more than a state financial market regulator with capacity and autonomy. It demands laws and mechanisms for dealing with each market failure that may arise, along with a society that accepts the verdicts of the state regulators. Nevertheless, there is no mistaking the fact that an effective regulatory system depends on state regulators who are autonomous and have the capacity to regulate financial markets.

The questions CEEC governments in transition have raised are: Given the costs in time, effort, money, and uncertainty, is it worth constructing a state regulatory administration over financial markets with capacity and autonomy? Or, is it possible to create an effective financial market regulatory system based on nonstate actors without first (or simultaneously) creating a strong state financial regulatory system?

The answers to those crucial questions turn on a more basic one: What are the risks of markets without effective financial regulation? From an economic perspective, one answer is probably diminished long-term growth prospects. Those who control financial assets—either through force or physical possession—will be tempted to seize them. At the extreme, this means that bank accounts may not be safe from bankers, shares may not be safe from financial intermediaries, and enterprise assets may not be safe from managers. These are classic principle-agent problems (Berle and Means 1932). The concrete risks to the nascent capitalism in CEECs are the delegitimacy of collective investment (for example, participation in pension funds, investment funds, or strategic partnerships), capital flight, and foreign investment shortfalls. The last is dangerous to the growth prospects of the region, given the shortage in advanced technology, market management skill, market access, and capital. This view shares North's insight—once embedded, a system of property rights that produces inefficient economic outcomes may endure (North 1981, 1990).

From a political perspective, one risk of ineffective financial regulation is a diminished quality of democracy. When state regulators are not autonomous, then the political system cannot be participatory (in the egalitarian sense defined here). Wealthy and well-connected groups will be able to influence state decision-makers while poor and unconnected groups will be excluded. Moreover, a rigged political system must invariably lose the confidence of its citizens, and thus eventually its stability. In this same vein, the poor economic results that may emerge from an ineffective regulatory system may also undermine the popular support for democratic institutions and instead provide support for ideologues, who espouse the kind of authoritarian solutions that almost no one in the West wants. We can already see the unfortunate political tendencies of inadequate financial regulation, not only in the Czech case, which we analyze in detail here, but also in the cases of some of the former Soviet Republics where indifference to market regulation of all sorts has limited economic growth and endangered political reforms (Cohen and Schwartz 1993; Cohen, Schwartz, and Zysman 1998). Unregulated capitalism may produce nondemocratic politics.

NOTES

1. Attributed to Tim Campbell in Riordan 1963, 13.
2. Such as managers, workers, state bureaucrats, and foreign interests.
3. Advocates for an active state role emphasized the developmental potential of the state (see Amsden, Kochanowicz, and Taylor 1994) rather than its regulatory possibilities at the outset of transition.
4. Unipath thinking has been common in transition analysis beyond privatization (and economics). Many analysts have spoken about the progress of the former communist states in building capitalism and democracy, as if Western institution building followed a known and measurable course (see, for instance, Elster, Offe, and Preuss 1998).

5. "Medium-size and large enterprises should target sales to strategic outside investors. . . . Although several transaction methods may be used, including negotiated sales, this can be brought about most effectively through competitive 'case-by-case' methods, more deliberative than voucher schemes or rapid, small auctions."

6. "Except for Dabrowski, we supported voucher privatisation at the time, wrongly as it turned out."

7. A possible exception is the role of McDermott in designing the Czech Restructualization Agency.

8. Institutional approaches have become popular in analyses of economic policy-making in CEECs (Stark and Bruszt 1998; Elster, Offe, and Preuss 1998; Hausner, Pederson, and Ronit 1995).

9. One could also add to this list some remarkably poor business decisions by the prospective new plutocrats, the new regulatory fervor of Social Democratic government, and the foreign bank privatizations.

10. In retrospect, one may characterize the financial upheaval in 1998 as a great "plutocrats war," in which some of the new financial groups benefited enormously while others were forced into bankruptcy, their chiefs sometimes fleeing the country.

11. In between these two groups falls a group of middle countries, including Bulgaria and Romania, that share characteristics of Group 1 and Group 2 countries. We could call these Group 3 countries; their developmental trajectory is likely to trace an intermediate pattern from the other two country groups.

12. Note that the following four factors are not intended to be exhaustive. For instance, privatization may force an immediate change in an asset's basic characteristics via function, line of business, fungibility, or value. Moreover, telecommunication assets differ from banks and strategic assets differ from the "family china." I consider the nature of the asset to be secondary to the four ownership regime characteristics above.

13. This formulation and wording is extracted from a personal memo written by Professor Robert Kagan to the author in 1999.

3

Ownership Regimes—The Basic Model of How They Form

The next set of issues concerns the sources and variations of privatization. Specifically, it is necessary to identify the critical state privatization decisions, understand their consequences, learn why they were chosen, and be able to compare privatization experiences across countries. Given the complexity and experience necessary for the West to operate modern market regulatory systems (and hardly smoothly at that), important background questions revolve around whether it was possible for the CEECs to develop a financial market regulatory system for a rapid privatization trajectory.

STATE CHOICES AND PRIVATIZATION

The model begins with the institutional premise that state officials determine the mode of privatization and thereby the first-ownership regime (the privatization outcome or "dependent variable"). The key state decisions concern the role and organization of the state administration and the privatization speed. In practice, state decision-makers are faced with a menu of privatization choices, each of which can be assigned to a "centralized path" or "decentralized path" category (see table 3.1). The saliency of state decisions focuses the model on identifying the state decision-makers, their motivations, as well as the pertinent nonstate actors and influences.

I. Nonstandard, Centralized Privatization Methods
   A. Voucher Privatization—Masses
      1. *Without intermediaries—individuals*: The state offers individuals enterprise shares for free (or for a nominal charge). In this case, individuals may not pool their shares.
      2. *With intermediaries—voucher investment funds*: As above, but individuals may pool their shares into spontaneously formed institutions.
   B. Institutional Privatization—National Investment Funds. The state creates private (nonstate) institutions to act as enterprise owners.

Table 3.1.　The Privatization Menu

Nonstandard, Centralized Privatization Methods (Mass Privatization)	*Standard, Decentralized Privatization Methods (Case-by-Case Privatization)*
1. Voucher Privatization 　(a) Without Intermediaries 　(b) With Intermediaries 2. Institutional Privatization	A. Insider Privatization 　(a) Manager Preference 　(b) Worker Preference B. Market Privatization 　(a) Public Sale, Domestic Buyers 　(b) Public Sale, Foreign Buyers 　(c) Public Sale, Open C. Tender Privatization D. Reprivatization E. State Residual Shareholding F. Other Methods

II. Standard, Decentralized Privatization Methods
　　A. Insider Privatization—Enterprise Insiders[1]
　　　　1. *Manager preference—managers*: The state transfers enterprise stakes according to manager preferences, that is, usually to enterprise managers or their agents.
　　　　2. *Worker preference—employees*: The state transfers enterprise stakes to enterprise employees. Worker privatization may be organized as an ESOP (employee share ownership plan).
　　B. Market Privatization—Moneyed Groups
　　　　1. *Public sale, domestic buyers—domestic interests*: The state sells enterprise stakes to the highest national bidder. Techniques may include public auction and closed bidding or direct sale (so-called envelope methods).
　　　　2. *Public sale, foreign buyers—foreign interests*: The state sells enterprise stakes to the highest foreign bidder.
　　　　3. *Public sale, open—foreign and domestic interests*: The state sells enterprise stakes to the highest bidder.
　　C. Tender Privatization—Various Claimants. Public tenders are the common examples of tender privatization. Situation-specific criteria, such as financing arrangements, access to Western markets, price, workforce changes, and introduction of new technology, set the winning claimants.
　　D. Reprivatization—Former Owners. The state offers ownership preferences to owners (or their descendants) of assets seized by the communists.

E. State Residual Shareholding—Central State. State residual shareholding is manifest by state enterprise stakes. Note that enterprise stakes can remain in state hands, while the economy as a whole is privatized.

F. Other Methods—Various. Other privatization methods may include transfers to local government or to charitable organizations, reprivatization, debt-equity swaps, and insolvency proceedings.

Path Dependence

A path-dependent framework situates the factors that motivate state decision-makers. *Path dependence*, as used here, is "a process of evolutionary change in which choices are heavily conditioned by earlier choices."[2] Or put differently, path dependence "depends heavily on the structure of already existing institutional arrangements and rationalities" (Campbell and Pedersen 1995, 31, fn. 1).[3]

Privatization decisions have an internal logic or rhythm that conforms to a path-dependent logic. When state officials have decided to privatize large numbers of enterprises, they must first determine a general approach, next decide which enterprises to privatize (and by what means), and then implement the privatization approach. In organizing privatization decision-making as a *sequential* process, I allow that privatization can be analyzed as a series of distinct and incremental stages that are path dependent. Privatization may be conceived of as path dependent once state actors embark on a particular privatization path, say a centralized or decentralized path.

Privatization may, on the other hand, fail the path-dependent criteria depending on the costs to a state policymaker(s) for switching privatization paths in midstream. Thus in the Czech Republic, the political costs accrued to Klaus would have been prohibitive for changing from a centralized to a decentralized privatization path at virtually any point in privatization. In Poland, on the other hand, major politicians often refused to commit to a single privatization approach, though Poland had been achieving substantial (path-dependent type) progress toward its institutional privatization approach (see chapter 11).

Path dependence is an attractive analytic device to model privatization decision-making for two reasons. First, it provides a mechanism to identify when and how political and economic constraints and opportunities for state decision-makers may shift in the course of privatization. Initial decisions are usually critical, because they lock in options for policymakers. In particular, early privatization decisions activate a sequence of tasks or functions that structure (constrain and enable) later options for state decision-makers. A path-dependent framework of privatization thus represents an analytic means to draw hypotheses regarding the sources of privatization preferences, how they might change over time, and how those preferences might translate into state policy choices. Second, a path-dependent model of privatization—by stressing process—avoids misleading and simplistic characterizations of reform as a single "big bang" or "shock therapy."

The path-dependent privatization model still may draw the internal options for privatization actors narrowly for two reasons. One, not all to-be-privatized enterprises will move through the privatization process as one bundle. State policymakers invariably will decide to handle some enterprises differently than others. This consideration means that the timing of privatization of enterprises will vary and that the privatization path traced by individual enterprises will also vary. Given differences in timing and privatization path over enterprise privatization, it is easy to imagine that the privatization process will stray from one single path and that privatization stages might overlap one another.

Two, the path-dependent privatization model considers the course of privatization in isolation from external factors. For instance, it minimizes the pressure on state policymakers stemming from other economic problems (such as an overhang of foreign debt), from ethnic disputes, and from privatization developments in other CEECs (which may impact learning).

Ideology and Nationalism in Privatization

The explanation for privatization outcomes places special emphasis on factors apparent at the very outset of transition. In particular, I contend that ideology, both at the elite and at the popular levels, partly accounted for early privatization choices of state officials.[4] It was natural that the dominant ideology would be neoliberalism and that neoliberals would be popular during the transition period, given the then-pervasive enmity toward all things communist. At the same time, the significance of ideology in privatization decision-making fluctuated over time, and it varied cross-nationally. For instance, neoliberal ideology was more apparent at the beginning of the transition period than later on; and it was more apparent in the Czech Republic and Russia than in Hungary. Historical legacies play a critical role in the propagation of neoliberal ideology, as is noted when the chapter expands on the privatization model.

Since its emphasis on ideology is somewhat unusual for contemporary studies that analyze the development of capitalist institutions, we need to define the term.[5] *Ideology*, as used here, is shorthand for the system of ideas that people use to interpret events. It is usually expressed as models or theories, yet I assign it no claim on rationality or organization. Ideology may reveal itself in policy statements or opinion polls, though the evidence of ideology in a particular policy domain is ultimately a matter of judgment. Economic theories, political theories, environmentalism, religions, cults, and nationalism (see below) are examples of ideologies, as the term is used here. The aggressive purveyor of ideology is the *ideologue*, a person who believes in his ideology fervently and has no reservations about expressing it.

Ideology may be contrasted with pragmatism. *Pragmatism*, as used here, emphasizes instrumental rationality. Pragmatists don't necessarily reject ideology; rather, they use it to achieve instrumental aims. Pragmatists reason from experience (inductively), whereas ideologues reason from first principles (deductively). James's distinctions between the "tough-minded" pragmatist and the "tender-minded" ideologue frame this divergence. The tough-minded pragmatist is "empiricist, sensationalist, materialistic, pessimistic, irreligious, fatalistic, pluralistic, and skeptical." The tender-minded ideologue is "rationalistic, intellectualistic, idealistic, optimistic, religious, free-willist, monistic, and dogmatical" (James 1907/1991, 9). Neoliberals tended to be ideologues; the Czech leadership led by Klaus was among the most extreme, at least just after the fall of communism.

Life experience shows that the attraction of ideology may change over time. An ideologue, for instance, may switch ideologies or become a pragmatist. North suggests that changes in the ownership regime is one possible stimulus: "an alteration in property rights which denies individuals access to resources which they had heretofore come to accept as customary or just (the enclosure of common land, for example)" (North 1981, 50). North's example carried special relevance in Central and Eastern Europe, where the communist government had over decades seized personal property amid failed promises of economic revitalization, to say nothing of state-sponsored terror. It was then little wonder that many men and women who were ideologues first later switched ideologies or became pragmatists.

The transition period also was a time when ideologies were likely to be fluid. Neoliberal reformers were making big promises, yet they were facing economic slowdown and increased domestic political competition. Populations that were initially ideologically very receptive to the neoliberals could presumably reverse loyalties quickly if the transition period went badly.[6] And, as popular opinions changed, so might the ideological commitment of the reformers. From a neoliberal vantage, the great risk of transition was that ideological momentum for the "combat task" would dissipate, both at the elite and popular levels.

The aesthetic of neoliberal theory is that it allowed reformers to "square the circle," to be both ideological and pragmatic.[7] Neoliberals could violate democratic and free-market norms in the short run, so long as they pursued the long-term objective of a capitalist economy. How neoliberal reformers responded to the tension between ideological ends and short-term pragmatism would determine the course of economic liberalization, including privatization.

Neoliberal theory was pragmatic in another sense. Unlike communism, which was based on a utopian vision, neoliberalism was founded on a developmental model that was "proved," to cite Czech reformer Klaus. Fundamental theoretical principles of free markets and democracy presumably had produced Western prosperity—especially in the United States. Moreover, adherence to neoliberal ideology would hasten the entry of CEECs into the global capitalist system, particularly the European Union. These considerations added a pragmatic, "empiricist" component to neoliberalism to go along with the ideological, "rationalistic" component represented by the likes of Friedman, Hayek, and other free-market theorists. Neoliberal pragmatism would become an effective rhetoric weapon in privatization debates, because it allowed reformers to repudiate both the failed communist experiment of the past and the "third way" utopianism proposed by those seeking a compromise between communism and unfettered markets.

Nationalism also played an important role in the determination of privatization policy. *Nationalism* is "a particular perspective or a style of thought. The idea that lies at the core of nationalism is the idea of the 'nation.' "[8] Nationalism embeds collective psychological feelings of pride, resentment, superiority, and inferiority—sometimes causing delusions of national grandeur among elites and citizens. There is little doubt that nationalism influenced privatization decision-makers in CEECs.[9] Consider that in the Czech Republic surveys showed that most Czechs opposed selling companies to Germans, a fear based mostly on historical animosity. Privatization xenophobia was also apparent in Poland, where citizens were averse to selling assets to most categories of foreigners, including Russians and Jews (Orenstein 1996, 131). Or consider that the ruling privatization decision-makers of Poland, the Czech Republic, and Hungary competed with each other to see which country's privatization approach was the best. National hubris partly explains why these countries were rivals.

Nationalism may be very difficult to separate from alternative explanations of privatization outcomes. The decision to limit privatization booty to nationals and exclude foreigners is a case in point. Which "cause" is the greatest culprit: Is it nationalism?

Or is it political expediency (to satisfy influential local interests or to boost popularity for policy initiatives)?

Or is it corruption (to reserve property for themselves or for friends)?

Or is it neoliberal ideology (to put assets in the hands of a domestic "middle class")?

Isolating causality in the context of privatization analysis will necessarily require more detailed work than exists in a single study. The point here is that nationalism is a variable too frequently neglected in political economic analyses.

THE PRIVATIZATION DECISION-MAKING MODEL

The privatization decision-making model orders state choices into elite approval, public legitimization, supply-side tasks, and implementation stages (see figure 3.1). Although stage outcomes reflect earlier choices, a stage constitutes an environment of functions, routines, actors, organizations, formal laws and regulations, and mechanisms of enforcement and compliance. Stages represent significant breaks in the privatization process and identify spots where material shifts in orientation and policy may occur.[10]

The initial major state choice is the role and organization of the state administration in privatization. It sets privatization on a path that can be categorized as *decentralized* or *centralized*. Centralized privatization paths keep decision-making in the hands of senior state officials. Decentralized privatization paths delegate decision-making—to state bureaucrats, consultants, or enterprise insiders. Each path admits variation in the organization of privatization—privatization rules, ministry roles, and privatization methods. In practice, CEECs followed privatization paths with both decentralized and centralized components; we can label these *mixed privatization paths*. A decision tree describes possible privatization paths (see figure 3.2).

The second major state choice is privatization speed. Privatization speed may be defined as the amount of enterprise assets (measured by number or value) privatized over a given time period. Privatization in the Czech Republic may be considered rapid—the state privatized about two-thirds of large enterprises[11] "all at once" from 1989 to 1995. Privatization in Poland may be considered gradual—the state privatized about one-third of large enterprises "case-by-case" over about the same period (Schwartz and Haggard 1997). Privatization speed may amplify or overwhelm the natural tendencies of a centralized or decentralized privatization path. For example, a rapid privatization approach may lower the discretion of state bureaucrats by forcing them to review decisions hastily. In sum, two variables may identify a privatization path—the centralization or decentralization of privatization and the privatization speed.

Elite Approval → Public Legitimization → Supply Side Tasks → Implementation

Figure 3.1. The Privatization Stage Sequence.

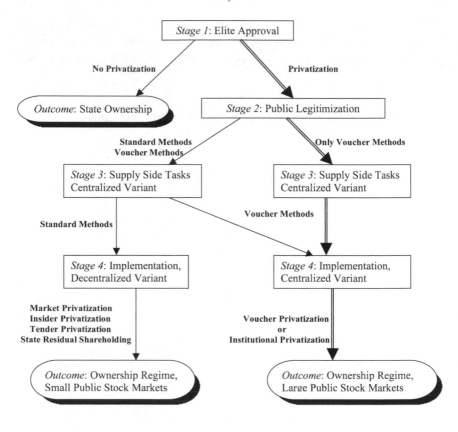

Figure 3.2.　**Privatization Decision Tree, Generic.**

Historical Legacies

The methods of social control exercised by the former communist regimes in the 1970s and 1980s shaped the opportunities of neoliberals to influence privatization politics in the "elite approval stage." Although all communist regimes suppressed basic civil rights, some were more aggressive than others. Two critical factors were: (1) limitations on citizen contacts with the West during communism, and (2) the latitude granted civil society (individuals and groups operating outside of state control) during communism. I label the more repressive regimes *conservative*, and the more mild regimes *reformist*. The

Czechoslovakian and Soviet communist regimes were unambiguously conservative; the Hungarian and Polish communist regimes were unambiguously reformist.

The first legacy from the communist methods of social control was ideological. Conservative communist regimes tended to engender extreme antipathy to communism and extreme passion for Western capitalism and democracy during the transition period. Those strong feelings translated into popular support for radical reform proposals, such as rapid privatization. They also helped constrain the organized interests of the communist past (trade unions, managerial associations, and the state bureaucracy) from effectively lobbying for reforms. These interests with clear roots to the communist past frequently lacked legitimacy from their own memberships. Meanwhile, the leaderships of these organizations were sometimes too preoccupied by turf battles to articulate a coherent policy agenda. Consequently, neoliberals had especially good chances to ascend to power and to implement a rapid privatization strategy where anticommunist ideology was pervasive.[12]

Consider, on the other hand, the situation in countries with reform communist regimes. The same groups that the communists had offered latitude just prior to 1989 emerged in the reform debates during transition. Since those groups typically included enterprise insiders (managers or workers), the obstacles to a rapid privatization strategy may have been close to insurmountable. A major problem was that ideological reformers could not overcome local enterprise opposition to rapid privatization. Indeed, the bargaining position of interest groups after transition proved decisive for the general privatization approach, as in the Polish and Hungarian cases.

In sum, transition countries that experienced a conservative communist regime tended to be associated with a radical pro-market ideology and weak interest groups; and, transition countries that experienced a reformist communist regime tended to be associated with a weaker pro-market ideology and strong interest groups. Historical legacies established a baseline for the privatization debates to come.

Stage 1: The Elite Approval Stage

State policymakers debated general privatization approaches during the elite approval stage. The proposals on the table concerned the dominant methods of privatization, the function of established state bureaucracies, the creation of new privatization authorities, and the orientation of the privatization approach with regard to speed and the role of pertinent interest groups (especially enterprise insiders)—the usual suspects. The local elite (including neoliberal economists) and, nearly always, Western advisors were the protagonists. Western advisors usually advocated a rapid privatization strategy, and in some cases, Western lenders reportedly "insisted" on one. The output of the elite approval stage was a general blueprint that the government agreed upon. It usually took the form of an official policy statement or government resolution.

Stage 2: The Public Legitimization Stage

Once a transition state agreed on a general privatization approach, it tended to seek public legitimization. State policymakers sought public approval on major policy decisions during the transition period as a counterweight to the communist past. The political pressure to legitimize the general privatization approach usually went hand-in-hand with its refinement. State policymakers commonly assigned bureaucratic competencies, set aside resources, prepared accompanying laws and policies, and commercialized enterprises (that is, they brought enterprises under formal state ownership). Public legitimization normally came in the form of a law ratified by the local legislature and/or public approval in the course of an election.

The potential costs state privatization decision-makers would incur by abandoning the general privatization approach once it had passed through the elite approval stage and the public legitimization stage could increase markedly. The general privatization approach mobilized interests in search of asset ownership (these may be called *claimants*), bureaucrats, and consultants, once it reached this point in the process. It also put political careers and egos at stake. These potential costs indicate why state officials were reluctant to cancel legitimated privatization strategies despite government turnover, as in Poland, Slovenia, or Hungary.[13]

Stage 3: Supply-Side Tasks

Supply-side tasks concerned how the state assigned privatization methods to specific enterprises assets. What criteria would the state use to privatize enterprises? Would the state privatize all enterprises by the same means? Which bureaucracies would make those decisions? Would foreigners be allowed to participate in the choices? How much time would be allotted for supply-side tasks? How would the state regulate the supply-side tasks? The empowering document was the general privatization blueprint, as legitimized in a public forum.

First-level supply-side outcomes were *privatization implementation methods* mapped according to classes of claimants and the pool of first private owners (see table 3.2). These could be subdivided into two categories consistent

Table 3.2. Privatization Paths and Ownership Regimes

Privatization Path	Associated Privatization Method	First Owners	First-Ownership Structure	Financial Markets	Level of State Autonomy & Capacity Of Capital Market Regulator	Of Financial Markets
			Ownership Regime Parameter			
Centralized	Voucher	Masses, Investment Funds	Cross-holding, Dispersed at Enterprise Level	Public Equity Markets	Low	Low
Decentralized	Standard	State, Enterprise Management, Investors, Multinationals	Direct, Concentrated at Enterprise Level	Bank/Finance Capital	High	Indeterminate

with the privatization literature. The first category comprised *voucher* or *non-standard privatization methods*, and it included voucher privatization and institutional privatization. Nonstandard privatization methods involved the privatization of many enterprises simultaneously, often automatically. Major decisions surrounding nonstandard privatization methods therefore normally took place among a few senior state officials. The second category comprised *standard privatization methods*, and it included market privatization, tender privatization, insider privatization, and reprivatization. These tended to be case-by-case implementation methods that demanded detailed administrative attention to the nature of the enterprise and the claimants. Standard methods were therefore associated with decentralized privatization paths. The state implemented nonstandard and standard methods in the next stage.

The supply-side task stage resolved more than "who gets what." It also provided a context for claimants to mobilize and for policymakers to set down administrative competencies and an ethic of privatization governance. Senior state decision-makers determined privatization procedures and they organized state institutions consistent with the implementation of the supply-side tasks stage. Senior state officials, for instance, typically created a privatization ministry. Other government ministries as well as enterprise insiders inevitably were involved in the supply-side tasks, particularly if the blueprint mapped called for a decentralized privatization path. The crucial point is that the movement from the elite approval and public legitimization stages to the supply-side task stage was a shift to an entirely different, less public, and more bureaucratic political environment. This was an environment in which the politics of economic interests would naturally become more salient and ideology would give way to pragmatism.

Stage 4: Implementation

Implementation concerns how the state (or an institution acting on behalf of the state) actually privatizes individual enterprise assets. How would the state qualify, recruit, and register claimants? Which criteria would the state use to admit some claimants but exclude others? Would the state offer privileges to foreigners or would the state discriminate against them? Which bureaucracies would implement privatization? How would the state regulate implementation?

Implementation, like the supply-side tasks, resolved more than "who gets what." It also provided a context for claimants to mobilize and for policymakers to set down administrative competencies and an ethic of governance. The state normally created a state agency (sometimes, but not necessarily, a privatization ministry or national property fund) to distribute property and to implement privatization. Like the supply-side tasks, it was inevitable that other government ministries and enterprise insiders would participate in implementation. Bureaucratic involvement would be substantial if the implementation process mapped out in the privatization blueprint was decentralized and the government officials designated large amounts of assets for standard privatization methods in the supply-side tasks stage. In any case, the movement from the elite approval and public legitimization stages to the supply-side task stage and then to the implementation stage represented yet another shift to an entirely different, less public, and more bureaucratic political environment. The first-ownership regime complete with first owners (and "first" losers) was the direct output of implementation.

FIRST-OWNERSHIP REGIMES

Particular privatization paths yielded variations in the four parameters of the ownership regime. Below is a speculative but representative depiction of the immediate impact of privatization implementation on first-ownership regimes.

- *Attributes of Owners.* Centralized (rapid) privatization paths tended to favor ownership for individual citizens, owners who lack resources, expertise, and market experience.

  Decentralized privatization paths tended to favor private ownership for enterprise insiders (managers or workers) or investors, especially Western investors who, as in the Hungarian case, approached the privatization ministries with individual "case-by-case" privatization proposals. Those owners were far more likely to bring capital, expertise, and market experience to the enterprise.
- *Systems of Corporate Governance.* Centralized paths tended to break enterprise stakes into small pieces, with a multitude of different brands of ownership. For instance, owners typically included individuals, investment privatization funds (to invest the shares of third parties), workers, and managers. Centralized privatization paths precipitated share trading as investors and investment funds alike searched for the best returns. Trading, in turn, bred cross-holding among investment funds, banks, and enterprises. It also raised tricky principle-agent issues between individual shareholders and investment funds and between investment funds and enterprises.

  Decentralized paths, on the other hand, tended to preserve enterprise stakes in larger chunks; often, the state privatized the enterprise to a dominant owner (50 percent-plus). Decentralized paths showed reduced cross-holding and principal-agent problems than centralized paths, and if the

Hungarian and Czech cases are contrasting illustrations, better economic results.

- *Financial Markets.* Centralized paths tended to generate market economies with broad-based capital markets covering hundreds or thousands of share issues, public corporations, and share investment funds, as in the U.S.-British institutional model. Brokerage firms, traders, security analysts, and speculators naturally developed around those basic institutions. Centralized privatization paths tended to generate public stock markets on top of a layer of privately held companies.

  Decentralized paths tended to generate market economies with far smaller capital markets and public financial industries. Markets in these countries consequently tended to be more efficient and transparent than in countries that adhered to centralized (rapid) privatization paths. Instead, private contracts between individual parties (with banks taking an active regulator role) regulated the transfer of investment in ownership shares in privately held corporations. Decentralized privatization paths generated financial markets less complicated to regulate.

- *The State Financial Market Regulator.* Centralized paths often produced markets—in particular, stock markets—that were neither autonomous nor exhibited high levels of capacity. The regulation of large public stock markets is daunting in mature market economies, but it is inconceivable when the market participants are inexperienced, liquidity is minimal, and resources of state regulators are low, as is the case in CEECs (Cohen and Schwartz 1993). The hazards of large stock markets are complicated further by their character as *public* markets. Everyone can see when investors are ripped off. People can lose faith in the system and the market reformers who sponsored it.

  When the privatization path was decentralized, the state administration could develop expertise (capacity and perhaps autonomy), which it might use to regulate markets. Decentralized paths were more demanding on the state regulator *during* privatization since they entailed detailed, case-by-case privatization decision-making. From a collective action perspective, the average state official might perceive that the involvement of other state officials reduces the point at which the net benefits for corruption would exceed the net costs for being caught and punished (Granovetter 1978; see also Shefter 1977). From a sociological perspective, the average state official might rationalize that since everyone else is colluding, then it also must be appropriate to make private arrangements for him. Consequently, both centralized and decentralized privatization paths posed threats to effective state regulation, though in different ways. Neither path offered reformers a perfect solution.

The privatization decision-making model showed that state privatization choices established ownership regimes. The privatization path (decentralized or centralized), including the privatization speed (rapid ["all at once"] or gradual ["case-by-case"]) were critical decisions. Those choices set the institutional arrangements and terms of interaction for state officials and economic and political interest groups after the state completed privatization. Privatization was more than a simple transfer of ownership from state to private party, more than just the creation of a regulatory system, but the generator of political and economic interests and their relationship with the state.

NOTES

1. Insider privatization approaches—privatization methods that granted privatization preferences to managers and/or workers—fall into the rapid or gradual privatization category depending on how they were administered. That is, if the state granted workers or managers enterprises automatically, then we might call these rapid methods since state privatization administrators were uninvolved in the share allocations. If, on the other hand, insiders were merely given advantages (for example, the rights to buy enterprise shares cheaper than others) in a standard privatization procedure, then insider privatization may be categorized as a gradual approach.

2. *Evolutionary* in this definition equates to incremental; no reference to natural selection is intended.

3. Formally a path-dependent process satisfies the following condition: if given two samples from the observer's set of possible historical events $\{ti\}$ and $\{t'i\}$, with corresponding time paths $\{xn\}$ and $\{x'n\}$, then $|x'n - xn| \to 0$ with probability one, as $n \to \infty$. Contrast the difference between path dependence and *predictability*. If a process is predictable, then an observer can *ex ante* construct a forecasting sequence $\{x^*n\}$ with the property that $|xn - x^*n| \to 0$, with probability one, as $n \to \infty$ (Arthur 1989, 128).

4. The evolution of privatization and regulation in the postcommunist societies suggests that the literature on the rationalization of state bureaucracies may usefully reconsider the role of ideology. In nineteenth-century United States, France, Great Britain, and Japan, the rationalization of state bureaucracies reportedly took place without "design or ideological coherence." Leaders then did not act "on the basis of a coherent ideological or utopian view of administration or bureaucratic role. . . . Each decision was determined primarily by strategic considerations" (Silberman 1993, 413–414).

5. An enlightening exception is Roe's emphasis on American populism to explain the development of corporate governance structures in the United States (Roe 1994).

6. This was the case in Poland, for example, where initial enthusiasm for markets dimmed radically from 1991 to 1993. For survey data on workers and trade unions, see Ost and Weinstein 1999.

7. In this regard, neoliberalism represented a somewhat eerie reversal of communism, which justified the sacrifice of civil rights in the short term for the long-term construction of socialism.

8. The term "nation" refers to the set of ideas that a group of people use to distinguish themselves as a "unique sovereign people" (Greenfeld 1992, 1–26).

9. This theme is consistent with Greenfeld's contention that nationalism was a driving force behind the creation of economic and political structures (Greenfeld 1992).

10. The model's emphasis on changing institutional environments (represented by stages) implies that the privatization process shapes the sociological frames and rational incentives of actors. From a sociological standpoint, actors reorient conceptions of appropriateness, including but not limited to ideological appropriateness. From a rational choice vantage, actors recalculate costs and benefits according to a pragmatic judgment of instrumentality. The privatization model presented here synthesizes theoretically diverse aspects in a way that presents the institution-building process as both constraining and enabling (or empowering). It is this synthesis that yields privatization policy outcomes—ownership regimes.

11. Assets by value.

12. For a different view, one that emphasizes the "method of extrication" on transition policies, see Stark 1992.

13. Outside factors such as a jolt in economic conditions or in political leadership do not force privatization or an entirely new path unless that jolt is very severe. The shift in Slovak privatization strategy is the exception that proves the assertion. Most Slovaks opposed voucher privatization prior to the formal split of Czechoslovakia in January 1993. Yet, Slovakia, then a Czechoslovakian Republic, faithfully implemented the first round of privatization. It wasn't until the Mečiar government established control over independent Slovakia that the privatization course was shifted. Even then, the Slovak government first postponed voucher privatization before canceling it altogether.

4

The Two Trajectories of Ownership
Regime Evolution

The privatization story doesn't end necessarily with the completion of privatization or the creation of a first-ownership regime. Rather, it may also depend on the nature of the first-ownership regime and the encapsulating economic and political environment that structure the evolution of ensuing ownership regimes. Privatization may be viewed as an asset competition between politically connected interests seeking assets from the state under a state-designed set of incentives and constraints.

The means of privatization and the subsequent competition of claimants[1] for assets in the context of the evolving ownership regimes and political contests determine the efficacy of markets. Institutions (rules, organizations, routines) may be fleeting during this period. Ownership regimes may undergo radical changes as first owners transfer assets to other owners, as cross-holding arrangements shift, as new laws and regulations come into effect, and as the state regulator gains autonomy and capacity. In addition, as ownership regimes evolve radically during this period, so do politics. Political parties consolidate, routines establish, and politicians gain experience. One could speak of permanent institutional progress in the CEECs only after the key battles over the ownership of state enterprises are settled.

Czech transition, for instance, became economically rational when the domestic competition for the valuable enterprise assets ended. Functional and honest capital markets, financial intermediaries, and banks became possible only at that point. Ironically, it was the political enemies of the neoliberal reformers, including the Social Democrats, who instigated stability and economic rationality in Czech finance. Contrary to the two institutional schools of thought, Czech capital markets now resemble Poland and Hungary, both in scale and regulatory scrutiny. These more recent trends are clear after 1998 (see chapter 11).

THE EVOLUTION OF OWNERSHIP REGIMES

First-ownership regimes (the ownership regime just after privatization) may be said to evolve according to one of two logics. One may call the first rationale neo-Coasian or economic; one may call the second rationale non-Coasian or political. Countries whose ownership regime evolves according to an economic logic such that assets eventually find their way to owners who can extract the most value from them are deemed to fit the Coasian or neoliberal pattern. Plutocracies are unlikely to thrive under Coasian conditions. Countries whose ownership regime evolves according to a political logic such that assets find their way to owners who have the strongest political connections (including perhaps the strongest handle on violence) are deemed to fit the non-Coasian or political pattern. Plutocracies are likely to become the rule when non-Coasian political patterns are the rule. The first-ownership regimes of Central European countries—Group 1 countries—may tend to evolve according to a neo-Coasian or neoliberal logic; while the first-ownership regimes of the FSU—Group 2 countries—may tend to evolve according to a non-Coasian or political logic.

Neo-Coasian Evolution

Countries with first-ownership regimes that may evolve according to Coasian logic may offer first owners an economic opportunity set replete with revenue possibilities. Although privatization may delay or even undermine those possibilities by sabotaging enterprise value, foreigners may pay substantial money for enterprises after privatization or domestic new owners may be able to extract maximum operating value from those businesses. In addition, new owners may have only rare chances to take advantage of long-term government subsidies. CEECs are often saddled with budgetary pressures, thereby reducing incentives on managers (and workers) to lobby politically. Plutocracies, which are based on the new owners' monopoly control of government and commerce, may be unlikely to endure given economic incentives that encourage inefficient owners to exit the market, foreigners to enter the market, and an autonomous and capable market regulator.

Political risks may discourage the development of plutocracies just as economic opportunity may drive ownership regimes in a Coasian fashion. To the extent that countries have created a decent quality of democracy, so citizens may limit the plutocrats' power by forcing them from positions of power at the ballot box or by pressuring influential elites.[2] The possibilities of entry into the EU (and NATO) for several Central European countries imply that any plutocracy may face not only domestic popular opposition but also European- and American-wide opposition should it seek power and riches openly and often. The economic opportunity set and political risks described here tend to match the situation in Central European/Group 1 countries better than in the East European/Group 2 countries.

The privatization approach impacts the evolution of ownership regimes and the nature of asset competition. Consider a first-ownership regime in which the state sold most enterprise assets to foreigners during privatization (à la Hungary). In this case, the main asset competition may have occurred between domestic and foreign interests (or between foreign interests) *during* privatization. After privatization, it seems likely that many enterprises may have fulfilled their Coasian fate and operated efficiently.

In countries that adhered to centralized paths, the main asset competition games may have been biased toward the continual readjustment of the ownership regime. In the Czech Republic, as the following chapters illustrate, the stealing that characterized the ensuing ownership regimes after privatization undermined current and future economic investment as well as the political base of the reformers. That competition for assets finally ended with the winners selling out to foreigners or local interests, and with the reformers losing in the 1998 elections, as the economic (and political) Coasians might have expected. Therefore, although the Czech ownership regime may have evolved according to Coasian logic, the result was a relatively low quality of capitalism and democracy that depended on the privatization strategy the state had chosen.

Non-Coasian Evolution

The logic that animates the evolution of Group 1 ownership regimes is completely reversed with regard to Group 2 countries. The economic opportunity set, for instance, is turned on its head. The greatest and easiest riches for the first owners in Group 2 countries lie with state support. Some plutocrats milk the state for direct benefits, such as subsidies or preferential treatment during privatization sales. In other cases, plutocrats use political connections to take advantage of distortions in the market. For example, the price of one ton of crude oil in the Soviet Union at the end of 1991 was $0.50, as compared with $100 on the world market (Åslund 2002, 172). Producers with powerful political allies could make easy money by utilizing government-provided export privileges that allowed them to take advantage of these massive differences in domestic and world prices. These opportunities for wealth creation based on political connections evolved both during and after the privatization process. Price differentials and other market distortions declined as economic reforms proceeded. Many other sources of state largesse dried up following the 1998 financial crisis in Russia. The nature of state interest group relations and competition for assets changed significantly after 1998, but asset competition has not ceased nor does it occur according to the dictates of economic rationality. Russia, like other Group 2 countries, continues to evolve according to a non-Coasian political logic.

The forms of politically connected wealth creation that are now prevalent differ from the strategies that plutocrats employed prior to 1998. Plutocrats lobby state officials for support in their battles with other plutocrats either by bribery or physical intimidation. Another tactic is for plutocrats to seek political office, thereby marrying political tactics with economic expediency. FSU plutocrats increasingly hold governorships and head city administrations. Also, the political influence peddling does not always involve interactions between plutocrat and state officials, but instead may explode into direct conflicts—sometimes violent ones—among plutocrats competing over assets (Volkov 2002).

First private owners in Group 2 countries faced a much more constrained economic opportunity set than Group 1 owners outside of state support. At the macroeconomic level, Group 2 countries' government finances were generally under dire strains as in Group 1 countries, but the same outside pressures to get those budgets in order were largely missing. At the level of the firm, the possibilities that plutocrats in Group 2 countries may have to obtain FDI money[3] or to operate profitable service or manufacturing businesses still are rare. Group 2 economic plutocracies are not tempted to sell out (To whom? At what price?), but rather, they have incentives to ally with one another and with the appropriate state bureaucrats to ensure that the political environment will be to their advantage as asset competition battles continue. Economic exit along Group 1 lines is not then usually the best option; incentives exist for the plutocracy to remain.

Finally, the low quality of democratic politics (defined as limited civilian participation in government) in Group 2 countries contributes to the lack of restraint that these plutocracies may have had in playing nefarious political games. Group 2 country plutocrats still usually face only a minimal threat that their political allies will be voted from office (unless a more powerful plutocrat seeks to place his political allies in power) or that favored bureaucrats will suddenly shun their advances due to popular discontent. Consider the difference from Group 1 countries, in which the regular shifts in political party hegemony posed a constant threat to a prospective plutocracy. Prospective plutocrats in Group 1 countries may have sought to maintain stable long-term relations with an entrenched political order, but more democratic political conditions made this difficult to impossible in the long run.

The book's (final) comparative chapter, chapter 11, considers two hypotheses from a comparison among Group 1 countries (Hungary, Poland, and Czech Republic) and Group 2 countries (Russia and Ukraine). The first hypothesis is that the ownership regimes in Group 1 countries developed according to neo-Coasian (or economic) logic while those in Group 2 countries developed according to non-Coasian (or political) logic. The result was that CEECs were evolving into different "varieties of capitalism," as some institutionalists suggested might occur. Timing was especially critical in that evolution. Centralized, rapid privatization strategies may have ironically generated an ownership regime that might appear as if germinated from a delayed development strategy, for instance, as in the Czech Republic.

Next, the chapter considers the hypothesis that Group 1 and Group 2 countries may need to be analyzed distinctly in terms of the impact of privatization. Privatization strategies may have greatly impacted the developmental trajectory of ownership regimes in Group 1 countries, but may have had relatively little lasting impact on the ownership regimes of Group 2 countries. Asset competition in both Group 1 and Group 2 countries occurred during privatization and as ownership regimes evolved. The reigning logic in Group 1 countries was first political and then (somewhat predictably) economic. The dominant rationale in Group 2 countries, however, remained political even as their ownership regimes continued to evolve in the postprivatization period. The result, this chapter contends, is that institutional stability will remain a remote possibility in the FSU until the political battles among the plutocrats are settled. Progress toward a system of a truly higher quality of capitalism and democracy will be possible only at that point.

INTRODUCTION TO THE CZECH MATERIAL

Chapters 5 through 10 present the material on Czech privatization (see table 4.1). Chapter 5 considers the role of historical legacies in the development of the Czech privatization approach. It shows that the conservative communist Czech regime was a likely cause of weak interests and strong proprivatization public opinion.

Chapter 6 shows how early state decisions set Czech privatization on a path that was partly centralized and partly decentralized (see figure 4.1).

Chapter 7 shows that the supply-side component of Czech privatization was a rapid decentralized process that undermined the capacity and autonomy of state officials.

Chapter 8 shows that the implementation of Czech privatization was a largely centralized process that created conditions for corruption after privatization. To the extent that the implementation process was decentralized, state officials proved vulnerable to the entreaties of claimants.

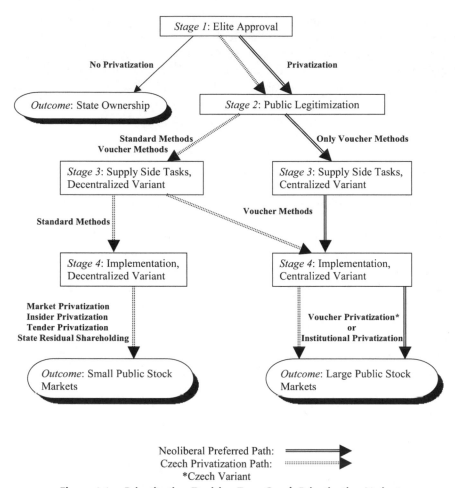

Figure 4.1.   **Privatization Decision Tree, Czech Privatization Variant.**

Chapter 9 shows how the Czech ownership regime evolved first into pluto-cratic capitalism, a political economy with a low quality of capitalism and a low quality of democracy. The tangible results were poor economic performance and popular contempt for government.

Chapter 10 examines the Czech comeback of 1998 through 2002 in light of the ascendancy of the left-wing Social Democrats. It argues that the Czech approach ironically appears to have been crafted by a delayed development strategy that put the country behind where it would have been had it followed a slower, more decentralized privatization path.

Table 4.1. Chronology of Czech Privatization

Privatization Stage	Time Period
Elite Approval	November 1989 to May 1990
Public Legitimization	June 1990 to February 1991
Supply-Side Tasks	February 1991 to May 1992
Implementation	January 1996 to December 1995
Plutocratic Capitalism	January 1996 to December 1997
Revival	January 1998 to December 2002

The Czech chapters and the comparative chapter reinforce the theme that rapid privatization strategies may delay subsequent moves to markets and democracy, counter to current best practice. They also imply that a preferable privatization approach would be a gradual strategy sensitive to state capacity and autonomy, with a prominent role for FDI. The broad policy lesson is that modern capitalism comprises more than financial markets; it also includes state institutions. The historic risk of economic reform is a permanent state of collusion between private competitors for economic resources and state officials. The book concludes that the roots of modern markets are historically derived prejudices, skills, happenstance, politics, self-interested economic rationality, and economic planning. A historical theory explains why local actors may behave contrary to Western expectations and why the relationships between capitalism and democracy may be more complex than the Washington consensus or its offspring, the post–Washington consensus, presume.

NOTES

1. Also managers, workers, state bureaucrats, and foreign interests.
2. Chapter 10 makes this case regarding the Czech Republic's comeback after 1998.
3. With the obvious exceptions of natural resource extraction and distribution.

Part III

CZECH PRIVATIZATION AS THE ILLUSTRATIVE
CASE OF THE OWNERSHIP MODEL OF
POLITICAL ECONOMY

5

Elite Approval—November 1989 to May 1990

Czechoslovakia announced one of the twentieth century's most ambitious and controversial economic reforms—the mass giveaway of the country's largest industries through vouchers—in April 1990, not even six months removed from November's "Velvet Revolution." Czechoslovakia seemed an unlikely candidate to plunge headlong into private ownership and presumably into market capitalism. The country had minimal experience in the free market, limited advanced technology, only dishonest native capital, and it was led by V. Havel, a person widely suspected of left-wing inclinations. Why did the Czechoslovakian government embark on that most daring of privatization strategies?

This chapter and the one that follows argue that the conservative Czechoslovakian regime's extreme anticommunism and extreme regard for the West played a major role. These passions drove the then-Czechoslovakian government to embark upon a voucher privatization strategy. This chapter considers one half of the argument: The Czech public's extreme anticommunism and extreme regard for the West provided neoliberals with the support necessary to seize the government's economic policymaking agenda. The next chapter completes the argument by showing that voucher privatization was destined to become law once the neoliberals had seized the government's economic policymaking agenda. In combination, these two chapters validate the broad hypothesis that a recent conservative communist past was conducive to voucher privatization becoming the dominant privatization method in CEECs.

Supporting evidence for the chapter argument is presented in four sections. The time period under evidence covers the abdication of Czechoslovakian communism in November 1989 to the government's approval of the voucher privatization development schedule in April 1990. I label this period an elite approval stage because the Czech elite agreed to support a single privatization approach during this time.

The first section links the Czech public's antipathy for the communist regime and its isolation from the West prior to 1989 to its support of dramatic market reform measures afterward. The section also shows that the Czech experience under communism translated, first, into weak organizations of managers and workers and, second, into the emergence of a galvanized, disappointed generation of young and middle-aged and educated Czechs amenable to neoliberal appeals. As we shall see, these factors were critical in facilitating the neoliberals' influence in privatization policy.

The second section argues that the background and orientation of Havel and the new Czech elite facilitated the penetration of neoliberals into economic policymaking circles. According to their own admission, the elite were generally people of the arts and therefore impressionable about economic issues such as privatization. Moreover, they needed a large cadre of professionals to carry out the historic changes, which given their small number would have to come from outside dissident circles. These factors offered neoliberals, the country's recognized economists, good chances to shape privatization policy. The section also establishes that the new Czech elite and especially Havel were in a position to make key privatization decisions. The new Czech elite's leadership on economic issues in the National Government of Understanding emanated from the public's extreme anticommunist and pro-Western sentiment.

The third section examines the competing privatization proposals in detail. It argues that the neoliberals' voucher privatization proposal best coincided with the anticommunist and pro-Western sentiments of most Czechs. It also best satisfied the burgeoning feelings of Czech nationalism by severely restricting the access of foreigners to enterprise assets. The ideological appeal of voucher privatization versus that of standard privatization would prove a decisive advantage for neoliberals.

The fourth section shows that the privatization debates played out as a political struggle between Valtr Komárek, the "gradualist," and Klaus, the neoliberal. Klaus won the battle mainly because of the broad ideological appeal of his radical economic policy prescriptions, including voucher privatization. The Czech elite around Havel found it politically expedient to close ranks around the neoliberal voucher privatization proposal in response to public opinion that favored a radical move to private property. Other contributing factors were the personal idiosyncrasies of the major competing advocates, Klaus and Komárek. In this regard, Klaus held the clear advantage because of his apparent professionalism and clean past. A contributing factor was Havel's decision to opt out of the privatization debates, which weakened opposition to neoliberal privatization initiatives. Finally, the weakness of enterprise interests—managers and workers—kept the debate on an ideological plane. Enterprise interests abstained from the debates out of strategic political considerations linked with the public's prevalent anticommunist and pro-Western predilections. The behavior of enterprise interests uncovers no evidence for Frydman and Rapaczynski's interest-based explanation—that political constraints on neoliberal privatization decision-making emanate from the de facto control of enterprises by managers, workers, or the state (Frydman and Rapaczynski 1994). Had the enterprise interests been able and willing, it is likely that the privatization approach would have included privileges for workers and managers. In the end, Havel favored Klaus's voucher privatization proposal over the competing standard privatization proposals, and thereby committed his government to neoliberal leadership over economic policy issues.

Klaus used his privatization victory over Komárek to consolidate neoliberal influence within the elite and eventually into nationwide political power. In this way, Czechoslovakia's turn to a neoliberal privatization agenda addressed the two core puzzles of postcommunist Czechoslovakian (later Czech) politics:

- How did Klaus obtain the support of nearly every level of society for an economic strategy and a privatization program that could cause suffering for many?
- How could Klaus push aside Havel, the president of the Czech Republic and hero of resistance against the communist normalization, even as Havel continued to prove far more popular than Klaus in every public opinion poll until Klaus's own demise in December 1997, eight years after the revolution?

COMMUNIST-ERA ORIGINS OF CZECH RAPID PRIVATIZATION

The months following the fall of communism in Czechoslovakia witnessed an extraordinary outpouring of bitterness toward the past regime and an equally strident determination to move toward capitalism, even by the standards of Central and Eastern Europe. These two passions were critical factors behind the Czech government's adoption of dramatic economic reform measures, such as voucher privatization. I attribute these passions mainly to the harsh method of social control of the communist regime and the public's isolation from the West since the failed Prague Spring of 1968. Czechoslovakia was a *conservative communist regime*; that is, its government was repressive by the standards of other CEECs. By contrast, neighbors Poland, Hungary, and the former Yugoslavia were *liberal communist regimes*; that is, these governments were relatively lenient (Rupnik 1989; Elster, Offe, and Preuss 1998) (see table 5.1). As we shall see, the communist background may explain why governments choose privatization strategies.

Comparative survey evidence supports the proposition that the Czech public may have been angrier at the communist rulers than were the Slovaks, Poles, or Hungarians. At the depth of normalization in 1975, the Czech respondents

Table 5.1. Communist Regime Types, 1968–1989

Conservative Regimes	Liberal Regimes
Czechoslovakia	Hungary
East Germany	Poland
Romania	Former Yugoslavia
Bulgaria	
Former Soviet Union	

regarded the level of social justice far below that in Poland, Hungary, and Slovakia (see table 5.2). An indication of the Czech public's euphoria at the demise of communism is the dramatic reversal of Czech public opinion two years after November 1989 (see table 5.3). In the future, the Czech public's extraordinary antipathy to communism would undermine the attempts of neoliberal foes to institute policies that smacked of a reconciliation with past practices and leaders.

In Slovakia, antipathy toward the past regime was somewhat muffled because normalization disproportionately benefited many Slovaks. The president of the Czechoslovakian Federal Republic was renowned Slovak nationalist G. Husák. During normalization, there was a separate Slovak Central Communist Bureau, a Federal Central Communist Bureau, but no Czech Communist correlate.[1] In the late 1970s and early 1980s, the mayor of Prague was Slovak; he was an enforcer of the post-1968 purges.[2] The state directed funds to Slovakia in nearly equal proportion to the Czech lands, despite the fact that Czechs outnumbered Slovaks nearly two to one. The Czechoslovakian state concentrated development in Slovakia; the share of national income created in Slovakia rose from 19 percent in 1948 to nearly 31 percent in 1989 (Průcha 1995, 62). Attitudes toward the communist past were secondary considerations in Slovakia owing to the Slovak ethnic bias of the prior regime. The relatively muted antipathy to the normalization regime partly explains the lack of Slovak fervency for dramatic economic reform.[3]

Not just anger and rejection of the past influenced the Czech public's support of measures promising a dramatic turn to Western capitalism. The degree

Table 5.2. Comparative Perceptions of Social Justice in CEECs

	Prewar	Communism (1975)	Present (1991)	Future
Poland	8	6	−7	−16
Czech Rep.	27	−54	30	14
Slovakia	−10	1	−18	−19
Hungary	−30	41	−8	14

Source: Hartl 1991, 273.

Table 5.3. Comparative Perceptions of the Present Regime (1991) versus the Communist Regime

	How Does the Present Regime Compare with the Past One?		
	Better	*Worse*	*Same*
Poland	41	23	26
Czech Rep.	71	14	14
Slovakia	44	35	22
Hungary	31	29	40

Source: Hartl 1991, 272, and chart 3 in Hartl 1991, 271–273.

of public and elite isolation from the West was also a critical consideration in shaping the postcommunist Czech mentality. The exposure of the Czech public to Western habits prior to 1989 and its impact on economic and political reform debates during the transition period has been frequently misinterpreted by Western analysts. The view is common that, like Hungary and Poland, "Czechoslovakia had already experienced a modicum of Western rationalization. . . . [As a result, Czechoslovakia] was more inclined to favor neoliberal economic discourse afterward than others such as Russia, Romania, and Bulgaria" (Campbell and Pedersen 1995, 11).

The facts fly in the face of the Czech reality. As a matter of state policy, Czechs (and Slovaks) were offered few chances to interact with Westerners, a penalty for and a safeguard against the excesses of 1968. The contrast in the extent of isolation from the West was especially sharp with neighboring countries—Hungary, Poland, and Slovenia. Citizens of these CEECs had greater opportunities to go abroad and to read foreign literature than Czechs (and Slovaks). One Czech economist complained that while there were fewer than fifty qualified Czech economists in the Czech Republic when communism collapsed, there were probably over two hundred in Hungary. In Slovakia, there may have been fewer than ten.

Pre-1989 Czechoslovakia was not only far more isolated than either Hungary or Poland but it was that isolation that promoted the neoliberal discourse that followed in the post-1989 period. Isolation stimulated most Czechs to seize upon the material outputs of capitalism. They learned from watching Western movies, listening to Radio Free Europe, reading the texts of neoliberal American economists, or hearing from relatives and friends who may have traveled or emigrated to the West and returned telling stories of bountiful riches. The moral wretchedness and technological backwardness of the Czechoslovakian communist system could not compete with the idealized West. The national conviction that Czechs were not Eastern Europeans, but rather civilized Central Europeans or even civilized Europeans reinforced their urgency to pull away from communism after 1989.[4] In keeping with a long

historical tradition, the isolation of communist Czechoslovakia and the public opprobrium that it attracted suggested that Czechs might support radical
changes in the wake of the ancien régime's fall. Tocqueville's famous analysis
of the French Revolution paralleled the situation in Czechoslovakia in the early
transition period:

> [If the French] had succeeded in gradually modifying the spirit of their ancient
> institutions without destroying them, perhaps they would not have been so prompt
> to clamor for a new order. As it was, however, every Frenchman felt he was being
> victimized; his personal freedom, his money, his self-respect, and the amenities of
> his daily life are constantly being tampered with. . . . Nor did he see any constitu-
> tional remedy for this state of affairs; it seemed as if the choice lay between meekly
> accepting everything and destroying the whole system. (Tocqueville 1955, 141)

Weak Enterprise Interests

Public antipathy to the Czechoslovakian communist regime incapacitated
claimants who would presumably lose in a program of drastic privatization
reform. Czechs commonly regarded such claimants—state bureaucrats, senior
officials, security apparatus officials, enterprise managers, workers, and to
some extent Slovaks—as stalwarts of the old regime and therefore as obstacles
to Czechoslovakia's return to Europe. Distrust extended doubly to the representative claimant organizations—the state, political parties, secret police
(Stb), manager confederations, trade unions, and Slovak nationalist groups.
Consequently, Czech privatization took place in an environment of weakened
claimants, a clear advantage for supporters of voucher privatization.

Anticommunist public sentiment retarded the organizational coherence of
enterprise interests—managers and workers. By *organizational coherence*, I
refer to the ability of an organization to articulate and to press a consistent
agenda. A small number of organizations—organizations with long histories, low leadership turnover, stabile memberships, and consistent goals and
means—indicated a high organizational coherence. The correspondingly low
level of organizational coherence of Czech enterprise interests translated into
a subordinate position in the face of neoliberal reforms, such as voucher privatization.

Enterprise Managers

The precarious position of individual enterprise managers (owing to the
prevailing anticommunist public sentiment) was a main cause of the low organizational coherence among representative organizations of managers in the
first half of 1990. The public generally regarded enterprise managers as accom-
plices of the communist regime and therefore as illegitimate beneficiaries of

economic reforms. At the time, moreover, there was intense public debate over the treatment of communist collaborators (such as enterprise managers) and there were whispers of an impending lustration campaign targeted at enterprise managers.[5]

Manager vulnerability was evident in large enterprises. These enterprises had been directed exclusively by senior communists and consequently were prime targets for public vengeance. Many enterprise managers were forcibly removed by newly energized workers or by activists from Civic Forum, the great Czech political movement of the time. Even in Slovakia, where the anticommunist regime sentiment was less intense than in Czech regions, angry Slovak workers, energized political activists, and careerist middle-managers engaged in a "cadres war" (*kádrová vojna*) to boot enterprise directors from their posts. The situation became so dire that, in March 1990, an alarmed Public Against Violence (the Slovak political counterpart to Civic Forum) issued a proclamation to stop the denuding of enterprise leadership (Gál 1991, 59–70).[6] Many managers reacted to the tension of the times by retreating into pension or by simply abandoning their posts.[7] Others sought to fortify alliances with the enterprise workforce. Others less threatened tried to spin off the enterprise's most valuable assets.[8] In any event, many enterprise managers were concerned more about corporate survival than about national policy.

The low level of organizational coherence reflected managers' individual jeopardy. More than a dozen organizations competed for a manager's membership. None of these organizations could boast of a significant recent history prior to 1989 or of large, stable memberships. Many managers chose to remain underrepresented. What would become the major lobbying arm for large enterprise managers, the Czech Confederation of Industry (*Svaz průmyslu*), was not founded until May 1990. Even then the Czech Confederation of Industry boasted only 153 founding members. In addition, R. Baránek's Association of Czechoslovakian Entrepreneurs, the major representative organization of mostly small- and medium-sized businessmen, disagreed with the Czech Confederation of Industry over privatization strategy, thus further dividing the managers. Due partly to the ineffectiveness of independent organizations, the most important vehicles for enterprise manager interests remained the Federal industrial ministries. Yet these ministries in 1989 and 1990 mimicked the remainder of the Czechoslovakian state—disorganized, in flux, illegitimate, ashamed, and on the defensive. The low level of organizational coherence relegated managers to a minor role in privatization decision-making early in transition.

Trade Unions

The compromised past of the trade unions was the primary reason for the workers' low organizational coherence just after the fall of communism.

Czechoslovakian communist trade unions did not represent workers in any real sense. Instead, they were "transmission belts" to keep the workers in line, either by granting generous wage packages or vacation benefits, or else by enforcing discipline. The social and political alienation of workers from the communist trade unions discredited the entire notion of collective worker action and ensured that trade unions would be suspect in the eyes of workers. One 1994 survey indicated that only 55 percent of the national membership trusted the trade unions to any degree and only another 15 percent fully trusted them; the 1990 figures would have been more unfavorable for the trade unions (Holub 1994–1995). It was even immaterial to the Czech public that the workers' general strike of November 27, 1989, was the event that broke the old communist regime (Pleskot 1994; Falbr 1994; Vejvodová 1990). The trade unions' compromised past put workers under relentless ideological pressure in the first months after November 1989 and they remain so as of this writing.[9]

The legacy of the trade unions' compromised past also preoccupied Czech worker-activists with the task of creating a legitimate representative organization for workers.[10] They were limited by their own inexperience, the personal connections of the old guard with enterprise managers and with mafia, workers' suspicions of the trade unions, and workers' apathy. Rivalries between Czech and Slovak trade unionists, between the trade union center and its branches, and between old trade unionists and new ones further complicated the task of the worker activists. Worker activists had little time to devote to matters of state policy because of the need to sort out basic issues.

The low level of organizational coherence of the trade unions largely explains why Czech workers showed little class consciousness just after the fall of communism. Union and nonunion members showed nearly identical views concerning voting preference, the evaluation of politicians, and political orientation (Rutland 1993, 14–17; Juraj 1994; Boguszak and Rak 1990, especially table 18, 33). Workers' views also mirrored the public acceptance of privatization. A May 1990 survey showed that 48 percent of workers supported privatization for their enterprise while only 30 percent were opposed.[11] Author interviews with union officials suggested that support may have been even higher. R. Falbr, who was the trade union boss then, wrote, "In our country trade unionists don't behave like trade unionists. There is absolutely no difference between the standpoint of citizens and of trade unionists" (Falbr in *RP*, February 12, 1993, as quoted in Myant 1993, 59).

The weakness of the trade unions is an important reason why, despite a membership of 7.5 million and substantial financial resources and an obvious interest in directing privatization, workers' interests were unlikely to be represented in privatization policymaking in the early transition period (Pleskot 1994, 1).[12]

The Disappointed Generation

The fist in the critique of the old regime came disproportionately from one demographic group—middle-aged (thirty-five to fifty years old) and technically educated Czech men.[13] This group entered government ministries, Parliament, local government, business, unions, and media for the first time in their lives after 1989. During the transition period, this "disappointed generation" staked out uncompromising positions on issues related to the restoration of the old system—concerning anticommunist laws, restitution laws, and concerning the neoliberal economic policies (including voucher privatization) that eviscerated the state from people's lives.

The reservoir of dissatisfied middle-aged, technically educated Czechs was connected to locked-up resentment against the regime.[14] Communist normalization limited people to a comfortable—not better, not worse—lifestyle.[15] The disappointed generation kowtowed to superiors in their professional life whom everyone knew were intellectually inferior. Some referred to communist Czechoslovakia as "Absurdistan." In a 1988 survey, 79 percent of Czechs and Slovaks claimed that their ability to reach their potential was either limited or virtually nil; 75 percent responded that their ability to participate in societal organizations was either limited or virtually nil (Vaněk 1994, 50). One result was that many ambitious people fled the country. From 1968 to 1989 emigrants left Czechoslovakia primarily due to economic dissatisfaction; prior to normalization, emigrants had left the country to escape political persecution (Vaněk 1994, 52). The deprivation of economic and career opportunities, not the squelching of political rights, motivated the disappointed generation.

A comparison of demonstrators in 1968 versus those in 1988 and 1989 identifies the disappointed generation. Most of the early demonstrators were very young (fifteen to twenty-three years of age) while those in the later period included significant numbers of slightly older (though still relatively young) protesters. The 1988 and 1989 protesters were typically thirty to forty-five; these same demonstrators were only nine to twenty-four years old in 1968 (Tůma 1994, 30–31).[16] To be sure, the 1988 and 1989 demonstrators were familiar with the Prague Spring invasion, but many still were too young in 1968 to be involved. Regrettably, these protesters were old enough to be victims of normalization. Interview evidence shows that the Warsaw Pact's merciless trampling of Prague Spring's reform initiatives shaped the formative memories of many new parliamentary delegates (Mansfeldová 1993).[17] The activists demanding change in 1989 evidently represented a delayed and a more radical continuation of the 1968 protests (Tůma 1994).

The Czech antipathy toward the past regime among the disappointed generation was matched by their fervency for capitalism. The disappointed generation—joined by the youngest Czech adults—justified capitalism as a program of change, a plan of action that would return the nation to the West. To these Czechs, capitalism was not some utopian ideology, like socialism, that had existed mostly in the minds and manuscripts of nineteenth-century philosophers. Capitalism was a pragmatic economic development strategy that had proved successful in the startling economic growth of Western Europe since World War II and the obvious, though rarely witnessed, prosperity of the United States. Klaus, the unofficial chieftain of the disappointed generation, states as much: "We are not interested in new experiments. . . . We've just ended 40 years of one failed economic experiment and now we want to stick with what has been proved" (quoted in *Business Wire*, March 17, 1992).

The Czech passion for capitalism was matched by a shared innocence of "really existing capitalism." Many young Czech economists learned contemporary economics from classic economic texts such as Friedman or Samuelson or from the sometimes cloudy memories of aging mentors, most of whom hadn't been allowed to venture west themselves since the late 1960s. Klaus's own foreign professional exposure, for example, was limited mainly to Italy in 1966 and the United States in 1969 (Klaus 1995b, 181). Few Czechs were well versed in (or took seriously) the modern discourses of institutional economics nor in the growth of the Asian economies.[18] Even as late as 1993, only two of the country's top twenty-five business and finance students knew the difference between debt and equity.[19] The disappointed generation supported a capitalist agenda with strikingly little regard for the opinions of those with market expertise, though they themselves came to political life with minimal market experience.

The Heir Apparent

The disappointed generation found common cause in the ranks of macroeconomists and mathematically oriented economists who had existed in normalization obscurity. Among them were Klaus, Ježek, and Tříska (the three fathers of Czech privatization), as well as other influential neoliberals, including V. Dlouhý, J. Zieleniec, R. Salzmann, J. Stráský, and K. Dyba. These economists worked in the state bureaucracy and were consigned to a life of mediocrity with no hope of career advancement. The economists acted like normal, frustrated people trapped within a crazy system. In short, the economists were just like the disappointed generation.

But the economists had an extra qualification for the adoration of the disappointed generation. They could plausibly claim a technical, scientific, and indeed Western measure of understanding that stood in sharp contrast to the Marxist babble of their superiors. Like religious priests, the economists claimed special dispensation from the trinity of Friedman, Thatcher, and Hayek.

Qualification became opportunity when normalization loosened in the early 1980s. The first tentative opening came with the ascension of Y. Andropov as Russian Communist Party chief. Andropov sought to relax the planning system to encourage economic growth. Andropov's approach prompted L. Štrougal, the Czechoslovakian prime minister, to ask V. Komárek, a luminary of 1968 and also a person the communists trusted, to organize a reform-minded institute. Andropov died suddenly in 1983 and his initiative was stillborn.

Štrougal revived the idea of a reform-minded policy institute when Gorbachev assumed the post of Soviet Communist Party chief in 1985. He commissioned Komárek to gather the best Czech economists and social scientists, regardless of ideological bent. The objective was to develop forecasts for the Czechoslovakian economy and society and to propose solutions for the problems that would lie ahead. Komárek recruited the Western-oriented economists for what would become known as the Prognostics Institute.

It was in the Prognostics Institute and the neighboring Czechoslovakian Academy of Sciences that the economists became widely recognized as legitimate, viable, and Western alternatives to the communist economists. There they conducted seminars and published papers that attracted the attention of regime opponents. Klaus published in the dissident newspaper *Lidové noviny* under the pseudonym F. M.—Friedman, Milton. During this time, the economists evolved into a cohesive and recognizable group (including a layer of young followers) committed to the development of a Western economic system in Czechoslovakia. Visibility, orientation, and solidarity offered the economists of the disappointed generation as an alternative leadership when the communist regime toppled in November 1989.

The antiregime dissidents were not an obvious partner for the disappointed generation. The dissidents were outsiders, unlike the disappointed generation. These true heroes openly battled the hated communists for years. In addition, the dissidents communicated in a discourse unintelligible to the disappointed generation. The dissidents were intellectuals—men and women trained in philosophy, mathematics, physics, literature, and the law. The dissidents spoke of morality, of human dignity, and of ethics—ethereal matters presumably linked with man's existential crisis. The rule of law, not the rule of men, was at the heart of the dissidents' message. The dissidents were the public defenders of Czech souls.

The problem for the dissidents was that the disappointed generation was more furious over earthly concerns—money, career, travel—than over moral ones. To be sure, the disappointed generation acknowledged the dissidents' points of argument and respected their bravery and self-sacrifice. At the same time, many of these people regarded the dissidents as "out of the real world" and therefore unable to relate to the concrete, pragmatic concerns of common people. The disappointed generation sought to better their lives and only secondarily to cleanse their souls.

Thus it was the neoliberals rather than the dissidents who loomed as the communist heir apparent on the eve of upheaval in 1989. The dissidents never recognized the profound appeal of the neoliberals to the disappointed generation until it was too late, the fall of 1990; by then, their passing relevance was a foregone conclusion. The neoliberals' path to power was through control over the economic agenda, and especially over privatization policy.

THE NEW CZECH ELITE

The power vacuum that emerged when Czechoslovakian communists abdicated power in November and December 1989 was filled first by the dissidents and especially by Václav Havel. Havel was the revolution's acknowledged moral authority owing to his well-chronicled resistance against the hated communist regime and to his public exposure of that regime's absurdity and illegitimacy. He preached that the Czechoslovakian communist state had lost sight of, and further, had trampled, the fundamental virtues of man. In Havel's view, and most Czechs and Slovaks agreed, the communist state had forfeited its authority to rule.[20] Havel felt (and the dissidents agreed) the only way forward was to institute reforms that would reestablish Czechoslovakia as a bona-fide Western nation.

Three factors connected with the composition and orientation of the dissidents worked in favor of the penetration of neoliberals into elite economic policymaking circles. First, Havel and most dissidents, according to their own admission, were persons of the arts and did not understand Western economics. The gap in the education of the dissidents made them willing to listen to the advice of acknowledged "objective" economists, such as the neoliberals. Moreover, the dissidents regarded (in the Central and East European tradition) economics as a nonpolitical, technical field that could not serve as an avenue for political power for its experts. Consequently, they did not fear the neoliberal economists, at least at the outset of transition.

Second, the dissidents were a very small group—perhaps 250—sitting astride a bureaucracy filled with Communist Party members.[21] To counterbalance the communist influence, the dissidents sought reliable outside help. The obvious source was the disappointed generation of professionals who worked in the state institutes and enterprises. Out of the Prognostics Institute, for instance, the dissidents appointed Klaus as finance minister and Dlouhý as head of the State Planning Commission. Along with the disappointed generation—which by itself could not provide the necessary personnel—the dissidents appointed to high government posts reform-minded communists, women, and Slovaks. While what we may call the new Czech elite was then a very heterogeneous group, it was a group distinguished by its resolution to reverse the past and install capitalist and democratic institutions.

Third, it would be an overstatement to say that dissidents spoke in one ideological voice. The ideas of Havel and many dissidents were formed in the failed effort to give socialism a human face in the 1960s. Others, such as D. Kroupa, philosopher and student of Charter 77 author Jan Patočka, co-founded (with P. Bratinka) the political party ODA to promote free-market liberalism. The unifying feature of the dissidents then was not an ideological consensus over economic reform, but rather the general (and vague) idea that a return to communism was unthinkable and a transformation of institutions along Western lines necessary. Therefore, the neoliberal economists whose views on economic reform (including privatization) were likely to cause social hardship did not meet strenuous objection from the dissidents.

In sum, the lack of economic expertise among the dissidents, the dissidents' small size, and the dissidents' strong anticommunist and pro-Western proclivities created an opening for the neoliberal economists to become Czechoslovakia's top economic policymakers.

THE GOVERNMENT OF NATIONAL UNDERSTANDING

The public and the various elite factions supported Havel's Government of National Understanding (*Vláda národního porozumění*) until the June 1990 elections. The major reason was that it embraced an anticommunist and pro-Western orientation.[22] On a more pragmatic level, some elites switched allegiance from the old regime to the new one because it had become quite clear that the new leaders were backed strongly by public opinion.[23] Warnings issued from initial and vindictive public reactions against leading communists, even in Slovakia, the region many Czechs dreaded as a potential site of nostalgia for the past. The communists in the Government of National Understanding, too, could read the popular tea leaves. One dissident reported that the Communist Party members performed in the first noncommunist government as patriots—"in the societal interest . . . over the political party interest, over particularistic or egoist interests, and over personal political ambitions" (Jičínský 1993, 163). Furthermore, the Havel government was acceptable to all factions so long as the Government of National Understanding was an interim solution awaiting popular public legitimization in free elections in June 1990. All agreed that a normal political life, with political parties and distinguishing political platforms, could begin only later—aggressive reformers around

Klaus thought after the June 1990 elections; the dissidents and more cautious advocates around Havel believed that it would occur after the June 1992 elections. Consequently, political and economic actors accorded the Government of National Understanding free reign in establishing institutional bases for a free-market economy and democracy.

The consensus about orientation and tasks explained why the complex decision-making structure of the Government of National Understanding was illusory. A decision-making chart counted no less than twelve sites of influence in the new Government of National Understanding—four Federal, six Republic, and two political organizations—yet the new Czech elite, and especially Havel, consequently made most key economic and political decisions, often unilaterally. A brief review of the configuration of the main actors illustrates that authority was concentrated at the Federal level (see table 5.4).

Czech Republic–level institutions—that is, the Czech premier, Czech ministers, and the Czech National Council—ceded important decision-making to Federal-level actors—the Federal ministries, the Federal Parliament, and Havel (Syllová 1992; Siváková 1992).[24] The impotence of Czech-level actors derived partly from the consensus that Czechoslovakia could best achieve the fundamental tasks of setting up free markets and a Western-style democracy from the political center. Also important was the reality that the most prominent Czechs were already running the country from the Federal level. Thus, most people regarded the Czech government level as subordinate.

Slovaks—that is, the Slovak premier, Slovak ministries, the Slovak National Council, Public Against Violence,[25] and also Slovaks in the Federal

Table 5.4. Sites of Influence in the Government of National Understanding, January 1990 to June 1990

Federal Level—Czechoslovakia
President, V. Havel
Premier M. Čalfa
Federal Ministries
Federal Assembly (Two Chambers)

Republic Level—Czech Republic
Czech Premier, P. Pithart
Czech Ministries
Czech National Council (Parliament)

Republic Level—Slovak Republic
Slovak Premier, J. Čarnogurský
Slovak Ministries
Slovak National Council (Parliament)

Political Organization Level
Civic Forum (OF)
Public Against Violence (VPN)

government—generally played a subordinate role in most policymaking decisions. They usually took their cue from the Czechs. This was a consequence of
the leading role of the Czech dissidents, the communist past of many leading
Slovak leaders, the dearth of Slovak expertise on technical matters, and the
disorganization of Slovak institutions.[26] An important exception to this rule
centered on the political rights and obligations of Slovaks and Slovak institutions in united Czechoslovakia.[27] Starting with the notorious "hyphen war"
in January 1990,[28] and continuing through the constitutional debates in 1990
through 1992,[29] Czech and Slovak disagreements escalated until the two sides
agreed to formally split Czechoslovakia in January 1993.

Civic Forum, the dominant Czech political organization founded by Havel
(among others) in November 1989, was not a major policy instrument in the
first half of 1990.[30] The withdrawal of Havel from Civic Forum in the winter of 1990 and the neglect of founding members such as P. Pithart, the new
Czech premier, or J. Dienstbier, the new Federal foreign minister, limited
Civic Forum's policy role. These Civic Forum founders soon became too embroiled in the affairs of state to participate deeply in the movement's business.
The effective leadership core of Civic Forum numbered under twenty people
by the spring of 1990.[31] The founders' neglect and Havel's abandonment of
Civic Forum during the crucial initial period precipitated the movement's later
dissolution. More important, Civic Forum mainly was a vehicle to win the
June 1990 elections against the Communist Party. In this capacity, the new
Czech elite designed Civic Forum to appeal to the maximum public following.
They feared alienating the voting public and losing the June 1990 elections
to the Communist Party. The Civic Forum election program thus omitted the
controversial issues that would define the post-June government—full privatization, restitution, and lustration (Krejčí 1994, 210–211).[32] As an umbrella
organization, Civic Forum was not destined to be the source of legislative
oomph.

The anticommunist and pro-Western consensus of the times allowed the
Federal-level actors in the Government of National Understanding to install
what most would agree are fundamental building blocks for a democratic
and a capitalist society.[33] On the political side, the new laws included provisions that allowed "citizens the right to associate in a democratic spirit in
political parties";[34] established a political movement such as Civic Forum or
Public Against Violence as a legal entity;[35] established the election period
for republic and Federal parliamentary elections;[36] established an electoral
system founded on proportional representation and set minimal voter acceptance levels for entry into Parliament;[37] canceled state censorship;[38] and
created institutional relationships (such as the tripartite) between employers,
employees, and the state.[39] On the economic side, the new laws included
provisions that changed and supplemented the commercial code;[40] allowed

for joint stock companies;[41] allowed for private companies;[42] changed and supplemented rules on economic arbitration;[43] changed and supplemented income tax and pension laws;[44] and changed and supplemented the law on the use of agricultural land and property.[45] Most Czechoslovakians regarded this work as uncontroversial and technical, unless one were nostalgic for the past regime.

The anticommunist and pro-Western consensus of the new Czech elite guiding the Government of National Understanding and the authoritative position of Havel provided ideological parameters for the privatization debates. As we shall see, Havel and the new Czech elite adopted the neoliberals' privatization proposal primarily because it best matched an anticommunist and pro-Western orientation. Voucher privatization, in turn, helped propel the neoliberal economists into political prominence.

THE IDEOLOGICAL PRIVATIZATION DEBATE

The neoliberal voucher privatization approach appealed to the anticommunist and pro-Western consensus of the Government of National Understanding and of Czech society more generally. It charted a simple, clear transition from the communist past to the capitalist future. In addition, voucher privatization stressed equal opportunity for everyday folk to become owners in the new system. To many in the Czech elite, standard privatization methods such as insider privatization—which could be implemented rapidly but would be privatized to presumably left-leaning managers and workers—smacked of socialism. The neoliberal plan had another advantage that Western analysts have frequently underestimated. For many Czechs, a fire sale of native assets to foreign interests, especially German ones, was unacceptable. Neoliberal voucher privatization thus promised more than rapid privatization; it also promised *national privatization*—that is, for Czechs (and Slovaks) only. The genius of Klaus and his neoliberal cohort was to devise a privatization approach that fit the mood of the new elite and the people.

Sometimes it is remarked that Klaus's and the neoliberals' success came at the expense of feckless losers—Valtr Komárek (the leading gradualist), left-wing intellectuals, enterprise claimants, and Slovaks. I would agree that the defeated displayed a blend of unfortunate strategic choices and inept leadership. Still, I question whether even the shrewdest opponents of neoliberalism could have prevailed against the Czechoslovakian neoliberals at a time when the new political elites were so keen to avoid the mistakes of 1968. Fought as it was on ideological—not political or material—grounds, the privatization battle clearly favored neoliberals in the elite approval stage.

Early Privatization Ideas

Czech (and Slovak) intellectuals and professional economists gave little thought to privatization before 1988 (Klaus 1991a, 10).[46] "It wasn't possible then to speak about the formation of large private enterprises" (Šik 1991b, 4). Communist leaders had tolerated little deviation from the state-dominated economic model since the Warsaw Pact invasion of 1968. Most domestic economists, including Klaus, had worked only on minor structural changes or on macroeconomic policy initiatives rather than on privatization (Klaus 1991a, 10).

When Czechs did begin thinking about privatization strategies, the one point that everyone could agree upon was that privatization should proceed gradually (Komárek 1990; Zieleniec 1990). In November 1989, a team of leading free-market economists led by J. Zieleniec—and including Ježek and other adherents such as R. Češka, V. Rudlovčák, J. Jonas, K. Kříž, and J. Kotrba—recommended that the state banks temporarily hold state enterprises until the time was ripe for privatization (Zieleniec 1990). In December 1989, Klaus said, "Privatization is not the word I would push today. . . . It's definitely not on the agenda for the next few years" (as quoted in the *New York Times*, December 1, 1989, A8).

The first stimulus to develop a Czechoslovakian voucher privatization program was the scheme devised by the Polish economists Lewandowski and Szomburg in 1988 (Lewandowski and Szomburg 1989). It was, for instance, discussed openly at a conference in Prague in summer 1989.[47] Yet it was J. Švejnar, a Czech émigré and an American economics professor, who presented it as a feasible alternative for Czechoslovakia. Švejnar introduced his voucher privatization framework to an audience of Czech decision-makers (absent Klaus) in the first week of February 1990 at the Kolodej castle in southern Bohemia. Švejnar's proposal offered Czechoslovakia a speedy method to transit from state ownership to private ownership (Švejnar 1989). Energized by the possibilities of Švejnar's approach, the neoliberal economists Ježek and Tříska (with Klaus's approval) began work on a Czechoslovakian voucher privatization version.[48]

In the first months of 1990, most Czech policymakers still favored standard privatization approaches along the lines of Hungary, East Germany, or even Great Britain. A team of economists under F. Vlasák, the first vice-chairman of the republic-level Czech government (as opposed to the Federal Czechoslovakian government), began an important effort to devise a pragmatic alternative based on standard approaches. Still other standard privatization approaches would be proposed after February 1990; it seemed that nearly every interested person had his own pet privatization scheme in the closet, ready if called upon.

Table 5.5. The Privatization Menu

Voucher Privatization Methods	*Standard Privatization Methods*

Voucher Privatization
  a) Without Intermediaries
  b) With Intermediaries
Institutional Privatization
	Insider Privatization
	  a) Manager Preference
	  b) Worker Preference
	Market Privatization
	  a) Public Sale, Domestic Buyers
	  b) Public Sale, Foreign Buyers
	  c) Public Sale, Open
	Contingent Privatization
	Reprivatization
	State Residual Shareholding
	Other Methods

Quite early in the transition period, lines were drawn between advocates of standard privatization approaches and the new, radical, voucher privatization approaches.

The Privatization Menu

The privatization debate offered the Czech elite clear alternatives between voucher privatization approaches and a variety of standard privatization approaches. The Czechoslovakian privatization menu approximated those simultaneously appearing in each of the other former communist countries (see table 5.5).

Voucher Privatization Approaches: The Proposals of Švejnar and the Czech Neoliberal Economists

Švejnar's voucher privatization scheme was the departure point for the Czech neoliberal economists. For Švejnar, the critical problem was how to privatize enterprises quickly when the people were poor. Of course, the state could simply sell the enterprises to the highest bidder, as was happening already in Hungary and would happen in Estonia. The dilemma for Švejnar was that foreigners, the only apparent source of large capital, would buy the local enterprises for bargain-basement prices. This would unnecessarily transfer local resources abroad. It would not do if the winning claimants would be foreigners in a country dominated variously over the centuries by Austrians, Germans, Russians, and more recently (some said) by Slovaks.[49]

    (a) *Voucher Privatization without Intermediaries*—Švejnar proposed to "augment the wealth of the population by distributing a part of ownership of firms/farms directly to the population at large." He proposed, first, that each enterprise be "declared a joint stock company with a given number of shares." Next, the government would create a trust fund to hold the enterprise shares. Finally, the trust fund would distribute shares to citizens as *individual diversified portfolios*. Švejnar's plan created instantaneous shareholders—winning claimants—of masses.[50]

(b) *Voucher Privatization with Intermediaries*—Klaus collaborators Ježek and Tříska built on Švejnar's framework to propose a "purer" voucher approach. Like Švejnar, they believed that the first priority was for a rapid and complete privatization—without direct sales. Fortunately, the relatively positive macroeconomic balances (as opposed to Poland and Hungary) allowed the government increased privatization options. Tříska argued, "In postcommunist countries privatization should be an end in itself, the aim is to strip the state of property rights . . . raising money is not an issue. The state budget is in relatively good shape, and both Czechs and Slovaks do not have that much in the way of savings already" (quoted in *Business Wire*, December 22, 1990).

Ježek and Tříska added another step to Švejnar's voucher framework. The Czechs argued that voucher holders, like investors in a market, should have the right to choose which enterprise share portfolio. They believed that the government or a trust fund should not be assigning share portfolios to individuals, as Švejnar had proposed. That would lead to undue state interference. It should be for the market, underpinned by individual preferences, to determine the valuation of shareholdings. Ježek and Tříska therefore developed an alternative scheme through which voucher holders could convert preferences into shares. The Ježek and Tříska voucher privatization scheme would occur without state interference and thus it would be fair.

In addition, Ježek and Tříska's privatization proposal was easily amenable to the introduction of intermediaries—collective institutions that would pool citizen voucher points. Presumably, intermediaries were more focused, more skilled, and more knowledgeable than inexperienced citizens. Later, this element was added explicitly into the Ježek and Tříska privatization scheme. Masses—and intermediaries—were the claimant winners under Ježek and Tříska's scheme.[51]

Institutional Privatization

No faction within the privatization debates seriously proposed institutional privatization for the Czech Republic, though it received support in the West and became a concrete part of Poland's privatization strategy in 1995 (Blanchard et al. 1991; Frydman and Rapaczynski 1994; Sachs 1993). The Czech neoliberals opposed this method on the grounds that the national privatization funds were an unnecessary parastatal. Market incentives would do better when popular investment demand would force the spontaneous formation of voucher intermediaries. The institutional privatization method might be rapid, but it was not readily apparent that it was fair or that it completely eliminated state influence in the economy. National rivalry may have also played a part in the rejection of the Polish solution. Institutional privatization was discredited in part on merit, but also in part as an approach designed by Poles and not by Czechs. The source of the idea made it less acceptable for Czechs than a homegrown approach.

Standard Privatization Approaches

Standard privatization approaches invariably involved many privatization methods, sometimes even allowing voucher privatization a minor role. The following paragraphs briefly introduce the major privatization schemes, those of the Czech Government, V. Komárek, and Enterprise Insiders, respectively. Then, as above, I break down the schemes into their component parts. This exercise allows a comparison with voucher privatization (see table 5.6).

(a) *The Czech Government Proposal.* The proposal of the economic team of P. Pithart's Czech government was by far the most influential of the early approaches. A man closely associated with Prague Spring, Czech first vice-chairman F. Vlasák was the team organizer. The Czech government team submitted its gradual privatization proposal to the Czechoslovakian government in April 1990 (Dvořák and Vlasák 1990; Valeš, Pithart, and Číč 1990; Šulc 1993).

The Czech government embraced privatization, contrary to the objections of the neoliberals. It modeled its privatization proposal explicitly on the German *Treuhundanstalt.* The Czech government proposed that privatization could take place immediately when enterprises were sufficiently capitalized, typically via market privatization. The state would retain ownership stakes in undercapitalized enterprises. The Czech proposal also stressed the role of foreign capital and expertise to modernize Czechoslovakian enterprises.[52] While the Czech government's German-inspired approach made good practical sense, it fell short of Ježek and Tříska's proposal, if equal share distribution to citizens was going to be a decisive criterion.

The Czech government proposal's heavy reliance on case-by-case privatization methods left it vulnerable to the charge that it was potentially

Table 5.6.   A Comparative Evaluation of Czech Privatization Proposals

	Criterion			
Privatization Method	Benefit to Former Communists	Speed	Chance of Completed Privatization	Nationalist Appeal
Voucher Privatization Methods (Advocates: Švejnar, Klaus, Polish Economists)				
Voucher Privatization				
(a) Without Intermediaries	None	Fast	Excellent	Excellent
(b) With Intermediaries	None	Fast	Excellent	Excellent
Institutional Privatization	Small	Fast	Excellent	Good
Standard Privatization Methods (Advocates: Czech Government, Claimants, V. Komárek)				
Insider Privatization				
(a) Manager Preference	Considerable	Fast	Excellent	Good
(b) Worker Preference	Considerable	Fast	Excellent	Excellent
Market Privatization				
(a) Public Sale, Domestic Buyers	Considerable	Slow	Medium	Good
(b) Public Sale, Foreign Buyers	None	Slow	Medium	Poor
(c) Public Sale, Open	Medium	Slow	Medium	Fair
Contingent Privatization	Medium	Slow	Medium	Fair
Reprivatization	Small	Fast	Excellent	Excellent
State Residual Shareholding	Considerable	Slow	Low	Excellent

too slow—privatization could take "537 or 612 years" (Ježek, as quoted in *SS*, August 24, 1990, "Kde drhne reforma?"). Privatization Czech-government style then would be susceptible to manipulation or even derailment by the bureaucrats. It also would offer managers increased chances to siphon off valuable enterprise assets in so-called spontaneous privatization, a process well underway in Czechoslovakia, and also in Hungary and Poland.[53]

The neoliberals dismissed the apparent successes of German privatization by noting smugly the vast resources devoted to transforming East Germany. The German strategy simply was not viable in Czechoslovakia. The Czech government privatization strategy offered a "third way to the third world," or so the neoliberals famously asserted.[54] In the last analysis, the Czech government proposal fell short of the neoliberal proposals on grounds of speed, fairness, and nationalism.

(b) *Komárek's Plan.* Komárek, who was the vice-premier of the Czechoslovakian Federal government and the leading gradualist, advocated a privatization approach somewhat similar to the Czech government plan. But Komárek's plan emphasized the role of the state as the central enterprise administrator. Komárek's approach alienated neoliberals and also other advocates of standard approaches who distrusted Komárek's statist pretensions. Komárek came across as a "Gorbachev," a gradual reformer of the old system, rather than a progressive, careful builder of a new system to Vlasák's team of Czech economists. To the neoliberals, Komárek came across as a "Galbraith" (Dlouhý, as quoted in Simonian 1992, 32). This was damning praise indeed to the Czech Chicago-school acolytes.

(c) *Enterprise Insiders.* Claimants such as enterprise insiders baldly advanced narrow privatization proposals that privileged themselves. The common line of argument was that the particular claimant was the best owner, either on grounds of fairness or of efficiency. The most active claimants were the enterprise managers. The trade unions, however, were surprising absentees in the privatization debates; they presented no alternative privatization approach. Slovak claimants also remained on the sidelines.

(i) *Privatization Plans with Manager Preferences.* All standard approaches incorporated an important role for managers in privatization. Still, large-enterprise managers and medium- and small-enterprise managers offered contrasting proposals. The large-enterprise managers frequently opposed the neoliberals; the medium- and small-enterprise managers generally were partners. So far as privatization was concerned, there were two categories of manager-claimants.

Along with other representatives of large enterprise managers, M. Grégr, the founder and president of the Czech Confederation of Industry (*Svaz průmyslu*), argued that voucher privatization proposals were inappropriate (Grégr, Berghauer, and Hrabě 1990). The new owners—the masses—would bring neither capital nor know-how to the enterprise. He argued that voucher privatization would stretch ownership too thin for concerted enterprise decision-making.

Grégr argued that the best way to promote enterprise restructuring was to allow the managers to become enterprise owners.[55] Grégr recommended that the government first establish a parastatal organization—a Fund of National Property—independent of the state budget and of state ministries to oversee enterprise management and privatization. He referred to the process of transferring enterprise stakes into the Fund of National Property as "de-etatization" or *deetatizace*.[56] Grégr intended that managers would have wide decision-making latitude under *de-etatization*. Management could, for example, rent enterprise facilities for its own private benefit, though the Fund of National Property would be entitled to payment in the form of rents, dividends, and the like (Grégr, Berghauer, and Hrabě 1990). Grégr's privatization approach resembles the Hungarian experience in this regard (Stark 1996).

Privatization would follow de-etatization under Grégr's approach. Managers also would be the leading figures in privatization.[57] The privatization decision should be "in every case a decision of existing economic subjects in cooperation with potential investors and support of the staff of enterprises" (Grégr, Berghauer, and Hrabě 1990, 3). In Grégr's scheme, the managers would shape the post-privatization stages.

Grégr's proposal was neither fast nor egalitarian, important criteria for the elite. Just as damaging to the proposal's approval, Grégr envisioned a critical role for state bureaucrats. Furthermore, Grégr's approach was suited to large enterprises with thousands of employees, but it made no provision for the wide variety of other state businesses, such as research laboratories, where managerial control might prove unpopular. For these accumulated reasons, Grégr's proposal was destined to be rated poorly by the Czech elite.

R. Baránek, the chairperson of the Association of Czechoslovakian Entrepreneurs (*Sdružení československých podnikatelů ČR*), a representative organization of small- and medium-sized businessmen, agreed with Grégr that managers deserved special privatization preferences. From a practical standpoint, only managers knew enough and cared enough about their businesses to be active owners. From a moral standpoint, managers deserved ownership because of the years in operating enterprises under communism (Baránek 1994).

However, Baránek argued along with Ječck and Tříska against Grégr's notion of de-etatization. Like the neoliberals, Baránek argued that privatization must take place immediately; the state is always and forever an inefficient owner. Selected trade associations, like the bakery association, also supported privatization with manager preferences.[58]

The neoliberals excluded the ideas of Baránek and the trade associations from the original privatization scheme. Still, the small- and medium-sized business organizations agreed with the principle of rapid privatization. That agreement would prove invaluable to the entrepreneurs in the public legitimization stage. According to J. Muroň, the deputy minister of privatization from 1990 until 1992, the business lobbies persuaded privatizers to adjust the privatization rules.

(ii) *Privatization Plans with Worker Preferences.* Expatriate Czech economists and left-leaning members of Civic Forum were among the prominent supporters of worker preferences.[59] The voice of O. Šik, the leading Czech economic reformer of the 1960s and the Federal deputy prime minister in 1968, was perhaps the most influential one.[60] Like many of the reform economists from that earlier period, Šik argued that Western-style capitalism was an unjust system.[61] He developed an ideal political economy that he labeled *Humane Economic Democracy* or, unfortunately as it would turn out, *The Third Way* (Šik 1991a). Šik's approach emphasized market mechanisms in combination with worker safeguards, the most important ones being general worker participation and worker ownership.

> [I]n order to prevent the formation of large concentrations of private capital, combined with a simultaneous alienation from capital of wide sectors of society, direct equity participation by employees in all market enterprises should be aspired to from the outset. Joint equity ownership, profit-sharing and co-determination by employees is what I would describe as general participation. (Šik 1991a, 13–14)

M. Zeman, then a Civic Forum deputy in Parliament and now chief of the Czech Social Democratic Party (and as of the June 1998 elections, prime minister) also supported worker ownership. He advocated American-style employee stock ownership plans (ESOPs) in parliamentary debates as early as the spring of 1990 (Jičínský 1993, 153). Zeman supported employee ownership on the grounds of fairness and protection, like Šik, but also on efficiency grounds. He believed that workers could drive corporate restructuring as well as outside owners. Zeman's support of worker ownership schemes persists to this day.[62]

If privatization schemes that offered preferences to managers conflicted with the objectives of market creation, so privatization schemes that favored workers would face worse comparisons. Not only did worker privatization carry the major disadvantages of manager privatization—it unfairly favored workers of valuable enterprises[63]—but it privatized to a class widely regarded as naturally antagonistic to the market. Neoliberals contended that worker incentives pushed management to raise wages to the detriment of expanding profits. The neoliberals constantly pointed to the Yugoslav case as the example of failed worker ownership (see Tříska's comments in Páral 1990). Finally, the indifference of the workers to worker ownership undermined the cause of worker privatization.

All standard approaches, whether considered separately or bundled for sensitivity to reflect individual enterprise conditions, were bound to struggle against the neoliberal juggernaut for acceptance. No justification for standard privatization approaches could match the parsimonious logic of the neoliberals. Only voucher privatization claimed to deliver private ownership irreversibly, without undue interference of the state, and to deliver ownership to native Czechoslovaks in equal measure, without the input of managers (read: *nomenklatura*), workers, and foreigners.

Market Privatization

The self-proclaimed neoliberal market economists did not support public sale methods, the most free-market of methods. Public sale methods collided with a common fear amongst neoliberal economists and amongst the Czechoslovakian elite as a whole. Domestic assets would be sold cheaply to foreigners or to undesirable domestics—mafia or well-connected *nomenklatura*.[64]

(a) *Public Sale, Domestic Buyers.* Entrepreneurs' unions, including Baránek's Association of Czech Entrepreneurs, were among the strongest advocates of public sales to domestic buyers. These groups argued that domestic auctions offered enterprise managers excellent chances to obtain ownership. Proximity to enterprises guaranteed that managers would have the best information to offer the right price. Managers were likely to prove indispensable to the enterprise owner, even should an outsider buy an enterprise. Few foreigners could operate a small- or medium-sized Czech enterprise without the local manager.

(b) *Public Sale, Foreign Buyers.* Czechs who emphasized the backward technology and market inexperience of Czech enterprises—Komárek, Grégr, Valeš, and Vrba, Czech minister of industry from 1990 to 1992— advocated aggressive promotion of foreign direct investment via trade sales.

(c) *Public Sale, Open.* Advocates of standard methods, such as the Czech government, supported open public sales when the nationality of the owner seemed immaterial. The objective was to raise money for the public treasury. Yet, in 1990, Czechoslovakia showed minimal foreign debt on its books and a state budget in rough balance. Consequently, the state never prioritized raising money through privatization. The Czech approach contrasts with "highest price wins," the dominant Hungarian approach.[65]

Contingent Privatization

The voucher privatization advocates also had no place for contingent privatization, a method that privileges criteria other than money in awarding ownership. They opposed contingent privatization because it offered the state leeway in choosing the new owner. Voucher fanatics argued that the state was unable to choose amongst owners. However, some neoliberals—Ježek was the most important one—later broke ranks by suggesting that the state should privatize selected enterprises to owners likely to restructure. As a rule, these enterprises were in "strategic" (Schwartz 1997) sectors such as automobiles, telecommunications, steel, and utilities. This led eventually to neoliberal proposals of public tender privatization, though not in the first half of 1990.

The Czech government economic team, the privatization designers most concerned about enterprise restructuring, advocated wider use of contingent privatization methods than the neoliberals. They recommended that the state use these methods to privatize nonstrategic companies as well as "strategic companies." Supporters of contingent privatization generally supported direct sale to foreigners since foreigner companies would be best able to restructure Czech firms.

State Residual Shareholding

Advocates of indefinite state ownership of most enterprises were rare in post–November 1989 Czechoslovakia. They were associated generally with the hard line of the previous regime. Only the "strategic" enterprises prompted wide disagreement within the elite, including within the neoliberal camp, over whether the state should remain a permanent owner.[66]

Instead, the advocates of standard privatization methods usually endorsed temporary state ownership, that is, until privatization.[67] The state could perform as a passive owner, as in Grégr's scheme above, or as an active planner, as in Komárek's "Social Economic Program for the Development of Czechoslovakia," issued in December 1998 (Komárek 1990). Komárek had based his policy advice on the argument that the deformation of the Czechoslovakian economy was the most pronounced economic legacy of the communist regime.[68]

Deformation took the form of extremely large enterprise units, overemphasis on heavy industry, monopolization, dysfunctional pricing mechanisms, and protectionism from outside competition. Komárek therefore contended that first "unblocking" and then reorienting the Czechoslovakian economy could be accomplished only gradually so as to minimize social costs and then only through central state guidance. Komárek wrote, "[I]n the transition period, before a high quality market will exist, the economic center must assist. In this way, at least in the next years, the economic center must make concrete decisions from the perspective of economic activity and it must support the allocation of resources" (Komárek 1990, 217).

Czechs across the political spectrum suspected that Komárek's emphasis on the role of the "economic center" was matched by hostility toward privatization. Although Komárek strongly supported market mechanisms, his plan explicitly left open the options for ownership transfer (Komárek 1990, 219–230). Komárek's fuzziness on privatization coupled with his emphasis on the need for an interventionist state exposed him to the charge that he was a person from the old system.

A rendering of the competing privatization proposals according to the anticommunist and pro-Western bias of the new Czech elite illustrates the ideological appeal of voucher privatization (see table 5.6). Voucher privatization (with or without intermediaries) offered no benefit to former communists and it promised to quickly complete privatization. Moreover, voucher privatization ensured that Czech (or Slovak) citizens would become the owners of enterprise assets. No other privatization method offered an ensemble of ideological advantages. This conclusion turns conventional wisdom on its head by suggesting that politics in the early transition period had a deterministic quality. Put another way, if Klaus had not existed, circumstances might well have invented him.

POLITICS OF THE ELITE APPROVAL STAGE

The central political story of privatization during the Government of National Understanding is the struggle between Klaus and Komárek. I contended above that Klaus's privatization proposal resonated with the extreme anticommunist and pro-Western strain of the new Czech elite. That rendering omitted the political backdrop, however. Sometimes, political self-interest and economic self-interest intervene so that policies are rejected despite their merit. One might have expected such intervention in the case of voucher privatization in the Czech Republic. For one thing, Klaus loomed as a threat to the dissidents' and Havel's hold on power. For another, many sorts of claimants stood to lose under voucher privatization—workers and managers are only the most prominent examples. Two puzzles, then, underlie the discussion:

1. Why did the new Czech elite overlook the obvious political dangers of Klaus and of voucher privatization and why did they disregard the political advantages of Komárek and of standard privatization approaches?
2. Why did managers and workers opt out of the privatization debates? Once again, the best answers revolve around the anticommunist and pro-Western convictions prevalent in Czech society and especially among the new Czech elite. Ultimately, the new Czech elite's decision to favor voucher privatization represented a victory of ideology over politics.

The ideological competition between Klaus and Komárek was fought first over macroeconomic policy. The main disagreements revolved around monetary policy, currency policy, and state budgetary policy. Klaus argued for restrictive policies to lay the groundwork for capitalist development; Komárek supported expansionary policies to guard against the inevitable unemployment and drops in industrial output. Concerning privatization, their disagreements could not have been sharper. The respective policy stances posed a clear ideological choice between a gradual and a radical reform approach.

Klaus versus Komárek

Komárek was the person mostly likely to direct privatization policy in Havel's Czechoslovakia. First, Komárek was the senior economic policy-maker. Komárek's appointment as Czechoslovakia's deputy prime minister in December 1989 in the interim Government of National Understanding positioned him to dictate economic policy during the transition. Second, Havel and two of his top economic advisors, Václav Valeš and R. Wagner, knew Komárek personally before November 1989. Third, Komárek's economic positions favoring gradual, socially conscious reform coincided with the views of Havel and his top advisors. Fourth, Komárek had converted his position as chief of the reform-minded Prognostics Institute into general personal popularity. Indeed, Komárek's popularity was far ahead of Havel's in late November and early December (Wheaten and Kavan 1992, 103; Gál 1991).[69] Fifth, Komárek's belief in a mixed system, which borrowed elements of capitalism and socialism, conformed with the preferences of the population as a whole (Vaněk 1994; Hartl 1991). Carrying evident advantages in political position, personal connections, general popularity, and ideological disposition, Komárek appeared to hold Czechoslovakia's economic and privatization fate in his hands.

Klaus seemed destined for a supporting role in economic policymaking. First, Klaus emerged from the events of 1989 as the Czechoslovakian minister of finance, an influential position to be sure, but not one at Komárek's level. Second, Klaus was not well known among the dissidents or to Havel.[70] Third, Klaus founded his reputation on free-market positions, positions that seemed too harsh for Havel and for the public. In contrast to Komárek, Klaus's priorities were righting macroeconomic imbalances (via low inflation, a stable currency, and balanced trade and government budgets) and privatizing enterprises; Klaus's primary concern was not social justice. Fifth, Klaus lacked Komárek's name recognition either prior to or just after the revolution.[71] Lacking Komárek's advantages, Klaus seemed a sure political also-ran in the euphoria of revolution.

Yet, Klaus's appeal to the disappointed generation in the Czech elite proved decisive in the political struggle against Komárek. First, these Czechs recognized Klaus as a Western economist. Klaus was arguably the leading market economist among the neoliberals; he had been hibernating in the state bank for seventeen years. On the other hand, Komárek "never was kissed by the muse of economic education . . . [because] he studied in Moscow and he advanced as a cadre of the Communist economic system" (Dlouhý, quoted in Simonian 1992, 32). Second, Klaus's ideas represented a bold and simple strategy to transit to capitalism. Komárek's advocacy of a gradual reform approach exposed him as a "68er," a failed reformer from the Prague Spring afraid to take the necessary and drastic steps toward a market economy. Third, Klaus was one of a handful of members of the Czech Academy of Sciences who never joined the Communist Party. Komárek was a Communist Party member and a suspect one at that.[72] Komárek's economics degree (1954) is from Moscow; he advised the Cuban government for several years; and, he maintained close personal ties with L. Štrougal, the communist prime minister of Czechoslovakia. Fourth, Klaus was independent from Havel; Komárek nearly a confidante. Klaus's independence was a lightening rod for the disappointed generation, who invariably shared Czech neoliberalism's antipathy toward the past regime and romanticism for Western capitalism. Fifth, Klaus was regarded by all who knew him as a committed, hardworking professional (Havlík 1990). Komárck was charismatic, but a "lazybones" (Ježek, quoted in Husák 1997, 56). Klaus was substance over form; Komárek, the reverse. In Klaus, the elite saw a person who epitomized their experience and espoused their hopes; in Komárek, the elite saw a person who epitomized past failures and espoused fanciful dreams.

One elite after another turned away from Komárek toward Klaus as time passed. Komárek's perceived inability to articulate a reasoned argument was particularly devastating to the natural advocates of a "third way" approach, "natural lefties" P. Kučera, I. Fišera, or J. Urban of Civic Forum and Havel

confidantes such as Valeš or M. Čalfa. The contrast with Klaus and the cohort
of neoliberal economists who worked together for years, debating the issues of
capitalist economics again and again, was stark. Reading the competing proposals and the newspaper polemics of the period, one is struck by the difference
between Komárek's flowery, frothy writing and the precise, academic style of
Klaus. The differences in style mirrored distinctions in content. The left wing
reluctantly abandoned Komárek and threw their support to the neoliberals. The
loss of his natural supporters doomed Komárek's economic agenda, if it had a
chance, and also his political future.

What happened to the Czech government's privatization approach?
Komárek's theoretical mists essentially swallowed it. This proved to be a pity
for the Left since the Czech government proposal offered a viable alternative
privatization strategy. Four other political obstacles burdened the Czech government privatization proposal, in any event. One, the Czech government was
but a junior decision-maker in the Government of National Understanding.
Two, the authors of the Czech government proposal were relatively older men
who earned their spurs in 1968.[73] Vlasák, for instance, was well into his seven-
ties in 1989. The spectacle of veteran economists or "old boys" endorsing an
approach that promised a gradual undocking from the past system seemed per-
ilously close to the reform communism debacle. Three, the Czech economists
primarily were academic economists and not politicians. They made only
meager attempts to spotlight their alternative proposals. Indeed, the Czech
economists passively submitted their proposal to Klaus's team of neoliberals
in the expectation that their ideas would be incorporated as part of an integrated proposal. The neoliberal privatization proposal submitted subsequently
to the Federal government practically ignored the Czech government contribution. Four, the content of the Czech government privatization proposal—a
mixture of standard privatization approaches—simply did not meet the ideological consensus among the elite. This last proved to be fatal, especially as
the Czech government's privatization proposal misleadingly became entangled
with Komárek's ideas.

Why Havel Opted Out of the Privatization Debates

Havel, who evidently was aware of the political threat posed by Klaus and
the neoliberals, chose to opt out of the privatization debates for two reasons.
One was the pressure that emanated from the disappointed generation. They
openly discouraged Havel's involvement in the privatization debates for fear
that he harbored left-wing sympathies. Havel's frequent references to a "just
society" and his selection of advisors conscious of the social consequences
of economic reform aroused suspicions that he was a person of 1968. The

disappointed generation also worried about Havel's apparent willingness to forgive communists. He welcomed former communist ministers into the government. M. Čalfa, a deputy minister in the past regime, became the Federal prime minister.[74] Havel also (in public) backed A. Dubček, the fallen reform communist leader of 1968. The disappointed generation feared that Havel would halt radical transformation initiatives and support kinder but less ambitious economic reforms, such as standard privatization methods.

Two, Havel abstained from the privatization debates due to his unfamiliarity with Western economics. Havel reportedly believed that economics was to be handled by trained professionals. This belief was consistent with the traditional East European view that economics, like engineering or accounting, is a technical, bureaucratic chore. Havel's behavior may also have been predicated on his own demonstrated lack of facility with economic concepts. Havel was said to have remarked that the role of economists was to achieve zero percent unemployment and zero percent inflation, a goal generally considered undesirable and impossible by professional economists. Dlouhý, the newly installed chief of the State Planning Commission, effectively exposed Havel's ignorance of economics at an important Civic Forum meeting in spring 1990. Perhaps humbled, Havel chose to act as an arbiter among opposing sides in the economic debates rather than to join as an active participant. Havel's choice was in the style of T. Masaryk, Czechoslovakia's revered first president during the First Republic, 1918–1938.[75]

By stepping out of the economic debates, Havel unwittingly opened the space for the neoliberal reformers (and fervent anticommunists) to seize the economic agenda. The casualties of Havel's political mistake turned out to be the Social Democratic left, the unity of Czechoslovakia, and Havel's own programmatic relevance. The prime political beneficiary was, of course, Klaus.

Why Czech Enterprise Managers and Workers Opted Out of the Privatization Debates

Unlike Havel, who opted out of the privatization debates owing to his own shortcomings, enterprise managers and trade unions were hemmed in by the prevalent anticommunist and pro-Western sentiment. As we saw earlier, these claimants were under constant attack during the elite approval stage and were in no position to be asserting their privatization interests. The enterprise managers and workers earned only opprobrium from the new Czech elite in the few cases that they did offer privatization proposals. This section offers a very brief characterization of the strategic choices of enterprise managers and workers. It also addresses and largely dissents with the conventional wisdom that explains those choices.

The Strategic Choices of the Enterprise Managers

In those trying times, the representative organizations of managers chose not to oppose actively the proposed privatization reforms of the Government of National Understanding. This was true both at the individual and collective levels. Grégr and the Confederation of Czech Industry were exceptional in that regard. Grégr opposed the privatization proposals of the Czechoslovakian government, and as a result made quick political enemies of leading neoliberal reformers.[76] The Government of National Understanding consequently largely ignored Grégr's proposal, a result congruent with the prevailing antimanager consensus.

In addition, it is misleading to assume, as nearly all Western analysts once did, that enterprise managers necessarily felt threatened by a radical privatization (Sachs 1990a; Frydman and Rapaczynski 1991; Kitschelt 1992). Anecdotal evidence suggests that many Czechoslovakian managers were itching for the chance to operate enterprises in a market environment.[77] These managers wanted to test their own abilities and in many cases were as frustrated as everyone else by the rigidity of the prior communist regime. In the early days of transition, many managers resembled most of Czechoslovakian society; they were disgusted with the prior regime and ready for a change.

The Strategic Choices of the Trade Unions

The rabid anticommunism of worker members and the organizational disarray of the labor movement severely limited the strategic choices for the new central union leadership. When the trade unions criticized the neoliberal theory, they provoked a reflex countercharge. Anticommunists called the Czechoslovakian trade unions socialist. Outright opposition to neoliberalism might then further alienate the trade unions' already hostile membership.

The Czechoslovakian trade union leadership conformed to the ideological boundaries of the new game, and went so far as to stress its "antitotalitarian" and "anticentralization" orientation (Vejvodová 1990). The December 1989 measure banning political parties in the workplace—it was targeted at the Communist Party—made manifest that orientation. The repeated union statements in support of privatization were another indication (see, for example, the speech by I. Pleskot, June 1990). Rather than privatization, the trade union leaders focused their public activities on wages, pensions, and unemployment—the traditional and uncontroversial avenues for maintaining worker support. Pleskot, the first president of the Czechoslovakian Confederation of Trade Unions, wrote, "trade unions could by no means elaborate their own alternative concepts of privatization and reform ... [because these concepts] are not in their competence...and because [the trade unions] do not have experts qualified for this work" (Pleskot 1990, 14).

The anticommunist and pro-Western popular consensus dictated union policies to favor privatization, just as it did all other organizations in the first stages of the Czechoslovakian transition.

Alternative Explanation: Enterprise Power Argument

One explanation for the degree of enterprise insider participation in privatization is the decentralization of enterprise reform during communism (Frydman and Rapaczynski 1994, 155–159). I call it the *enterprise power argument*. The logic is as follows. Privatization supposedly favored enterprise insiders in cases where reform under communism had delegated autonomy to enterprise insiders. When it came time to privatize, the postcommunist state supposedly needed to recapture enterprise control in order to then privatize those stakes to nonstate actors (via a process commonly referred to as commercialization or corporatization). Why would enterprise insiders with enterprise control turn over enterprise ownership to the state? The reason was a preference in privatization.

Conversely, the state would not need to buy off the enterprise insiders when the prior regime had not decentralized ownership authority. The state could conduct privatization according to its own preferences. In short, this is the enterprise power argument as applied to Czechoslovakia. The Czechoslovakian state did not decentralize authority. Therefore, the Czechoslovakian government was able to institute voucher privatization largely without the consent of the enterprise insiders.[78]

The enterprise power argument conflicts with Czechoslovakian privatization experience. The historical premise underlying the enterprise power argument is that the Czechoslovakian state was the dominant and overwhelming enterprise actor in the pre-1989 period. Although this remains the prevailing point of view in the West, the work of L. Mlčoch argues that a coalition consisting of top enterprise managers, party leaders, and central state bureaucrats dominated corporate governance in most Czechoslovakian enterprises. The enterprise manager, not the state planner, was the *primer inter pares* of the enterprise coalition. Mlčoch's metaphor is the "upside-down pyramid," not the neat, ordered hierarchy (Mlčoch 1992, 1993; Klaus 1991b, 36–38). Interviews I conducted with Czech and Slovak industry officials, ministry officials, academics, and bankers in 1993 and 1994 confirmed Mlčoch's version of enterprise governance.[79] Mlčoch's work fits in a wider revisionist literature that emphasizes the manager's role during the communist period (Grossman 1994). If the manager was the dominant enterprise actor prior to 1989, then according to the enterprise power argument, the Czechoslovakian state should not have been easily able to commercialize—that is, assert formal state ownership rights. Instead, commercialization in the Czech Republic was a nonevent.

The enterprise power argument is more plausible if the enterprise insiders are Czechoslovakian workers. In pre-1989 Czechoslovakia, workers were excluded from enterprise management;[80] thus, the Czechoslovakian workers did not have property rights, de facto or de jure. Supporting evidence for the enterprise power argument is the lack of employee share ownership plans (ESOPs) and the discrimination against workers in the Czech Republic. By contrast, the heritage of activist labor officials in Poland enabled Polish workers to block privatization or to direct privatization to their advantage. ESOPs and high worker-share percentages are common in Polish privatized enterprises.

Yet, the enterprise power argument for worker activism is suspect in the Czech case. While it is true that trade unions largely were precluded from enterprise decision-making in pre-1989 Czechoslovakia, Czechoslovakian trade union local leaders and workers actually supported voucher privatization,[81] though they knew it might mean unemployment for them and their co-workers. I remember the words of one thirty-something trade union boss who argued that his factory should be closed in order to get rid of the communist management and methods, even if it meant the unemployment of thousands of workers—including himself. Indeed, the most vulnerable firms in a market economy—the heavy industry firms favored by the prior regime—actually were privatization's biggest supporters (Boguszak and Rak 1990). Despite the differences in worker activism in the Czech and the Polish cases, the core difference was in the worker attitudes toward privatization—antagonistic in the Polish case, sympathetic in the Czech case. The Czech case consequently does not support the enterprise power argument.

The absence of managers and workers from the Czechoslovakian privatization debates partly defined a "claimant-free" atmosphere for the elite approval stage. The elite judged privatization initiatives on their merits, that is, the degree to which they conformed with anticommunist and pro-Western orthodoxy.

How Public Opinion Settled the Issue in Favor of Voucher Privatization

Public opinion gave the new Czech elite the final go-ahead for voucher privatization advocates. It showed the elite that moving ahead with voucher privatization would not provoke widespread social unrest or, more importantly, meet with a resurgence of the Communist Party in the June 1990 elections. The elite hedged their bets by mounting a concerted public relations campaign through the media on behalf of voucher privatization and other radical transformation measures (Krejčí 1994). In Czechoslovakia, public legitimization accompanied elite approval.

The prospects of a radical privatization approach seemed dim at first, judging from public opinion. In November 1989, only 3 percent of Czechoslovakian survey respondents preferred capitalism over socialism or a mixed economy (Vaněk 1994). In December, 73 percent of Czechoslovakians were opposed to the return of "not only restaurants and small property, but also large productive enterprises" (Vaněk 1994, 58). In January 1990, 58 percent of Czechoslovakian respondents answered that economic reform measures should be mild and gradual rather than comprehensive and quick (Boguszak and Rak 1990, table 1.1). With the June 1990 elections on the horizon, voucher privatization would certainly not have won government approval had these figures persisted through the spring.

But the figures did not persist; public opinion reversed. By May 1990, Czechoslovakians (collectively) considered economic reform the highest priority and privatization the single categorical imperative of economic reform (Boguszak and Rak 1990). Fifty-eight percent of Czechoslovakians supported a harder, faster approach to economic reform; only 42 percent endorsed a milder, slower approach to economic reform. More important, Czechs and Slovaks increasingly realized that economic reform would entail real sacrifice, that the costs were not the figment of an economist's imagination. In January 1990, 52 percent of Czechoslovaks thought that large-scale unemployment was unavoidable; by May 1990, 79 percent of Czechoslovaks thought so (Boguszak and Rak 1990, chart 4, question 28). Yet, only a mere 19 percent of Czech (and 34 percent of Slovak) respondents answered that "unemployment should be avoided though it meant that economic reform would be slowed or stopped altogether" (Boguszak and Rak 1990, chart 4, question 31). This evidence conflicts with standard analyses, which routinely link low Czech unemployment rates with the decision to go ahead with voucher privatization. Full employment in the Czech Republic was a gigantic surprise to the Czech elite that came only later when the decision to go ahead with voucher privatization was irreversible. The public supported radical economic reform, including voucher privatization, in spite of its apprehensions about looming unemployment, not because there was no unemployment. The increasing willingness of Czechs (and Slovaks) to support radical economic reform, to acknowledge that radical economic reform would entail personal sacrifice, and to endure that sacrifice for the greater cause of economic reform gave the elite the green light to support voucher privatization.

Why did public opinion shift? One of the key reasons was the heavy hand of the elite in shaping public opinion through the media. The media came out strongly in favor of radical economic reform and voucher privatization. Television broadcasts seem to have been especially effective. At the same time, the media avoided the potentially divisive Komárek and Klaus power struggle. The media was more fifth column than fourth estate when it came to privatization.

The bald abuse of the media may seem surprising when democracy was supposed to have been the watchword. One Civic Forum leader, who also served as a newspaper editor, explained during an interview with the author that the elite used the media "to teach the people." Czechoslovakian reporters were "citizen-journalists, . . . reporters who put their civic duty and the health of the republic before their freedom to report. This attitude—and a basic lack of news gathering and delivery skills—caused the Czech press to remain not more than a bulletin board for government messages" (Kayal 1994, 1).

One Czechoslovakian newspaperman justified his acquiescence to the new correct line: "The truth is that [privatization] has problems, but the truth is also that privatization is the only way for a good economic system. . . . Not as a newspaperman, but as a citizen of this country, I want privatization to be successful" (quoted in Kayal 1994, 6).

Reaffirmed by public opinion, the Czech elite thus chose Klaus over Komárek as the country's economic and privatization czar. The Czech elite also gave Klaus the political opening he needed to eventually seize political power. The first choice was a conscious decision on the part of the Czech elite; the second one was an unintended consequence. The political ramifications of the choice would not become fully clear to Klaus's opponents until the public legitimization stage.

The Privatization Decision: Klaus over Komárek

Havel endorsed Klaus's economic program at the Aurora, a popular political club, in the spring of 1990.[82] This prompted the quick resignation of Komárek as deputy Federal minister. The denouement was the government acceptance of the Finance Ministry privatization *Harmonogram*—a schedule outlining a voucher privatization development plan.

Only a heroic counterfactual could assert that Czechoslovakian privatization policy would have met a different end had the standard-bearer for a softer privatization approach been a more able person than Komárek. It would require a person simultaneously of political stature and economic professionalism plus a young cohort of economists. From where would that young cohort emerge? How would this standard-bearer persuade the elite to support a moderate privatization approach when the elite were single-minded in their conviction to throw off all remnants of the past? Circumstances, more than the human beings, conspired to promote a voucher privatization program. The atmosphere of energized euphoria offered the neoliberals an unassailable advantage.

CONCLUSION

The analysis of the elite approval stage shows that historical legacies carried over from the conservative Czechoslovakian communist past—an extreme anticommunism and a passion for the West—facilitated neoliberal influence over privatization decision-making. The sentiments engendered by the past underpinned the public and elite backing for neoliberals, the purveyors of a radical turn from communism to the West. They also were responsible for the ineffectiveness of interests. Ultimately, a broad consensus over privatization policy emerged in the Czech Republic, an outcome of an "interest-free" and "institution-free" privatization decision-making environment.

The evidence nevertheless highlights the limitations of the historical legacies hypothesis and the appeal of "window of opportunities" formulations. Political tactics were crucial in the neoliberal ascendance. Perhaps, the critical political choices were those of the new Czech elite around Havel, who chose to close ranks around the economic proposals of Klaus, even though many disliked Klaus personally and distrusted his brand of economics. Yet they supported him and his neoliberal economic policies, in part, because the alternative economists seemed professionally incapable of conducting national economic policy. But they also supported Klaus's program because it was an ideal political weapon against the communists, whom most of the elite still regarded as the prime enemy in the first months after November 1989. Moreover, Czech nationalism surfaces during this period; the Czech elite and population were clearly at home with privatization procedures that kept the most valuable assets in native hands. In sum, historical legacies and political tactics and nationalism combined to account for why the Czech neoliberals were successful in the early privatization stages. The mixed result of the historical legacies hypothesis suggests that in its early stages, transition was part "window of opportunity" and part constrained politics.

NOTES

1. From 1968 to 1991 there was a Slovak Communist Party and a Communist Party of Czechoslovakia, but no Czech Communist Party.

2. Zdeněk Zuska (1931–1982) was the mayor of Prague from 1970 to 1981. Before becoming mayor, in the prior two years he was the chief of a bureaucratic department for the establishment of party justice (*prořizení stranické práce v č. zemích*) (*Malá československá encyclopedia: Š–Ž, Vol. VI*, 1987, 867). Zuska was one of many important Slovaks appointed to important posts within the Czech lands. He was killed in a suspicious car collision with a truck. It only seems like an insult in retrospect when it is unimaginable that a Slovak would be mayor of Prague. During normalization nobody seemed to care.

3. Ironically, the hard-line communist approach to the Czech lands and the relatively lenient communist approach to Slovakia may have precipitated a reform movement within the top layers of the Slovak Communist Party prior to November 1989 and the corresponding lack of a reform movement in the Czech Communist Party. For a discussion of this issue, see Grzymala-Busse 1998.

4. Evidence of the Czech self-image as European is apparent in important 1989 and 1990 documents. Consider, for example, the 1990 Civic Forum program that states the country's top priority should be a "Return to Europe." See also Rupnik 1989.

5. The failure of the 1960s reforms—the so-called managers' revolution—also undercut the case for managerial privileges in 1989 and 1990.

6. Czech enterprises were the sites of similar antimanagement agitation. Like Public Against Violence, Civic Forum stepped in to support managers against workers, whom party members saw as dangerous for the future of the enterprises (Pleskot 1994, 8).

7. Nonetheless, the routine of the enterprises may not have been impacted, since deputy managers frequently replaced the chief enterprise managers.

8. Evidence for this point is the significant growth in the number of state-owned enterprises from January 1990 to June 1990 (Charap and Zemplínerová 1993). Most spin-offs, however, occurred later in 1990 and early in 1991, not in the first months of 1990 (Lízal, Singer, and Švejnar 1995, 220–221).

9. The formal anticommunist stance of the trade unions was little more than a holding action against the continuous barrage of criticism from neoliberals and anticommunists alike. Anticommunists drew attention to the unions' compromised role during communism; and, the neoliberals attacked the trade unions for antimarket and "antidemocratic" proclivities.

10. Disparate groups of workers formally agreed upon a new structure at the March 1990 trade union conference.

11. Twenty-two percent of workers said that privatization of their enterprise was out of the question in 1990. Often, these were workers in state ministries, health organizations, and the like (Boguszak and Rak 1990, 23).

12. In 1990, the trade unions did no more than comment on the titanic amounts of legislation the Government of National Understanding was passing. Only in exceptional cases did the trade unions actually propose draft laws, and privatization was not one of those exceptional cases (Pleskot 1994, 9).

13. It is a neglected fact that the disappointed generation was almost exclusively male. In the early 1990s, Klaus's ODS party did not have a single woman who could be counted among its leadership. Also, prior to 1989 (in 1986) roughly one quarter of the deputies in the Federal Assembly were women (Wolchik 1991, 71); yet after the June 1990 elections the number had dropped to 11 percent (Leff 1997, 92). However, this may not imply better opportunities for women prior to the revolution. Just over two-thirds of women deputies in the 1986 Federal Assembly were workers, as compared to less than 20 percent of men (Wolchik 1991, 71). This suggests, as Leff points out, a quota-like inclusiveness. Ironically, the first noncommunist governments displayed a similar drive to include women in high positions in government, despite the mere 11 percent showing of women delegates.

14. The protest history against the communist regime impacted political perspectives throughout the CEECs. In Poland, for instance, the March 1968 strikes shaped the political perspective of the Polish intellectuals who rose to power after 1989 (Ekiert 1997, 320).

15. For Czechs, a comfortable lifestyle included, not insignificantly, the improvement of summer *chatas* and *chalupas*. *Chatas* (wooden, smaller) and *chalupas* (brick, larger) are vacation cottages. The Czech press reported that the Czechs own more vacation cottages per capita than any other nationality. During normalization, these cottages remained privately owned and were deliberately used by the communists as a way to channel discontent and energy away from the public sphere. Summer houses were commonly acknowledged as a form of "internal exile." This viewpoint is acknowledged readily by the Czechs.

16. Detailed comparisons of Prague demonstrations in 1989 and 1990 versus those of 1968 confirm that the thirty- to forty-four-year-old generation comprised the critical opposition group in 1989, but not in 1968. Moreover, opposition to the communist regime was greater in the Czech Republic in either period than in Slovakia (Tůma 1994). This fact is consistent with the point that Slovaks were relatively satisfied with the past regime as compared with Czechs.

17. Contemporary antiregime demonstrators covered only a minute percentage of the population, so we must be careful about drawing strong conclusions solely from this data.

18. Klaus referred to the institutional views of property rights literature as "babbling" (Husák 1997, 97).

19. These data emanate from a class I taught in financial markets at VŠE, the top business and economics university in the Czech Republic in spring 1993.

20. The most commonly cited influences on Havel's thought are Kant, Heidegger, and Jan Patočka (the latter two knew each other). For more information on Havel's thought, see, for example, Josef Šafařík (1992) and in English, Aviezer Tucker (1990) and Gellner in the *Czech Sociological Review*. Perhaps the most ardent Czech critic of Havel is Václav Bělohrádský, a former broadcaster on Radio Free Europe and a professor at Bologna, Italy. See, for example, *Přitomnost*, February 22–23, 1990; *MFD*, March 28, 1992; *MFD*, March 29, 1992; *MFD*, January 30, 1992, 11.

21. Over one-third of bureaucrats (50,000 out of 142,000) were Communist Party members in 1989 (Holub 1997). By contrast, according to Jan Urban, official spokesperson for Civic Forum in 1990, the core strength of the dissident community was only 250 (Leff 1997, 86). And, according to prominent dissidents interviewed by the author, the leadership core was no greater than five.

22. Three events founded the Government of National Understanding:

- The abdication of Czechoslovakian president G. Husák on December 10, 1989;
- The formal eradication of the constitutional statutes mandating the leading roles of the Communist Party (Article 4) and validating Marxism-Leninism as official state ideology (Article 16); and,
- The parliamentary election of Havel as president of the Czechoslovakian Republic on December 29, 1989.

23. Public opinion surveys in the first months overwhelmingly illustrated popular euphoria at the demise of the prior regime (Boguszak and Rak 1990; Hartl 1991).

24. An important exception concerned ethnic questions between Czechs and Slovaks. Most contentious issues revolved around the jurisdictions of the central federation and the constituent republics. Czech-Slovak disputes were tabled largely until after the June 1990 elections (see below).

25. In the June 1990 Federal parliamentary elections, Public Against Violence garnered 33 percent of the Slovak vote, as compared with 18 percent for the Slovak Christian Democrats (KDH), 14 percent for the Slovak Communist Party (KSS), and 12 percent for the Slovak Nationalist Party (SNS). However, for much of the period leading up to the election, Public Against Violence was less popular (as measured by election preference) than the Christian Democrats and sometimes less popular than the Communist Party. At the extreme point, a month before the election, the gap between Public Against Violence and the Christian Democrats reached 20 percent (30 percent to 10 percent), in favor of the Christian Democrats (Krejčí 1994, 238).

26. Indeed, the Slovak leadership often learned first of key state decisions from the media (author interview with a former leader of Public Against Violence).

27. Czech and Slovak parties assumed contrasting approaches to the nationality question. For example, Civic Forum ignored it entirely in its 1990 election program and Public Against Violence highlighted it as a main theme (Krejčí 1994, 210). Partly, Public Against Violence may have been reacting to the surging popularity of the Slovak Nationalist Party (SNS) and the activism of the political movement of ethnic Hungarians, ESWMK.

28. The "hyphen war" grew out of the controversy surrounding the proper name of Czechoslovakia. The issue arose because the term "socialist" in Czechoslovakian Socialist Republic was to be eliminated. Many Slovaks feared that their national identity was being swallowed up in the country name *Czechoslovakia.* One proposal was that the name be hyphenated to *Czech-Slovak Republic*; thus the dispute was entitled "the hyphen war." Ultimately, the parties settled for a state title of the *Czech and Slovak Republics.*

29. These debates centered initially on the applicability of the 1960 federal constitution and the 1968 amendments, which awarded the federation wide decision-making latitude. Slovak political elites advocated decentralizing decision-making rights to the republics. Czech political elites sought to maintain political authority at the federal level.

30. The declaration founding Civic Forum was signed on November 19, 1989, by members of the dissident group Charter 77, Movement for a Free Society, Independent Peace Movement, Circle of Independent Intelligence, Obroda, and representatives of the cultural community (Honajzer 1996, 14).

31. Author interview with Civic Forum leader.

32. Privatization was a component of the political program of both Civic Forum and Public Against Violence. Fedor Gál, the chair of Public Against Violence, considered that rapid privatization was the first pillar of the party (Gál 1991).

33. The following discussion draws heavily from Jičínský 1993 and from Jičínský and Jan Škaloud 1996.

34. zákon č. 15/1990 Sb. (*zákon* is "law" in English; *č.*, short for *číslo*, meaning "number"; and *Sb.*, short for *Sbírka zákonů*, meaning "collection of laws").

35. zákon č. 15/1990 Sb.

36. zákon č. 45/1990 Sb.

37. zákon č. 46/1990 Sb.

38. zákon č. 86/1990 Sb.

39. zákon č. 120/1990 Sb.

40. zákon č. 103/1990 Sb.

41. zákon č. 104/1990 Sb.

42. zákon č. 105/1990 Sb.

43. zákon č. 106/1990 Sb. changing and supplementing zákon č. 121/1962 Sb.

44. zákon č. 107/1990 Sb. changing and supplementing zákon č. 73/1952 Sb. and zákon č. 108/1990 Sb. changing and supplementing zákon č. 157/1989 Sb.

45. zákon č. 114/1990 Sb. changing and supplementing zákon č. 123/1975 Sb. A fuller list of important laws enacted during this period appears in Jičínský 1993, 138–158, especially 145–146.

46. Also based on author interview with privatization officials.

47. Author interview with privatization officials.

48. Klaus originally opposed the mass privatization idea (author interviews with privatization officials). Within only a week, possibly shorter, Klaus changed his mind and offered his blessing to the idea.

49. Polish and Czech privatization designers expressed analogous concerns (for instance, Frydman and Rapaczynski 1994, 23–24). One could also add the local mafia to this list of probable buyers, though Švejnar explicitly limits the comment to foreigners.

50. Švejnar's proposal also allowed for the government to hold selected enterprise shares in reserve for other claimants. He names as possibilities pension funds, local governments, or the central government. Švejnar proposed too that the government could sell selected shareholdings to domestic and foreign investors. Švejnar's voucher privatization scheme also made allowances for other claimants (Švejnar 1989).

51. Švejnar's scheme was also amenable to the introduction of intermediaries, though only *after* privatization. Recall that he proposed that the government assign voucher holders diversified share portfolios. Certainly, intermediaries could—and without restrictive regulations would—arise to manage the share portfolios. However, it is beyond the scope of this discussion to consider how Švejnar's postprivatization intermediaries would compare with the investment privatization funds since we are strictly outlining privatization strategies (Švejnar 1989).

52. More specifically, the Czech government contended that privatization must take place in two steps, de-etatization and privatization. De-etatization in this version required the state, under the direction of the Fund of National Property, to restructure Czech enterprises. The Fund of National Property would downsize enterprises (to de-monopolize) and recapitalize enterprises, including removing enterprise debts (Dvořák and Vlasák 1990).

53. The Czech government's proposal did seek to deflect the neoliberal criticism by withholding important privileges to managers, such as job guarantees. Yet, the

Czech government proposal also allowed managers to rent enterprise equipment (Dvořák and Vlasák 1990). Frydman and Rapaczynski argue against spontaneous privatization by speculating that "the pressure for this type of ownership change comes instead from an alliance between the workers and the management who are intent on resisting significant departures from the status quo: it is precisely the opposition to a restructuring that is likely to result from genuine privatization that motivates the alliance" (Frydman and Rapaczynski 1994, 62).

54. Czech neoliberals leveled those same charges at Hungarian reformers. Hungary was already in the process of implementing a case-by-case approach by 1990. Perhaps even worse, the Hungarian approach highlighted enterprise sales to foreigners and thereby facilitated the foreign "theft" of national resources.

55. Although Grégr explicitly mentions the role of unions in enterprise decision-making and privatization (he also supports ESOPs), Grégr is forceful in accentuating management benefits (Grégr, Berghauer, and Hrabě 1990). In general, I would expect that possible worker-management alliances would be grossly asymmetric in the Czech case (as in Russia), where the managers have tended to be far more influential in setting enterprise policy than workers.

56. Grégr's Fund of National Property would keep to a limited role though it would be technically under the control of Parliament. Grégr assigned the setting of management policy to representatives of enterprise unions and employees. Grégr's conceptualization of de-etatization closely followed the prior notion of the Czech government (Grégr, Berghauer, and Hrabě 1990).

57. Grégr reportedly also contributed to the writing of the *State-Owned Enterprise* (zákon č. 111/1990) of April 1990, which privileged manager interests. "This law permitted the transfer of property of state-owned companies to other companies, without imposing strict conditions. In practice, this [would have] paved a way for the possibility of transferring state property to the management" (Kotrba and Švejnar, n.d., 14). The easy transfer of state property to management—spontaneous privatization—was causing a public uproar in neighboring Poland and Hungary. However, the law was abolished in a later Czechoslovakian parliamentary session after the public careers of Grégr and Komárek had faded. (Grégr resurfaced in public life as minister of industry and trade under the M. Zeman government after the 1998 elections.)

58. Author interviews with privatization officials.

59. Oddly enough, trade unions seldom advocated worker ownership schemes. I will treat this issue in the next section.

60. Šik was the director of the Economic Institute of the ČR from 1961 to 1968. He immigrated to Switzerland in August 1968 and from 1970 on was a professor at St. Gallen in Zurich.

61. Komárek also begins his economic program with a criticism of Western capitalism (Komárek 1990; also Vanek 1990).

62. Švejnar also argued that "empirical evidence from Western countries . . . suggests that it might be desirable to combine [worker] participation with appropriately de-signed profit sharing and worker ownership schemes," given that "some form of worker participation in management" is inevitable (Švejnar 1989, 9–10).

63. According to the *Economist*, "Worker-buyout lobbyists argue that theirs is the fairest answer. It isn't: workers in viable businesses do well, the stalwarts of dud ones miss out" (*Economist*, April 14–20, 1990).

64. The neoliberals' animosity toward undesirables (such as the mafia) would mollify while their animosity to foreigners would stiffen. One factor that hardened the resolve of Czech decision-makers against foreign ownership was supposedly bad deals done in 1990 and 1991 (especially the Škoda-Volkswagen automobile deal and the [since aborted] CŠA/Air France airline deal). The elite believed that these deals unfairly advantaged the foreign partner (Schwartz and Haggard 1997). Opposition to foreign ownership proved more durable in Czechoslovakia over time, as we see in chapters 6 and 7.

65. Hungarian privatizers emphasized public sale to foreign buyers from 1990 to 1992 and from 1995 to 1997, and public sale to domestic buyers from 1992 to 1994 (Schwartz and Haggard 1997).

66. Although most Czechs, including the neoliberal economists, did agree that a small selection of enterprises should remain in state hands, the list invariably included nonnegotiables like the post office, the gas pipelines, national forests, and other traditionally state enterprises. However, the neoliberals disagreed amongst themselves in the first half of 1990 over which industries should be privatized and which should remain state owned. In February 1990, Tříska explicitly mentioned railroads, airlines, and communications as industries that should remain in state hands (quoted in interview in Páral 1990, 7). Ježek, in a March 1990 article, argued that the state should hold stakes in strategic companies (citation unavailable). In May 1990, Dlouhý argued that "in the beginning we should privatize just a small group of enterprises—those which are successful" (quoted in the *New York Times*, May 22, 1990).

67. One exception was Šik, who argued that shares must not be left in the hands of the state through which bureaucrats would intervene in enterprise economics.

68. The program is authored by Komárek and others. Who the others are is not specified precisely, though Komárek claimed that the program was a joint effort of the Prognostics Institute, including leading neoliberals such as Klaus, Dlouhý, and Ježek.

69. Komárek's lead over Havel in popular preference was especially large in Slovakia. One December 1989 television poll showed Komárek as the politician most associated with the identity interests of Slovaks. The percentages were: V. Komárek, 29.6 percent; M. Kňažko, 27.2 percent; J. Budaj, 25.6 percent; and V. Havel, only 6.2 percent (Gál 1991, 35).

70. There is disagreement over this point. One colleague of Klaus argues that "Klaus maintained contact with dissidents for many years; he wrote in dissident journals and in the unofficial Lidové noviny [the dissident newspaper in 1988 and 1989]" (Simonian 1992, 32). Klaus also claims a long relationship with Havel, dating from his membership on the editorial board of the magazine *Tvář* in the late 1960s, when Havel was chief editor (Klaus 1995b). However, my interviews with dissidents suggest that Klaus was not a dissident. The consensual story was that Rita Klimová, later the first Czechoslovakian ambassador to the United States, introduced Klaus to the dissidents in the late 1980s. Possible evidence of Klaus's unfamiliarity to Havel

and the dissidents is Havel's famous "misintroduction" of Klaus to the communist leadership as Volf in November 1989.

71. Klaus enhanced his personal popularity by his advocacy of the free market from the theater stages during the first weeks after the revolution. Klaus also spread his message by conducting special seminars on economic topics with parliamentary delegates in the first few post-November months (Jičínský 1993, 138).

72. Komárek renounced his Communist Party membership in December 1989 upon becoming Czechoslovakian deputy prime minister.

73. The team leader was K. Kouba; the original team members were J. Fogl, J. Hanzelka, J. Holec, V. Klusoň, K. Kouba, Č. Kožušník, L. Mlčoch, J. Řehak, S. Stuna, P. Ševčík, Z. Šulc, O. Turek, and K. Václavů. Later team contributors included M. Horálek, J. Kolář, M. Matěka, M. Pick, A. Suk, O. Šik, and V. Valeš (Šulc 1993, 33).

74. Čalfa was also Havel's close ally throughout the spring of 1990.

75. Similar to his role in other matters, patterned on Masaryk, with frequent references in 1990 speech to *Hovory z lán* (weekly Sunday), Masaryk's favorite place, the summer presidential estate. Masaryk left the task of day-to-day government to his ministers and to Parliament, interfering primarily in foreign policy and in domestic matters of the highest urgency.

76. Dlouhý wrote in a sanctioned Confederation of Czech Industry (*Svaz průmyslu*) publication several years later that the organization was not a useful partner for the government with Grégr (or his successor, Hanák) in office.

77. Author interviews with Czech Confederation of Industry officials and enterprise managers.

78. Frydman and Rapaczynski note that the Czech privatization approach received the "surprising" support of managers, though they do not integrate this observation into their theoretical premises (Frydman and Rapaczynski 1994, 155–159).

79. The most notable exceptions were industries in which the Soviet Union took special interest, such as defense.

80. A Czechoslovakian system of workers councils was instituted in the late 1980s. To all accounts, the workers councils never experienced meaningful participation in enterprise affairs.

81. As indicated by author interviews with an official of the KOVO (metalworkers) trade union, who commented that 60 percent of union locals supported rapid privatization. According to Pleskot, "the trade unions advanced to the coupon [voucher] privatization without any prejudice" (Pleskot 1994, 15).

82. Author interview with government officials.

6

Legitimating the Giveaway—June 1990 to February 1991

Public demands on the new democracies in Central and Eastern Europe required elites to legitimize the government's proposed privatization strategy. Direct elections, referenda, and legislative votes were common legitimizing procedures. The main political challenge for the Eastern European elites lay in convincing the public to trade current income and employment for privatization's promise of future prosperity and democracy. A product of the public's extreme anticommunist and pro-Western sentiment, early elite choices ensured that the public legitimization of privatization would not become a major political problem in the former Czechoslovakia.

Public legitimization took less than a year. In May 1990, the Czechoslovakian Government of National Understanding approved a schedule to launch voucher privatization; in June 1990, the voters supported advocates of voucher privatization; in September 1990, the Federal Parliament approved voucher privatization as the main privatization method (in the Scenario of Economic Reform); and, in February 1991, the Federal Parliament passed the Large Privatization Law. In other CEECs, such as Poland and Hungary, public legitimization lasted several years.

The public legitimization of Czech privatization encompassed two distinct phases. The first phase was political and did not much involve privatization directly. It included the new Czech elite's efforts to legitimate their own authority over the government and also to legitimize a radical economic reform agenda, including privatization. The consequence of these efforts was to present the neoliberals with an opportunity to build economic and also political influence. The second phase was also political, but it focused exactly on the legalization of privatization. In this phase, high neoliberal influence in privatization policymaking precipitated the privatization laws that established voucher privatization as the dominant privatization method. This chapter and the prior one, in combination, support the hypothesis that a recent conservative communist past was conducive to voucher privatization becoming the dominant privatization method—reservations notwithstanding.

Four sections present supporting evidence for the proposition that strong neoliberal influence in economic policymaking translated into voucher privatization becoming the dominant privatization method. The first two sections focus on the first phase of legitimization; the second two sections concentrate on the second phase.

The first section covers the first free Czechoslovakian elections in June 1990. It shows that two elements in the Czech elite's election campaign strategy benefited neoliberals. One was the new Czech elite's promise to support a quick return to the market; the neoliberals were the obvious orchestrators of this policy. The second was the new Czech elite's decision to present a unified face to the public and to suppress internal dissent until after the June elections— by which time the Parliament and not the public would decide policy. This frankly nondemocratic approach helped the neoliberals, who gained prestige and support in the elections. Ironically, it wasn't the clever political tactics of Klaus that opened this opportunity for the neoliberals, but the tactical choices of Havel and his advisors. The second section shows how Klaus, in the best neoliberal tradition, set about seizing political control of the state in the summer of 1990. Klaus's main recruits were the new Parliamentary members of the disappointed generation. Using them as a base, he commandeered control of Civic Forum and was elected the movement's first chairman in November 1990. Eventually, Klaus splintered Civic Forum and built his own political party, ODS. With the neoliberals' political savvy and support among the disappointed generation, ODS became the strongest party in the Czech Republic. Klaus's political moves set the stage for neoliberal legislative successes in privatization.

An honest reading of the initial two sections suggests that a deterministic theory explaining the rise of the Czech neoliberals is simplistic. More than anticommunist and pro-Western ideology was at play. Idiosyncratic factors— political tactics, economic policy creativity, and the personal character of Klaus, Havel, and other major actors—were critical. Therefore, although we can confirm broadly the hypothesis that the rise of the neoliberals was founded on anticommunist and pro-Western ideology, we must also acknowledge that this outcome was contingent on factors that are difficult to analyze systematically.

The third section shows that the neoliberals orchestrated the passage by the Federal Parliament of the Scenario of Economic Reform in September 1990. Sometimes referred to as the "Capitalist Manifesto," the Scenario of Economic Reform codified neoliberal reform principles (including voucher privatization). The fourth section shows that the Large Privatization Law of February 1991 followed upon the precedent established in the Scenario of Economic Reform to create a legal framework for privatization and voucher privatization, in particular. It was ensured from this point onward that voucher privatization would be the country's dominant privatization method.

An honest reading of the latter two sections reveals that it is analytically narrow to attribute voucher privatization solely to the will of the neoliberals. To be sure, the Scenario of Economic Reform and the Large Privatization Law established that voucher privatization would be the dominant privatization method. Still, these laws—particularly the Large Privatization Law—dictated that Czech privatization (including voucher privatization) would proceed in violation of neoliberal principles. The main reason is that these laws were products of compromise with opposing elite factions and the industrial ministries. First, the laws fixed a hybrid privatization path that decentralized the supply-side tasks (state bureaucrats would decide which enterprises would be privatized by which methods) and centralized the voucher privatization demand side tasks (a computer programmed and monitored by top neoliberals would assign enterprise shares to participating citizens). Second, the laws included a provision for standard privatization methods. Third, the Czech privatization laws established a Fund of National Property to hold and to manage state ownership stakes, provisions antithetical to the neoliberals' aversion to state intervention. Fourth, the laws deliberately neglected legal guidelines for state regulation of privatization. Although this particular omission was not a function of compromise—nearly everyone agreed that state regulation would unnecessarily slow privatization—"lawless" privatization eventually veered Czech privatization from neoliberal objectives.

The complicated legacies of the privatization laws sensitize us to the dangers of reducing the privatization strategy of a single country to one implemented method, such as voucher privatization. For even though voucher privatization was the major Czech privatization method, it was but one of several and it was implemented at the end of a complicated process that ultimately determined its character. Extrapolating from this observation, I conclude that while it may be a useful first approximation to categorize national privatization strategies by dominant privatization methods, a serious analysis must take into account the privatization path and the role of the state in managing enterprises and in regulating privatization.

THE JUNE 1990 ELECTIONS

The new Czech elite that stood astride the Government of National Understanding single-mindedly aimed to preserve its position and simultaneously to forestall a return of communism. They moved on two fronts. First, as we saw in the previous chapter, they began to institute the legal foundations of a new capitalist and democratic system (including rules for passing legislation, voting laws, censorship laws, a commercial code, and tax code). Second, they turned the June 1990 election into a plebiscite for the new leadership (and against the communists). The election did not offer voters a choice between competing social, political, and economic programs. Political conflict could wait for the election results, according to the new elite. The neoliberals, at this point still fighting for elite and public acceptance, were the primary beneficiaries of Civic Forum's election strategy.

The all-or-nothing strategy of the new Czech elite hinged on the election fortunes of Civic Forum. The new elite feared that the revolution would be lost should Civic Forum and the Slovak correlate, Public Against Violence, falter in June. In the weeks just prior to June, the possibility of a Civic Forum and Public Against Violence defeat was not as far-fetched as it might seem today, looking back at the 1990 election returns. In March, the election preference polls showed public support for Civic Forum at only 21 percent, and public support for Public Against Violence at a paltry 14 percent (Krejčí 1994).

To attract maximum voter interest in the June elections, the Czech elite cast Civic Forum (and Public Against Violence in Slovakia) as an inclusive political home, excepting communists. Civic Forum trolled for the widest possible net of voters through its political symbols, its political program, and the heavy-handed use of the media.

- First, Civic Forum was a political movement, not a political party. Under the slogans "Nonparty Politics" and "Civic Forum is for everyone. Political parties are for party members," the new elite designed Civic Forum so as to appeal to the antipolitical party preferences of Czechoslovakians—76 percent of Czechs (and 72 percent of Slovaks) refused to join a political party (Boguszak and Rak 1990, table 1.2).
- Second, Civic Forum drafted an election program designed to leave feathers unruffled. Civic Forum's election program advocated "the return to Europe," escape from totality, and regard for the legal state and the market—including privatization, social policy, and ecology (Civic Forum Election Platform; Krejčí 1994, 210; Honajzer 1996).
- Third, the elite used the media, especially television, unabashedly as "propaganda" for Civic Forum. The media was an advocate, not an impartial reporter (see above; see also Krejčí 1994, 240).

Civic Forum's encompassing strategy also applied to its privatization recommendations. Civic Forum advocated privatization, though it never specified in election documents precisely what privatization means—that is, what would be privatized, who the new owners would be, the terms of ownership, and the means of privatization. Neoliberal opponents insinuated that in avoiding the key controversies surrounding privatization (and also lustration and restitution), Civic Forum deliberately misled the public into believing that its standard of living would be protected in a radical reform program like voucher privatization.[1] The neoliberals themselves did nothing to dispel this impression. In a speech in front of ten thousand cheering steelworkers at Poldi Kladno, Dlouhý affirmed that the government must aid struggling enterprises; he said, "I do not want to be socially cruel" (quoted in *Financial Times*, April 12, 1990).

The decided neoliberal beliefs of Civic Forum candidates in June 1990 supported the accusation that the Civic Forum leadership misled voters. For the most part, Civic Forum candidates were more optimistic about the future than was the general population, more convinced that transition would be a long process, more convinced that economic transformation should be the top priority, and more apt to believe that the state should not be the guarantor of employment (Rak 1992, 208–209).[2] A Civic Forum win in the June elections portended a shift to the right.

The neoliberal orientation of the Civic Forum candidates nonetheless exaggerates the political influence of the radical reformers at the time. Although the candidate views did tend toward the neoliberal right, it was the candidates with a left-wing or social democratic orientation who occupied top rungs on the Civic Forum election lists. The success of the neoliberal candidates came as a result of the overwhelming electoral success of Civic Forum. A close victory in the June elections would have translated into many fewer neoliberal Parliament members. Neoliberals were not the dominant policymakers in the first half of 1990.

An important point that lurks in the background of the election analysis is that elite politics and Civic Forum politics were hidden and nondemocratic. This is certainly the case. Critical public policymaking wouldn't take place during the elections, but only after the public had already stamped its approval on parameters that carried little practical weight. Czechoslovakian politics began in earnest only after the June 1990 elections.

1990 Election Results: The New Turks of the Disappointed Generation

Civic Forum and Public Against Violence won smashing victories in the June 1990 elections (see tables 6.1 and 6.2). The Communist Party received only 13.5 percent of the popular vote. Popular support for Civic Forum and for Public Against Violence surged in the election's final weeks; the media campaign had certainly played a critical role in swaying popular opinion. The elections

Table 6.1.   How Czechs and Slovaks Voted in the June 1990 Elections

Party, Movement, or Coalition	Czech Republic (%)	Slovak Republic (%)
OF and VPN	50.9	33.1
Christian Democrats (KDU and KDH)	8.6	18.3
Communist Party (KSČ and KSS)	13.5	13.5
Slovak Nationalists (SNS)	–	12.1
Regional Party (HSD-SMS)	9.0	–
Hungarian Party (ESWMK)	–	8.6

Source: Krejčí 1994, 256.
Note: Aggregate of voting for both houses of Federal Parliament and Republic Parliaments.

vindicated the political strategy of the new elite. They also created a fabulous political opportunity for the neoliberals.

The neoliberal Civic Forum candidates wound up the biggest election winners (Honajzer 1996, 23–25). Probably the biggest Civic Forum winner was Klaus himself. Klaus ran in the heavily industrialized region of North Moravia, a district most prognosticators believed would present stiff opposition to the neoliberal program. Instead, Klaus, running unabashedly as a neoliberal, recorded a dazzling and surprising victory.[3] The election victory of the supporters of rapid transformation paved the way for Parliament's legitimization of voucher privatization in September 1990.

The election returns went beyond the victory of one ideology over another. A new and previously excluded Czech generation laid claim to leadership. This was the disappointed generation: highly educated, middle-aged, and ethnic Czech.[4] A "massive group around forty-three years of age" entered both the Federal Parliament and the Czech Parliament (Mansfeldová 1993, 7; see table 6.3).[5] Nearly half the new Parliament members had technical backgrounds.[6] Finally, the prominent neoliberals and new leaders were ethnic Czechs, including Klaus, Dlouhý, Zieleniec, Ježek, Kroupa, and Tříska.[7] Humiliated and marginalized by the prior regime, the disappointed generation wasn't going to be ignored in the next one.

The political emergence of the disappointed generation into Parliament undermined Havel and his supporters. For while Havel's popularity soared in the wake of the election, the political tectonics had shifted. Prior to the June 1990 elections, the most highly regarded politicians were associated with the dissidents of Civic Forum and the November 1989 revolution. After June, the political mood shifted in favor of the neoliberals and their "pragmatic" approach to liberalization. Most of the elite now believed—and the election reinforced this belief—that Klaus was the man to instill in Czechoslovakia the necessary capitalist ethic.

Table 6.2.   June 1990 Federal Parliamentary Election Results

A. *Czech Republic Chamber of the People*

Party, Movement, or Coalition	Popular Vote (%)	Mandated Seats
Civic Forum (OF)	53.2	68
Communist Party (KSČ)	13.5	15
Czech Christian Democrats (KDU)	8.7	9
Regional Party (HSD-SMS)	7.9	9
Others	16.7	–
TOTAL	100.0	101

B. *Slovak Republic Chamber of the People*

Party, Movement, or Coalition	Popular Vote (%)	Mandated Seats
Public Against Violence (VPN)	32.5	19
Slovak Christian Democrats (KDH)	19.0	11
Communist Party (KSS)	13.8	8
Slovak Nationalists (SNS)	11.0	6
Hungarian Party (ESWMK)	8.6	5
Others	15.1	–
TOTAL	100.0	49

Source: Krejčí 1994, 253.
Note: Although this data covers only the Federal Chamber of the People, the proportions closely track the results in the Federal Chamber of Nations and in the Republic Parliaments. See Krejčí 1994, 252–260.

Havel and his advisors tried to slow down Klaus's political momentum. They knew well that as Federal finance minister, Klaus could plausibly direct state economic policy, and acquire still more political popularity. Havel and his advisors tried to marginalize Klaus by appointing him to the invisible position of head of the Czechoslovak State Bank. Klaus refused the change in portfolio. He instead threatened to resign entirely from the government. Klaus's threat carried gravity, thanks to the election results and to the ringing public endorsement of Klaus's economic strategy.

The worst fears of the anti-Klaus elite came to pass. Federal Finance Minister Klaus ultimately solidified his political base. He moved to a position of political power unequaled in other former communist countries. In the next set of general elections in June 1992, Klaus's ODS political party won a popular mandate that vaulted him to Czech prime minister. Klaus's political ascent began in the fall of 1990 when Klaus was voted chief of Civic Forum. Simultaneously, Klaus pushed through Parliament a predominantly neoliberal Scenario of Economic Reform, the articulation of his economic vision.

Table 6.3. The June 1990 Elections

	Delegates, 1986	New Delegates, January 1990	New Delegates, June 1990	Total Membership
Federal Chamber of the People	2 (1.3%)	31 (20.6%)	117 (78.0%)	150
Federal Chamber of Nations, Czech Republic	1 (1.3%)	20 (26.6%)	54 (72.0%)	75
Federal Chamber of Nations, Slovakia	1 (1.3%)	17 (22.6%)	57 (76%)	75

Source: Reschová 1992, 234.

From Economic Policymaker to Political Kingpin

The political gloves came off immediately after the public repudiation of communism in the June elections. Just days later, Komárek wrote an article in the *Financial Times* assailing "naïve" neoliberal economic policy. Komárek's article was a bald attack on Klaus (*Financial Times*, June 8, 1990). With Komárek's thrust, a dispute hidden under the consensus of the Government of National Understanding boiled over.[8] Komárek's polemic signaled that the consensus of the Government of National Understanding was over, that conflict—the essence of politics—could begin. With the elections safely over, it was conflict that would occur primarily at the elite level.

Klaus and his allies barnstormed Czechoslovakia in the summer and fall following the general election. They gave countless speeches, even venturing to Slovakia, a part of Czechoslovakia ventured into by few Czech politicians. They presented the neoliberal economic program to local government officials, bankers, enterprise managers, trade unionists, Civic Forum regional leaders, new Parliament members, and ordinary citizens.

Klaus's political energy earned grudging respect from friend and foe. P. Havlík, Klaus's first campaign manager and organizer of ODS, rallied around Klaus because Klaus was "professional and hardworking" (Havlík 1990). Civic Forum opponents also revealed tremendous regard, if studied personal contempt, for Klaus's drive.[9] Consistent with the traditional Czech pattern, most of these people retired to their summer homes in July and August 1990 while Klaus tirelessly worked to build a political basis of support. The lax communist work ethic illustrated that the country desperately needed such people. Komárek's long-whispered laziness was an obvious counterpoint to Havlík's feelings.

Klaus used a "carrot and stick" political approach to recruit political support in the summer and fall of 1990. On the other hand, he co-opted potential opponents with assurances "that going along" would translate "as getting along." For instance, Klaus reportedly promised enterprise managers that they would retain their positions after voucher privatization. Later, Klaus created registers of likely supporters and offered them positions in his political party (ODS) if they would fulfill specific political tasks. There was a veiled threat behind Klaus's reassurances, however. Klaus pointed out to recruits and potential opponents that the political tide was moving in the neoliberal direction and that opposition to his political rise would later prove counterproductive. Klaus's political approach over this period presaged the patronage politics of the transition period.

Klaus's energy and tactics paid dividends in the fall of 1990 when it was time to vote on a chairman for Civic Forum.[10] Civic Forum then was divided between neoliberals and neoliberal opponents who disagreed over economic policy and over political strategy. The neoliberal opponents were a potpourri of dissidents, Social Democrats, reformed communists, and in some cases, people who harbored personal grudges with the neoliberals. Anti-Klausians included M. Palouš, P. Rychetský, J. Dienstbier, I. Fišera, V. Sedláček, D. Burešová, and P. Kučera. When the vote was tabulated at the Civic Forum Assembly in Hostivař in October, Klaus emerged with nearly 70 percent of the 167 valid votes, much to the surprise of much of the Civic Forum elite (Honajzer 1996, 33).

Klaus and the neoliberals set out to split Civic Forum. They argued that modern political organizations are not inherently collegial. Political organizations should promote an ideology and policy program, be organized hierarchically, and select a representative slate of leaders. Political parties are appropriate political organizations, not political movements. The problem was that Civic Forum was a political movement that pursued an amorphous ideological program. Therefore, in the neoliberal view, Civic Forum was the wrong vehicle to drive radical economic reform. Consequently, Klaus and the neoliberals provoked the division of Civic Forum into the interparliamentary clubs. These interparliamentary clubs prefigured the demise of Civic Forum and the subsequent emergence of political parties.

On October 12, 1990, the day before the Hostivař assembly of Civic Forum, the Interparliamentary Club of the Democratic Right announced its basic principles (Honajzer 1996, 25–28). Klaus's "Interparliamentary Club of the Democratic Right" was composed of thirty-three members of the Federal Parliament (out of 118 Civic Forum members) and thirty-three members of the Czech Parliament (out of 127 Civic Forum members). Klaus designed the Interparliamentary Club of the Democratic Right to advocate a neoliberal economic agenda and to reverse the declining popularity of Civic Forum.

Neoliberal opponents were late to join the elite political competition. It wasn't until two months later, in December 1990, that Klaus's opponents organized interparliamentary clubs. One group formed the Liberal Club on

December 13. The Liberal Club included ministers of the Federal and Czech governments as well as Parliament members. Many Liberal Club members were dissidents and nearly all opposed Klaus and the neoliberals, for personal as well as ideological reasons (Honajzer 1996, 25–28). The Liberal Club comprised believers in a more gradual program of economic change combined with a socially conscious agenda. The late start of the anti-neoliberal opposition to form a coherent organization was one of several indications just how far ahead Klaus was in mobilizing political support and how much more seriously Klaus considered politics than did his opponents.[11]

Klaus's political strategy reflected a profoundly undemocratic view of the political economy of reform. Klaus and the neoliberals argued that stringent economic reform measures demanded a politically insulated taskmaster who could enact the necessary legislation and protect liberalization from the selfish challenges of societal groups. Real democracy could come after the market institutions were in place. This view matched those perspectives of prominent Western neoliberals who argued that the institutional endpoint was the critical variable; the scars of liberalization would not endure. The means of liberalization were fleeting, fodder for historians.

But we should also note that Klaus's disdain for citizen participation in government (the defining criterion for democracy) during the transition period was shared by Havel and the dissidents. Their whole legitimization strategy, as indicated in the June 1990 elections, was predicated on the view that the public was unprepared to rule on the advisability of one policy versus another. The public could decide only whether the country should move forward, presumably to the West, or backward, presumably to communism. Seen with the understanding that the new Czech elite also chose to exclude public participation in government, Klaus's political success can be attributed not only to a favorable ideological climate but also to political tactics—the neoliberals' as well as those of Havel and the dissidents.

THE CAPITALIST MANIFESTO: THE SCENARIO OF ECONOMIC REFORM

In July 1990, the Federal government charged the Federal Parliament to draft a comprehensive strategy of economic reform. The Federal Parliament was a plausible public legitimizing institution since it traced its authority to the general elections in June 1990. Prior to that time, neither the elite nor the population considered the Government of National Understanding an appropriate legitimizing institution since it governed without a popular mandate. All agreed that economic reform and especially "privatization must be approved by the people" (Tříska, quoted in *Business Wire*, December 1990). This did not mean, of course, that the voters should directly ratify a privatization approach (most elites thought they were incapable), for that was the paternalistic task of elites acting on their behalf.

What became known as the "Capitalist Manifesto," or formally as the Scenario of Economic Reform, represented the neoliberals' first major legislative success. The negotiations within the elite over the Scenario of Economic Reform reflected the rise to economic and political influence of the neoliberals over the previous half-year. Vested with popular legitimacy from the June elections, with elite support from a busy summer of lobbying, and backed by a Parliament that was filled with disappointed generation allies, the neoliberals wrote most of their priorities into a Scenario of Economic Reform. The Scenario of Economic Reform, ratified by the Parliament, codified the neoliberal principles, including voucher privatization, that would drive economic reform.

Outside Opposition

Five outside institutes—some with connections to the economists of the Czech government and to Komárek—proposed versions of a Scenario of Economic Reform.[12] Each alternative scenario rejected voucher privatization in favor of standard privatization methods administered by a Fund of National Property. This position was at odds with the prevailing view of the elite and the Parliament.

The fate of the alternative scenarios reflected the fallen political position of the moderate reformers and standard privatization advocates and the rise of the neoliberals. The gradualists had fought toe-to-toe with the neoliberals in the elite approval stage. In public legitimization, they were bit players, losers in a choreographed economic debate. As in the elite approval stage, the media played a crucial director role in the acceptance of the neoliberal Scenario of Economic Reform.[13] The outside proposals stood no chance without strong support from Havel and the dissidents.

Loyal Opposition

The elite within the Czechoslovakian government—which was expected to be hostile to voucher privatization—was surprisingly conciliatory. I refer primarily to Havel and the dissidents in Civic Forum. They supported the economic strategy of Klaus, despite the fact that they increasingly viewed Klaus's economic program as a threat to their own political fortunes. One reason was that the neoliberals were willing to compromise on principles in the Scenario of Economic Reform. The accepted Scenario of Economic Reform, as noted above, contained ample social welfare provisions. A second reason was public anxiousness. The popularity ratings of Civic Forum and Public Against Violence showed a steady decline after the 1990 elections—Civic Forum's support was down to 30 percent and Public Against Violence's support was down to 17 percent by November 1990 (Krejčí 1994, 242). Even the trade unions backed radical economic measures.[14] The elite rallied around a radical economic strategy, in part, to maintain popularity. But many neoliberal opponents genuinely believed in a rapid and spirited transformation approach. This faith was generally not founded on economic rationales—the neoliberal opponents were startlingly ignorant about economics. Rather, it was founded on the perception that Czechoslovakian society had not changed substantially since the revolution. Many of the same people remained in charge, often of the same communist institutions. Havel was known to question the economists about why his local pub was still state owned.[15] The elite sought dramatic change, and only Klaus and the neoliberals presented a clear plan.

The Scenario of Economic Reform

The Scenario of Economic Reform, ratified by the Parliament in September 1990, reflected neoliberal thinking on economic reform. The four main elements of the economic strategy—listed in the order they were presented in the actual document—which reflected the neoliberal agenda, are as follows:

1. Restrictive Macroeconomic Policy[16]
2. Ownership Changes in the Economy
3. Price Liberalization
4. Internal Currency Convertibility[17]

The Scenario of Economic Reform also incorporated compromises with elites who were concerned about the social fallout from radical economic reform. These elites still held influential positions throughout the Federal, Czech Republic, and Slovak Republic governments, and the neoliberals were in no position to dictate policy.[18] The "social democratic" elements in the Scenario of Economic Reform were:[19]

5. Social Policies Connected with Economic Reform[20]
6. Structural Policies[21]

The section on privatization also reflects social democratic influence. Although the Scenario of Economic Reform endorsed voucher privatization as the primary privatization, it also provisioned for standard privatization methods. It specifically allows the preferential sale of shares to employees and to municipal and community funds, the sale of shares to domestic and foreign investors at market price, joint ventures, and leasing. In addition, the Scenario of Economic Reform endorses the creation of a Fund of National Property. The Fund of National Property would be a state agency charged to hold and to manage state enterprises prior to privatization. It would be entitled to reorganize the finances of individual enterprises and to fire and hire management. The Fund of National Property was a major concession to the social democrats since state intervention was antithetical to the neoliberals' laissez-faire policy of economic management.[22]

Yet the Scenario of Economic Reform remains a neoliberal document concerning privatization, as it does on most economic reform questions. The section on the use of standard methods of privatization is an appendage to the pages extolling the virtues of voucher privatization. Even the separate section on the establishment of the Fund of National Property proposes that the Fund would act in support of privatization rather than as an instrument of industrial policy. Indeed, the pattern of neoliberal proposal followed by social democratic modification is pronounced throughout the Scenario of Economic Reform.

The compromises in the Scenario of Economic Reform have led some analysts to mischaracterize and overrate the social democratic features in Czech economic policy, especially prior to 1993. Elite politics and popular demands forced pragmatic compromises in the former Czechoslovakia. Moreover, the social democratic addenda in the Scenario of Economic Reform coincided with the recognition of the neoliberals that privatization might have dramatic and negative social repercussions. Soaring unemployment already was alarmingly apparent in Poland, Hungary, East Germany, and elsewhere in Central and Eastern Europe; and, in 1990, the unemployment rate in Slovakia was climbing rapidly and would soon reach 10 percent. Societal discontent arising from high unemployment, or so many neoliberals calculated, would inevitably scuttle economic reform. The Czech neoliberals invariably included social components to preempt social conflict in the Scenario of Economic Reform and in future economic reform documents.[23] It is therefore true that Czech policy matched the stark neoliberal rhetoric, but only in selected policy areas.

Czech social and economic policy is congruent with the revisionist thinking of neoliberals who advise transition governments to establish a social safety net so that radical reforms may go forward. Neoliberal social reforms in the former Czechoslovakia resembled the preemptive social initiatives of Bismarck in Germany in the 1880s rather than the progressive measures of the modern Scandinavian welfare state. The Scenario of Economic Reform was the first instance of a sequence of political give-and-take between the neoliberals and their opponents. But make no mistake: it was the Czech neoliberals who steered economic reform.

THE FORK IN THE ROAD

Klaus's team of neoliberal economists set about drafting a Large Privatization Law following Parliament's passage of the Scenario of Economic Reform in September 1990. The logic of privatization from this point mandated that the state assign specific competencies, create bureaucracies, and write privatization laws and regulations after the Parliament's passage of the Scenario of Economic Reform. Institutional actors—lawmakers, legal advisors, middle- and low-level state officials, local officials—played increasingly meaningful roles. Claimants entered the game; earlier, they had been bystanders. The politics of privatization shifted radically as privatization decision-making became more focused on the pragmatic issues of converting the principles established in the Scenario of Economic Reform into law. The first major legislation was the Large Privatization Law, approved by Federal Parliament on February 26, 1991.

The policy switch from a set of ideas to a set of concrete measures planted the institutional seeds that would subvert original neoliberal aims. The Large Privatization Law emphasized voucher privatization, but it also built on the Scenario of Economic Reform to incorporate room for standard privatization methods and to allot a major role for the Fund of National Property. These measures ensured that privatization would proceed on a case-by-case basis. Harried and corrupt bureaucrats would then have a say in privatization. Accelerating the process, as the neoliberals would propose, wouldn't avert state intervention.

The concessions embodied in the Large Privatization Law grew out of the neoliberal obsession with rapid privatization. In this theory, the threat to the neoliberal program was concerted opposition by voucher opponents and a subsequent delay in privatization—as was occurring in Poland. Neoliberals feared that a strategy of confrontation would delay, perhaps forever, market reform. The neoliberals chose to compromise with political opponents and push privatization along rather than to risk the Polish malaise.

Quite aside from the political risks of a delay in privatization, prominent neoliberals harbored private misgivings regarding the economics behind voucher privatization, though most publicly intoned the free-market line— "Privatization first, restructuring later." What would happen if the state privatized heavily indebted enterprises? Would private owners be able to restructure such enterprises? Would they want to? How will thousands of small shareholders bring desperately needed capital and expertise to enterprises? The most prominent dissenting neoliberal was none other than Tomáš Ježek, a "father" of the Czech voucher privatization approach. Doubts within the neoliberal camp over the advisability of no government role prior to restructuring provoked the Czech reformers to allot the state a role in privatization, a clear breach of neoliberal orthodoxy.

Neoliberals ultimately supported a Large Privatization Law that varied in important ways from neoliberal orthodoxy, owing mostly to political exigencies but also to the genuine belief that the state could play a positive, albeit limited, role in restructuring enterprises. Politics, common sense, and, as we shall see, nationalism combined to limit the extent of neoliberal ideology in the Large Privatization Law.

Issues and Compromises in the Large Privatization Law

In Czechoslovakia, debates over the privatization law revolved around three sets of issues: supply-side tasks, demand-side tasks, and the role of the state. *Supply-side tasks* establish the mechanisms that determine which enterprises will be privatized by which methods. *Demand-side tasks* establish the terms at which claimants may participate in the privatization of specific enterprises. There is a logical order between the supply-side and the demand side. The state can address demand-side tasks only after the state has decided which privatization methods it will apply to which enterprises, that is, after it has completed the supply-side tasks. The *role of the state* addresses two main issues in privatization: the obligations and possibilities of state ownership and the regulation of the process. How the Czech privatization law addressed the demand side, the supply-side, and the role of the state would determine the implementation outcomes.

The issues at stake in the Czechoslovak Large Privatization Law were:

A. *Supply-Side Tasks*—choosing which categories of enterprises are privatized by which privatization methods
B. *Demand-Side Tasks*—choosing the terms at which claimants may participate in a given privatization method
C. *The Role of the State*—
   i. As claimant: setting the possibility for the state to become an owner
   ii. As regulator: ensuring that the spirit and the letter of the supply-side tasks and demand-side tasks will be observed

Supply-Side Tasks

The Scenario of Economic Reform dictated that the state would privatize most enterprises through voucher privatization, though the state would retain the option to privatize via standard privatization methods. The open question was, "How did the state determine which privatization method to apply to which enterprise?" The Czech solution to this question sowed the seeds for the subversion of the neoliberal privatization agenda.

One wing of neoliberals advocated that the state should privatize all shares in all state-owned enterprises via vouchers. The most ardent representative of this view was Tříska, the close collaborator of Klaus and the most ideological of the neoliberals. Tříska contended that the state could allocate virtually all enterprise assets through vouchers by cybernetic wizardry. Arguing against a multitrack privatization approach, Tříska believed that the state should not decide which shares of which enterprises would be privatized via which methods. Politics invariably would overcome economics if bureaucracies presided over privatization. No enterprise shares should be privatized via market privatization, contingent privatization, or any other standard privatization method. Tříska, supported by Klaus, promoted the slogan "97 and 3"—97 percent of the enterprise assets should be privatized by vouchers and 3 percent by reprivatization.[24] For his extreme position, Tříska was branded alternatively a "privatization skinhead," an appellation he carried proudly, and a "computer jockey," which he did not.

Government officials who advocated a differentiated approach to privatization opposed those neoliberals. The differentiated view accepted a multitrack privatization strategy—voucher privatization would be appropriate in selected cases; standard privatization methods would be appropriate in all other cases. In this view, the state should privatize threatened steel industries using a different method than, say, dairies or research institutes.

The industrial ministries were keen supporters of the differentiated, multitrack approach to privatization. Jan Vrba, the Czech minister of industry and trade, former director of a textile enterprise (Textilana), and former deputy minister under communism, was a prominent representative for this theory. The representative organizations both of large- and small-enterprise managers joined the industrial ministries in support of differentiated privatization.

The subtext of the differentiated privatization view was that standard privatization methods were preferable to voucher privatization. Arguing in an economic vein, Vrba and the other advocates of the differentiated view contended that masses of small shareholders wouldn't provide real, active owners. Neither ownership by the state nor by the masses would provide the capital and expertise necessary to restructure and invigorate Czech enterprises. Generally, the best active owners would be managers and foreign multinationals. B. Ošt'ádal of the Czech Confederation of Industry summarizes the position, "I am of the opinion that it is necessary to quickly privatize . . . but that [it] is necessary to leave privatization decisions to management" (*HN*, September 24, 1991, 18). The arguments advanced by the industrial ministries and the enterprise managers were founded on economic sense, not merely on self-interest couched as nostalgia.

At first glance, the battle within the government between the advocates of voucher privatization and of a differentiated, multitrack privatization approach merely reprised the earlier struggles between the neoliberals and Komárek or the Czech government. When the debate was replayed this time—after the conceptualization and legitimization of voucher privatization—no one doubted that voucher privatization had won the war; the question concerned the extent of that victory. The supporters of standard privatization methods conceded that voucher privatization would be an important, if not the critical, privatization principle. That concession opened the door to a compromise between the opposing positions.

The edge went to the advocates of the standard privatization methods. The surprising swing factor was Tomáš Ježek, the neoliberal Czech privatization minister. Ježek sided with Vrba and the other advocates of a differentiated privatization approach. Ježek evidently believed that so long as voucher privatization was the dominant privatization method, targeting owners for specific enterprises would permit restructuring. He reasoned that "standard methods are slower, more difficult to implement, but perhaps are a more favorable economic vehicle" (*HN*, September 24, 1991, 12). "The fact that coupon privatization would not be the one and universal method of privatization and would include public auctions, public competitions, direct sale, and free transfers to communities appeared in the end only as a loss to the computer fanatics [meaning Tříska]" (quoted in Husák 1997, 178).

The split in the neoliberal camp between Klaus and Tříska on the one side, and Ježek on the other, predetermined that Czech privatization would proceed on a multitrack basis. Václav Valeš, Komárek's replacement as the Federal deputy prime minister and, significantly, a recognized supporter of a differentiated privatization approach, brokered the deal between the two factions.[25]

The compromise between the two opposing camps was a decision-making procedure—concocted by Tříska and Ježek—designed to match a given enterprise with a given privatization method. The compromise was necessary to have "voucher privatization in full swing (before the election) and at the same time to allow enough enterprises to be privatized via standard privatization methods to ensure that some people would become direct property holders" (Macháček 1992, 6).

Demand-Side Tasks

The next question was how the state would distribute the ownership stakes to the winning claimants. The answers were standard and straightforward regarding standard privatization methods. The main alternatives to voucher privatization should be market privatization, either by direct sale or public auction, or contingent privatization, usually by a public tender. Nonetheless, the alternative of insider privatization to workers was studiously neglected, and it does not explicitly appear anywhere in the Large Privatization Law.

The state was committed to voucher privatization, a method with neither solid theoretical nor empirical bases, to distribute assets. Surprisingly, the main debates concerning the preparation of voucher privatization were remarkably restrained at this time. One reason was that the Czech privatizers hadn't as yet devised the details of the voucher privatization implementation plan; there was little for voucher privatization opponents to target. Tříska didn't start work on the detailed organizational blueprint of voucher privatization until January 1991, well after the presentation of the first government privatization draft proposals in November 1990. A second reason was that the parliamentary deliberations of the Large Privatization Law were suitably general and rushed to foreclose a debate on the details. As a result, the Large Privatization Law was only the skeleton of voucher privatization. The Parliament intended that voucher privatization's flesh and bones would be filled in by the privatizers, and notably by Tříska.

Discussions did occur among economic policymakers about specific features of voucher privatization, including the price of the vouchers, the eligibility of Czech nationals and foreigners, the role of the republics in voucher privatization decision-making, and the possibility of shareholder representatives.[26]

Should the vouchers be distributed free of charge? The consensus was that people should pay a nominal fee to participate. Tříska's opinion was representative on this point: "[Y]ou have to prove that you are seriously involved in the process and one indicator for that is that you have to pay something for this package of vouchers" (quoted in *Business Wire*, 1991, 2). Nonetheless, the price shouldn't be too high to discourage local participation; after all, one of the explicit purposes of voucher privatization was to harness popular support for economic reform, in general, and for neoliberal politicians, in particular. A similar, politically motivated rationale motivated the below-market pricing of vouchers elsewhere, most significantly in Britain and in France. In the Czech Republic, 1,035 CZK (about a week's wage) was the final figure.[27]

Another question concerned eligibility. All Czechs agreed that foreigners should not be eligible to participate in voucher privatization. The designers of voucher privatization expected that the 1,035 CZK participation fee would be far below the market value of the assets. They believed that only Czech nationals should be allowed to reap the rewards of purchasing national assets below value. The ever-present concern—that foreigners would run off with the most valuable national assets if given the chance—permeated privatization decision-making.

A third question concerned the role of the republics. The Slovaks insisted that only the respective authorities had the right to privatize property in their republic; Czech neoliberals argued that privatization should be administered wholly by the center. One Czech concern was that the Slovak gambit for decision-making power would compromise the integrity of what they considered Czechoslovak privatization. Klaus also may have feared losing the political benefits that he stood to gain in mass privatization. In the end, Klaus partly conceded that point to the Slovaks. The Slovaks could delay, if not derail, the entire privatization effort by blocking the law in Federal Parliament or at the republic level. The resolution was that the republics' privatization ministries would determine the privatization methods for specific enterprises, though the Federal government would administer voucher privatization.[28]

A last question concerned the option that voucher holders could be represented by intermediaries. The issue arose from the concern that dispersed ownership would amount to a lack of ownership control. That would mean that enterprise managers would lack incentives to improve enterprise performance, as before. The Czech privatizers allowed for intermediaries in order to solve the corporate governance puzzle, though they tabled the details surrounding the rights and responsibilities of intermediaries.

Overall, it was not obvious that the demand-side arrangements undermined neoliberal privatization. The resolutions over the voucher price, the eligibility of the claimants, the role of the republics, and the opportunity for masses to be represented by investment intermediaries seemed to conform to the neoliberal vision of privatization. It is hard to say, even in hindsight, that the demand-side compromises embedded in the first phase of legalization jeopardized the neoliberal objectives of a fast, fair, and complete privatization.

The State as Claimant

Czech economic decision-makers acknowledged that there was a set of enterprises in which the state should remain the sole or majority owner for the foreseeable future. The so-called *strategic enterprises* included the national airline, communications, nuclear and electric power companies, coal mines, banks, and steelmakers.[29] The consensus that the Czech state must remain a selective owner ensured that the Czech public sector would not disappear.

The more contentious questions concerned the state holdings in what would become the temporary portfolio, not the permanent portfolio. Those questions concerned how the state should administer the portfolio of shares in enterprises before privatization was implemented. Should the state have the right to restructure enterprises, perhaps by breaking them up into more economically manageable units or by relieving oversized debt burdens? Should the state have the right to dismiss managers? Should the state have the right to intervene in enterprise operations? Should the state create a new ministry to manage state property?[30] These questions attracted two varieties of answers.

Neoliberals argued that the central state should not intervene into the affairs of individual enterprises.[31] Therefore, the creation of a new government ministry to administer property—a Fund of National Property—was an unnecessary step. First, the business of a Fund of National Property would be hidden from central authority. The likely trustee of a Fund of National Property, the Czech Parliament, was incapable of monitoring the complicated operations of such an agency. The Czech Parliament could not even control the state budget expenditures. The Czech ministries regularly changed budgets without securing parliamentary approval (M. Tuček [then, general director of IPB] *HN*, September 9, 1991, 3).

Worst of all, a Fund of National Property would put the lives of individual enterprises into the hands of, by neoliberal definition, incompetent and corruptible bureaucrats. The possibility that a government official would have the authority to pick winners and losers was anathema to the neoliberals. This position is consistent with the disdain for state management of any type, including the phobia that the state should direct an industrial policy and the belief that once established, bureaucracy will not fade away.

On the other side of that ideological divide stood the advocates of a differentiated privatization approach (standard privatization methods). A Fund of National Property, in this theory, would play a useful role by encouraging the restructuring of firms prior to privatization. A suitable restructuring program might involve debt relief or subdividing enterprises for the purpose of de-monopolization.

Furthermore, the main advocates of a differentiated privatization approach were concentrated in the Czech Republic government, not the Federal center. Recall that in conceptualization, the Czech government proposal emphasized standard privatization methods.

The two sides compromised over the Fund of National Property, as with other aspects of privatization. The compromise came about because the neoliberals at the center were not able to impose their will on the constituent republics. It was the Republic ministries, not the Federal center (a.k.a., Klaus's Ministry of Finance), that had nominal control over the enterprise shares. Consistent with this logic, the Czech government insisted that a Czech Fund of National Property would hold all Czech enterprise stakes, though the fund would only be authorized to implement standard methods of privatization, as specified by the Czech Ministry of Privatization. Echoing the neoliberal position, Ježek stated, "We don't want in any case for the fund to do business" (*HN*, November 11, 1990, 1).

The compromise over the Fund of National Property differentiated Czech privatization from privatization approaches that emphasized the explicit restructuring role targeted for the state. The German correlate to the Fund of National Property, the *Treuhundanstalt*, represented an activist state approach. The *Treuhundanstalt* was empowered to close, restructure, and sell the enterprise stakes in its portfolio. By contrast, the Czech neoliberal aversion to state intervention in individual enterprises remained consistent policy throughout the transition.

Government agreement allowed for Czech state ownership under two conditions: on a permanent basis, concerning stakes in strategic enterprises, and on a temporary basis, concerning stakes in enterprises prior to privatization. The Czech state was then destined to be an owner in the next phase, though it was unclear just how large a role it would play. Czech privatization would be incomplete, in spite of its neoliberal origins.

The State Regulator

Whereas the Czech privatizers engaged in lively debates over the proper organization of the supply-side tasks, demand-side tasks, and the future ownership status of the state, they neglected the state's regulatory role. All sides in the privatization debates accepted the view that the legal foundation of privatization largely was a secondary consideration during this period. According to Ježek, "this special, transitional period . . . justifies things that would be unthinkable in capitalist economies" (quoted in Reed 1996, 23).

The view that the state should withdraw from formal responsibility over privatization was prevalent in surprising places. Consider the position of P. Rychetský, a persistent foe of Klaus, and a supporter of the dissident wing of Civic Forum. Rychetský tacitly supported a privatization approach that fell beyond state laws and therefore beyond state enforcement at the time.[32] Rychetský's support was critical since he was vice-premier of the Czech government and, more importantly, chairman of the Czech government's Legislative Committee. Rychetský was in a position to hold up laws that failed to meet legal standards of acceptability. Tellingly, Rychetský was silent regarding the constitutional integrity of the Large Privatization Law.

The reason for Rychetský's surprising silence was that he, like the neoliberals and like nearly everyone else in the Federal government, regarded rapid privatization as a national imperative. Recall that nearly all Czechoslovakians, not only neoliberals, shared the ideological sentiment that state ownership was the great evil, and that rapid privatization was the only way to purge the society of the past. E. Klvačová, then-spokesperson for the Ministry of Privatization and previously editor of *Ekonom*, the Czech Republic's leading economic journal, expressed this theory: "[I]t is not too important what rules are accepted. They are not capable of creating ideal owners, and it does not make sense to attempt this" (Klvačová 1992, 19).

At the same time, both state officials and the population exhibited an "incredible naiveté"[33] over the ability of the privatizers and the bureaucrats to carry out an expeditious and honest privatization strategy. "[A] feeling of good will"[34] toward the new government characterized the public mood. Public confidence in "good supervision"[35] guaranteed a felicitous result and obviated the need for the time-consuming enactment and exercise of an exhaustive battery of privatization laws, to say nothing of the necessary enforcement procedures. The exaggerated confidence—some would say arrogance—that so many in the Czechoslovakian government had of their own capabilities to manage and control as complex and inherently unruly a process as transformative privatization lies at the root of the Czech Republic's hijacked privatization.

The Large Privatization Law of February 1991

The Large Privatization Law and the Scenario of Economic Reform were similar documents. Both documents reflected neoliberal principles. Both documents were borne of compromise. Both documents emerged from internal debates within the government. The Czechoslovakian Parliament approved both documents quickly—after only a few days of debate. One keen observer of the Czech political scene remarked that "Finance Minister Václav Klaus and his team appear to have got their own way, with only minor concessions" (Oberman 1991, 12–15).[36]

There were two essential differences between the Scenario of Economic Reform and the Large Privatization Law. First, the content of the Large Privatization Law specified a legally binding framework for privatization, whereas the Scenario of Economic Reform outlined a general economic and social program of which privatization was but a part. Second, the Large Privatization Law was offered to the Parliament without alternative, whereas the Scenario of Economic Reform was offered to the Parliament as one of several possible scenarios. The Large Privatization Law was a document open to parliamentary amendment, not rejection.

The fact that the Parliament abdicated its active legislative function in favor of the government testifies to the dominating influence of the Federal government in Czechoslovakian politics. It also testifies to the good faith of common people in the government. Popular euphoria supported parliamentary acceptance of what was widely conceived of as a neoliberal program.

Ironically, the Large Privatization Law embedded the compromises that would ultimately subvert the neoliberal aims of privatization. The meaning of those compromises wasn't then clear to the interested parties, least of all the neoliberals. The neoliberals lost control of privatization even before the beginning of the first wave, in the spring of 1992.

Finally, the privatization law and the privatization negotiations that preceded Parliament's consideration of the privatization law deliberately subordinated two groups of claimants—workers and foreigners. Most Czechs linked workers, especially the previous trade unions, to the communist past. The draft privatization law awarded workers the right to discuss with managers the terms of the privatization project. The Large Privatization Law reduced still further this already symbolic gesture to the workers' rights to be "kept informed" of the terms of the privatization project (Section 7, Paragraph 4).[37] If one set of enterprise insiders were to be rewarded preferences in privatization, pragmatism dictated that it would be the enterprise managers rather than the workers. Enterprise managers, though former communists, were widely viewed as necessary to operate the enterprises. As for foreigners, Czech nationalists (including the neoliberals) successfully argued against widespread foreign participation in voucher privatization, despite the obvious advantages of foreign expertise and money to the Czech economy (Section 24).[38] The law's prejudice against workers and foreigners indicated that Czech privatization was becoming more pragmatic and nationalistic and less ideological.[39]

CONCLUSION

The compromises between the neoliberals and the government officials who favored standard privatization approaches cemented the Czech privatization trajectory. We can summarize the main features:

- Regarding the *supply-side*, business lobbies influenced both sides in the dispute to accept a privatization strategy that awarded enterprise managers key decision-making roles. As part of this compromise, neoliberals opted for a privatization strategy that was not streamlined, but rather was overly complex and bureaucratic.
- Regarding the *demand side*, privatizers laid the groundwork for a voucher approach that favored masses (and Slovaks), but left the door open for intermediaries.
- Regarding the *role of the state as claimant*, the privatizers tacitly agreed that strategic state enterprises would remain either wholly owned or majority-owned by the state. In addition, the privatizers agreed to establish a Fund of National Property to administer state property before privatization and to implement standard privatization methods. These decisions

ensured that the Czech state would be a significant player in the postprivatization stage.

- Regarding the *state regulator,* government officials remained silent. Privatization was a transformative task that needed to be fast, and if legal niceties were not observed, then . . . what of it? A regime of private property must precede the formation of a proper legal state.

Those four sets of compromises and arrangements—involving the supply-side, the demand side, the state as claimant, and the state as regulator—established the immediate terms of the critical privatization document, the Large Privatization Law of 1991, and ultimately the long-run trajectory of Czech privatization process.

The Czechoslovakian Parliament's passage of the Large Privatization Law in February 1991 marked a watershed in Czech privatization decision-making. Neoliberals emerged as the unchallenged Czech privatizers from that point. Simultaneously, privatization decision-making decentralized to involve state bureaucrats and claimants. The manifestation of this decentralization was a shift in decision-making venues from broad public arenas—the June 1990 elections, Civic Forum meetings, and Parliament—to bureaucracies and to closed meetings of government. The cause of the change was the natural progression of privatization tasks from grand policy design to implementation and its preparation. The decentralization of privatization involved new sets of incentives, a new cast of privatization actors, and new privatization politics.

NOTES

1. Krejčí, who referred to the Civic Forum election program as "social democratic," advances this argument (Krejčí 1994, 211).

2. Also, 83.4 percent of Civic Forum candidates preferred a faster reform variant coupled with an immediate decline in the standard of living to a gradual reform variant with a more modest decline in the standard of living. By contrast, only 58 percent of the population responded in favor of the radical variant (Rak 1992, 209).

3. His name was the most-cited on the so-called preferential votes, the only way that voters could select individually favored candidates. Nearly 400,000 cast preferential votes for Klaus. The order nationally (including Slovakia) was Klaus, Čalfa, Dienstbier, and Dubček (Havlík and Stoniš 1998, 15).

4. The survey shows that the relative support of Civic Forum within the categories of education, size of domiciled city, age, and "socio-professional group verticality." It is noteworthy that Civic Forum got its highest percentage of voters in the forty-five- to fifty-four-year-old category (27 percent of the sample) and second highest percentage in the thirty-four- to forty-four-year-old category (23 percent in the sample). While

the forty-five- to fifty-four-year-old category is a bit high for our characterization of the disappointed generation, this age group certainly qualifies as a group of people who suffered and was still suffering virtually their entire careers under communism (Boguszak and Rak 1990, table 4, 9–10 in appendix).

5. The average age of the Federal Parliament members was forty-five. A similar generation pattern was found among new local elected elites; the average age was forty-two. During the June 1990 elections, even the Communist Party fielded a much younger slate of candidates; the average age of Communist Party candidates was forty-four (Rak 1992, 217).

6. These people had backgrounds as engineers, scientists, economists (which was considered a technical occupation in Czechoslovakia), doctors, and researchers. (Mansfeldová 1993, table 2, 22). In the new Czechoslovakian government in June 1990, eleven of sixteen cabinet members had either technical or economic backgrounds. In the Czech government the ratio was eleven of twenty-one; in the Slovak government twelve of twenty-three (Wolchik 1991, 138).

7. The prominent ethnic Slovaks after November included men who did not match the aggressive profile of the Czechs. I speak in particular of A. Dubček, the reform communist leader of 1968 and M. Čalfa, the Federal deputy premier during the communist regime. Moreover, the Slovak Parliament was far older than the Czech Parliament; there the average age was fifty-two. Not "radical thinkers," these "up-and-coming" Slovak leaders would prove preoccupied by issues of nationality first, political and economic change second.

8. By the time of the attack, Komárek himself had already lost whatever long shot there was to influence state policy. The influx of the disappointed generation in the wake of the June elections effectively nullified any chance for Komárek to garner support.

9. Based on author interviews.

10. This section draws heavily on interviews with Civic Forum members; also Honajzer (1996), especially 26–35.

11. Another telling example came when P. Havlík, Klaus's deputy, came unannounced to a Civic Forum meeting and baldly claimed that Klaus had sufficient popular support within Civic Forum to seize the agenda. Although Kučera registered the dismay of the current leadership of Civic Forum, of course, as Klaus's right-hand man, Havlík knew what was coming. Klaus overwhelmingly won the election as Civic Forum's first chairman. (This dispute was played out in the Czech press; see also Havlík and Stoniš [1998].)

12. The institutes were Prognostický ústav ČSAV Praha; Prognostický ústav SAV Bratislava; Ekonomický ústav ČSAV Praha; Vysoká škola ekonomická Praha; and Československé ekonomické fórum.

13. M. Matějka, the author of the VŠE proposal, went so far as to call the media an orchestrator of a "disinformation campaign." As evidence, Matějka claimed that his testimony before Parliament was intentionally distorted by *Mladá Fronta Dnes*, one of the major Czechoslovak daily newspapers (Matějka 1992, 9).

14. Newspaper interview with then-chief of trade unions, Vladimír Petrus, date unavailable.

15. Author interview with privatization officials.

16. Policy recommendations included tight monetary, balanced-budget fiscal policy, and exchange rate measures designed to ensure a positive real interest rate. The "macroeconomic priority in the process of transformation is the blocking of inflation and this priority must to a reasonable extent override all other foundations of macroeconomic aims—economic growth, employment, and the balance of payments" (Scenario of Economic Reform 1990, 5). The section entitled "Macroeconomic Framework of Economic Reform" also includes topics on stabilization policy, tax reform, and budgetary policy (Scenario of Economic Reform 1990, 5–13).

17. Internal currency convertibility meant the relatively free access of Czechoslovakian subjects to currency, but the Scenario of Economic Reform restricted the use of foreign currency by domestic subjects doing business with foreign subjects, including trading on foreign markets (Scenario of Economic Reform 1990, 25).

18. Elites skeptical of the neoliberal approach included Federal ministers such as M. Čalfa, the Czechoslovak prime minister, V. Valeš (Komárek's replacement) as Federal deputy premier, P. Miller as labor minister, V. Stěpová as trade and commerce minister, and P. Rychetský, chair of the Federal legislative commission. We must also consider Federal President V. Havel as a neoliberal opponent.

19. The Scenario of Economic Reform also included a section on particularities related to the agriculture and food-processing businesses. Orenstein reports that the social policy section was drawn up by an advisor with social democratic inclinations, P. Miller (Miller later became a Social Democratic Party member) (Orenstein 1996, 81). Miller's prominence was based on his role in November 1989 as the representative of the workers and his alleged friendship with Havel.

20. This section featured an active incomes policy designed to speed the changeover from unemployment to employment, to support the founding of new workplaces, to promote the benefits of hard work and small enterprises, and to support the requalification of workers (Scenario of Economic Reform 1990, 29).

21. This section included specific programs for restructuring industries such as coal, steel, energy, and various branches of engineering. Such programs included a special State Fund for Structural Changes on the Republic level. However, the Czech government gradually abandoned programs calling for active state intervention at the enterprise level in favor of privatization.

22. The neoliberal authors of the Scenario of Economic Reform did not anticipate an important role for the banks in privatization. According to the Scenario of Economic Reform, "it is impossible to assure that the domestic banks will extend credit to the domestic population for the purchase of property due to the banks' capital inadequacies" (Scenario of Economic Reform 1990, 17). Moreover, there is no mention of the banks in the Scenario of Economic Reform as owners. Analysts who associate the equity-holding role that banks now play in the Czech Republic confuse result with intention. Citizens (and later investment intermediaries [that is, funds]), not banks, were the intended owners.

23. These social components included active incomes policies, institutions of labor negotiation like a tripartite commission, a minimum wage, and regulation of energy and

housing prices. In the ensuing years, the fear of popular pressure arising from growing unemployment would also influence the neoliberals in the Czechoslovak government to suspend bankruptcy legislation, to subsidize selected industries and banks, and to offer generous unemployment benefits.

24. In practice, all shares of all enterprises meant 97 percent of individual enterprise shares since the government reserved 3 percent of enterprise stakes to satisfy restitution claims. At this point, restitution was the "third-rail" of Czech politics, and like other overwhelming popular initiatives (such as Social Security or Medicare in the United States), it was untouchable. Moreover, all enterprises excluded certain traditionally state enterprises (such as the post office) as well as certain "strategic" enterprises (Schwartz 1997).

25. Valeš was also a minister of foreign trade in the 1960s and thereby a "68er." Moreover, Valeš was thought to be very close to Havel, having shared a prison cell with him during the 1980s.

26. A faction within the neoliberals warned of the possible risk of inflation stemming from the issuance of vouchers. Nonetheless, most neoliberals argued that the risk of inflation was minimal since the vouchers would in any event represent only a small fraction of the money supply (based on author interviews).

27. Although one early draft proposal of the Large Privatization Law called for a 2,000 CZK participation fee, the 2,000 CZK figure did not appear in the privatization law.

28. Ježek claims that the need to administer voucher privatization federally grew out of Klaus's ego and political ambitions (Husák 1997).

29. The decision of what shares should remain in state hands was guided in part by zákon č. 100/1990, which stated that the state should own "mineral wealth, basic energy resources, forestry land, natural underground water supplies, water courses, and natural medicinal resources." The law also stated that other property necessary to secure the needs of the whole of society, the development of the national economy, and the public welfare can only be owned by the state or by a legal entity to whom the state entrusts them. The reader should not overestimate the impact of laws on the decision of what assets should or should not be owned by the state. The Czech leadership often took liberties with the law. Reed points out, for instance, that while legal provisions for state ownership were required under the List of Basic Rights and Freedoms adopted as part of the constitution, the Czech government announced in the first half of 1995 that such a law was unnecessary (Reed 1996, 55).

30. A related question concerned the financing of the new ministry and especially the disposition of revenues collected by the new ministry. At this point, it was generally agreed that the new ministry's finances should be outside the state budget. The Large Privatization Law also mandated that revenues would be targeted for debt relief to the banks or to foundations, for instance. Ježek was an important supporter of privatization revenues to the banks.

31. Of course, there might exceptions to this policy recommendation, as to de-monopolize or to relieve a strategic enterprise of staggering debt burdens (including banks).

32. Rychetský, for instance, was almost certainly aware that the Large Privatization Law did not adequately resolve the jurisdictional issues raised by privatization. Those issues concern which ministries would be legally empowered to administer which privatization rules. The critical law on the books that considered the jurisdictions of ministries dated from 1968; and, the government's flagrant disregard of this law, as in the case of privatization, rendered it no more than a "piece of paper," according to one senior justice department official. The disregard of the 1968 law—it was sometimes amended after the fact—also was manifest in the areas of foreign trade and social policy. In these cases, the government (typically Klaus) personally chose which ministries would write and enforce given laws. With regard to privatization, Rychetský was soon to reverse his position and become one of the most ardent supporters of legal oversight of privatization (Rychetský "Odvrácena tvář privatizace" [undated]). His reversal and subsequent efforts turned into a case of "too little, too late."

33. Author interview with member of parliament.

34. Author interview with member of parliament.

35. Author interview with member of parliament.

36. The Large Privatization Law did pass through parliamentary committees prior to reaching a vote in Parliament. This process resulted in only minor changes to the law.

37. Moreover, the writers of the commercial code buried a small section that severely limited the ownership preferences of workers (Section 158, Czech Commercial Code).

38. The Large Privatization Law does not specify the rights of foreigners concerning standard privatization methods, however.

39. Czechoslovak small privatization, the program by which the state privatized relatively lower capitalized assets, also underpinned the biases versus workers and foreigners. First, the small privatization program offered no preferences in auctions (the sole method elaborated in small privatization) for employees or shopkeepers. The shopkeepers and employees staged a brief strike in response to their lack of privilege in small privatization. Contrary to many expectations, though, the public sided with the government. Consequently, the shopkeepers and employees ended their work action, but without having influenced the law. Concerning foreign interests, small privatization explicitly barred foreign participation in the purchase of an asset in the all-important first round of auction. Only in the case of assets that remained unsold after the first round could the foreigners participate in auctions. After that round, though, foreigners were not likely to have interest in the remaining assets, since most of the best assets would likely have been sold already. In practice, foreigners participated in small privatization by finding Czechs literally willing to do their bidding in the auctions.

7

Creating Plutocracy—February 1991 to May 1992

Supply-side tasks are the means senior state officials and state bureaucrats use to assign privatization methods to enterprises. First-level supply-side outcomes are *privatization methods* that can be mapped according to classes of claimants. Winning claimants are first private owners.

Supply-side issues provide a context for special interests to mobilize and for policymakers to set down administrative competencies, rules and procedures, and an ethic of governance. What criteria would the state use to privatize enterprises? Would the state privatize each enterprise by the same means? Which bureaucracies would make those decisions? Would foreigners be allowed to participate in the decision-making process? How much time would be allotted for supply-side tasks? How would the state regulate supply-side tasks? The state implemented privatization based on how it executed the supply-side tasks.

The Czech Large Privatization Law locked the supply-side tasks into a decentralized trajectory. The legalized procedures called for the Czech bureaucrats to examine and to rule on over ten thousand privatization proposals and to assign privatization methods to thousands of enterprises.[1] The law guaranteed that the supply-side tasks would consume the attention of enterprise managers and nearly the entire Federal government and both Republic governments—particularly, the economic ministries, the newly formed privatization ministries, and the senior government officials.

A significant administrative role for state bureaucrats in privatization was unacceptable to the Czech neoliberals. They believed that Czech (and Slovak) bureaucrats lacked the skill, resources, and honesty to privatize enterprises fairly and in the best economic interest.[2] The Czech privatizers consequently sought to marginalize state interference. They used time pressure as a bludgeon, setting state institutions on an impossibly tight schedule to make privatization decisions on individual enterprises. Free markets presumably would correct whatever inequities, inefficiencies, illegalities, and mistakes were created from the excessive speed. Rapid decentralized privatization, as we shall see, increased the chances for collusion between bureaucrats and influential claimants.

The Large Privatization Law's supply-side procedures gave the enterprise managers special advantages to become owners by insisting that enterprise managers make the initial privatization proposals. Enterprise managers naturally responded by tailoring proposals to their own interest. Their typical proposal subdivided the enterprise stakes by privatization method, and included at least one ownership stake with a privatization method that would benefit them.

The role and behavior of the enterprise managers during the supply-side tasks had two impacts on the ownership regime. First, the Large Privatization Law ensured that enterprise managers would be substantial first owners. Enterprise manager-owners were not necessarily good for corporate restructuring since they lacked capital and market experience. Second, the participation of enterprise managers and the subdivision of ownership stakes by privatization method ensured that the first-ownership structure of individual enterprises would be fractured. Most Czech companies therefore would have important minority owners but lack majority ownership immediately following privatization. The fractured ownership structure set in motion a frenzy of asset sales just after privatization, which complicated corporate governance and delayed corporate restructuring.

The Czech neoliberal supply-side strategy unwittingly encouraged collusion between bureaucrats and claimants. The decentralized decision-making procedures created access points for local politicians, small business associations, enterprise managers, and other claimants to influence state bureaucrats. In combination with the massive amounts of enterprise data and tight time schedule, the input of claimants into the supply-side tasks pushed bureaucrats to make privatization decisions based on criteria other than merit. Collusion was exacerbated by the neoliberals' honor system for privatization decision-making. The honor system insulated bureaucrats from accountability by removing legal boundaries, by withdrawing authority and the resources from policing agencies, and by eliminating court recourse. In these ways, the Czech rapid privatization approach made collusion between bureaucrats and claimants all but inevitable.

The Czech reformers' supply-side approach generally was consistent with neoliberal rapid privatization strategy. This argument refutes the common charge (Stark and Bruszt 1998; Macháček 1998) that Czech reformers were social democrats.[3] This is a charge that wrongly, in my opinion, stems from looking at policies irrespective of political context and neoliberal priorities. Recall that neoliberalism is not merely belief in free markets but also a pragmatic philosophy that admits of compromises with opposed interests and antidemocratic practice in pursuit of political power. In the early 1990s, the Czech reformers behaved as neoliberals in issue areas that they considered crucial;

as time went on, though, critics of the neoliberals may correctly question the reformers' neoliberal credentials.

Evidence shows that Czech neoliberals accommodated claimants who would be useful allies in pushing privatization forward. Their only caveat was that claimants be rewarded on an individual basis. In the spirit of post–World War II German reformers, Czech neoliberals regarded claimant organizations as market enemies as well as competitors for political power. Besides, market incentives would overwhelm claimants in the next stage, or even better, markets would transform claimants into a productive and democratic middle class. Public speeches, press articles, and author interviews also indicate that Czech neoliberals distanced themselves from the public in their conduct of supply-side tasks. Private owners eventually would erase these antidemocratic beginnings. (It is only when reformers violate core liberalization principles that the sincerity of neoliberals must be called into question.) Political circumstances and neoliberal strategy rather than moral turpitude guided Czech neoliberals at that time.[4]

SUPPLY-SIDE PRIVATIZATION PROCEDURES AND INSTITUTIONS

The procedures and institutions as outlined in the Large Privatization Law set the context for supply-side decision-making. They decentralized the supply-side tasks, involving much of the Czech (and Federal and Slovak) government. Simultaneously, these procedures and institutions created access points for politically connected and rich claimants to influence and in some cases collude with bureaucrats. Enterprise managers were bound to be the most favored of all claimants in the supply-side system due to their initiation role in the process and their prior connections with officials in economic ministries and in the Czech Ministry of Privatization. Social conditions and policies that encouraged experienced bureaucrats to flee the government ministries only to be replaced by inexperienced and often dishonest bureaucrats augmented the opportunities for claimants to influence government decision-making. The vulnerability of the supply-side procedures and institutions to manipulation by claimants was exacerbated still further by the speed of the process, the lack of a legal framework, and lax policing procedures.

The Supply-Side Routine

The supply-side tasks formally began when an enterprise (nearly always an enterprise manager) wrote a privatization proposal. The central component of the privatization proposal was the matching of enterprise ownership stakes with a privatization method. The privatization proposal often called for the subdivision of the enterprise before assigning enterprise stakes privatization methods. This raised the question not only of who would get ownership but also what form the enterprise would take after privatization. The proposal was called a *privatization project* or, simply, a *project*.

Next, the enterprise submitted the project to the appropriate Republic branch ministry—called a *founding ministry*. For instance, a Czech industrial enterprise normally would submit its project to the Czech Ministry of Industry and Trade; a Slovak agricultural enterprise would submit its project to the Slovak Ministry of Agriculture. The founding ministry would then evaluate the project and, following that evaluation, send a recommendation on to a Republic Ministry of Privatization.

The Republic Ministry of Privatization would then approve the privatization method as specified in the project or else reject the project entirely. In the rejection case, the project would return to the founder and ultimately to the enterprise for revision. In the approval case, the property would be transferred to the ownership of the Fund of National Property, where it would await privatization by the privatization method(s) specified in the project. The Federal Finance Ministry governed voucher privatization; the Fund of National Property privatized under all other methods. The Federal Czechoslovak government, the Czech Republic government, and the Slovak Republic government could intervene in any privatization project, and in cases of direct sale would be legally obligated to do so (see Part 2, Sections 5–10, Large Privatization Law 1991).

A closer look at the main actors and institutions in the supply-side privatization process—enterprise managers, founding ministries, and the Czech Ministry of Privatization—offers a first perspective into the dynamics and implications of the Czech system.

Enterprise Managers

Most analysts underrate the advantages of enterprise managers in Czech privatization by focusing only on the demand side and particularly on the voucher side of the Czech privatization approach. The conclusion of a recent academic paper is typical:

> The absence of preferences given to managers and employees of enterprises and the relative lack of opportunities for *nomenklatura* or "spontaneous" privatization in the Czech program . . . stand in striking contrast to the practice in most other East European countries of granting special preferences . . . to favored groups— through both formal and informal means. (Earle et al. 1997, 13)

Actually, the supply-side decision-making procedure put tremendous power in the hands of the enterprise managers, many of whom were former *nomenklatura*. The major advantage was that Czech enterprise managers (who monopolized enterprise decision-making) wrote the basic privatization project. They could and consequently did propose privatization methods to coincide with their interests. In practice, the enterprise manager's privatization project served as the basis for privatization decisions since, as we shall see, the founding ministries and the Czech Ministry of Privatization were overworked and under severe time pressure.

The decision-making procedure incorporated another element that would dramatically work to the benefit of the enterprise managers: the option to privatize one piece of the enterprise via one method and another piece via another method. A hypothetical enterprise might be privatized 50 percent by vouchers, 20 percent by insider privatization to managers, 15 percent by direct sale, 10 percent by other privatization to local governments or former owners, and 5 percent by insider privatization to workers. The enterprise manager could propose that the enterprise be split up into discrete units or privatized whole. He could propose a small piece of equity for himself and a large piece of equity for vouchers.[5] Either way, the flexibility inherent in the kinds of projects the enterprise managers could propose offered the enterprise manager a nearly infinite number of games to play that would satisfy the broad aims of privatization, but that would also allow the enterprise managers the best chances to maintain control. The legal latitude to use more than one privatization method on a single enterprise gave the supply-side process the feeling of a negotiation between stakeholders rather than a winner-take-all affair in which the state was the sole arbiter.

The variety of privatization methods applied to a single enterprise ensured that Czech enterprises would have a fragmented ownership structure. Different privatization methods invariably invited stakeholders of varying abilities and resources. Often, there would be no majority owner. Although the dispersed ownership sometimes benefited the enterprise manager after privatization, more often it precipitated a time- and resource-consuming struggle for enterprise control. Chapters 5 and 6 address issues connected with fragmented ownership in detail.

Further analysis of the supply-side procedures reinforces the theme introduced here that enterprise managers were unusually privileged claimants in Czech privatization. Next, we will show that the privatization procedures and organization of the founding ministries and the Czech Ministry of Privatization benefited enterprise managers. Later, the chapter shows that Czech enterprise managers benefited from the haphazard and rushed style in which the Czech neoliberals conducted the supply-side tasks. The fluidity of Czech society at the time and the reformers' disregard for legal procedure and enforcement magnified the chances of enterprise managers to influence the system and, in particular, to collude with state officials.

The Founding Ministries

The supply-side protocol ensured that thousands of projects made their way to the founding ministries and then to the Ministry of Privatization. As first evaluators of privatization projects, founding ministries played a critical, even determinative, role in setting the privatization method for individual enterprises. The Ministry of Privatization was not allotted the weeks or months necessary to properly evaluate each project. Consequently, the Ministry of Privatization's decision leaned heavily on the recommendation of the founding ministers (who themselves were pressed for time).

The founding ministers were the consolidated and reorganized ancestors of the communist industrial ministries. After November 1989, the Czech reformers had extraordinary authority to shape the state system to their own design, as Dlouhý would demonstrate in his closing of the State Planning Commission. The reformers merged, trimmed, and eliminated ministries. The reform objective was to destroy the communist-state system.

The collapse of the communist-state system and the expectations for the new one precipitated a veritable flood of bureaucrats out of the ministries, into retirement, and into private business. All too often, the fleeing bureaucrats were the most able. Many senior bureaucrats left because they feared being tried as communists under the new regime. Rapidly forming businesses, especially banks, hired them straightaway. Other former communists went into business for themselves. As the bureaucrats were abandoning the ministries, so the ministries themselves were seeking purpose in the new regime. One found purpose was the evaluation of privatization projects.

Ministries were the logical state institutions to offer privatization recommendations. Under communism, ministries allocated resources, planned production targets, and set enterprise input and output prices. Yet incestuous ministry-enterprise relations were as much of a curse as a blessing during privatization. Founding ministry bureaucrats were reluctant to oppose the enterprise managers, who loomed as potential employers after privatization.[6] Managers also typically would enlist moneymen, consulting firms, and friends and family to co-opt founding ministry bureaucrats. The reality that the remaining founding ministry bureaucrats were often among the least able also increased the managers' clout and that of other claimants. Against these pressures, the efforts of founding ministry officials, such as Vrba, the Czech minister of industry and trade from 1990 to 1992, to limit collusion or other forms of undue influence by subjecting projects to extensive intraministry review, must be seen as limited measures. In many cases, the founding ministries' recommendations often reflected the managers' (and their allies') priorities.

Despite the ineffective and easily compromised founding ministry bureaucrats, the upheaval in Czech society was proving a double-edged sword for the state managers. State enterprise managers, much like the ministry bureaucrats, were potential victims of their compromised pasts and of their market inexperience. A survey of 243 enterprises over the 1991 to 1993 period showed that the lead managers were replaced in nearly 80 percent of the cases (*Privatization Newsletter of Czechoslovakia* 1994). Many replacements were deputies or lower-ranking officials from the same enterprise. Anecdotal evidence suggests that many replacement managers were uncertain how to proceed in the societal turbulence and were equally uncertain how to advance their own personal interests in lieu of the transformation tasks. One well-traveled management consultant remarked that many of the new enterprise directors were "scared" during this initial period of privatization. Later on, during the second privatization wave, the managers defended their interests much more aggressively, thereby demonstrating the steepening of the transition learning curve. In some cases, the communist-era managers even returned to reclaim the enterprise. In the early privatization stages, however, some state enterprise managers made a retreating and fearful lot, not the aggressive clique corrupting the bureaucracy.

The Czech Ministry of Privatization

The Czech Ministry of Privatization (or the Ministry of Privatization) arose de novo, unlike the founding ministries.[7] The neoliberals appointed one of their own, Tomáš Ježek, first minister of privatization in July 1990 to insulate the ministry from claimants. The Czech reformers were loathe to expose this critical ministry to the possible infiltration of the hard-to-see blocking interests that were lurking in the reconstituted industrial ministries. The Ministry of Privatization, itself, began operations in August 1990.

The Ministry of Privatization was a rushed and underfunded affair. It started with only twenty employees from an employees list from the Ministry of Finance. Mundane issues like finding secretaries and suitable offices were complicated endeavors (Husák 1997, 127–129). There were only six computers. Ministry of Privatization salaries paled next to those of the burgeoning private sector, and the ministry jobs were destined to be temporary, canceled when privatization was complete. Consequently, many new employees proved to be not only young and untrained but also unprincipled, especially at lower levels.[8] Finally, the fact that—as some have argued—Ježek was not an altogether effective administrator, even though he was a well-respected and probably principled one, meant that the Ministry of Privatization would function in an increasingly out-of-control manner. These factors favored the interventions of managers and other claimants with easy access into the Ministry of Privatization. They also proved conducive to collusion between bureaucrats and claimants.

SUPPLY-SIDE PRIVATIZATION DECISION-MAKING ON THE FLY AND WITHOUT RULES

The neoliberals orchestrated the supply-side tasks emphasizing speed. The rationale was to privatize everything as fast as possible so that the perceived opponents of privatization would not block reform. Privatization also should proceed apace, at a strict time schedule that allowed the bureaucracies little discretion over privatization. The neoliberals (Tříska was the main author) wrote a government *Harmonogram* (schedule) of June 1991 that put privatization on a forced march up until the end of the year ("Zásady vlády České republiky pro sestavení návrhu seznamů podniků a majetkových účastí státu určených pro privatizaci," *HN*, June 4, 1991, 9).

Neoliberals argued that the creation of a detailed legal framework and credible enforcement would take time and delay privatization; the need for speed justified disregard for law. They argued that privatization was inherently a complex and evolutionary process suited to quick decisions and policy shifts. Maneuverability was essential. It would be impractical to force privatizers to refer to the legal codes each time a choice was needed. A few minor indiscretions and winks at the law would be a small price to pay for capitalism and democracy. Ježek wrote, "The application of normal laws to the privatization process is inadmissible. Privatization is here so that normal laws can be valid after it is finished" (*ČD*, Oct. 15, 1993, 26).

In consideration of the need to privatize quickly and the understanding that laws would be not be binding, the neoliberals established a privatization "honor system," though it was never formally put in those terms. Privatizers asked society to trust them to privatize the economy. They knew best. The honor system represented a "social contract" that most people were willing to accept in order to effect the transformation of the system.

The honor system was evident in all aspects of the privatization process, from the government's approval of privatization projects, to the implementation of privatization, to the management of the state's residual shareholdings. In this section, we analyze how the supply-side tasks operated under the honor system, paying particular attention to the categorizing of enterprises prior to privatization ("composing the lists") and the privatization approval process in the Czech Ministry of Privatization.

Composing the Privatization Lists

The first task of the Ministry of Privatization was to divide the enterprises into general categories prior to privatization: (1) enterprises privatized in the first wave; (2) enterprises privatized in the second wave; (3) enterprises not privatized; and, (4) enterprises liquidated (Husák 1997, 151). The two privatization waves corresponded to two branches of enterprises that would be offered in the course of voucher privatization.

First-wave enterprises generally consisted of the more valuable enterprises and those enterprises unlikely to attract political controversy. The more problematic second-wave enterprises often came with high debt burdens, large workforces, and uncompetitive products. Many second-wave enterprises were engaged in heavy industry, chemicals, agriculture, and health care. The Ministry of Privatization postponed the more serious privatization problems until the second wave when the government would have maximum public support and presumably more latitude for unpopular privatization choices.[9]

The Ministry of Privatization would take no chances with the controlling share packages of the largest enterprises, invariably the most politically sensitive of all enterprises. The fate of those shares was tabled indefinitely and the shares were housed in the Fund of National Property. The Ministry of Privatization published the first enterprise lists in July 1991.

The effort to categorize state enterprises provoked concerted lobbying. The founding ministries were one lobbying source. Sometimes acting on behalf of managers, the founding ministries recommended that some enterprises should be transferred from the first to the second wave. Enterprise managers were seeking to buy time until they could find themselves the best privatization deal. Founding ministries also recommended that certain enterprises be excluded from large privatization. In some cases, founding ministry officials believed that the enterprise would be better served if the state would restructure the balance sheet or the management team prior to privatization.[10] Typically, the Ministry of Privatization accommodated the founding ministries and the enterprise managers, especially when it came to moving enterprises into the all-important first wave (Husák 1997, 151).

District Privatization Councils were another important lobbying source. The state originally conceived these councils to conduct the auctions of relatively small enterprises and other assets. District Privatization Councils lobbied the Ministry of Privatization to have selected enterprises (or more properly, parts of enterprises) removed from the large privatization lists and transferred to small privatization. District Privatization Councils sought to break up enterprises—some were unwieldy mastodons from the past era that needed a drastic pruning—and to sell the pieces at auction. Ježek claims that the District

Privatization Councils acted out of ideology. According to Ježek, the district councils regarded large privatization as a "betrayal" of the revolution since it protected the integrity of the existing enterprise and consequently the authority of the enterprise manager (Husák 1997, 137–139).[11] It is equally likely that some district committee members (and unseen allies) saw possibilities to obtain valuable enterprises at reduced prices. What is often not publicly admitted is that small privatization was dominated by unsavory elements who rigged property auctions. Sometimes the unsavory interests were foreign mafia or local thieves. In practice, the negotiations over whether and how enterprises should be broken up were complicated affairs in which economic interest played a determinative role.

Competitive Privatization Projects and the Politics of Privatization Delay

Tříska's *Harmonogram* required first-wave enterprises to submit privatization projects to the founding ministries by the end of October 1991, only three months after the publication of the privatization lists (see table 7.1). Most enterprise managers were pressed to write projects within the time schedule. The time crunch was more severe regarding outside projects—the so-called *competitive projects*.

Competitive projects were privatization projects proposed by claimants other than by the enterprise managers speaking on behalf of the enterprise.[12] The neoliberals created competitive projects on economic grounds—to keep the enterprise managers from dictating the privatization method—and on justice grounds—"every citizen should have the chance to manifest interest in the purchasing of a state property by a formal means" (Husák 1997, 150).

The problem was that Tříska's *Harmonogram* didn't allow time for outsiders to submit a viable competitive project. Ježek claimed that by the time the deadline for the submission of projects had come and gone, privatization rules had not been widely distributed (Husák 1997, 154). Consequently, not one private entrepreneur had submitted a competitive project by the October 1991 deadline.[13]

The privatizers at the Ministry of Privatization were swayed by the entrepreneur associations to extend the privatization submission deadline. The most persuasive ones were industry associations—Deputy Minister of Privatization J. Muroň mentioned the bakery association.[14] Baránek, chairman of the Association of Czech Entrepreneurs, also was active. Baránek besieged the ministry with petitions and speeches, and through the press. He argued for rapid privatization, but he also argued that many enterprises were unsuitable for voucher privatization. Some enterprises such as dairies or hotels simply would function better with sole proprietors than as shareholding companies with thousands of owners. Baránek pushed the envelope hard for privatization methods that allowed for enterprise managers and money interests to become the owners. In the fall of 1991, Ježek persuaded a majority of the government cabinet members to extend the privatization deadlines (Baránek 1994).

It is hard to escape the speculation that the competing views of Tříska and Ježek—each one a dedicated neoliberal—were shaped by the posts they occupied during privatization. As minister of privatization, Ježek assigned privatization methods to individual enterprises. Ježek, a confident and conscientious person, sought to privatize in the fairest and most efficient manner, while maintaining an eye on the higher goal of rapid reform. Ježek steered a middle privatization course. On the other hand, Tříska managed voucher privatization. Tříska's priority was to maximize the amount of enterprise assets privatized by vouchers. Why would a man in Tříska's position concern himself with the details of the supply-side that so preoccupied Ježek? There is no apparent answer. Tříska's impatience with Ježek's delays then seem entirely understandable. The conflict between Ježek and Tříska is one between institutions as much as between conflicting ideas.[15]

Klaus fiercely took up Tříska's cause in reaction to Ježek's "stalling." His concern was that the delay could raise opposition to voucher privatization. Prospective buyers were slated to begin registering for voucher privatization the first week of November 1991. Who would register for the program not knowing which enterprise shares would be offered, yet knowing that the whole endeavor was in bureaucratic turmoil? Klaus assailed Ježek's stalling as tantamount to "sabotage."[16] "[I]t will make the citizens lose trust in the government's ability to handle the existing problems," Klaus argued (quoted in *ČTK*, November 7, 1991).

Surprisingly, Ježek won the day. In the fall of 1991, Klaus was the most imposing politician on the Czech political scene, but contrary to popular belief, he could not dictate policy. The Czech government voted to move the start of voucher privatization from January 1992 to May 1992. The extra time gave Ježek's team at the Ministry of Privatization two months to receive and to evaluate privatization projects. Still, two months was several years short of the time the Ministry of Privatization needed to properly evaluate privatization projects.

How did the Ministry of Privatization choose among competing projects? In January 1992, at a castle in Lnář, in picturesque southern Bohemia, sixty-five Ministry of Privatization bureaucrats embarked on what was to become a two-month marathon to decide the fate of the Czech economy.[17] The bureaucrats were charged to sift through uncountable piles of enterprise documents, including the founding ministry recommendations, and then to decide how to privatize individual enterprises.

Table 7.1.   The First Wave of Privatization

Task	Harmonogram	Achieved
Publication of list of first-wave enterprises	July 15, 1991	July 15, 1991
Deadline for project submission to founding ministry	October 31, 1991	January 20, 1992
Coupon registration for first wave	November 1, 1991	November 1, 1991
Deadline for receiving project from founding ministry	November 30, 1991	Through March 20, 1992
Rulings by Ministry of Privatization	December 15, 1991	January 20, 1992, to March 20, 1992
First wave begins	January 1, 1992	May 18, 1992

The obvious challenge was the massive volume of materials. The Ministry of Privatization received 11,252 projects for 2,727 enterprises—roughly four projects for every enterprise—by the January 20, 1992, deadline for the submission of privatization projects (Czech Ministry of Privatization 1993, 4). Thousands of projects translated into roomfuls of stacks of papers. How could the bureaucrats go through all this paperwork and decide the best ways to privatize enterprises? The short answer is that careful, deliberative decision-making was next to impossible (see table 7.1).

How did the Ministry of Privatization officials choose among competing privatization projects? What happened if no privatization project seemed appropriate? What happened when the Ministry of Privatization officials disagreed with the recommendations of the founding ministry? How did the Ministry of Privatization's decision-making process fare in the face of fantastic time pressures and staffing inadequacies? The short answer is that the Ministry of Privatization officials made privatization decisions hurriedly, asystematically, and often against the spirit and the letter of existing laws. Among the consequences were enterprise owners who obtained enterprise ownership stakes, collusion between claimants and bureaucrats that persisted after privatization, and enterprises with a fragmented ownership structure. But, from the neoliberal vantage, the most important supply-side outcome was the readiness of enterprises for privatization—particularly voucher privatization. We will evaluate whether rapid privatization was worth the sacrifice in later chapters.

The Absence of State Control: The "Honor System"

The honor system was perhaps most consequential in the decisions revolving around the privatization decisions in the Ministry of Privatization and the management of state property in the Fund of National Property. Four aspects characterized the honor system as it pertained to the privatization decision-making in the Ministry of Privatization.

- The first aspect of the honor system was that the decisions of the Ministry of Privatization were secret. The state announced privatization decisions without explanation. After (illegal) adjustments, again no word. A series of amendments passed following the June 1992 elections institutionalized the secrecy.
- The second aspect of the honor system was that the Ministry of Privatization could (and did) adjust privatization projects, though this practice was against the law.[18] The Ministry of Privatization legally was charged to approve or disapprove projects, not to adjust them.[19] Ježek estimated that only 5 percent of all projects were accepted as written; otherwise, ministry bureaucrats "completed, supplemented, or remodeled" projects.
- The third aspect of the honor system was that the state would lack the authority and the resources to police privatization. R. Češka, then a deputy minister of privatization, admitted that the ministry was simply "too busy" and lacked "enough employees" to monitor the privatization process.

> The state doesn't have the capacity [to investigate potential abuses]—we aren't able to observe whether someone is not selling something, to document [the abuse], or to remove enterprise directors. If someone put into the hands of our minister materials which showed that this or that director did something, I am 100 percent certain that the minister would team up with the minister from the appropriate other ministry and fire the director. (quoted in *Respekt*, February 17, 1991)

Interviews with Ministry of Privatization officials and control officers indicated that the control officers were engaged in a constant and futile battle with the privatizers to police privatization (Reed 1996). Officials from the Federal government's control bureau complained that it was nearly impossible to get the resources and information necessary to monitor privatization.[20] Pavel Hájek, chief of the Prague Bureau of Investigation department that deals specifically with corporate crime, remarked, "Since the Velvet Revolution, mechanisms for controlling economic criminality have been basically eliminated" (quoted in Lešenarová and Reed 1997, 17). A 1993 law ended the independence from government meddling of the Control Office, once and for all (Müller 1994, 11). Milan Pohanka, head of the Legal Department of the Supreme Audit Office of the Czech Republic, concluded simply, "There are no control mechanisms in the privatization process" (quoted in Reed 1996, 65).

- The fourth aspect of the honor system was that the losing claimants would lack recourse. The Large Privatization Law is written so that no one takes legal (or even political) responsibility for a controversial privatization, such as occurred when the Ministry of Privatization sold an enterprise for a strangely cheap price. For example, Nestlé could only grit its teeth when it bought shares in the Czech company Čokoládovny at one price, while a Czech investor (IPB) was purchasing Čokoládovny shares at a fraction of Nestlé's price. Ježek stated later that the IPB purchase came as the product of an "administrative error." Concerning recourse for losing claimants, the crucial question was recourse to whom?

The Czech privatizers extended the honor system as Klaus's popularity grew. A 1992 amendment to the Large Privatization Law brought privatization decision-makers beyond the reach of the courts. "General determinations emanating from administrative proceedings do not concern a privatization decision. The privatization decision is not subject to review by a court" (zákon č. 210/1993, Sb., Section 10, Paragraph 3). Previously, privatization decisions had been reversed or delayed by the courts, as in the cases of Obalex Děčin and Karlovarský Porcelán (Reed 1996, 61). That same 1992 amendment also removed the privatizers from public accountability. It states flatly, "Privatization decision-making is not public" (zákon č. 210/1993, Sb., Section 10, Paragraph 4). The privatizers legalized what had previously been illegal or, in the best case, extralegal in order to discourage outside interference (Reed 1996, 61).

The Czech honor system aroused the popular suspicion that many state officials were corrupted and that the privatization system was rotten. One common speculation was that privatization benefited "dirty money," including money laundered from criminal activities. Klaus and Ježek's frequent public assertions that "money is money" did nothing to assuage those suspicions. Another common speculation was that the conflict of interests of privatizers and bureaucrats were regular and pernicious. Finally, outsiders speculated that political parties were lining their coffers with privatization bribes. The persistent and largely successful efforts of privatizers, bureaucrats, and their allies in the Parliament to postpone toothy "dirty money," conflict of interest, and party financing legislation lent credence to that speculation (Reed 1996, 68). The profusion of scandals in the coming years confirmed that privatization had proceeded unfairly.

The Czech honor system was partly a policy of circumstances and neoliberal ideology, despite the sinister, antidemocratic overtones. Consider, for instance, the 1992 amendment that removed the courts as a check on the privatization approval process. The then-existing Czech court system was dysfunctional. Courts and judges were horribly overburdened by an explosion of civil litigation cases. Privatization cases threatened to clog the system for years; privatization would then be stalled, perhaps indefinitely. That would be a disaster for rapid privatization. In the cases that would come before the courts, the judges were patently incapable of ruling on complicated cases involving market issues. The judges were as inexperienced in market rules and practices as the rest of the society. Neoliberals were probably right when they argued that courts were the wrong forum to adjudicate privatization disputes. The view that the Czech honor system was more than political chicanery for personal enrichment emphasizes the importance of neoliberal principles in the exercise of Czech privatization.

How did the ministry of privatization choose among competing projects? Or posed differently, the question is: Given the time demands on the privatizers in the Ministry of Privatization and the honor system, what criteria did they use to select privatization methods for enterprise stakes?

The first answer is that Ježek's Ministry of Privatization favored privatization projects that devoted large ownership stakes to voucher privatization over those that emphasized standard privatization methods; state officials had warned enterprise managers earlier that this would be an important approval criterion. The Ministry of Privatization followed the prior agreement of Ježek and the Federal Finance Ministry that at least 140 bn CZK ($5.0 bn) in enterprise book value would be privatized through vouchers in the first wave. It actually allotted over 200 bn CZK ($7.1 bn) in enterprise book value to vouchers in the first wave and another 155 bn CZK ($5.5 bn) in the second wave.[21] That was nearly half the asset value of all property targeted for large privatization.

In deciding between projects that proposed standard privatization methods, the Ministry of Privatization officials claimed to prefer projects with a "sensible" business plan. As always, what qualified as "sensible" was a matter of taste and political influence. Founding ministry recommendations and the recommendations of the District Privatization Councils (which purportedly knew well the local claimants and the conditions of the enterprise) factored into decisions of Ministry of Privatization officials (Macháček 1992).[22] By and large, the Ministry of Privatization looked askance at market privatization proposals, which might lead to a return by the former communist management, asset stripping, or to a "flip" sale to foreigners.[23]

In interviews and in the press, Ministry of Privatization officials made great pains to assert their immunity from outside influence, including collusion. But given the time pressures, the sheer volume of paperwork, and also the lack of market experience and honesty of many Ministry of Privatization officials, it is imaginable that they were influenced far more than they have admitted. Collusion was definitely a problem, though no one is sure about its reach. Klvačová, a former deputy ministry of privatization, described the pressures of the unsupervised supply-side procedures:

> The absence of rules has regular results: a perpetual state of siege for everyone who reviews and decides about projects; continuous persuasion of decision-makers by arguments and promises of future advantages; evident desperation and arrogance of decision-makers in dealing with authors of projects and their spokesman; escapes of authors or projects to less accessible places and locked doors; the fulfillment or unfulfillment of attempts at corruption; and, court disputes. (Klvačová 1992, 19)

Personal gain motivated some privatization bureaucrats. Benefits came as bribes or as promises of future employment. Senior ministry officials openly admitted that some of the junior members of the ministry were not of the highest moral fiber.[24] Yet, the constant stream of scandals in the coming years indicated moral turpitude at the senior level.[25] Ježek dismissed one senior privatization ministry official, M. Křmář, for suspicious dealings; and, Muroň, Ježek's right hand and deputy minister of privatization, resigned over (never proved) accusations of corruption.

The following anecdote illustrates how claimants could infiltrate the privatization bureaucracy. When it came time to privatize the Czech Republic's cement businesses, among the most valuable assets in the country, a man with a business card claiming to be an expert from the European Union showed up at the door of the Ministry of Privatization to volunteer his services. For the next several weeks, this man allegedly participated in the formation of privatization policy at the Ministry of Privatization. All seemed to be in order. The problem came when, on a visit to the European Union in Brussels, one of the senior privatization advisors learned that this man was a fraud. He was not in the employ of the European Union. Having learned of the deception, the advisor immediately tried to rectify the situation by having the man removed from the Ministry of Privatization—but without success. The man had ingratiated himself with the bureaucrats to the point where they defended his contribution. So he remained. In the end, the cement companies were sold to foreign investors, and for a song. As for the mysterious advisor, he vanished, and was never heard from again.[26] It would, however, be unfair to say that Ministry of Privatization decisions were based wholly or even largely on the results of collusion. The truth is that no one knows collusion's extent. It was, though, apparent that the pressure of having to decide quickly combined with the access points in the system biased Ministry of Privatization officials toward privatization projects submitted by enterprise managers.

The managers' greatest advantage was enterprise information. In noncommunist economies, enterprises usually display meaningful and documented histories of profit and loss, of past investment, of projected investment, and of book value for gauging corporate value and prospects. By contrast, standard benchmarks were often meaningless in the transition period. Enterprises had recently operated in an environment where market prices were largely beside the point. Most enterprises had never bothered to keep accurate books. During the transition, the enterprise managers invented financial data to create a self-interested picture of the enterprise. No one knew the better. And, to the extent it existed, reliable enterprise information thinned out as the privatization project moved from enterprise to founding industry to Ministry of Privatization. Muroň, Ježek's close deputy, called the protection of information the "most delicate aspect of privatization" (quoted in Marek 1991, 3). How in good conscience could the founding ministry or the Ministry of Privatization claim to know a better method of privatization than that proposed by the enterprise manager? Especially when—thanks to the information bias— the management-submitted projects were often far more comprehensive and sensible then competing projects?[27]

Time pressure swelled the enterprise managers' information advantages. It translated into a lack of direction and a lack of supervision from top personnel at the Ministry of Privatization.[28] Although the bureaucrats took two months to evaluate projects for the first wave instead of the fifteen days originally allotted by the *Harmonogram*, there were sometimes only minutes to devote to an individual project. The bureaucrats in the Ministry of Privatization tried to mitigate this problem by organizing themselves into branches corresponding to the founding ministries.[29] Yet the decentralization of decision-making meant that Ježek and his senior deputies were dependent on the judgment of the ministry staff. And the staff was vulnerable to collusion on the one hand, and it didn't have the training or experience necessary to judge privatization proposals on the other hand. In practice, Ježek would formally approve projects that he knew virtually nothing about.

Predictably, most of the projects Ježek approved were submitted disproportionately by enterprise managers. Central enterprise management or plant managers submitted 24.3 percent of the total number of privatization projects; manager projects accounted for 87.5 percent of those approved by the Ministry of Privatization. Outsiders—including potential buyers—submitted 48.2 percent of the total number of privatization projects; outsider projects consisted of only 7.4 percent of those approved by the Ministry of Privatization (see

Table 7.2. Claimant Success Rates in Privatization Project Approvals

Claimant	Share in Submitted Projects	Share in Approved Projects
Enterprise Management	21.3	81.8
Plant Managers	3.0	5.7
Consulting Firms	2.3	1.9
Outsiders, Potential Buyers	48.2	7.4
Restituents	2.7	0.9
Municipalities	7.2	0.4
Others	15.3	1.8
Total	100.0	99.9

Source: Zemplínerová and Laštovička 1997, 208.
Note: These figures include second-wave statistics. The first-wave breakdown of 11,252 submitted projects was management, 25%; plant managers, 4%; consulting firms, 3%; potential buyers or outsiders, 39%; restituents, 4%; others 14%; commissions, 7%; and, regional bodies, 4%.

table 7.2).[30] Enterprise managers controlled their destiny far more than Czech privatizers admit. The privatization flowchart (figure 7.1) that shows the state as the unchallenged authority is therefore misleading, much as it was in central planning.

In concluding this section, I should note that the simple fact that the enterprise managers shaped the privatization of their enterprises did not by itself determine that the new ownership regime would be dominated by rich enterprise

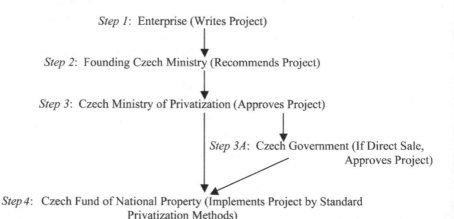

Step 1: Enterprise (Writes Project)

Step 2: Founding Czech Ministry (Recommends Project)

Step 3: Czech Ministry of Privatization (Approves Project)

Step 3A: Czech Government (If Direct Sale, Approves Project)

Step 4: Czech Fund of National Property (Implements Project by Standard Privatization Methods)

OR

Ministry of Finance (Implements Project by Voucher Privatization)

Figure 7.1. The Typical Path of a Successful Privatization Project: From Origination to Approval to Implementation.

managers intent on restructuring companies. First, as we noted above, close to half of the property bound for privatization went to voucher privatization. Second, the privatization methods that managers favored did not specify the conditions under which managers could assume ownership. In some cases, they ended up as "losers" in a game of their own choosing. For example, though some managers proposed and later took advantage of market privatization, they ended up buying enterprise stakes at inflated prices. In the process, they borrowed money from the banks that they couldn't pay back. Many of these enterprises bankrupted; virtually none restructured. Still, the enterprise managers were active privatization participants, contrary to conventional wisdom.

Exceptions to Neoliberalism

Naysayers to the argument that the neoliberals were ideologically motivated point to the fact that the state retained ownership of large amounts of property and also that state bureaucracies operated a closet industrial policy.[31] Without disputing these facts, I argue instead that they were the results of neoliberal pragmatism in combination with genuine confusion. The essence of neoliberalism in CEECs was its flexibility in making compromises over "minor" issues so that the main liberalization policies would progress. Moreover, we should not make too much of policy inconsistencies when both political and economic outcomes were uncertain.

The State Claimant: Incomplete Privatization

Surprisingly, the Ministry of Privatization, an institution designed to eliminate the state, entrusted controlling enterprise stakes to the Fund of National Property. Overall, the Fund of National Property, the repository for nearly all state shares, retained shareholdings in 1,426 (82 percent) of the enterprises privatized by the end of the second wave in December 1994.[32]

The state kept most enterprise stakes for innocent reasons—for modest employee share purchases, for foreign strategic investors, for former owners, or for private farmers. The Ministry of Privatization also assigned the state shares based on the wishes of management, who hoped to control large stakes. In "family jewels" such as beer producers, the Czech neoliberals argued that the state should be a partial owner partly to satisfy the incumbent management and partly to appeal to Czech nationalism. Although neoliberal best practice would contradict the state's residual shareholdings, the transgression is minor compared with the whole privatization endeavor.

Perhaps more substantial, but on the whole understandable, were the controlling stakes the state maintained in "strategic enterprises." The state owned at least a 46 percent share in fourteen of the twenty largest Czech industrial enterprises as of the middle of 1996 (ING Bank Archive, cited in *MFD*, May 25, 1996, 15).[33] The residual share portfolio ensured that the Czech state's ownership role in the economy would endure, in spite of the Czech government's rabid emphasis on private sector development. On the other hand, the Czech government's portfolio of banks, airlines, coal mines, steelmakers, power companies, and the like puts it in a class of economies such as France or Italy, economies that are hardly of the Soviet state–socialist variety. Privatization in the Czech Republic was not finished, but it was substantial.

Czech Privatization and Industrial Policy

Ministry of Privatization bureaucrats used privatization as a vehicle to restructure enterprises, contrary to neoliberal dogma, which rejected state intervention. They invariably dissolved enterprises into constituent parts:[34] many enterprises had been messy amalgams of unrelated businesses that enterprises had accumulated over four decades of communism. The Ministry of Privatization sometimes separated out economically unsalvageable divisions and unpayable debts from enterprises to facilitate privatization.[35] A prototypical case was Poldi Kladno—incidentally, now bankrupt. Poldi Kladno was composed of nineteen divisions including a heating plant, an engineering consultancy, a trucking company, and the country's most famous steelworks. The bureaucrats subdivided Poldi Kladno into separate companies. The data confirm that enterprise splitting was common ministry practice. The Ministry of Privatization's decisions were part of a shadow government policy of industrial restructuring.[36] No doubt that this minimal level of restructuring was sensible (see table 7.3).

Perhaps the most hitting charge of heresy against the neoliberals concerned the use of privatization revenues to shore up the banks (see table 7.4). In 1992, the Fund of National Property recapitalized Czech and Slovak banks by 50 bn CZK in the form of five-year bonds (8 percent of all bank credits to enterprises). By October 1993, the fund had transferred to the large banks (and the state Consolidation Bank) 65 percent of large privatization revenues (77 percent of expenses) or 5.2 percent of GNP. These privatization transfers were part of a wider policy to support the banks.[37]

To be sure, the Czech government's financial support of banks resembled the German approach rather than the U.S.-British one. And, I don't believe that it can be explained away by claims of pragmatism—"the banks will go bankrupt, causing disaster." It is patently inconsistent with neoliberalism. With that said, I also don't believe that the Czech government's bank policy negates

Table 7.3. Enterprise Splitting in Privatization

Industry	Number of Enterprises Prior to Approval of Privatization Projects	Number of Enterprises Following Approval of Privatization Projects
Ferrous metallurgy	20	51
Nonferrous metallurgy	16	50
Chemical and rubber	57	131
Machinery	303	676
Electronics	74	212
Building materials	119	280
Wood-processing industry	81	230
Metal products	18	41
Paper and cellulose	22	84
Glass, china, and ceramics	55	159
Textiles	94	409
Apparel	23	72
Leather	19	72
Printing and publishing	31	50
Food processing	198	683
Other	49	93
Total	1,179	3,293

Source: Zemplínerová and Stíbal 1997, 237.

the main thrust of privatization, that of creating first private owners. After privatization, however, the government's bank policy emerged as more than just a side issue. And it is at that point that the neoliberals' credentials must be seriously questioned, not before. Chapter 9 addresses this issue in detail.

Table 7.4. Debt Clearance and Recapitalization for Selected Banks by Bonds Issued by the Fund of National Property, 1991–1993

	Debt Clearance in 1991 (billion CZK)	Recapitalization in 1991 (billion CZK)	Recapitalization in 1992 (billion CZK)	Recapitalization in 1993 (billion CZK)
KB	15.0	0.6	13.0	–
IPB	2.7	2.3	10.2	–
ČS	–	3.8	–	1
ČSOB	2.2	1.1	–	–
Konsolidační banka	2.3	–	–	16 + 3 (reserves)
TOTAL	22.2	7.8	23.2	20

Source: Mejstřík 1997, 149.

NEOLIBERAL POLITICAL TACTICS

Remarkably, the public seemed satisfied, even gratified, by the privatization supply-side preparations in 1991 and 1992. With the help of a cooperative and "passive" (Češka, quoted in *Respekt*, 1991) media, the privatizers were able to convince most Czechs (and nearly all foreign observers) that the supply-side of privatization was a huge success, warts and all.[38]

Privatization's rave reviews were due partly to the neoliberal convictions of the journalists and the naïveté of the Western analysts and the Czech public. The favorable press supported "distancing"—the conscious strategy of government officials to insulate policy creation and policy implementation from public scrutiny. A government that conducts policy hidden from the public, that is above the law, that offers no recourse to the wronged, and that sabotages all intragovernment efforts at control is evidence of successful "distancing." One could also rightly assert that it is evidence of a society and state that are not democratic. The Czech privatizers' creation of the supply-side privatization honor system was a manifestation of distancing.

Another dimension of "distancing" was the calculated public arrogance of the Czech neoliberals. The rhetoric of the renowned privatizers—Klaus, Ježek, and Tříska—was punctuated by occasional bizarreness. Klaus, for instance, claimed that the question wasn't whether the Czech Republic was ready to join the European Union, but whether the European Union was ready to join the Czech Republic. Extreme arrogance of the Czech sort seems fitting for the British tabloids, not for reformers of transition economies. The privatizers' extreme arrogance earned the name the "Czech Syndrome": "The Czech Syndrome is manifest in the inability of dialogue [between opposing sides] and it is manifest by the psychologically urgent need to stick a label of enemy on one's opponents or to say 'Go to Hell' to anyone who thinks otherwise, so that no one will be engaged" (Palouš 1997, 10).

It easy to overlook the political ramifications of Czech arrogance through all of the boasting and the name-calling. The privatizers' political objective was to pound their philosophy into the popular belief system and to convince the West of their own ideological purity. Theirs was the arrogance of a neoliberal pantheon—Hayek, Friedman, and Thatcher. The privatizers were liberal economists, and therefore only they, the privatizers, were capable of interpreting the great texts. The Czech privatizers distanced themselves from potential opposition by asserting a monopoly on truth, much like priests who preached the Holy Scriptures to the unenlightened flock. There was no room for a difference of opinion. Disagreement was patently absurd and due to the excesses of the past, immoral. The privatizers' message to the public was paternalistic—"Stay away. Only we can manage economic reform. Trust us to be competent and fair. You will reap the benefits." The striking success of the arrogance tactic was manifest both in the marginalization of the political opposition and the passivity of the Czech population toward economic reform. Of the latter, some say that the "distancing" tactic reinforces a centuries-old Czech cultural trait, a Švejk-like resignation to the unassailable power of outsiders.[39]

From a political tactics vantage, the Czech neoliberals preferred to grant concessions to potential opponents as individual entities rather than as organized interests. Thus the privatizers refused to satisfy the public demands of the enterprise managers' major association to subordinate the voucher privatization. On the other hand, the privatizers simultaneously chose to mollify individual enterprise managers by offering them input in the supply-side tasks.[40] Klaus epitomized the neoliberal political approach in his tribute to the postwar German reformer, Ludwig Erhard:

> Erhard understood, consistent with German orthodox-liberalism, that the role of the state was to defend the interests of the *entire society* against the *particular interests* of strong and organized societal groups. He knew that democracy and the market system were creating a substantial area and perhaps too lively a ground for the rise and activity of such groups and for their ability to pressure the state. The pressure on the state would be only to the benefit of their own particular interest to the detriment of all citizens. (Klaus 1997, 45)

Yet the core of Czech neoliberalism is not its arrogant liberalism nor its political tactics, but its seemingly contradictory claims on pragmatism. Czech neoliberals argued that real-world politics and economics forced them to make short-run choices that seemed contradictory to liberal philosophy. In this view, transition inherently is unpredictable and evolutionary. Neoliberal economic reform strategy admits to no blueprint, but only to a liberal philosophy or ideology. It also does not admit to accountability. It was acceptable for the privatizers to make pragmatic accommodations to potentially antagonistic claimants in order to achieve long-run liberal objectives. The core of neoliberalism is its blend of pragmatism and ideology.

Consider how the pragmatic side of the privatizers' neoliberalism applied to supply-side policymaking. Privatization was designed to usurp enterprise decision-making power from the enterprise managers and turn that power over to the market, or to be specific, to the new owners. Almost universally, analysts believed that the threat of a free market would turn the enterprise managers into opponents of privatization. Instead, the Czech supply-side privatization procedures transformed the enterprise managers into allies by offering them a stake in the next regime. As testimony to the success of Czech neoliberalism, we can observe a dramatic change in orientation by the Czech Confederation of Industry, the organization of large enterprise managers founded by that implacable opponent of voucher privatization, M. Grégr. As privatization unfolded and the managers' association changed leadership, the Czech Confederation of Industry's originally acerbic antigovernment rhetoric became conciliatory.[41] Similarly, we can observe active cooperation between Vrba's Ministry of Trade and Industry and Ježek's Ministry of Privatization during the privatization preparations.[42] The neoliberals made it more profitable for the managers to work within the neoliberal privatization system rather than to fight it. The blooming relationships between government and business started in the supply-side stage paved the way for antidemocratic practice to continue after privatization.

CONCLUSION

The analysis of the supply-side tasks shows that the most serious threats to the neoliberal agenda in the Czech Republic did not arise from special interests who would oppose reform for self-interested reasons, nor did they emanate from a public that would lose from market reforms. The threats of unemployment or price increases that play such a prominent role in other analyses are somewhat beside the point in the Czech case. In the Czech Republic, ideological persuasion substituted for economic prosperity as a short-term expedient.

The pregnant threat to the neoliberal agenda in the Czech Republic instead loomed in the countless hidden accommodations to claimants who may have welcomed the onset of markets on propitious terms. The immediate consequence of accommodation was a privatization policy that was delayed, biased, and incomplete. The longer term consequence was an ownership regime characterized by collusion between bureaucrats, moneymen, and enterprise managers, by first private owners who would be unable and unwilling to restructure enterprises, and by a fractured enterprise ownership structure. In this way, the Czech neoliberal privatization strategy ensured that the Czech ownership regime would encourage the emergence of plutocrats rather than modern capitalists and democrats. Ultimately, the accommodations made in the supply-side tasks (and later in implementation) brought down the neoliberal government and Václav Klaus.

Analysis of the Czech neoliberal supply-side strategy reveals that the central tension is not between neoliberals and Social Democrats or between rapid privatization advocates and gradualists. Rather, the contest is between neoliberals and state builders, or between a captured state and a capitalist state, or between modern Western capitalism and plutocratic market development. These themes echo still louder in the analysis of the implementation of privatization, and especially in the implementation of voucher privatization, the centerpiece of the entire reform agenda in the Czech Republic.

NOTES

1. A similar process was underway in Slovakia at this time.

2. The contrast with Germany, the one regional exception, could not have been sharper. German expertise and money enabled the state privatization agency, the *treuhandanstalt*, to close and to restructure thousands of Eastern German enterprises.

3. Also based on author interview with an advisor to Havel.

4. After December 1994, the case that the Czech reformers had largely abandoned neoliberalism for selfish interests is more persuasive. Indeed, I will argue in the following chapters that the Czech reformers' corruption of neoliberalism probably is rooted in the antidemocratic precedents and illicit connections established during the supply-side tasks and implementation.

5. This was a modified version of the 1990 spontaneous privatizations in the Czech Republic. At that time, enterprise managers and division managers separated valuable subsidiaries from the whole. The number of enterprises doubled or tripled in some industries (Zemplínerová and Laštovička 1997). Spontaneous privatization took place throughout the former communist world, most notably in Hungary and Poland.

6. This rationale was well understood by the Czech reformers, and it was the basis for withholding the right of privatization approvals from the founding ministries. It was one thing for the enterprises to have the power to propose enterprise privatization, but quite another thing to decide (through the founding ministries) the enterprise privatization.

7. The official name of the Czech Ministry of Privatization is the *Ministry for the Administration of the National Property and Its Privatization of the Czech Republic*. This unwieldy name grew out of the 1990 compromise between the Czech neoliberal reformers who emphasized privatization and those supporters in the Czech government (spearheaded by F. Vlasák, then–deputy head of the Czech government) who emphasized the need for a state agency to administer state enterprises prior to privatization. The ensuing long name combines both points of view (author interview with privatization officials).

8. Author interview with privatization officials.

9. One study has shown that the first wave attracted relatively larger enterprises, more profitable enterprises, and enterprises in branches with relatively more competitive structures than were privatized later (Buchtíková and Čapek 1993, 21–22). Nonetheless, many analysts estimated that as many as a third of first-wave enterprises may have entered the first-wave program functionally insolvent.

10. Usually, the greatest interest of the enterprise managers was in avoiding having their enterprises hived off and sold in pieces in the small privatization auctions. Only

by keeping the enterprise in one piece could the managers hope to control enterprise assets in the postprivatization phase.

11. The power of the district committees was derived from the Small Privatization Law, which stated that an asset only can be included in large privatization if a district committee has not included it in small privatization (Husák 1997, 138).

12. Enterprise managers could and did propose privatization projects alongside the official enterprise privatization project. Sometimes they hid their involvement in competitive projects.

13. Ironically, the idea of a competitive project was Tříska's (author interview with privatization officials).

14. Author interview with member of parliament.

15. This struggle was most evident in the first weeks of November as policy opinions became more pronounced. See, for example, the debate in *Respekt* 1991 between Jurečka and Češka.

16. It was also during this period that Klaus and Tříska introduced the "97 and 3" campaign as a means to pressure Ježek into abandoning his circumspect privatization approach (Husák 1997, 155).

17. The approval process actually began before the January 20 deadline for project submission. Ježek reports a three-way discussion including J. Stráský (then-vice-prime minister of the Czech government) and Baránek in which enterprises were identified that would not be receiving competitive projects. The assignment of privatization methods began immediately for these enterprises (Husák 1997, 161).

18. Typically, the amount of vouchers in a privatization project was raised upward. This action was part of the Ministry of Privatization's policy to encourage vouchers as opposed to other privatization methods.

19. The law was amended in July 1993 to allow "the responsible organ to change the conditions, extent, and method of privatization contained in the proposed privatization project." Moreover, the Fund of National Property can adjust a privatization project when the condition of the enterprise significantly differs from that presumed when the original privatization decision was reached (zákon č. 210/1993, Sb., Section 10, paragraphs 6–8).

20. Author interview.

21. The Slovak Ministry of Privatization agreed to privatize 70 bn CZK of book value via vouchers. It actually privatized 79 bn CZK of book value via vouchers.

22. Also based on author interviews with Ministry of Privatization officials.

23. The fear of sale to foreigners was particularly sensitive in the so-called family silver enterprises. The state considered these enterprises very close to the Czech heart. Family silver enterprises included producers of beer, glassware, porcelain, and jewelry. In some cases, a "flip" sale occurred anyway, despite the original protestations of the first owners.

24. Author interviews.

25. For now, I will short-list the enterprises that made Czech headlines in the ensuing years in connection with questionable privatizations: Knižní velkoobchod (bookseller), Rakona rakovník (consumer products), V. J. Rott (hardware), Karlovarský porcelán

(porcelain), Poldi Kladno (steel), Mlékárny klatovy (dairy), Čokoládovny (confectionery products). See Reed 1996 for detailed information on these and other cases.

26. Author interview with advisor at the Ministry of Privatization.

27. Successful competing projects usually incorporated the input of management or former management.

28. Another factor that exacerbated the time pressure on the Ministry of Privatization was that many projects were incomplete or filled out incorrectly. This was the case despite the fact (or, in some cases, due to the fact) that the founding ministries and outside consulting firms often were involved in the checking and preparation of projects (author interview with privatization officials).

29. Large privatization was organized on a branch principle while small privatization was conducted on a regional principle. In small privatization, the critical actors were the regional privatization committees, not the Ministry of Privatization, as under large privatization.

30. I must repeat here the warning that the figures in table 7.2 may be misleading, even though the conclusion is not. One factor, as noted in the text, is that enterprise managers may have been represented surreptitiously in other projects. In a survey of 257 projects, the privatization agencies approved 62 percent of the projects submitted by managers against only 17.3 percent submitted by other parties (Kotrba 1994, 15).

31. Some analysts add another factor, namely the postponement until 1993 of bankruptcy legislation passed by the Parliament in 1991.

32. The FNP still owned shares in 968 enterprises, as of April 22, 1996 (Schwartz 1997).

33. The state share does not include shares held by local governments, which in certain cases (for example, the gas and electric distribution companies) can be substantial.

34. Large privatization was hardly the only means that enterprises were subdivided. Small privatization was another device, as were the aggressive spontaneous privatization practices of many enterprise managers.

35. These enterprise fragments (*zbytkové podniky*) often became the administrative duty of the appropriate branch ministry, usually the Ministry of Industry and Trade (Tůma and Dotson 1995, 1–3).

36. One of the most important such choices concerned the dispensation of privatization revenue. The Czech reformers decided to use the privatization revenue to retire old debts and to finance the banks. In this way, the Czech reformers practiced a de facto policy of industrial targeting.

37. In addition, the state offered credit guarantees for particularly risky loans; other loans were removed from the bank's books, typically by the state Consolidation Bank. The state also has supported banks by postponing potentially destabilizing bankruptcy legislation. Finally, the state has consciously protected the (large) domestic banks by carefully controlling the issuance of bank licenses. Careful monitoring has allowed the large banks protection both from small domestic start-ups and from foreign competition (Schwartz 1997).

38. The public's enthusiasm for Czech-style privatization was also aided by the beginning of voucher program privatization at this time. Voucher privatization

promised that all Czechs would share in the pie as owners. In the fall of 1991, the government began its distribution of coupon books; and in January 1992, egged on by the promotions of voucher investment funds that promised manifold returns, the public jumped into ownership with both feet.

39. This is a common theme of the famous Czech cartoonist V. Renčin.

40. The privatizers locked out union ambitions for ownership—as noted earlier, Section 158 of the Czech Commercial Code limited employee ownership preferences to a maximum of 10 percent of the total shares outstanding. Indeed, the most visible neoliberal concession to unions throughout the first years of economic reform was the creation of a tripartite commission, which largely turned out to be a sham.

41. Author interview with association officials.

42. Author interview with privatization officials.

8

Implementing the Ownership Regime— February 1991 to December 1995

How would the state qualify, recruit, and register claimants? Which criteria would the state use to admit some claimants, but exclude others? Would the state offer privileges to foreigners or would the state discriminate against them? Which bureaucracies would implement privatization? How would the state regulate implementation? The central argument of this chapter is that *how* the state implemented privatization determined the ownership regime after privatization.

The centerpiece of Czech rapid privatization and the basis of the country's miracle reputation was *voucher privatization*. The Czechs claimed to have solved the riddle that had puzzled other former communist countries—how to transform poor people into owners, and fast. Czech voucher privatization was a centralized means to distribute enterprise stakes quickly and fairly to citizens; it excluded managers, workers, and foreigners.

The evidence shows a mixed picture. Czech voucher privatization achieved its primary objective—the rapid privatization of the economy. By the end of 1995, approximately 70 percent of GNP was produced by the private sector. In addition, the regime and the neoliberal politicians in charge had obtained wide popularity. On the other hand, Czech voucher privatization had generated a specific ownership regime of first owners, a first-ownership structure, capital market institutions, and state regulatory capacity and autonomy that would prove inimical to capitalism and democracy. Czech voucher privatization illustrates why and how neoliberal strategies may yield specific ownership structures and weak states, and therefore weak markets.

The evidence regarding voucher privatization covers three implementation phases—the preparation of voucher privatization (February 1991 to September 1991), the preliminary stage of the first wave (October 1991 to April 1992), and two privatization waves (May 1992 to December 1994). It shows that the reformers conducted voucher privatization in a centralized format, in haste, with a readiness to compromise with politically influential claimants and court Czech public opinion. Furthermore, it shows how rapid privatization produced a very specific ownership regime that was likely to undermine the quality of democracy and capitalism.

Similarly, the chapter shows that the Czech government's implementation of standard privatization methods also was likely to undermine the quality of democracy and capitalism. Surprisingly, the Czech Fund of National Property still held title to over 32.6 percent of the large-scale ownership stakes by December 1995, including major stakes in the country's strategic enterprises. The Czech state administered its ownership stakes and privatized ownership stakes virtually without oversight, without a coherent strategy, and without regard for the law. That is, the state operated standard privatization in a manner consistent with rapid privatization principles. The Czech implementation of standard privatization methods showed how decentralized privatization conducted without regard to state autonomy and capacity may undermine future attempts at enterprise restructuring and at developing an honest and capable state bureaucracy.

THE PREPARATION OF VOUCHER PRIVATIZATION, FEBRUARY 1991 TO SEPTEMBER 1991

A small team led by Tříska supervised voucher privatization preparations in parallel with the Ministry of Privatization's (Tomáš Ježek was the minister) execution of the supply-side tasks.[1] Voucher preparations consisted of a registration procedure for eligible citizens, an information system to disseminate enterprise data and voucher privatization procedures to citizens, and a pricing mechanism for enterprise shares. They also included legal provisions for the inclusion of intermediaries: investment privatization funds or IPFs. Czech voucher preparations were designed to create a fast and fair distribution system of enterprise shares to all citizens.

Voucher preparations were centralized. Tříska managed the demand-side preparations with only a small network. Three graduate students in mathematics comprised Tříska's core staff. Moreover, key decision-making was centralized in the Federal Ministry of Finance, where Tříska was a deputy minister. Ježek, by contrast, oversaw a complex decision-making hierarchy that included enterprise managers, founding ministries, and privatization bureaucrats. In addition, the neoliberals were relatively free of claimant pressures. The significant voucher privatization beneficiaries were masses who were willing to let the government manage privatization. The others were IPFs, which didn't yet exist. Enterprise managers, ministry officials, moneymen, management consultants, and political operatives were otherwise preoccupied in "helping" the Ministry of Privatization and other government agencies approve privatization projects. The isolation of Tříska's team immunized voucher privatization from scandals—to the degree his small team was honest. Finally, Tříska prepared voucher privatization out of the public eye. Tříska's proprietary approach exemplified the neoliberal tactic of distancing.[2] The public would leave Tříska alone so long as the voucher preparations were complete by the deadlines or, as it would happen, when Ježek's Ministry of Privatization supply-side tasks were complete.

Voucher preparations also were rushed. Tříska adjusted his system on the fly and he made changes with little regard for equity or for the law. Improvisation was the rule. A significant omission concerned the regulation of IPFs, the intermediaries designed to collect citizen voucher points. The danger in the omission didn't become clear until after privatization, when IPFs blocked corporate restructuring, foreign capital, and stock market regulation.

Voucher preparations were essential to the *public* political interests of the privatizers. Tříska's team appealed to the masses by producing what appeared to be an honest, efficient means to distribute state ownership stakes quickly and fairly. The result was extraordinary public satisfaction with voucher privatization and a decisive neoliberal political victory in the June 1992 elections.

THE AUCTION SYSTEM OF DUŠAN TŘÍSKA

The core of Tříska's voucher distribution system was the pricing mechanism for enterprise shares. True to his market principles and his background as a mathematically oriented economist, Tříska devised a computerized auction system to match the preferences of voucher holders with the price of enterprise shares.

Tříska's auction system was complex. From the voucher holder vantage, the objective of this game was to buy enterprise shares at the lowest price. Voucher holders received 1,000 voucher points as a starting stake. The voucher holder bid her voucher points on enterprises, according to prices set by Tříska's computer or by a pricing commission.[3] The voucher holder's success would depend on the demand of other voucher holders. If the total demand was high, then the voucher holder's bid would not be satisfied; if the total demand was low, then the voucher holder's bid would be satisfied. In the latter case, the voucher holder would become a shareholder; in the former case, the voucher holder would have to bid her points again, in a future round.[4]

Tříska conceived the auctions as a series of iterative rounds. After the first round, enterprise prices would be reset according to the revealed voucher holder preferences of the prior round. Eventually, the price of the enterprise and the preference of the voucher holders would match and the supply of enterprise shares and the supply of voucher points would clear (see table 8.1).

Table 8.1.   The Privatization Rounds of Tříska's Auction System

1. In the first auction round, the state assigns all enterprise shares the same price. The voucher holders then express their preference for enterprise ownership by bidding their voucher points (up to 1,000) for particular enterprise shares.
2. If the resulting demand for an enterprise is higher by over 25% of the offered supply of shares, then the enterprise is considered oversubscribed. In this case, the demanding voucher holders are issued no shares.
3. If the resulting demand for an enterprise is lower then the offered supply of shares, then the enterprise is considered undersubscribed. In this case, the demanding voucher holders are assigned shares.
4. If the resulting demand for an enterprise equals (or is not over 25% higher than) the offered supply of shares, then the enterprise is considered fully subscribed. The market clears, and the state issues all the enterprise shares.
5. Shares remaining from the oversubscribed and undersubscribed enterprises are then repriced, as adjusted according to a computer algorithm based on the demand in the first auction round.
6. The shares, with the recalculated prices, go on auction in the second auction round. The second auction round proceeds precisely as the first. The successive rounds proceed according to the first-round procedures.

THE PRELIMINARY STAGE OF THE FIRST WAVE, OCTOBER 1991 TO APRIL 1992

The main task prior to the first wave was the registration of claimants. The key issue revolved around eligibility, and this the Czech neoliberals handled in predictable style. To enhance public acceptance of privatization and to enhance their own political stature, they set wide eligibility requirements and excluded foreigners. The population of eligible voucher participants was nearly identical with the population of eligible voters.

All over-eighteen Czech (then Czechoslovakian) residents were eligible to participate in voucher privatization. In addition, voucher privatization did not discriminate on the basis of income. A citizen did not have to be wealthy to participate in voucher privatization. The participation price was only 1,035 CZK (about $37), about a week's wage.[5] Moreover, voucher participants received the same basic information on the enterprises eligible for privatization.[6] Every Czech citizen presumably had an equal chance to pick winners (or losers). Finally, voucher privatization was a Czechoslovakian affair, at least for the first wave (the second wave took place after the split of the country). This meant that Czech and Slovak citizens were eligible to participate. In all, voucher privatization seemed fair to all Czechoslovakians.

Czech voucher privatization excluded foreigners, including Czech expatriates.[7] Why should foreigners be allowed to obtain Czech assets virtually for free? The controversial issue was whether the vouchers, prior to

Table 8.2. The Demand-Side Timetable

Task	Achieved Date
Government issues voucher privatization guidelines (zákon č. 393/1991, Sb.)	September 5, 1991
Sale of voucher books and stamps begins at post offices	October 1, 1991
Voucher registration for first wave begins	November 1, 1991
Voucher registration for first wave ends	February 17, 1992
Preround begins	March 1, 1992
Prewave ends	April 26, 1992
First wave begins	May 18, 1992

their conversion into shares, could be sold by Czechs to foreigners. Determined to keep privatization a domestic affair, the Czech reformers decided against voucher transferability.[8] Foreigners could only participate in Czech privatization through one of the other privatization methods.[9]

The New Players: Investment Privatization Funds

The only institutional players participating in voucher privatization were IPFs. The Czech privatizers designed IPFs to solve an economic puzzle. The mass distribution of vouchers promised to create thousands of shareholders for each enterprise. Who would manage the mass-owned enterprise? Who would provide the invigorating capital or technical expertise? Mass ownership of enterprises easily translated into no ownership of enterprises. Ironically, the corporate governance dilemma echoed the earlier concerns of the Czech government economists who had opposed voucher privatization in the elite approval stage.[10] The Czech privatizers encouraged the development of IPFs partly to ensure that enterprises would have active owners. IPFs would manage enterprises and add value by recruiting management experience, capital, and expertise. Alternatively, IPFs would sell share blocks to a strategic investor, a final owner, who would then restructure the enterprise for maximum profit.

The idea of a financial intermediary to concentrate ownership originated in the Polish version of voucher privatization (see Lewandowski and Szomburg 1989, chap. 3). The Polish schema is top-down. That is, the state creates the financial intermediaries. The Czechs imagined instead that market incentives would inspire entrepreneurs spontaneously to organize IPFs in order to capture profits from aggregating citizen vouchers into controlling enterprise stakes (Žák 1997, 16). The Czech schema is bottom-up. Consistent with market logic, Tříska wrote laws that placed liberal limits on the entry of IPFs. IPFs needed only 100,000 CZK (about $3,500) in basic capital in order to solicit vouchers.[11] Markets, not regulation, would determine the size and number of IPFs.

The Czechs tried to hedge bets on IPFs so that they wouldn't become dominant owners. One major hedge was a 20 percent limitation on IPF holdings in individual enterprises.[12] Privatizers worried that IPFs might acquire too much enterprise control. Simultaneously, the Czech privatizers restricted individual IPF shareholdings to no more than 10 percent of the total portfolio. The privatizers designed this restriction to force IPFs to diversify, and thereby to limit IPF vulnerability to the permutations of a single share issue (amendments 67/1992 and 69/1992).[13] Despite these regulations, the legal framework for IPFs must be considered liberal. It prompted 439 IPFs to register with the Ministry of Finance.

IPFs fit into two general categories. First, there were very well capitalized investment funds, typically financed by domestic banks or insurance companies.[14] *Bank IPFs* were attracted by the acquisition of valuable information about individual enterprises and by the fees they might earn by investing the voucher portfolios. Bank IPFs also entered the fund business because bank management saw other financial institutions getting involved. Evidently, the risk from being left out of voucher privatization was dangerous, though bank management often couldn't articulate why.[15] It should also be noted that the state owned (and still owns) controlling stakes in banks that happen to own the largest bank IPFs.[16] The state therefore retained a major ownership stake in the Czech economy through the bank IPFs. Moreover, many IPF fund managers were publicly recognizable as former *nomenklatura*, especially from the Ministry of Foreign Affairs. As we shall see in the remainder of this study, bank IPFs were controversial actors in Czech privatization and in the ensuing ownership regime.

Second, there were *nonbank IPFs*, financed by "who knows" or simply undercapitalized.[17] This category included V. Kožený's famous Harvard Capital and Consulting Company, which reportedly started with almost no capital. Presumably, the nonbank IPFs were attracted by the investment fees, and also by the possibility of collecting cheap assets from voucher holders and selling them to foreigners at close to fair market prices.[18] Perhaps because they were unaffiliated with a state institution, most nonbank IPFs operated closest to the legal fringe, as unregulated cowboys.

Harvard Saves the Day

IPFs burst onto the voucher scene in December 1991 and January 1992, when voucher privatization had the look of a potential disaster. On January 1, 1992, the number of registered voucher holders was shy of one million. The privatizers originally had hoped that four million Czechs (and Slovaks) would register for voucher privatization. Without many more participants, neoliberals presumed that voucher privatization would be a failure and that the reform agenda would die.

The saving catalyst for voucher privatization was the bold advertising campaign of a heretofore unknown company, Koženy's Harvard Capital and Consulting. Harvard guaranteed voucher holders ten times their original investment (1,035 CZK) in a year's time, if the voucher holder would entrust his or her 1,000 voucher points for investment to a Harvard IPF.[19]

The Harvard guarantee made perfect sense on its face. The estimated book value of the enterprises in voucher privatization for each 1,000 points was close to thirty times the cost of the voucher book. Harvard was promising to pay 10,035 CZK for assets valued at 30,000 CZK! The Harvard gamble seemed like no gamble at all. Skeptics, though, fretted that the enterprise book values vastly overstated the quality of the assets. Book value was not in any case market value. Could Harvard deliver on its promises?

The privatizers were wary about the Harvard guarantee. The strenuous efforts of some privatizers, especially Ježek, to vet voucher privatization of Harvard are well documented in the press. Reportedly, the minister of finance hired investigators to seek the source of Harvard's capital and to look into Koženy's background. Rumors about secret police ties and bribes swirled around Harvard. Nothing was proved publicly. Otherwise, the findings of the Harvard investigation are not public record.

Events overtook the privatizers. The Harvard guarantee galvanized voucher privatization.[20] The promise of a guaranteed profit of ten times grabbed public attention. Other funds matched or even exceeded Harvard's offer soon thereafter; some funds offered voucher holders fifteen times their original investment. Citizens rushed registration places in order to entrust their vouchers to IPFs. By December 16, 1991, about thirty thousand citizens per day were registering for voucher privatization; by January 20, 1990, over 500,000 Czechs and Slovaks were registering for voucher privatization (estimated from a report to Federal Parliament 1992). Over 8.5 million Czechs and Slovaks participated in voucher privatization by the time the fun had ended (Centrum kuponové privatizace [CKP] 1995, 26).[21]

Harvard had boosted the popularity of voucher privatization tremendously, and privatizers feared discrediting or antagonizing Harvard, especially since the June 1992 elections were on the horizon. Consequently, they refused to regulate sternly either Harvard or the other IPFs. The state did not force IPFs to reveal even rudimentary information, such as the identity of all the IPF managers or the IPF financial resources (Bláha et al. 1992).[22] Prior to February 1992, IPF regulations, such as they were, were bundled in government decrees (*nařízení vlády*) together with the general voucher procedures (zákon č. 383/1992 Sb. plus amendments). It wasn't until February 1992 that the Federal

Parliament passed a law (*zákon*) that founded legal bases for IPFs (zákon č. 248/1992 Sb.). Is it any wonder that IPFs operated with impunity during the first months of voucher privatization?

In response to that question, many privatizers intoned the neoliberal litany. Markets were certain to be imperfect at the outset. Market logic in time would overwhelm legal glitches or alleged bad apples, such as Koženy. I believe that a genuine response would have emphasized that compromises are necessary with dishonest claimants so that privatization would progress. The IPFs' free reign was one such compromise.

Otherwise, IPFs were busy attracting over two-thirds of the voucher holders; individual voucher holders entrusted IPFs with 73.3 percent of the voucher points in the prewave of privatization.[23] Bank IPFs attracted by far the most investment points thanks to their high capitalization and sometimes thanks to their extensive local banking networks. ČS (the Czech Savings Bank), with the most bank branches, attracted the most voucher holders.

Harvard was the most successful nonbank IPF; it was one of three nonbank IPFs to crack the top fourteen funds. In all, 423 IPFs participated in the first wave of voucher privatization (Mejstřík in Mejstřík 1997a, 156). The corporate governance problem, owing to the extraordinary involvement of IPFs, seemed to be solved before it ever emerged.

Who could have known that IPFs, as a rule, would not only perpetuate the corporate governance problem, but would also sabotage deep corporate restructuring? Who could have known that IPFs, as a rule, would block attempts to institute transparent, liquid, and honest capital markets? Who could known have known that IPFs, as a rule, would steal from their voucher holders and thereby undermine the very political legitimacy of Klaus's neoliberal government?

Actually, I believe the Czech privatizers should have known.

The privatizers deliberately ignored warnings that voucher privatization would go out of control.[24] They banked instead on a quaint and naïve conception of market power. Market theory presumes that economic actors compete for scarce resources and, moreover, that competing economic actors will regulate the market by checking the cheating of competitors. One shortcoming in the application of market theory to reality is that actors may decide to collude rather than to compete. Another shortcoming is that market theory presumes perfect information among consumers and producers. A third shortcoming is that most market theories presume a continuing or iterative market relationship between economic actors. The realities of transition and of postvoucher privatization highlighted these shortcomings. Unfortunately, the privatizers were wearing ideological blinders.

VOUCHER PRIVATIZATION IMPLEMENTATION, MAY 1992 TO DECEMBER 1994

The apparent smoothness of the two voucher privatization waves testified to the wisdom and the technical preparedness of the Czech privatizers. Czechs and Slovaks orderly registered for vouchers and bid for ownership stakes in a sequence of choreographed privatization rounds. To be sure, Tříska's voucher system prompted justifiable criticisms over the speed, the equity, and the completeness of voucher privatization, but the criticisms were minor in the views of most Czechs and foreign observers. I also agree that Czech voucher privatization was a magnificent political and economic success, if one confines one's focus strictly to the neoliberals' implementation objective—share distribution.

The First Wave

On May 23, 1992, 8.6 million registered Czechs and Slovaks, acting on their own behalf or represented by IPFs, bid for enterprise shares in the first round of the first wave. The first round was the first investment decision for nearly everyone involved. The first-round bidding process finished a month later, after which time Tříska and his team went about tallying the results.

The goal of the first round was to establish voucher holder preferences so that the reactive pricing of enterprise shares could begin. It was not to match voucher holder bids and enterprise shares. Tříska's technical team set identical prices for all shares—three shares per 100 voucher points—understanding, of course, that not all shares are worth the same price. Patently valuable shares consequently were oversubscribed and patently inexpensive shares were undersubscribed. Using the demand information gathered from this initial round, the technical team and the computer adjusted enterprise prices for the second round. In the second round, then, the serious matching of bids and shares would take place.

The state launched the second round two months from the beginning of the first round. Thanks to the first-round adjustments, the share prices correlated closer to the now revealed voucher holder preferences. The technical team consequently assigned many shares in this round. The second round took Tříska's team two months to complete, including collecting the voucher holder bids, assigning share rights, and recalculating (again) enterprise prices.

So it went for five rounds. Voucher holders bid for enterprise shares, the technical team tallied those bids, assigned share rights, and then calculated new enterprise share prices for the next round. The technical team halted the process after five rounds to coincide with the split of the country on

January 1, 1993. Ninety-three percent of the enterprise shares were assigned to voucher bidders, and 98 percent of the voucher points were exhausted.

In the second half of 1992, the Czech privatizers successfully and with minimal disruption authorized the first mass share distribution in history.[25] It was little wonder that Ježek boosted to a Polish newspaper, "We are the stars" (Zagrodzka 1993, 4–5) or that the cover of the 1989–1993 Ministry of Privatization Report was adorned with pyrotechnics over Prague Castle.

The Second Wave

The entire process rewound from July 1993 to December 1994. The second wave proceeded even more smoothly than the first wave in the minds of the Czech privatizers and most analysts. Voucher privatization seemed like old hat to the masses and to the privatizers after the fanfare and novelty of the first wave.

The implementation of the two privatization waves revealed differences. In the second privatization wave, the set of enterprise shares was new and IPF bidders were a mix of the experienced and inexperienced. The changes in enterprise stakes reflected a riskier blend of enterprise shares as predetermined by the Ministry of Privatization. The shifting composition of enterprise stakes also reflected the increasing supply-side influence of claimants, especially enterprise managers.

Alterations in the composition of IPFs reflected rule changes as well as the first-wave experience of masses and IPFs. IPFs competing for voucher holder points generally were of a different structure than in the first wave as a result of additions to the law. First-wave IPFs were organized as share companies. In the second wave, the Czech privatizers allowed IPFs to be organized as open-ended and close-ended investment trusts as well as share companies. IPF managers of these new investment trusts were tied to investors by a long-term management contract; in share companies, the management was subject to a shareholder vote. Although the change appeared minor at the time, the next section shows that it was crucial.

Also, IPFs marginally were less successful in attracting voucher points in the second wave, despite continued offers to voucher holders. The bank funds were less successful relative to the nonbank funds in this wave; the total proportion of shares of the four large Czech banks and the Czech insurance company dropped from nearly 30 percent to 22 percent overall (see tables 8.3, 8.4, and 8.5). Overall though, second-wave voucher holders exercised a growing confidence in their own investment capabilities, a product of increasing skepticism over IPF investment acumen. IPFs garnered 63.5 percent of the voucher points in the second privatization wave against 73.3 percent in the first wave (CKP 1995, 26).

Table 8.3.   The Fourteen Largest Privatization Funds' Financial Groups in the First Wave of Privatization

Fund Group	Voucher Points Acquired (in millions)	Voucher Points as a Percentage of IPF Total Points	Voucher Points as a Percentage of Total Points
1. SIS ČS	950.4	15.60	11.10
2. PIAS IPB	724.1	11.90	8.45
3. Harvard CC	638.5	10.50	7.45
4. VUB	500.6	8.19	5.84
5. IKS KB	465.5	7.62	5.43
6. KIS CP	334.0	5.47	3.90
7. SI	187.9	3.07	2.19
8. SSK	168.9	2.76	1.97
9. CA	166.3	2.72	1.94
10. SIB	145.1	2.37	1.69
11. PPF	117.5	1.92	1.37
12. ZB	117.5	1.92	1.37
13. SLP	116.7	1.91	1.36
14. AG	111.1	1.82	1.30
Top 14 Groups	4,744.2	77.63	55.39
Total IPFs	6,112.0	100.00	71.35
Total Points	8,566.0	—	100.00

Source: Mejstřík 1997, 158, table 6.6 "Emergence of Institutional Owners."

Notes: 1. SIS is the investment company of ČS; 2. PIAS is the investment company of IPB; 3. Harvard Capital and Consulting Investment Company; 4. VUB is the investment company of VUB (Slovakia); 5. IKS is the investment company of KB; 6. KIS is the investment company of České pojišťovna, a Czech insurance company; 7. SI is Slovenské investice (Slovakia); 8. SSK is the investment company of the Slovak Savings Bank and VSŽ Košice, a Slovak industrial company; 9. CA is the investment company of Creditanstalt, an Austrian bank; 10. SIB is the investment company of the Slovak Investment Bank; 11. PPF is an independent investment company; 12. ZB is the Investment company of Živnostenská banka; 13. SLP is the investment company of the Slovak Insurance Company; and 14. AG is the investment company of Agrobanka.

Table 8.4.   IPF Participation in Voucher Privatization

	Total Voucher Points (%)	
	First Wave	Second Wave
Largest IPFs	11.1	5.2
Largest Five IPFs	38.0	21.1
Largest Fourteen IPFs	55.4	36.7
Bank IPFs	39.8	11.8
All IPFs	71.4	63.5
Individuals	29.0	36.5

Source: Desai and Plocková 1997, 191.

Table 8.5.   The Fourteen Largest Privatization Funds' Financial Groups in the Second Wave of Privatization

Investment Company within a Fund Group	Voucher Points Acquired (in millions)	Voucher Points as a Percentage of IPF Total Points	Voucher Points as a Percentage of Total Points
1. A-invest	320	8.2	5.2
2. Expandia	306	7.8	5.0
3. Harvard CC	292	7.5	4.7
4. OB Invest	198	5.1	3.2
5. KIS, CP	187	4.8	3.0
6. IS entrepreneur	157	4.0	2.5
7. YSE	156	4.0	2.5
8. Czech coupon	152	3.9	2.5
9. PPF	130	3.3	2.1
10. SIS	124	3.2	2.0
11. IKS	124	3.2	2.0
12. MorCE IS	113	2.9	1.8
13. PIAS	98	2.5	1.6
14. CS Funds	94	2.4	1.5
Top 14 Groups	2,451	60.1	38.2
Total IPFs	3,920	100.00	63.5
Total Points	6,170	—	100.00

Source: Mejstřík 1997, 161, table 6.7 "Emergence of Institutional Owners."
Notes: Of the fourteen funds, there are six bank-affiliated funds: 1. A-invest is affiliated with Agrobanka, then a wholly private bank; 4. OB Invest is the investment subsidiary of ČSOB, a Czech and Slovak bank; 5. KIS is the investment company of Česká pojist'ovna, a Czech insurance company; 10. SIS is the investment company of ČS; 11. IKS is the investment company of KB; and, 13. PIAS is the investment company of IPB. The remaining eight funds are nonbank IPFs. Of these eight IPFs only Harvard Capital and Consulting Investment Company and PPF were among the top fourteen funds in the first wave.

In addition, competition among the IPFs was fiercer in the second wave than in the first wave. The IPF offers started immediately in the second wave; by contrast, Harvard's guarantee came two months into the first wave. Consequently, the dispersion of voucher points among the IPFs was far greater in the second wave. Also, bank IPFs were far less successful in attracting voucher

Table 8.6.   Voucher Privatization Summary Statistics

	First Wave (1992–1993)	Second Wave (1993–1994)
Participating enterprises	988	861
Enterprise book value (bn CZK)	200	155
Shares (mn)	973	867
Participants (mn)	5.98	6.17
Eligible citizens registering voucher books	78%	81%
Investment funds	429	353
Voucher points entrusted to investment funds	73.3%	63.5%

Source: Various national sources.

points in the second wave (see table 8.5). Nonetheless, the second wave's major change was the absence of the Slovaks, due to the split-up of Czechoslovakia in January 1993. Most neoliberals thought, and most Czechs agreed, that it was a good thing.[26]

Fast and Fair Privatization in the Czech Republic

The smoothness of the two privatization waves vindicated the neoliberal line. Suddenly, the Czech Republic had the world's highest percentage of shareholders, and by far the highest stock market capitalization of any former communist country.[27] On its face, the voucher process conformed to the miracle version of Czech privatization. Czech voucher privatization seemed fast, fair, and complete.[28]

Fast Privatization

The Czech reformers privatized by vouchers over 343 bn CZK (Fund of National Property 1995) of the Czech Republic's largest enterprises in just over four years.[29] Parliament passed the Large Privatization Law in February 1991; privatization investment funds distributed the second-wave shares in the spring and summer of 1995 (see table 8.7). The Czechs had implemented voucher privatization virtually without practical market experience and lacking advanced computer facilities. At the same time, the Czech reformers were occupied with other demanding tasks, including the privatization of small businesses and agricultural cooperatives; the restitution of thousands of assets nationalized by the communist regime; the freeing of most prices; the transformation of the banking system from a monobank to a competitive market system; the creation of a modern tax structure; the writing and ratification of a constitution; and the establishment of an entirely new political system. The Czech reformers did all that and also privatized while orchestrating the peaceful split of Czechoslovakia.

Table 8.7.   The Time Frame of Voucher Privatization

Task	Achieved Date
Large Privatization Law	February 1991
First Wave Begins	May 1992
First Wave Ends	December 1992
First Wave Shares Distributed	May 1993
Second Wave Begins	April 1993
Second Wave Ends	December 1994
Second Wave Shares Distributed	February 1995 (individuals)
	April 1995 (IPFs)

Fair Privatization

The local population was the jury of import, and it deemed the voucher process as fair. Surveys conducted well after the completion of the first wave revealed that most Czechs regarded voucher privatization as the fairest method to distribute state property.[30] Czech voucher privatization evidently considered the rights of the Czech population. Klaus wrote, "Our public rightly demands that privatization is carried out as cleanly as possible, that privatization discriminates against no one, and that people do not break laws or act unethically in order to enrich themselves in the course of privatization" (Klaus 1994, 61).

The apparent fairness of Czech voucher privatization brought extraordinary popularity to Klaus's reform-minded ruling party.[31] Hardly a dissenting word could be heard regarding the genius of the Klaus policies in the halcyon days of 1993 and 1994. I can vividly recall one televised question-and-answer section with Klaus and the media. The participating journalists repeatedly punctuated soft queries with deferential remarks respecting the brilliance and success of the neoliberal policies. The interview resembled a coronation. Such was the uncritical state of the Czech public and the Czech media.

Complete Privatization

The Czech government privatized a total of 1,664 Czech enterprises in the two voucher privatization waves.[32] The change in percentage of GDP produced by the private sector testifies to the completeness of Czech privatization. In the late 1980s, the former Czechoslovakia's private sector accounted for approximately 3 percent of output, perhaps the lowest of the former communist countries. By 1996, privately owned businesses generated as much as 90 percent of the Czech Republic's GDP, the highest of the former communist countries.

POLITICAL OUTCOMES OF VOUCHER PRIVATIZATION

Cynics say that the neoliberals' prime purpose in voucher privatization was to garner support for the 1992 elections and for political contests beyond. It was easy to come to the conclusion, as many did, that the distribution of cheap vouchers was tantamount to vote buying. The neoliberals did crudely attempt to transform participation in voucher privatization into neoliberal votes at the ballot box—Klaus's signature was on every voucher; the government distributed pens and balloons to promote voucher privatization. Voucher privatization was a ballyhooed "event," an event, in fact, that distracted the popular attention for nearly four years. Finally, all agree that the "coincidence" of the first-round voucher privatization and the June 1992 elections was not coincidental (Macháček 1998).

Although voucher privatization buttressed public support for Klaus's reform-minded ruling party, public opinion surveys suggest that the groundwork for its political popularity was established long before. Klaus's ideological victory over Komárek in spring 1990, the subsequent 1990 Civic Forum election victory, and the neoliberal capture of the economic agenda in the 1990 Scenario of Economic Reform cleared the field of credible opposition to voucher privatization. Surveys also illustrate that the June 1992 election results were not the short-term consequence of political manipulation—admittedly, political expediency did play a role—but the result of a two-and-a-half-year neoliberal crusade to plant market concepts among Czech society. In the Czech Republic, privatization started with ideology; ideology then had political consequence.

Czech support for comprehensive large privatization—recognized in the public as voucher privatization—remained roughly unchanged. In May 1990, 56.9 percent expressed support; in December 1990, 59.9 percent; in June 1991, 56.2 percent; in December 1991, 56.8 percent; and, in June 1992, 57.2 percent. IPF guarantees and the neoliberal election push in June 1992 show no appreciable impact on that support (see table 8.8).

The wide popular support for voucher privatization was *not* due to vote buying. Although the percentage of Czechs likely to participate in voucher privatization rose from December 1990 to December 1991, as late as December 1991, many Czechs still had no intention of buying voucher books—though 57 percent continued to support comprehensive large privatization on principle (see table 8.9). IPFs induced Czechs to participate in voucher privatization—80 percent of eligible Czechs actually purchased coupon books by February 1992—but not to change their opinions. The share of the population that did not consider voucher privatization a fair method of distribution of national property remained at over 40 percent.[33]

Table 8.8. Popular Support for Czech Large Privatization, May 1990 to June 1992

Q? Is it necessary to change all large enterprises in state ownership to share companies or to private firms?

	May 1990	December 1990	June 1991	December 1991	June 1992
Surely Yes	17.1	24.0	22.2	22.4	23.7
Rather Yes	39.8	35.9	34.0	34.4	33.5
Rather No	33.9	29.2	34.3	33.2	32.0
Surely No	9.2	10.9	9.6	10.0	10.8

Source: Ekonomické očekavaní and STEM.

Table 8.9. The Likelihood That Czechs Will Participate in Voucher Privatization, December 1990 and December 1991

Q? Do you expect that all the adults in your family will purchase investment coupons?

	December 1990	December 1991
Surely Yes	9.6	23.9
Rather Yes	13.0	12.6
Rather No	32.4	24.1
Surely No	45.0	39.4

Source: Ekonomické očekavaní and STEM.

Likely voters for Klaus's ODS party (or one of the coalition partners) were voucher privatization supporters. The most enthusiastic Czech voucher privatization supporters and Klaus supporters were from large cities, highly educated, and under thirty-nine years of age. By contrast, opponents of voucher privatization were predominantly concentrated in the "leftist" opposition. The voucher opponents hailed from small cities or from the countryside, had only basic education, and were older (the greatest opposition was in the over-sixty-years-old category). Also, voucher opposition was far stronger in Slovakia than in the Czech Republic (various surveys, courtesy of Jan Hartl). The predictable pairing of ideological preference and economic policy suggests that class politics played an important role in Czech politics at an early stage in the transition period. It also suggests that voucher privatization was a critical policy in distinguishing one party from another (see table 8.10).

In the June 1992 elections, Klaus's ODS party—formed in the 1991 split of Civic Forum—combined with like-thinking parties to thrash the opposition. The most prominent loser was OH, another Civic Forum spin-off party. OH

Table 8.10. Support for Voucher Privatization by Political Party, July 1993

Q? Do you think that voucher privatization is a fair form of dividing the national property?

		Coalition Parties		Left Parties	
	Total	ODS	ODA	Christian Parties	Social Democrats	Left Block
Surely Yes	13.7	25.9	13.9	11.2	3.1	1.5
Rather Yes	45.8	57.8	53.8	56.2	35.1	18.3
Rather No	27.5	12.7	24.9	23.6	41.2	50.4
Surely No	13.0	3.6	7.5	9.0	20.6	29.8

Source: Trendy 1993 and STEM; data only included parties in the Czech Parliament, and does not include the far right party (SPR-RSČ) and the Communist Party.

was the political home of many pre-1989 dissidents, and it counted among its members several Federal and Czech ministers, among them Jan Vrba, the Czech minister of industry and trade. It is sufficient to note that important OH members, such as Vrba, also were vocal skeptics of voucher privatization. The neoliberal political victory was so crushing that OH failed to muster even the 5 percent of the electorate needed to enter the next Federal Parliament. The 1992 June election results ensured that the neoliberals would dominate economic policymaking over the next several years.[34]

THE CZECH *FATA MORGANA*: THE OWNERSHIP REGIME THEORY

Czech privatization was not so much miracle, but *fata morgana*, as seen from an ownership regime theory that emphasizes the characteristics of the first owners, the first-ownership structure, the capital market institutions, and especially, the autonomy and capacity of the state regulator. The Czech ownership regime that emerged from privatization does not appear here as a formula for markets and democracy, but rather as a means for unscrupulous claimants and state officials to seize state assets. The analysis implies that the neoliberal strategy may be deeply flawed.

It is necessary to gauge the extent and the quality of the assets offered in voucher privatization prior to sketching its impact on the ownership regime. Voucher privatization actually covered less than half of all large- and medium-sized enterprises; 48.2 percent of Czech assets in joint stock companies were privatized using the voucher privatization method.[35] In all, 40.2 percent of large assets were privatized through vouchers (see table 8.11 and table 8.12 for an overview of Czech privatization). Consequently, although this chapter sketches the ownership regime produced by Czech voucher privatization, it also sketches the ownership regime produced by standard privatization methods. The relevant ownership regime features are: the first owners, the first-ownership structure, the capital markets, and the autonomy and capacity of the state regulator of the capital markets.

First Owners

Who were the winning claimants? Who were the losing claimants? The intention of these questions is to establish both who were and who were not Czech first owners. Claimants in Czech privatization fall into seven categories: masses, IPFs, Slovaks, managers, workers, foreigners, and the state. I argue in this section that the winning claimants or first owners (as well as the losing

Table 8.11. An Overview of Czech Privatization

Czech Privatization Programs	Property Value (bn CZK)	Property Value (%)
Restitution	95	6.2
Small Privatization	30	1.9
Cooperatives	215	14.0
Large Privatization	(850)	(55.2)
Joint Stock Comp.—Voucher Privatization	343	22.2
Joint Stock Comp.—Other	363	23.6
Non–Joint Stock Comp	144	9.4
Free Transfer to Local Government	350	22.7
Total	1540	100.0

Sources: Mejstřík, *Privatization Newsletter of the Czech Republic and Slovakia* 1994; *HN*, January 23, 1995; Fund of National Property 1995, 9–12; Češka in *Privatization Newsletter of the Czech Republic and Slovakia* 1993; Mládek 1994.

Notes: Restitution figures are average of 70–120 bn CZK, Cooperatives are average from 200–230 bn CZK. Property values are book values except joint stock company values, which are nominal values. Includes state shares in FNP. Includes 230 bn CZK of joint stock company still at FNP as of December 31, 1995 (Fund of National Property 1995, 12). Does not include state shares held by ministries and central bank.

claimants) were a function of the voucher privatization design, the rapid privatization strategy, and happenstance.

Data on industrial enterprise profitability suggest that voucher participants were significant privatization winners or first owners. Privatized industrial enterprises had higher profitability ratios than the overall average for Czech industry (*PlanEcon* 1992–1993). Nevertheless, the mere fact that the Czech privatization authorities removed over half of the privatized assets from voucher privatization sustains the nagging suspicion that the masses or IPFs may have been unfairly discriminated against. Moreover, analysts estimated that perhaps a third of the enterprises the Ministry of Finance offered in voucher privatization were functionally bankrupt.[36] Although a perfunctory examination of voucher privatization assets does not conclusively determine whether they were treated fairly, voucher participants unequivocally were offered stakes in valuable enterprises. The evidence below argues that the winning voucher participants were masses, IPFs, and Slovaks; on the edge are managers; the losers are the workers and foreigners.

Table 8.12. Czech Privatization: More Than Just Vouchers

Voucher Privatization (by Value) as a Percentage of . . .

—Joint Stock Company Privatization	48.5%
—Total Large Privatization	40.2%
—Total Privatization	22.2%

Table 8.13. The Worth of a Voucher Book

	First Wave	Second Wave
Total Book Value (bn CZK)	200	155
Total Voucher Holders (mn)	5.86	6.16
Cost of Voucher Book (CZK)	1,035	1,050
Book Value per Voucher Book (CZK)	36,000	25,000
Individual Voucher Holders (CZK)	40,700	33,800
IPFs (CZK)	26,500	19,000

1. Masses

Masses collected nearly thirty-five times the value of a voucher book in the first wave and nearly twenty-five times the value of a voucher book in the second wave. Masses certainly were claimant winners on an absolute scale (see table 8.13).

Nonetheless, Tříska's auction system disallowed voucher holders chances to make rational investment decisions. One reason was that Tříska's auction system was opaque. The Ministry of Finance enjoyed extraordinary flexibility to set and then to change the auction rules (zákon č. 248/1992 Sb.). Voucher holders could not know the auction rules for certain. Given imperfect information, voucher privatization therefore could not match the preferences of voucher holders with the volume of offered shares. Voucher holder investment decisions could not be rational.

Consider the question of whether a voucher holder should bid points for his favorite enterprise in later rounds or earlier rounds. The answer depends on the projected number of rounds. If the voucher holder (correctly) guesses that the prices for his favorite enterprises would drop as the rounds proceed, this voucher holder would run the risk that the Ministry of Finance would suddenly announce that the next round would be the last. Precisely, this strategy risked that the enterprise shares would be oversubscribed in the last round; in that case, the voucher holder would be left with nothing since no enterprise shares would be distributed. Indeed, this example was not hypothetical speculation. In the first wave, the Ministry of Finance did suddenly announce that the fifth round would be the last; 7 percent of enterprise shares and 3 percent of voucher points did go unallocated.

Voucher holders also could not express rational preferences because they lacked precise information on the price-setting mechanism. The Ministry of Finance printed the technical information in unofficial publications that were neither widely distributed nor clear about the computer algorithm (Bláha et al. 1992). Additionally, voucher holders lacked key information concerning subsequent taxation and also where and when it would be possible to begin trading shares (Bláha et al. 1992).

The dearth of voucher holder information was compounded by the fact that in several cases, though the number is not publicly known, a Ministry of Finance price commission (not the computer algorithm) established the share auction prices. Neoliberals, including Tříska, R. Češka, then a deputy minister of privatization, and V. Rudlovčák, a long-time Klaus collaborator, sat on the price commission. The existence of the price commission raised key questions. What criteria did the price commission use to set auction prices? Which share prices were set by the price commission? Which prices were set by the computer algorithm? The existence of the price commission and the deliberate hoarding of information fanned suspicions that the neoliberals followed a hidden strategic agenda or else followed a private, corrupt agenda.

In retrospect, the suspicion that the price commission, or those close to the price commission, may have acted to set enterprise prices for personal gain does not seem implausible, though nothing has been proven or even formally alleged against the neoliberal privatizers. It raised eyebrows, for instance, that V. Kožený's Harvard Fund got close to its legal 20 percent share limit in preferred enterprises without illicit assistance (Reed 1996). The 1994 allegations and subsequent bribery conviction of J. Lizner, the chief of the Center for Voucher Privatization and the senior computer technician, strongly suggested that the monopoly of information had become too much for self-seeking bureaucrats to resist.[37] It is hard to imagine that the 1994 incident was Lizner's first and only acceptance of a bribe, or that he was the only bad apple.

Voucher privatization didn't provide voucher holders reliable information for reasons that were out of Tříska's control. For instance, Ježek's delay of the supply-side tasks meant that when citizens registered for voucher privatization, they were unaware of the enterprise stakes that would be privatized by vouchers. Furthermore, many enterprises submitted information that was either incomplete or highly suspect. As it was, the state required that enterprises only release to prospective bidders dog-tag data: industry segment, number of employees, book value, and recent profit history. Other information critical to a reasonable investment decision, such as the quantity and structure of enterprise debts, was secret.

The hoarding of enterprise information, like the opaque auction process, reinforced the suspicion that neoliberals were uninterested in assisting the voucher holders to make informed, market-based decisions—pretending that Tříska's auction system was a market when it really was an artificial game, or pretending that market-based decision-making was realistic in a society that hadn't experienced functioning markets in half a century. To be sure, the main neoliberal intention of voucher privatization was to achieve just enough popular acceptance to distribute the enterprise shares rapidly.

2. IPFs

The prominence of IPFs must temper judgments about the success of masses in voucher privatization. Individual voucher holders entrusted IPFs with 69.0 percent of the total voucher points; 73.3 percent in the first wave and 63.5 percent in the second wave (CKP 1995, 26). Consequently, mass success depended to a considerable degree on the sophistication of IPF investment practices. Mass success also depended on the efficiency of postprivatization capital markets and the financial regulatory environment. Voucher privatization and IPFs enticed the masses to enter into share ownership. Selling the ownership shares and actually collecting the voucher profits was another matter entirely.

Did IPFs buy shares more cheaply than individual voucher holders? The IPFs would seem to have bidding advantages in voucher privatization due to their disproportionate (compared with individual voucher holders) ability to gather enterprise information. The circumstantial evidence is contrary to the betting line. IPFs actually paid higher prices than masses for the same shares. IPFs bought shares in the early rounds of each privatization wave when shares were comparatively expensive. Evidently, IPFs were determined to make sure that their voucher points were exhausted. Individuals tended to buy shares in later rounds when shares were comparatively cheap.[38]

Investment research at many IPFs was remarkably superficial. One major bank IPF claimed that it hired five investment "professionals" from the Prague Economics University (VŠE) to recommend promising enterprises. These professionals, according to the bank IPF, did not make enterprise visits or contact enterprise management prior to making investment recommendations.[39] It would have been unthinkable in the West that an investment house would *not* inspect personally a potential investment before committing funds. The average book value of individual voucher holders was approximately 40,700 CZK as against 26,500 CZK for IPFs in the first wave and 33,800 CZK versus 19,000 CZK in the second wave (CKP 1995, 26).[40] Individual voucher holders appeared to be better investors than the IPFs.

The demand-side regulations also discriminated against IPFs. The IPF law limited IPFs to a 20 percent ownership stake in any individual enterprise; the law added the stipulation that no IPF could have more than 10 percent of its portfolio in any one enterprise. These restrictions placed IPFs at a relative disadvantage in placing its shares. Only workers and foreigners faced restrictions that limited share purchases during privatization.

Still, IPFs automatically were winners due to the large ownership stakes acquired through voucher privatization. The IPF share portfolio comprised 58 percent of the book value of all voucher privatized companies, as against 42 percent for individual voucher holders (CKP 1995, 26). IPFs owned

38 percent of all enterprise shares by the completion of the second wave in 1994 (Desai and Plocková 1997, 193). Masses and the state owned most of the remaining shares.

The high ownership share of IPFs in the postprivatization economy guaranteed that IPFs would earn high management fees, and it introduced the possibility that IPFs would manipulate enterprise finances for selfish purposes. Yet the extent to which voucher privatization benefited IPF managers could not be answered at privatization's close. The benefit to IPFs of voucher privatization was eventually a function of the postprivatization regulatory environment and the moral integrity of the individual IPF managers.

3. Slovaks

Slovaks also gained disproportionately (as opposed to Czechs) from voucher privatization. The Slovak side contributed far fewer valuable assets to voucher privatization than the Czech side. "While the Czechs contributed prime, undervalued assets such as hotels and breweries, Slovaks threw in grossly overvalued dinosaurs like the Eastern Slovakia Iron and Steel Works" (*PlanEcon* 1992–1993, 11). The consequence of the different values of the portfolios was that Slovaks invested nearly four times as much into Czech assets (26.3 bn CZK) as Czechs invested in Slovak assets (6.4 bn CZK). Slovak individual voucher holders bought approximately 50,000 CZK of assets—versus only 41,000 CZK for their Czech counterparts—by disproportionately investing their voucher books in Czech enterprises. Ultimately, the Czech privatizers gained nothing by appeasing the Slovak voucher holders; the country formally split on January 1, 1993.

4. Managers

Managers did not enjoy special privileges in voucher privatization implementation. Instead, enterprise managers worked from the supply-side of Czech privatization. Managers normally preferred standard privatization methods that offered them, or a close collaborator, clear title to assets. The enterprise manager payoff occurred primarily in the implementation of standard privatization methods, not in the implementation of voucher privatization.

Voucher privatization was not an unfortunate second-best privatization solution for many enterprise managers. The dearth of management ability in the country was one factor that supported the position of managers in Czech enterprises. Some enterprise managers feared the threat of foreign owners who would bring in Western management expertise. Voucher privatization served as a refuge in these cases. The Tatra (a truck manufacturer) manager reportedly

Table 8.14. Interrepublic Investments in Voucher Privatization

	Enterprises in Voucher Privatization (By Book Value—bn CZK)		
Investments	Czech-Based	Slovak-Based	Total
By Czech Voucher Holders	171.7	6.4	178.1
By Slovak Voucher Holders	26.3	73.3	99.6
Total	198.0	79.7	277.7

Source: CKP 1995, 14.
Note: Figures include investments of vouchers by Czechs and Slovaks both directly and through IPFs.

cut off negotiations with the German company Mercedes to protect his position. Moreover, many enterprise managers expected that voucher privatization would produce a dispersed ownership structure. Dispersed ownership would translate into no active owner and therefore no ownership control. The manager would remain as the controlling authority. Ironically, the main new owners in the end were IPFs.

The data also indicate that managers apparently learned to use the Czech privatization system over time. Table 8.14 shows that the state offered fewer bundles of shares for vouchers in the second wave. The logical assumption is that managers were gaining more influence in the Ministry of Privatization's selection of the privatization method. To evaluate precisely whether Czech enterprise managers were winners requires analysis of standard privatization methods, not voucher privatization.

5. Workers

Czech voucher privatization discriminated against organized workers. The trade union leaders' choice to opt out of privatization decision-making in 1990 and 1991 effectively subordinated the workers in voucher privatization. Absent trade union pressures for worker ownership, the government adopted the stance of a close Klaus advisor.

> As for worker's shares, I think that they would be a poor alternative to voucher privatization. . . . At first, the authority of the management and the discipline of the workers would lag. Then, there would be the tendency to overextend worker benefits and even to split the capital among the workers in the form of higher wages or as dividends. (Robert Holman in *HN*, February 6, 1992, 9)

Discrimination against workers appeared as the 1992 Czechoslovak Commercial Code paragraph that restricted the free transfer of shares to employees

Table 8.15. Enterprise Ownership Stakes Offered in Voucher Privatization

Shares Offered in Voucher Privatization (%)	Total Number of Joint Stock Companies (%)		Asset Value (%)	
	First Wave	Second Wave	First Wave	Second Wave
<34	4	29	12	28
34–50	8	13	10	23
51–96	46	46	50	43
>96	42	12	28	6
Total	100	100	100	100

Source: Czech Ministry of Privatization 1993, 31.

to not more than 5 percent of the nominal value of the capital stock.[41] Some privatization projects did offer workers chances to buy up to 10 percent of the enterprise shares at book value.[42] Yet this was not generally a good deal for the workers, since most enterprises were worth less than book value.[43] Consequently, many shares designed to go to workers went unallocated and ended up at the Fund of National Property. Workers did not become owners when they were "supposed to" (see table 8.16).[44]

Note the comparison between how workers made out in Czech voucher privatization as compared with Polish institutional privatization and Russian voucher privatization. In Poland, the state awarded workers 15 percent of their own enterprise. In Russia, the state offered managers and workers the option to buy majority ownership stakes at preferential prices. As of 1994, employees controlled via ownership only three Czechoslovak companies. This compares with 187 employee-controlled companies in Hungary (from self-privatization), and approximately 600 in Romania, 1,478 in Poland, and 6,300 in Russia (Earle and Estrin 1994, 83).

6. Foreigners

Czech voucher privatization openly discriminated against foreigners. Simply, foreigners were ineligible. The Czech privatizers also forbade foreigners to purchase vouchers from the voucher holders.[45]

Table 8.16. The Voucher Privatization Scorecard

First Owners	Losers	On the Edge
Masses	Workers	Enterprise Managers
IPFs	Foreigners	
Slovaks		

It is an open secret that Czech privatization was "marked by an aversion to the sale of national property to foreign capital" (Klvačová 1991, 1). Furthermore, foreigners had to jump through special hoops to obtain shares through standard privatization methods. These hoops included complicated approval privatization procedures that had to pass through several government agencies. This was a serious hurdle given that "Czech governmental bodies are often prejudiced in favor of Czech bidders versus foreign bidders."[46] The process is also very time intensive, a serious barrier when competing neighboring countries are willing to expedite privatization procedures to attract a foreign strategic investor. The direct purchase by foreigners of privatized Czech shares amounts to less than 2.0 percent of enterprises (Fund of National Property 1995, 12).

The First-Ownership Structure

Analysts using an institutional or network approach have been among the most vocal critics of Czech voucher privatization. They latched on to the state's still substantial shareholdings in individual enterprises including its sharepackages in the four dominant Czech banks (IPB, KB, ČSOB, ČS) and the national insurance company (Česká pojišťovna). The logical chain of enterprise in these analyses is straightforward. Each of these financial institutions controlled a bank IPF, either directly or through subsidiaries. These bank IPFs, in turn, became large shareholders from voucher privatization. The ownership chain immediately after voucher privatization was: the state owned the banks; the banks owned the bank IPFs; the bank IPFs owned the enterprises. The state owned the enterprises, q.e.d. (see tables 8.17 and 8.18).

The most sophisticated of these critics further contended that voucher privatization had created a cross-holding ownership structure (Stark and Bruszt 1998). Bank IPFs were the largest bank shareholders. Furthermore, banks also directly owned enterprise shares (from debt to equity swaps) or else were tied to enterprises by large outstanding loans. Very large enterprises, in turn,

Table 8.17.   The State Ownership Share in the Banks

Institution	State Share
1. IPB	32.88
2. KB	48.74
3. ČSOB	90.10
4. ČS	45.00
5. Česká pojišťovna	26.27

Note: As of April 26, 1996.

Table 8.18.   Cross-holding in the Czech Republic after Voucher Privatization

Czech Bank IPFs	Financial Institutions Privatized through Vouchers (%)			
	ČS	IPB	KB	ČP
ČS	–	0.5	4.9	2.0
IPB	8.8	17.0	10.8	4.1
KB	3.9	–	3.4	–
ČP	0.2	3.0	0.7	1.0
Total: Four Bank IPFs	12.9	20.5	19.8	7.1
Total Ownership Privatized by Vouchers	37.0	49.6	53.0	15.0

Source: Mejstřík in Mejstřík 1997, 163; author calculations.
Notes: Does not include FNP sale of ČP shares: 14% to ČSOB, 10% to KB, 10% to IPB, 10% to ČS, and 10% to Interbanka. ČP is Česká pojišťovna, the largest Czech insurance company. PPF, a nonbank IPF, later bought virtually the entire share of ČS and Interbanka; this share was 19.4%.

controlled IPFs or owned large stakes in other enterprises. The network consequences of voucher privatization are represented by the ownership flowchart outlined in figure 8.1.

The division of enterprise stakes among many different kinds of first owners—individuals, IPFs, managers, municipalities, the central state, restituents, foreigners, and workers—is part of the privatization story. Table 8.19 illustrates concrete examples. The existence of many owners within a single enterprise translated into indecisiveness in corporate decision-making in some cases, and gambits by financially powerful owners to marginalize weaker owners or to steal enterprise assets in other cases. The variety of ownership stake configurations in Czech privatized companies portended a plethora of games among and between owners and managers for control of enterprise assets.

Financial System

The immediate outputs of Czech voucher privatization were nearly 1,700 share issues, over 8 million individual shareholders, and over 400 IPFs. Most share issues were unlikely to be actively traded because they represented tiny companies by international standards; average market capitalization for the smaller 1000 issues was under 7.5 mn CZK ($270,000). Two new stock markets emerged simultaneously with shares and shareholders. One new stock market, the Prague Stock Exchange, came with modern electronic technology and advisors from France.[47] The other, the RM-System, used much of the same technology as voucher privatization and was designed as a clearinghouse for

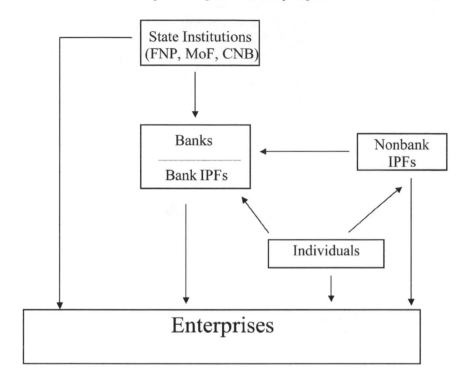

Legend

Owner ⟶ Holding

Figure 8.1.   The First Czech Ownership Structure, 1993.

Table 8.19.   Variation in Enterprise Ownership: Division of Ownership Stakes in Selected Automobile Suppliers, 1992

	Firm		
Mitop	*Asbestos Zvéřínek*	*Buzulak Komárov*	*ČZ Strakonice*
IPF 73% (25 IPFs)	State 71% (for direct sale to foreign partner)	IPF 75% (5 IPFs own more than 5%)	Individuals 48%
Individuals 16%	State 21%	Individuals 14%	IPF 26%
Community 5%	Restituents 3%	State 12%	State 20%
Restituents 3%	Community 2%	Restituents 3%	Restituents 3%
Employees 3%			

Note: The shares of most automobile suppliers were sold in the second wave and/or stakes were sold to foreign investors.

Table 8.20.   Extent and Liquidity of Selected
Equity Markets, 1995

	Number of Traded Firms
Central Europe	
Czech Republic	**1,635**
Hungary	42
Poland	65
Slovakia	18
Asia	
Malaysia	529
Korea	721
Taiwan	347
Indonesia	238
Latin America	
Argentina	149
Brazil	570
Chile	284
Mexico	185
European Union	
Greece	212
Portugal	169
France	450
Germany	678

Source: Filer and Hanousek 1996, 22.

small traders. It was operated by none other than Tříska. If those choices weren't sufficient for investors, investors could always trade directly at the Government Center for Securities, in the so-called Czech OTC. A host of brokerage houses, trading companies, and advisory organizations sprouted to service the new financial industry. On the surface, Czech financial capitalism appeared prepared to attract and to productively put to work the investment needed to bring the country back to the West (see table 8.20).

Financial System Regulation

The Czech neoliberals' attitude about regulation derived from their conviction that the state should abstain from markets, and that included regulating them. Tříska would label capital market regulation an anachronism of "American socialism" (quoted in Holub, Macháček, and Mlynař 1997, 10). Consequently, the neoliberals made no effort to reinvigorate the control mechanisms that had been de-emphasized during privatization, nor did they seek to construct a regulatory apparatus commensurate with the scope of the new capital markets. Much of the regulatory authority was concentrated in the Ministry of Finance and directed by officials who had little or no previous experience in markets, and who believed that the state did not have the right to closely regulate markets. Ježek recalled, "[Capital market regulation] wasn't merely neglected. The guys didn't even hide it. They refused regulation. I had an active dispute with Klaus, Tříska, Rudlovčák, and Kočárník. There wasn't disinterest. There was active resistance. This period was driven by the false philosophy of *laissez faire*, absolute liberalism" (*RP*, 1998, 4).

Specifically, the Czech capital market regulations required minimal disclosure requirements of enterprises and IPFs, including ownership, changes in ownership, or intentions to change ownership. The regulations also omitted provisions governing insider trading. What was worse, the regulators were empowered to impose only minor penalties on regulation violators. These regulatory lacunae were exacerbated by the inconsistencies in the Czech tax code and in the Czech Commercial Code. For example, the Czech tax system rewarded successful share trading and allowed enterprises and IPFs wide latitude in reporting profits and loss. This encouraged scarce resources to go into share trading on the one hand, and it allowed enterprises and IPFs opportunities to manipulate share prices and corporate finances for their own benefit. The possibility of manipulation of the Czech capital market system was further augmented by the Czech Commercial Code and, in particular, the implicit discrimination against minority shareholders. Finally, the Ministry of Finance (although the responsible market regulator) delegated regulatory authority to the exchanges. As the exchanges, and the Prague Stock Exchange in particular, were dominated by banks and IPF's member-owners,[48] the stage was set for influential owners to manipulate capital markets. The result, as we shall see in the next chapter, was that unscrupulous market players successfully corrupted the Czech capital markets.

The Ownership Regime: Voucher Privatization

The output of privatization in Central and Eastern Europe is the ownership regime. In the case of voucher privatization in the Czech Republic, it can be summarized by first owners who are primarily masses and investment funds, a first-ownership structure characterized by cross-holding at the economic level and dispersion at the enterprise level, a capital market system centered around public equity markets, and a state without the capacity and autonomy to regulate either the nascent capital markets or the new owners (see table 8.24 later in this chapter). The next chapter shows how the ownership regime produced by voucher privatization precipitated the capture of politics and economics by first owners who showed little interest in building either modern capitalism or democracy.

STANDARD PRIVATIZATION METHODS

Standard privatization methods produced a second ownership regime, distinct from voucher privatization. Standard privatization methods (including continued state ownership) comprised just over half (51.3 percent) of Czech privatization, so the ownership regime produced by standard privatization methods was consequential (see table 8.21).

Table 8.21. Czech Privatization by Privatization Method, 1995

Privatization Method	Share Value (bn CZK)	Portion of Total Value (%)
Voucher Privatization Methods		
Voucher Privatization	342.6	48.5
(a) Without Intermediaries		
(b) With Intermediaries		
Institutional Privatization	—	—
Voucher Privatization Total	342.6	48.5
Standard Privatization Methods		
Insider Privatization	2.2	0.3
(a) Manager Preference		
(b) Worker Preference		
Market Privatization	37.6	4.9
(a) Public Sale, Domestic Buyers		
(b) Public Sale, Foreign Buyers		
(c) Public Sale, Open		
Contingent Privatization	9.9	1.4
Reprivatization	21.4	3.0
State Residual Shareholding	230.1	32.6
Other Methods	64.1	9.1
Standard Privatization Total	365.3	51.3
Large Privatization Total	706.4	99.8

Source: FNP 1995, 9–12; author's calculations.
Notes: (1) Columns 2 and 3 may not add due to rounding; (2) The Shares Values are from Joint-Stock Companies; Large Privatization also included the privatization of property valued at 144.1 bn CZK. However, these properties were generally among the lowest value in the portfolio, under 50 mn CZK (Klvačová 1992, 6); (3) These shares are only those in the FNP portfolio. State ministries and the central bank also hold share portfolios (Schwartz 1997); (4) Share values are nominal values. The book value of these shares was 751.4 bn CZK. In the Czech system, part of the company assets are placed in reserve, thereby lowering the nominal value below the original book value; (5) Czech voucher privatization is voucher privatization with intermediaries thanks to the inclusion of IPF's shares; (6) Market privatization combines shares privatized by public offering (8.3 bn CZK), direct sale to domestic buyers (16.3 bn CZK), and direct sale to foreign buyers (13.1 bn CZK); (7) Reprivatization combines shares privatized to the restitution investment fund (19.7 bn CZK) and shares for individual restitution cases (1.7 bn CZK); (8) State Residual Shareholding includes strategic company shares (176.4 bn CZK) and nonstrategic shares (47.6 bn CZK); and (9) Other Methods includes free share transfers to local governments (50.1 bn CZK), to the agricultural support fund (12.2 bn CZK), to the nonprofit foundation fund (.07 bn CZK), as well as unallocated shares (1.7 bn CZK).

Over 60 percent of the assets privatized by "standard privatization methods" (or 32.6 percent of total assets) were "state residual shareholding" as of December 1995. How can the state remain a major owner in a privatized economy? The confusion centers on the term "privatization." By a privatized economy, we refer to the privatization of an *economy*, one in which most enterprise stakes, 70 percent is a sensible rule of thumb, are transferred to nonstate hands. In a privatized economy, then, the state can remain an important owner—as, for instance, in France.

The large state ownership after privatization indicated that Czech privatization was incomplete. Critics have gone so far as to cite the large Czech state shareholdings after voucher privatization as evidence that voucher privatization was a ruse to corral public opinion rather than a sincere effort to transform the Czech economy. It also indicated that the Czech government (to the extent it remained willing) would privatize a high percentage of Czech assets well after the completion of voucher privatization.[49] Inevitably, a large chunk of Czech privatization would take place over a long period of time. Most important, the large Czech state stake in the economy locked the Czech government into a dual role as administrator and privatizer of state assets. This dual role created a tension that the Czech state was unable to resolve to economic and political benefit.

The Czech Fund of National Property (FNP)

The Czech neoliberals created the FNP to implement the standard privatization methods approved by the Ministry of Privatization.[50] The FNP conducted auctions, public tenders, direct sales, free transfers, enterprise consolidations, and reprivatization.[51] Or, in terms of the typology used here: market privatization, contingent privatization, and other methods. The FNP also was responsible for what has been called the state's "residual" shares.

Like so much of the institutional machinery of Czech privatization, the FNP was established quickly, without regard to law. Indeed, the privatizers explicitly registered the FNP as a legal entity in the Corporate Register rather than as a state body. This legal trick allowed the privatizers to conduct business in the Fund of National Property without regard to the laws that pertain to state institutions.[52] It also allowed the Czech neoliberals to privatize a large chunk of assets to claimants who might otherwise try to derail privatization. In this way, the FNP's implementation of standard privatization methods was an integral political component of Czech rapid privatization.

The predictable result was that the FNP earned a reputation as a dishonest and slipshod institution. Rumors of bid rigging in auctions and bribes to FNP officials were rampant. For instance, Jan Suchánek, managing director of the investment fund YSE, publicly declared that several investment funds (including Koženy's Harvard Capital and Consulting) bought information from the FNP and other state institutions (Reed 1996). Real repercussions accompanied the accusations. Ježek dismissed M. Křmář, head of the Shares Department at the Fund of National Property, for allegedly disclosing to IPB the other bids in the competition for shares in three enterprises. IPB reportedly resubmitted (and after the deadline) revised bids according to Křmář's information (Reed 1996). In another case, IPB bought shares of Čokoládovny for book value just as Nestlé and the EBRD were paying three times book value. When revelations of the dicey sale hit the newsstands, Ježek dismissed the well-below-market sale as an administrative error.[53] Finally, key privatization cases evidently attracted payoffs to political party slush funds. The December 1997 discovery of a slush fund stashed in Switzerland linked to Klaus's ODS party prompted Klaus's resignation and the fall of the neoliberal government. The FNP's implementation of standard methods illustrated that privatization had matured into a clientalistic policy that benefited lucky and opportunistic state officials.

As administrator of state assets, the FNP was known for the mismanagement of state assets and often for corruption. Part of the reason was that the FNP's official approach to residual share ownership was indifference to enterprise affairs. FNP's guidelines grew out of the obvious fact that the FNP had neither the manpower nor the capital and expertise to supervise enterprise restructuring. Besides, the neoliberal idea was that enterprises would be privatized sooner or later, and that therefore the short-term decisions of the FNP would qualify as no better than inappropriate meddling. Real enterprise restructuring was best left for the first owners.

The absentee ownership practiced by the FNP meant that enterprise managers were typically the decision-makers. Without a serious mandate, FNP employees were available as allies and in practice enterprise managers often hired cooperative FNP employees. The most serious damage of the Czech policy of "state ownership *sans* responsibility" concerned the state banks, as we saw in chapter 7 and shall see below. In the Czech Republic, collusion and incompetence in one sphere—privatization—easily transferred to another—state administration.

First Owners (Standard Methods)

1. The State

The largest Czech shareholder, even after the two privatization waves, remained the Czech state. The FNP retained shareholdings in approximately

Table 8.22. FNP Share Portfolio Profile, 1996

	State Ownership Share of Enterprises (%)						
	100	*67–99*	*51–66*	*34–50*	*20–33*	*0–19*	*Total*
Nonstrategic Enterprises (By Number)	19	33	42	62	113	650	909
Strategic Enterprises (By Number)	4	11	7	28	4	3	59
Total (By Number)	23	44	49	90	117	653	968

Source: Schwartz 1997.
Notes: (1) Unless otherwise noted, all figures are from April 22, 1996; (2) The share of ČSOB incorporates all Czech and Slovak government shares, 90.1% in all; (3) 100% FNP-owned holding company UNIPETROL is included. Its shares in KAUČUK and CHEMOPETROL are counted as part of the individual companies; (4) 100% FNP-owned holding companies Prisko and Poldi are included; and (5) the twenty-eight enterprises listed in the 34% to 50% category include sixteen gas and electricity distributors, each of which excludes an additional 34% share owned by local government.

82 percent (1,426) of the original 1,738 enterprises, as of December 1994. The FNP retained at least a 20 percent share in 410 of these enterprises; and, as of June 1996, the FNP still retained at least a 30 percent stake in seventeen of the largest twenty industrial enterprises. By the end of 1997, the FNP had sold much of its residual shareholdings in nonstrategic shareholders, but had done virtually nothing in selling its strategic stakes. The existence of these large residual state shareholdings ensured that the state's ownership role in the economy would endure (Schwartz 1997).[54] (See tables 8.22 and 8.23.)

2. Managers

At a first glance at table 8.21, it may appear that managers were losers in privatization, including the Czech implementation of standard privatization methods. This table shows that insiders (including managers and workers) accounted for only 0.3 percent of privatized assets. Even if we assume that the 4.9 percent of assets privatized by market privatization and the 1.4 percent of assets privatized by contingent privatization benefited only managers, then the total of privatized assets accruing to managers would stand at a mere 6.6 percent.

Nevertheless, as designed in the political compromises during legalization in 1990 and 1991, the managers did benefit disproportionately from standard privatization methods, though perhaps not as much as elsewhere in the region. The small value of total assets accruing to managers (6.6 percent) is a deceptive indicator. One reason is that managers were nearly always the de facto authority in enterprises when the state was a very large shareholder, even in the country's largest companies. That authority offered managers opportunities to surreptitiously transfer enterprise assets to their personal accounts or

Table 8.23.   Major Czech State Shareholdings, 1996

Sector	Percent Stake	Managing Ministry
Banks		
IPB	32.88	Finance
KB	48.74	Finance
ČSOB	90.10	Finance
ČS	45.00	Finance
Utilities		
ČEZ	67.46	Industry
16 Regional Energy Distributors	45.27–49.21	Industry
Insurance		
Česká pojišťovna	26.27	Finance
Airlines		
ČSA	89.55	Transportation
Telecommunications		
SPT TELECOM	51.83	Economy
České radiokomunikace	70.49	Economy
Steel		
NOVÁ HUŤ	68.25	Industry
VI'TKOVICE	68.31	Industry
Coal		
Mostecká uhelná	46.29	Industry
OKD	54.00	Industry
Severočeské doly	55.00	Industry
4 others	31.47–47.00	Industry
Refineries and Petrochemicals		
CHEMOPETROL	61.00	Industry
KAUČUK	73.00	Industry
Sokolov	73.74	Industry
Manufacturing		
Aero Holding	61.83	Industry
ŠKODA PRAHA	54.77	Industry
ŠKODA—Mladá Boleslav	30.00	Industry

Notes: (1) Unless otherwise noted, all figures are from April 22, 1996; (2) ČSOB share includes 26.5% Czech National Bank, 19.6% FNP, 20% Czech Finance Ministry, and 24% National Bank of Slovakia (*HN,* April 16, 1996, 1); (3) The capital distribution of the oil and gas distributors is virtually identical: The approximate proportions are 45% (plus a percentage point) FNP, 15% private voucher holders, 34% communities and municipalities, and 6% other. Twenty percent of the 45% of the FNP share is set aside for a foreign strategic partner; (4) The state announced that as of the June 1996 shareholders meeting, the state's share in OKD will decline to 45%; (5) These figures include the holdings of now 100% state-owned oil company UNIPETROL. In 1997, KAUČUK and CHEMOPETROL were merged into UNIPETROL. The state will retain from approximately 67%–70% depending on whether the residual shares of chemical company Spolana are included. International oil consortium will own 49% of the oil refining subsidiary of UNIPETROL; (6) Shares are owned through Prisko, a holding company 100% owned by the state Konsolidační banka (Consolidation Bank) as of December 31, 1997. Prisko also holds the debts of ŠKODA—Mladá Boleslav, accrued before the alliance with Volkswagen.

to companies under their control. It also put the managers in excellent position to take in hefty bribes in return for enterprise influence and information. Moreover, when the FNP finally got around to privatizing its share portfolio, managers were more often the beneficiaries.[55] From a manager's viewpoint, Czech privatization, however, may compare unfavorably with privatization strategies implemented elsewhere in the region. For example, the Russian state turned over majority ownership to three-quarters of the large enterprises to insiders (including managers and workers).[56] The Polish state turned over 30 percent of enterprise assets to insiders through "liquidation," including liquidation through bankruptcy and privatization through liquidation (Schwartz and Haggard 1997). Nonetheless, it would mischaracterize their position to say that enterprise managers were losers in Czech privatization.

First-Ownership Structure (Standard Methods)

Czech standard privatization methods produced a first-ownership structure dominated by the FNP, owing to the state's large shareholdings. The FNP, despite its passive stance toward enterprise management, still administered the lion's share of the 32.6 percent share of the Czech economy's enterprise assets after the completion of voucher privatization. The neoliberals intended, however, that state ownership of enterprise stakes would be temporary, its role declining as the FNP sold off share blocks. The FNP was merely a transitional institution under this scenario, and the true first-ownership structure would be dominated by owners with decisive blocks of shares and underpinned by banks who would provide financing and direction. The state's privatization of the country's largest enterprises ground nearly to a halt from 1995 to the winter of 1998, though the FNP did privatize its ownership stakes of many smaller enterprises during this period.

Financial System (Standard Methods)

The financial system regarding the state ownership stakes depended on state choices. The first state choice was that the FNP should privatize its ownership stakes via the existing capital markets or through auctions, public tenders, and the like. The resulting financial system from FNP's implementation of these privatization methods is then the capital markets created by voucher privatization, and also a batch of privately held companies that would presumably raise capital through private share placements or through bank financing.

The FNP proved to be a slow privatizer. Lassitude meant that the main financial system—if we can still call it that—resulting from standard privatization methods revolved around the state. Here we encounter the second main Czech state choice, namely, that the FNP should be a passive owner. FNP representatives (and state officials from competent bureaucracies) should sit on company boards to monitor state shareholdings, but do little more. Under this arrangement, the FNP would delegate control of Czech corporate finance to enterprise managers or to outside owners (typically IPFs in the case of companies privatized by vouchers). In the cases of the critical strategic industries, however, the state lacks consistent policy. In practice it vacillated between financial restructuring (refineries and petrochemical firms), subsidies (banks, coal, steel), and passive monitoring (telecommunications, automobiles, national airline). Consequently, we can not refer to a financial system per se in these cases, but to a set of institutions and individuals whose priorities, resources, and strategies may vary over time.

Financial System Regulation (Standard Methods)

Regulation of the state's residual shareholdings addressed the capital market system generated by voucher privatization. The state was subject to the same low level of regulation as a public shareholder, no different than IPFs or ordinary citizen-shareholders. Circumstances—everyone knew the state would sooner or later sell its share blocks—exposed it more than most to the barely regulated capital markets, as we saw in chapter 7.

Regulation of the state's residual shareholdings also addressed how the state managed its residual shareholdings internally. Since the state and the FNP, in particular, usually delegated responsibility to enterprise managers or to other owners, state regulation was almost nonexistent. The danger of an absentee owner was particularly relevant to economic development regarding the state's bank shares. Since the state did not see fit to exercise hands-on bank supervision, the life-or-death development decisions about where and how much to invest lay with the bank managers and loan officers. That raised a gigantic moral hazard problem. The absence of regulation offered bank officials easy chances to get rich quick—give a bribe, get a loan. The chain of bank governance resulted in out of control lending policies punctuated by illegal and immoral arrangements between managers, bankers, and inevitably the FNP representatives charged to protect the financial integrity of the state portfolio.

The Ownership Regime (Standard Methods)

Czech standard privatization methods produced an unexpected ownership regime, thanks to the surprisingly large state residual shareholdings (see table 8.24). The natural supposition was that insiders, domestic investors, banks, or foreign strategic partners would become the new owners from

Table 8.24. The First Czech Ownership Regime

				Level of State Autonomy and Capacity	
Associated Privatization Method	First Owners	First-Ownership Structure	Financial System	Of Capital Market Regulator	Of Financial System
Voucher	Masses, Investment Funds	Cross-holding, Dispersed at Enterprise Level	Public Equity Markets	Low	Low
Standard	State, Managers	Simple, Concentrated at Enterprise Level	State Management, Bank/Finance Capital	Low	Low

Ownership Regime Parameter spans the top of the columns after the first.

standard privatization methods. Concentrated owners would then populate the economy, ownership stakes would trade hands in an opaque system of private placement, and regulation would be dominated by the commercial code, the sanctity of contracts, and perhaps bank intervention. Instead, an ownership regime predicated on state residual share policy took its place alongside the capital markets produced by voucher privatization. In that state policy, the managers remained the decisive actors, as they were under communism (Mlčoch 1992). Contrary to conventional wisdom in the West, state ownership did not translate into state control in the Czech Republic.

DANGER SIGNS

For Czech neoliberals voucher privatization was a great success, based on neoliberal principles. First, vouchers privatized a visible, critical mass of enterprises. Without controversy, it created first owners, the putative basis of capitalism and markets. Second, it bought citizen support for the economic reform process. As proof, masses rewarded the privatizers through the general elections of 1992 and of 1996. Neoliberals dismissed evident failures such as Klaus's resignation in December 1997 as the inevitable consequence of a temporary economic slowdown. Structural imperfections associated with IPFs and imperfect capital markets were temporary anomalies to be washed out by the power of market incentives. Furthermore, neoliberals could justify the slow implementation of standard privatization as a necessary political sacrifice for voucher privatization to move forward. Finally, they argued that the Czech privatization scandals were an inevitable, if distasteful, price of market transformation. Viewed through the prism of the Washington consensus, Czech rapid privatization hardly represented a policy that would go radically wrong.

It is easier to catalog the potential shortcomings of Czech rapid privatization when we view them from the alternative, ownership regime theory. If we consider Czech voucher privatization, we see that the first owners rarely came with capital and enterprise expertise. The first-ownership structure was a network of cross-holding ownership dominated by IPFs with no obvious incentives to restructure companies, but a lot of incentives to collaborate with other large shareholders (including representatives of the state) to strip enterprise assets. Finally, the financial system that vouchers produced was a hodgepodge of virtually unregulated capital markets that presented an invitation for corrupt operators.

If we consider Czech standard privatization methods, we see that the state was the primary first owner, and that it was a reluctant one. The first-ownership structure comprised enterprises with large state-share blocks, other shares usually divided among voucher shareholders. The Czech state, however, usually withheld capital and expertise (to the degree that it had them) from its enterprises, much like other first owners. The financial system was then the state institutions responsible for the residual share portfolio, and because of the state share management policy of benign neglect, the enterprise managers. Regarding regulation, the Czech state's purposeful neglect over its residual shareholdings tempted state officials, managers, and other owners to ally to seize and to strip assets. The privatizers' neglect of the FNP invariably translated into its ineffectiveness as administrator of state property.

In sum, the neoliberal privatizers brought little in the way of capital and expertise to enterprises that needed desperately to be restructured, and it offered first owners easy opportunities to strip enterprise assets by refusing to regulate privatization. Those opportunities, in turn, could best be realized by assistance from cooperative state officials, a group readily available in the Czech transition. In the following chapter, we will see how the ownership regime provided a template for further development that diverged from capitalism and democracy.

NOTES

1. The reader may notice the apparent incongruity of the analysis of demand-side procedures in the implementation stage. It would seem more appropriate to place the analysis in the legalization stage, both according to a time-line criterion—voucher privatization procedures were fixed in 1991—and according to a substantive criterion—the

development of demand-side procedures decidedly does not involve the actual implementation of voucher privatization. Instead, I chose to incorporate that analysis of the voucher privatization demand-side tasks in the voucher privatization implementation section. In the Czech case, the citizens began registering for voucher privatization in September 1991, and they began to entrust their vouchers to IPFs in January 1992. It was only in May 1992, however, that voucher holders and the IPFs began the process of actually bidding for shares. Under these circumstances, it is tricky to demarcate firm limits between privatization stages.

2. The detachment of Tříska and his team from the public and from other members of the elite prompted suspicions and rumors that Tříska managed voucher privatization for his own benefit (*Respekt*, 1993, 8–9). Tříska founded the stock market RM-System, provided software advice to PVT (the company that provided the software for voucher privatization), took partial ownership in an IPF (through his wife), and maintained connections with suspicious operators (such as Harvard Capital and Consulting's V. Kožený). I believe, however, that the notion that Tříska advocated voucher privatization for his own enrichment is far fetched, despite the obvious fact that he profited from the system he helped to create. Tříska embraced the idea long before anyone had an idea how voucher privatization would play out.

3. Tříska set all share prices 3/100 in the first round of the first wave, 2/100 in the first round of the second wave.

4. Shares were not technically issued until after all the rounds—that is, the entire wave was complete.

5. In the first wave, the costs were 35 CZK for coupon books (registration fee), 1,000 CZK for voucher points. In the second wave, the cost was 1,050 since the CKP raised the coupon book price to 50 CZK. However, due to the march of prices, the second-wave entry cost was less than 18 percent of a monthly wage (Mládek 1992, 11).

6. The "Informační příručka," published by Federal Ministry of Finance in Czech, Slovak, Hungarian, and English, provided basic information for the first wave. The price was 15 CZK. Over 1.2 mn were sold, making it the most popular publication of 1991 (CKP 1995, 12).

7. Some analysts also add *under-eighteen claimants* to the unfairly excluded; *PlanEcon* argued that "[T]he Czech Parliament in its infinite wisdom, disqualified anybody from 18 years of age from participating in the scheme although those under 18 years of age were the only ones with a guaranteed 'clean' political argument." Yet, this argument unreasonably presumes that "clean" under-eighteen claimants would invest independently of their "compromised" communist parents. It can, I believe, therefore be dismissed (*PlanEcon*, December 1992, no 4–5). The editor of *PlanEcon* is J. Vanouš, a Czech with a special familiarity with Czech-style privatization. Vanouš attended the first important privatization meeting at Kolodej in February 1990. Vanouš has written critically of rapid privatization approaches in the past, however.

8. Czechoslovak vouchers were transferable "only between relatives and/or on the death of the owner." Vouchers were (are) transferable in Albania, Armenia, Belarus, Estonia (after 1994), Kyrgyzstan, Latvia, Poland, Romania (1992 Plan), and Russia (Estrin and Stone 1996, 8–9).

9. E. Klvačová observed in 1991 that "[Czechoslovak] privatization is marked by . . . an aversion (manifested above all from the side of real and potential entrepreneurs) to the sale of national property to foreign capital" (Klvačová 1991, 1). Klvačová is a well-placed and keen observer. As noted earlier, she was a leading spokesperson for the minister of privatization and, as of this writing, is editor of *Ekonom*, a well-regarded economic weekly.

10. IPFs were not included in the first Czech voucher privatization schemes. Tříska claimed that the pressure to include IPFs as part of the privatization process emanated from Parliament, not from a neoliberal calculation (author interview with privatization officials).

11. The 100,000 CZK requirement was later raised to a still modest 1,000,000 CZK or about $35,000.

12. Initially, the limitation was 20 percent per IPF, but 40 percent per IPF company. In practice, this meant that a fund company could have several IPF funds that collectively may have owned as much as 40 percent of a particular company. This was a way in which a fund company could control more than the legally mandated 20 percent. Later, this loophole was eliminated, so that neither a fund company (collectively) nor an IPF could own more than 20 percent of a particular enterprise's shares.

13. Privatizers feared a "run on the funds," according to J. Coffee. He claims that this was the case for both amendments, though I believe that this was unlikely in the case of the 20 percent maximum (Coffee 1994, 17). More likely, the privatizers were seeking to prevent excessive power in the hands of the IPFs.

14. The only restriction on bank ownership eligibility was a law which mandated that banks could not directly own stakes in other financial institutions, yet banks easily got around this law by establishing IPFs as legally independent subsidiaries. The major exception was ČS, which goofed.

15. An indication of the poor planning of the bank IPFs was their general unpreparedness in analyzing companies. See the following chapter for details.

16. With the exceptions of CA, the investment company of Creditanstalt, an Austrian bank; ŽB, the investment company of Živnostenská banka; and, AG, the investment company of Agrobanka.

17. Several IPFs started as consulting firms to state ministries and to enterprises. Kožený's Harvard Capital and Consulting began in this manner (Szirmai 1993).

18. We could also add a third category of IPF participants: regional and industrial IPFs. Often, these IPFs were underwritten by enterprise management with specific interests in their own enterprise or in neighboring or competing enterprises.

19. The details of the arrangement were ambiguous. Harvard later argued the terms were one year and a day after the vouchers were transformed into shares. Thus, redemption day was not the winter of 1992–1993, but rather spring 1994, one year from the time vouchers became shares.

20. Ježek's point of view is that people were following human nature and waiting until the last moment. According to Ježek there is no doubt that interest in privatization grew, but in his estimation there would have been 6 million voucher holders rather than 8.5 million (Husák 1997, 159).

21. In the first wave of privatization, approximately 5.95 million Czechs bought share vouchers. The total number of participants was 8.54 million; 2.54 million Slovaks also participated in voucher privatization. In the second wave of privatization approximately 6.16 million Czechs bought vouchers (CKP 1995; Mládek 1994, 20).

22. Petr Vanouš, an IPF manager (and brother of *PlanEcon*'s Jan Vanouš), reported in 1993 that only about half of IPFs reported to the government the required information.

23. The prewave was designed for voucher holders to entrust voucher points to IPFs. Participants entrusted 63.5 percent of the voucher points to IPFs in the second privatization wave (CKP 1995, 26).

24. Bláha et al. 1992, for example, warned of possible abuses directed against small shareholders. Prokurátor (*prosecutor* in English) Ivan Gašparovič also warned the government about serious legislative shortcomings of voucher privatization in 1992.

25. The actual shares were distributed in the spring of 1993.

26. There was a brief moment of concern in the winter and spring of 1993 when the Czech privatizers temporarily balked at distributing shares to Slovaks. When the Ministry of Finance distributed the shares to the Slovaks, the moment passed.

27. By comparison, Slovenia 2.1 percent, Hungary 4.1 percent, Poland 4.3 percent, Slovakia 21.6 percent, Germany 25.1 percent, Czech Republic 33.9 percent, United States 62.8 percent, Great Britain 113.2 percent (Linne 1996, 11–15).

28. Fifty-nine percent of those Czechs surveyed (number of respondents: 1,623) responded rather dissatisfied or very dissatisfied to the question, "When you think about it in general terms, how do you think our privatization process is going?" (*Trendy*, February 1994).

29. The first wave incorporated both Czech and Slovak companies. Owing to the split of Czechoslovakia into the Czech Republic and Slovakia, the second wave included only Czech companies. The reported figures do not include Slovak companies.

30. Sixty-eight percent of those Czechs surveyed responded (number of respondents: 1,493) surely yes or rather yes to the question, "Do you consider that voucher privatization is the fairest form of dividing up national property?" (*Trendy*, July 1993).

31. Eighty-four percent of Klaus's ODS party (versus 68 percent of all Czechs) surveyed (number of respondents: 498) responded surely yes or rather yes to the question, "Do you consider that voucher privatization is the best form of dividing up national property?" (*Trendy*, July 1993). Only 33.9 percent of Klaus's ODS (versus 59 percent of all Czechs) surveyed responded (number of respondents: 494) rather dissatisfied or very dissatisfied to the question, "When you think about it in general terms, how do you think our privatization process is going?" (*Trendy*, February 1994).

32. The first privatization wave included the shares of 988 enterprises; the second privatization wave included the shares of 861 enterprises. The shares of 185 second privatization wave enterprises were also included in both privatization waves (CKP 1995, 26–27). Included in the first privatization wave were 503 Slovak companies (*PlanEcon*, December 31, 1992, 3).

33. Survey data implied that IPF offers uplifted Slovak support for privatization. Slovak responses to the question, "Is it necessary to change all large enterprises in state ownership to share companies or to private ownership?" show a jump in positive

answers (surely yes or rather yes) from December 1991 to the June 1992 elections from 38.2 percent to 45.7 percent. But, the jump was short lived: By January 1993, the positive answers were back to 39.4 percent (those figures are: 11.8 percent, *Surely Yes*; 27.6 percent, *Rather Yes*; 43.0 percent, *Rather No*; 17.6 percent, *Surely No*).

	May 1990	December 1990	June 1991	December 1991	June 1992
Surely Yes	15.2	15.4	14.7	9.9	12.2
Rather Yes	31.8	32.8	29.5	28.3	33.5
Rather No	38.8	36.8	38.0	41.9	38.5
Surely No	14.2	15.0	17.8	19.8	15.8

Source: STEM

34. Did voucher privatization, as the key economic reform, encourage the split of Czechoslovakia? After all, the Slovak leadership halted voucher privatization when the Slovak Republic became an independent state in 1993. Moreover, voucher privatization was demonstrably less popular among Slovaks then Czechs. In my judgment, the answer to this question is still no. The Slovak leadership and the Czech leadership had been operating on different wavelengths since the 1989 revolution. The Czechs emphasized economic and social policymaking presuming a whole state. The Slovak leadership, on the other hand, focused on how the consequences of policy would impact their state and, more importantly, their authority in their state. For instance, Ježek reports from a 1990 meeting between Czech and Slovak economic leaders, the concerns on the Czech side were on the proper reform steps; on the Slovak side, concerns centered on the progress of a common economy. Ježek later wrote about this meeting, "It was as if I were on Mars" (Husák 1997, 229–230). No doubt the Slovaks felt similarly. Voucher privatization was an excuse, not a cause, given the different agendas.

35. The FNP created joint stock companies, which then issued shares that could be privatized through several methods. As of December 31, 1995, the FNP privatized large property valued at 895.5 (bn CZK). The FNP transformed 751.4 (bn CZK) of enterprise shares directly into a joint stock company. The FNP transferred 144.1 (bn CZK) directly to private owners by nonvoucher methods (Fund of National Property 1995, 10–11).

36. Author interview with researchers at the Czechoslovak Management Center.

37. Lizner was caught with millions CZK in a briefcase leaving a Chinese restaurant in Prague in 1994. The money evidently was a bribe for facilitating the purchase of brewery shares by TWI, a Czech investment firm. Lizner was the highest public official in Czech history to be brought up and convicted on corruption charges.

38. American mutual funds face the same challenge in buying (or selling) large numbers of shares without moving the market; this problem may partly explain why American mutual fund performance typically lags the overall market.

39. Author interview with then-official at IPB.

40. Not including Slovak voucher holders and investment funds. In addition, two big "ifs" hang over the data. One is the uncertain meaning of book value in the Czech context. The book value of the Czech companies prior to privatization tended to grossly overvalue machinery and equipment and at the same time drastically undervalue land. Sometimes land values were not even listed on the corporate ledgers. A second is the nagging suspicion that particular IPFs may have unduly benefited in voucher privatization, as discussed earlier.

41. Section 158, paragraph 2, Czechoslovakian Commercial Code. The Federal Assembly of Czechoslovakia passed zákon č. 513/1991 Sb. which contains the new Czech Commercial Code. The Czechoslovakian Commercial Code went into effect January 1, 1992. The Czechoslovakian Commercial Law automatically became the Czech Commercial Law with the split of the country on January 1, 1993. Furthermore, workers could not buy more than 10 percent (later 5 percent) of an enterprise's privatized shares at a preferential price.

42. The fight over employee preferences was greater over the Small Privatization Law. The major issue in small privatization concerned whether to give shop employees special access to financing, lower prices, or preemptive purchasing rights. The small privatization resolution, consistent with neoliberal thinking, was to hold auctions—highest bid wins (Mládek 1992; Frydman, Rapaczynski, and Earle, n.d.).

43. The unsold portion of shares slated to be sold to workers was a major component of the ensuing state ownership share (author interview with a senior official at the Fund of National Property; Schwartz 1997).

44. The fate of Czech workers in privatization parallels their fate overall in the Czech transition period from 1990 to 1997. The Czech government in 1990 organized a tripartite commission that was regarded by nearly all locals as a sham. The real wages of workers plummeted in 1990–1992. Real wages didn't begin serious catch-up until 1994 when the tripartite commission failed to reach a general agreement of wages (Flek 1996). Only in 1997 did Czech real wages reach the 1989 level.

45. An important loophole was the lack of a provision to prevent the incursion of foreign institutions to act as IPFs. It was only necessary for a foreign institution to establish a domestic subsidiary. The domestic subsidiary could then act as a Czech IPF. However, only one major foreign bank, Creditanstalt of Austria, took advantage of this oversight in the law and participated in voucher privatization.

46. Observation of Creditanstalt Securities, a house with an excellent reputation in the Czech Republic (Creditanstalt Securities [Prague], "Introduction to the Firm," 1996, 9).

47. The Prague Stock Exchange formally opened on April 6, 1993. Active trading of voucher stakes began on June 22, 1993, with 622 issues; another 333 issues were added on July 19, 1993. Many IPFs are also traded on the exchange. Due to the exchange's listing requirements not all voucher issues and IPFs are traded on the Prague Stock Exchange. All issues are traded on the RM-System exchange and on the Czech OTC (Kotrba 1995, 7).

48. R. Salzmann, then-chairman of Komercní Banka and prominent ODS party member, was the first chairman of the Prague Stock Exchange.

49. As of December 31, 1994, the Fund of National Property had only sold off 63 percent of the assets approved for public competitions, 55 percent of the assets approved for public auctions, and 33 percent of the assets approved for sale on the capital markets. As of March 1995, the Ministry of Privatization has approved an additional 2.3 bn CZK of public competitions and 3.7 bn CZK of public auctions. And, the Fund of National Property is holding an additional 53.1 bn CZK of shares that will be probably be sold into the capital markets in the future (figures are from *Fond národního majétku* [FNP] *Newsletter*, March 1995, 2). Many analysts muddled the issue by reporting assets as privatized when the privatization method was *approved* by the Ministry of Privatization instead of *completed* by the FNP.

50. Originally, the FNP was part of the Ministry of Privatization. Ježek was then simultaneously FNP chairman and the minister of privatization. In 1992, when Skalicky became FNP chair, the positions were divided. In 1994, Ježek was dismissed for R. Češka.

51. The Large Privatization Law explicitly mentions ten allowable privatization methods. Tříska claims that the state used fifty-six privatization methods (Tříska 1994, 6). The Czech Ministry of Finance typically awarded RIF (Restitution Investment Fund) 3 percent of the shares of each enterprise privatized by vouchers.

52. A model case was the design of the Fund of National Property—the agency charged to administer state property before its privatization and to implement standard privatization methods (the Czech Fund of National Property was founded by zákon č. 171/1991 Sb.). The privatizers established the FNP as a legal entity in the Corporate Register rather than as a state body. This legal trick allowed the privatizers to conduct business in the Fund of National Property over the laws that pertain to state institutions (Rychetský 1993).

53. Indications that the relationship between the FNP and IPB might be rather more cosy than the public interest requires were also confirmed by a further sale to IPB for nominal price of shares in twenty-five enterprises—for example, in the world-famous brewery Plzeňské pivovary. In return, IPB gave the FNP a building on Prague's Rašínovo nábřeží.

54. The vast Czech state portfolio reflects the fact that in the Czech Republic, an approved privatization project is not a completed project. As of December 31, 1994, the Fund of National Property had only sold off 63 percent of the assets approved for public competitions (4.3 bn CZK out of 6.8 bn CZK) passed on from the Ministry of Privatization, 55 percent of the assets approved for public auctions (14.2 bn CZK out of 25.8 bn CZK), and 33 percent of the assets approved for sale on the capital markets (24.2 bn CZK out of 73.8 bn CZK). As of this writing, the Czech state does not have an explicit plan to privatize part of the remaining share portfolio, especially the strategic share portfolio.

55. Sometimes Czech managers who bought their enterprises from the FNP found out that they paid too much for the assets to the FNP and ended up heavily indebted. One Czech banker estimated that over 75 percent of the so-called privatization loans, as of 1997, were in default.

56. In practice, many Russian managers were able to gain enterprise control (Blasi, Kroumova, and Kruse 1997).

9

The Abuses of Plutocracy, the Failure of Czech Neoliberalism—January 1996 to December 1997

The preceding chapters showed how a rapid privatization strategy drove the Czech national privatization process trajectory. That trajectory, in turn, resulted in the first Czech ownership regime. This chapter argues that this first Czech ownership regime laid down the foundations for plutocratic capitalism, a political-economic system based on collusion between business and government and characterized by a biased or incomplete system of market regulation. The ensuing failure of plutocratic capitalism to sustain economic prosperity and to sustain popular faith in democratic government was a likely cause for the fall of the Czech neoliberals in December 1997. The Czech outcome suggests that plutocratic capitalism discourages outsiders (the source of money and votes) from participating in markets and politics, and thus undermines the quality of capitalism and democracy.

The failure of Czech neoliberalism came as a great surprise to virtually all domestic and foreign analysts concerned with the Czech Republic. Most forecast that the Czech economy would experience progressively better performance and Czech reformers would experience high popularity ratings after privatization. First owners would sell ownership stakes to an active, democratically inclined class of owners. The Czech Republic's bright prospects and its privatization achievement prematurely prompted Ježek to gush, "We are the stars" (Zagrodzka 1993).

What the neoliberals and their legions of supporters did not realize at the time is that Czech rapid privatization had created an ownership regime with too many holes for the state to regulate. These holes were manifest in controlling shareholder–minority shareholder gaps and principle-agent gaps (specifically, owner-agent gaps and employer-employee gaps) (Berle and Means 1932). They offered some new owners and managers easy chances to steal from minority shareholders and enterprises. The inevitable outcome was a reconstituted ownership regime pernicious to capitalism and democracy I call plutocratic capitalism.

Plutocratic capitalism evolved from share trading and asset movements just after the completion of voucher privatization. Managers, traders, and a diverse group of owners (particularly IPFs) used unregulated capital markets to drain assets from enterprises or from lending financial institutions. This exercise, locally referred to as tunneling, was manifest in the explosion of bad debt on bank and state agency books and in the transformation of the ownership structure into an opaque labyrinth of enterprises, subsidiaries, and trading companies. Worst of all, tunnelers transferred much of the stolen resources overseas or simply consumed them. Domestic investment was relatively rare. Tunneling indicated that the neoliberal experiment had gone wrong.

The tunneling phenomenon and the associated market abuses could not have occurred without the participation of state officials (including prominent neoliberals). Co-opted government officials worked in cahoots with tunnelers. They blocked legislation that would make markets more honest, such as shareholder rights, investment fund regulation, conflict of interest, and disclosure requirements. They also undermined efforts to enforce the market laws that did exist. Sometimes, state officials served on company boards and assisted tunnelers in extracting corporate assets from rightful owners or lien holders. Their major reward was wealth for themselves and for their political party. To be sure, some of the Chicago boys of Milton Friedman and Václav Klaus had mutated into the Chicago gang members of Al Capone.

The plutocracy's tawdry behavior provoked an effective public backlash of humiliation and disgust, fortunately for the Czech Republic. The discovery of a Swiss bank account at the disposal of Klaus's ODS party in 1997 was the mortal blow. Klaus's subsequent resignation as prime minister probably marked the end of the brief neoliberal era in the Czech Republic, though it remains to be seen whether the new rulers will raise the quality of capitalism and democracy. Many enterprises lack the capacity to compete on world markets. Many citizens feel contempt for domestic politicians. Irrespective of whether the country's quality of capitalism and democracy improve, the unregulated free market may never again be above suspicion in the Czech Republic.

SHARE TRADING AND ASSET MOVEMENTS, JUNE 1993 TO DECEMBER 1995

The first-ownership regime was the template for the transfer of ownership stakes after the completion of the first and second privatization waves. It is the starting point for an analysis of what came next (see tables 9.1 and 9.2, figure 9.1). The starting date is June 1993, when the two main Czech stock markets (the Prague Stock Exchange and the RM-System) began publicly trading

Table 9.1. The First Czech Ownership Regime

		Ownership Regime Parameter		Level of State Autonomy and Capacity	
Associated Privatization Method	First Owners	First-Ownership Structure	Financial System	Of Capital Market Regulator	Of Financial System
Voucher	Masses, Investment Funds	Cross-holding, Dispersed at Enterprise Level	Public Equity Markets	Low	Low
Standard	State, Enterprise Management, Multinationals	Simple, Concentrated at Enterprise Level	State Management, Bank/Finance Capital	Low	Low

the shares of the companies privatized by vouchers in the first privatization wave. The second wave augmented the number of traded shares in 1995.

The commencement of trading of first-wave voucher privatization shares inspired optimistic forecasts for the Czech Republic's nascent market economy and democracy. Czech stock markets would provide a venue for investors to participate in the development of companies with the greatest profit potential. They also would provide a venue for companies to raise investment capital for restructuring. It was hard not to agree that "one of the most important developments in the reform programme is the creation of an overnight capital market for thousands of companies participating in the voucher privatization scheme" (Arbess 1992). The Prague Stock Exchange rallied dramatically in the first months of trading, as if to confirm the wisdom of the Czech reformers.

Table 9.2. The Czech First Owners

Investment Privatization Funds	33.7
Bank IPFs	(14.8)
Nonbank IPFs	(18.9)
Individual Investors	15.1
Strategic Partners—Domestic	4.2
Strategic Partners—Foreign	2.0
Fund of National Property	32.6
Managers and Employees	0.3
Other	12.1

Source: Various national sources.
Note: Figures are from 1995 and reflect book values.

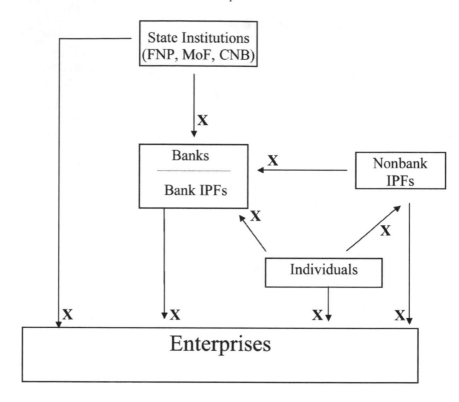

Legend

Owner      Holding

X = Potential Owner – Agent Gap (8 in Total)

Figure 9.1.   The First Czech Ownership Structure, 1993.

The neoliberals also expressed confidence in the country's major new owners, the IPFs. IPFs would drive Czech modernization and subsequent integration into the Western economic community, it was believed. A prominent Western lawyer who worked closely with the Czech neoliberals wrote,

> [The investment funds] will also want to maximise their investments, restructuring the old state enterprises by raising capital and negotiating for foreign management, technology and marketing commitments.
>
> All this should spell opportunity for many strategic and financial investors who have been waiting on the sidelines to see how the reform programme developed. (Arbess 1992)

IPFs and functioning capital markets appeared to form a solid base for modern capitalist development in the Czech Republic. The cross-holding ownership structure was judged to be ephemeral. A leading Czech neoliberal judged that "what will happen after privatization, how the shares will be grouped as exchange for coupons is a matter for the market" (J. Muroň, quoted in Marek 1991, 3). Some Czechs even mounted a campaign to nominate Klaus for a Nobel Prize in economics. From a political perspective, the creation of the new ownership class would support the development of democratic practice in the Czech Republic. Built on private ownership and capital markets, a period of free-market prosperity seemed at hand.

Portfolio Concentration and Minority Shareholding Risks

IPFs (and other large owners) began concentrating ownership stakes soon after share trading opened. Many IPFs had a widely dispersed share portfolio following voucher privatization.[1] SIS, the bank IPF associated with ČS, owned stakes in over 500 companies; IKB, the bank IPF associated with KB, owned stakes in over 200 companies.[2] By 1996, the SIS portfolio was under 200 firms and the IKB portfolio was under 100 firms. Considering the Czech economy overall: in 1993 the largest enterprise owner had collected over 50 percent in less than 1 percent of public companies and between 30 percent and 50 percent in 6 percent of public companies; by 1997 the largest enterprise owner had 50 percent in 38 percent of public companies and between 30 percent and 50 percent in 35 percent of public companies. In sum, while only 7 percent of public companies had decisive controlling owners in 1993, nearly three quarters had so four years later.

At first glance, ownership consolidation supported the primary neoliberal proposition: first owners would sell ownership stakes to active owners (or intermediate owners) soon after privatization. Prospective active owners generally demand controlling (often majority) stakes in enterprises before committing to a project. Ownership consolidation evidently indicated that first owners were amalgamating shareholdings into big enough packages that would interest prospective active owners.

Ownership consolidation hid defensive motivations on the part of shareholders. The first owners concentrated holdings in individual equities (and simultaneously divested small holdings), not only with the idea of selling out to prospective active owners but also because the risk of minority shareholding in the Czech market conditions was severe. Czech law granted controlling (and especially majority) owners extraordinary powers to hijack shareholder rights regardless of the impact on company finances or of the opposition of individual shareholders.[3] Legal safeguards held dear by Western investors such as due diligence or fraud had little meaning in the Czech context. For instance, majority shareholders could legally transfer company assets to personally owned dummy companies, or they could generate liens on company assets, and then simply pocket the loans. Minority shareholder stakes would in either case be vulnerable.

Capital market inefficiencies exacerbated the market vulnerability of minority shareholders, especially individual shareholders. Individuals generally did not control enough shares to interest most buyers and so were restricted to trading on the public markets, away from where the real action took place. Consequently, individuals almost certainly attracted only low prices on the public stock exchanges. Nobody knew the prices or the volumes of large share transactions.[4] Individuals were losers in the capital markets not because they made investments in lousy companies, but because of the particular institutionalized system of incentives existing in the Czech Republic just after privatization.

The risks of minority shareholding extended to IPFs that were shareholding companies (*akciové společnosti* or *a.s.*).[5] These IPFs were potentially vulnerable to outside shareholders gaining a controlling interest. To protect against that threat, IPF managers bought shares, sometimes using shadow companies, in their own IPFs. They also purchased shares in other IPFs and in the parent banks of bank IPFs to protect their positions. As a result, IPFs became entangled; cross-holding among IPFs and banks accompanied concentration in enterprise stakes. Naturally, cross-holding among the IPFs promoted common interests and strategies among IPFs and banks. The emergence of a new ownership interest group centering on the banks and IPFs was at hand.

Owner-Agent Gaps

Czech-style voucher privatization created owner-agent gaps that exacerbated the risks of shareholding, even for owners with large share blocks. Owner-agent gaps are situations in which agents could potentially exploit owners without legal recourse. In the Czech Republic, the combination of state indifference to capital market regulation and rules instituted during privatization offered agents extraordinary chances to take advantage of owners. To determine the impact of the owner-agent gaps on share trading and asset movements just after privatization requires a precise accounting. The X's in figure 9.1 identify three classes of owners and eight owner-agent sites in the first Czech ownership structure (see also table 9.3). An important result is that bank management, IPF managers, and some enterprise managers had extraordinary powers of control over assets. The next section shows how the problems associated with the owner-agent gaps evolved to disastrous proportions.

Table 9.3. Owners and Agents in the First Czech Ownership Regime

1. Individuals
    1a. Individuals/Bank IPFs
    1b. Individuals/Nonbank IPFs
    1c. Individuals/Enterprises
2. IPFs
    2a. Bank IPFs/Enterprises
    2b. Nonbank IPFs/Enterprises
    2c. Nonbank IPFs/Banks
3. State Institutions
    3a. State Institutions/Enterprises
    3b. State Institutions/Banks

Individuals/Bank IPFs and Individuals/Nonbank IPFs

Although they were owners, individuals who invested in IPFs in the first wave were powerless to control their agents, the IPF managers. This was due in part to the investment fund laws. First-wave IPFs were shareholding companies (*akciové společnosti*). Theoretically, then, IPF shareholders could remove the IPF manager by shareholder vote. Yet this avenue effectively was foreclosed by cross-holding among IPFs by other IPFs. Investors made only one attempt to remove a major IPF management team (Trend Fund), and though they "succeeded," these investors found an almost worthless shell (Weiss and Nikitin 1997, 7).

Individual investors in second-wave IPFs were no better off than those who invested in IPFs during the first wave. About 80 percent of second-wave IPFs were closed-end investment trusts. In these trusts, a management contract tied IPF managers to the investors. Management contracts typically lasted as long as twenty years and incorporated stiff penalties if the contract were broken. The management of closed-end trust IPFs was virtually impossible to remove since an investment contract cannot easily be annulled in court once agreed upon by both parties.

Both bank IPF and nonbank IPF managers took advantage of an owner-agent gap between IPFs and IPF shareholders. They charged their shareholders exorbitant fees. The charges were not evident in the 1.5 percent to 2.0 percent of assets under management—figures common for Western mutual fund management fees. Instead, excess charges were embedded in hidden brokerage fees, redemption fees, transfer fees, and the like. Most important, IPF managers made money both personally and for their corporate fund parents by trading their share portfolio. The IPF managers had privileged access to enterprise information and insider trading information, including efforts by outsiders to buy or sell share stakes. Needless to say, the profits earned by IPF managers did not trickle down to the IPF owners.

The obvious recourse for dissatisfied IPF investors was to sell IPF shares on the capital market. If IPF shareholders wanted to sell their IPF shares they could, but they would receive a paltry sum compared with the liquidation value of their IPF investment. Owing to the lack of control of IPF shareholders, the capital market usually valued IPF shares at heavy discounts to net market asset value—normally about 50 percent for bank IPFs and from 50 percent to 90 percent for nonbank IPFs. Therefore, citizens who entrusted their vouchers to either first-wave or second-wave IPFs were stuck with IPF management. They were victims of the owner-agent gap between IPF managers and IPF shareholders.

Individuals and Enterprises

Individuals lacked incentives to act as active owners. Just as in any Western capital market, it was very expensive in time and money for Czech individuals to influence enterprise behavior. Surveys confirm that individuals did not influence enterprise behavior (Schwartz 1997).

Bank IPFs/Enterprises

IPFs are hybrid institutions; they are simultaneously owners and agents. IPFs own enterprise shares, just as IPF shareholders own IPF shares. Although bank IPF managers could and did take advantage of their individual shareholders, their own position was more complicated. Bank IPF managers often wielded control, especially financial control, over enterprises in which the IPF owned large share blocks. The asymmetry in the owner-agent relationship between IPF shareholders and IPF managers on the one hand and between IPF managers and enterprise managers on the other gave IPF managers enormous control in the Czech economy. In practice, since bank management normally dictated the activities of its bank IPF managers (depending on the internal policy and control mechanisms of the parent bank), the real authority over asset movements was in the hands of bank management.[6]

The banks had special incentives to consolidate bank IPF ownership stakes after privatization. First, large ownership holdings allowed the bank to monitor its loan portfolio better. Enterprise information at this time was notoriously hard to come by, even for creditors; ownership helped to solve this information gap. In addition, bank IPFs could and ultimately did force enterprises to take on unneeded debt at high interest rates. That debt would be held by and thus benefit the parent bank of the bank IPF. The enterprise would lose because the added expensive debt would burden earnings; minority shareholders would lose because the debt would lower the underlying value of the enterprise. Debt loading was standard practice at PIAS, the "state-owned" IPB IPF.[7] Banks were critical players in the postvoucher privatization economy, a result unexpected and sometimes unwelcome to neoliberals.[8]

Nonbank IPFs/Enterprises

Nonbank IPFs' proportion of total shares increased relative to bank IPFs' during and after the second privatization wave. They continued to accumulate shares in the capital markets, while bank IPFs spread their portfolio to include a greater proportion of debt securities. Evidently, nonbank IPFs were trying to maximize management fees and trying to concentrate holdings in takeover candidates, presumably in preparation of selling to active owners. Although those motivations encouraged nonbank IPF managers, a more potent motivation was the possibility of stripping enterprise assets for their personal benefit. That possibility came about because the nonbank IPF managers normally had a decisive say in the financial fate of enterprise assets (like the bank IPF managers) and the nonbank IPF managers were relatively unencumbered by their own shareholders (also like the bank IPF managers). Moreover, nonbank IPF mangers were free to act without the interference of bank management, unlike the bank IPF managers. The added latitude separated conventional corruption and what was to become outlandish corruption, as we shall see in the following section.

Nonbank IPFs/Banks

One industry that nonbank IPFs were relatively unsuccessful in influencing was banking, referring particularly to the country's four largest banks. Many nonbank IPFs obtained shares in banks in voucher privatization, and so nonbank IPFs became bank shareholders directly and bank IPFs shareholders indirectly. Yet, the nonbank IPFs generally were unable to obtain seats on the large bank boards despite several infamous attempts. The best known were those by Motoinvest and Harvard to enter the board of ČS, the giant Czech savings bank. Coordinated efforts by the state and bank management blocked these and other attempts by nonbank IPFs to capture the management of the largest Czech banks. The nonbank IPFs/banks owner-agent gap is a rare case in which the Czech government intervened to prevent an owner from exercising ownership rights. By restricting the access of the nonbank IPF managers to bank assets, the state protected its economic authority and the authority of the bank managers.

State Institutions/Enterprises

The Czech state was a direct and indirect owner (mainly through bank IPFs) of large swatches of the Czech economy. Consistent with its neoliberal doctrine, however, the Czech state normally eschewed operational intervention in enterprises. Fund of National Property guidelines explicitly instruct its company board members to vote with managers and other owners. Surveys and interviews confirm that the state is a quiet owner. The state often found itself the financial loser when it ceded control to enterprise managers or to other owners.

In addition, the state failed to defend its minority share interest and thereby severely limited the value of its portfolio. Like other minority shareholders, the state wouldn't get fair market value unless it could sell its stake to another owner looking to create a strong controlling or majority shareholding. Consider the case of Spolana, a large Czech chemical company. The FNP, Chemapol, and Harvard (a nonbank IPF) each owned roughly 30 percent stakes. Chemapol wanted a majority stake in the company. Both Harvard and the FNP were willing to sell Chemapol their stakes. For obscure reasons, Chemapol decided to buy Harvard's stake. Spolana then was effectively Chemapol's. The FNP's 30 percent share was now worth relatively little. In addition, IPFs and other capital market players frequently convinced the Fund of National Property to sell shares at lower than fair market value (and often to shady investors). According to a widely distributed Ministry of Finance study,

> It can be pointed out that National Property Fund [FNP] is gradually selling shares in block trades through the RM-System (or on the Stock Exchange) at prices which are greatly under-priced; the prices should contain premiums, as these consist of significant portions. It can be observed that state share sales often occur when prices in the AOS PCPP (Prague Stock Exchange) drop to a minimum. (Czech Ministry of Privatization 1993)

The incapacity and unwillingness of the state to defend even its obvious interests signaled to market players that rules could be bent and broken in pursuit of assets.

State Institutions/Banks

The state's passive approach toward its residual share portfolio extended to banks and particularly to bank IPFs. The state's absentee ownership of banks was a precondition for bank IPF managers to abuse agent and ownership rights (and for bank lending policies to spin out of control). Nonsensical bank privatization policy was the second important underlying cause for these problems. The section below on Czech bank privatization addresses this contention. It is sufficient for this part to note that banks (and by extension bank IPFs) were the controlling agent, and the state was the passive (and vulnerable) owner.

Employer-Employee Gaps

The problems and abuses associated with owner-agent gaps were exacerbated in the Czech Republic by employer-employee gaps. These are situations in which the employer cannot control the employee. Employer-employee gaps are factors that explain share trading and asset movements. For instance, the existence of a bank IPF within the bank also sets up an owner-agent relationship *within* the bank. How can the bank manager monitor the bank IPF manager? In the transition period, when not all bank employees were competent or honest, the functional answer was sometimes that the bank IPF manager had carte blanche over the management of bank IPF assets. Consequently, although we spoke earlier about the influence of bank managers on bank IPF managers, we added the caveat that bank IPF manager autonomy depended on the internal policy and control mechanisms of the parent bank. In general, bank IPF managers of IPB were regulated more closely than those of KB, who were regulated more closely than those of ČS. Similarly, state-appointed enterprise board members frequently pursued their personal interest at the expense of the state, contrary to FNP guidelines (Schwartz 1997). Czech-style privatization helped encourage and perpetuate employer-employee gaps such as those by neglecting state regulation and by leaving company restructuring to the first owners. I propose that the employer-employee gaps would have been less prominent if the state had directed more privatizations to foreign corporations, which would have been better able to regulate their own employees. The concluding chapter considers this solution in more detail.

The minority shareholding risks, owner-agent gaps, and employer-employee gaps encouraged many first owners (and first agents) to behave perversely to what Czech neoliberals had envisioned. They did not sell to final owners; they sought instead to take advantage of the holes in the system to drain enterprises for their personal benefit or for the benefit of the managing institution. They made little or no effort to restructure enterprises in most cases. Nor, we must add, were the capital markets the efficient mechanism of price discovery. Instead, they were rigged. The state had effectively abdicated its role and indeed its very ability to regulate the markets. The ensuing evolution of the ownership regime reflected the opportunities and hazards of the unregulated free market.

Motoinvest and Harvard Up the Stakes

Ownership reshuffling became nasty business when a new player tried to crash the consolidation and cross-holding game. Motoinvest, a shady nonbank IPF based in Plzeň, surreptitiously purchased shares in Czech enterprises and IPFs in the spring and summer of 1995.[9] Motoinvest next mailed out letters to six million "dissatisfied" small shareholders. Those letters exhorted shareholders to sell their holdings to Plzeňská banka, Motoinvest's ally.[10] It accompanied these letters with a two-stage advertising campaign captured by the slogans "Small Shareholders Cry" and the "Third Wave." Motoinvest accumulated substantial stakes in the IPFs of Creditanstalt, KB, ČSOB, Živnobanka, and Agrobanka over time. Creditanstalt eventually sold its IPF to Motoinvest. KB paid an undisclosed sum of greenmail to buy back its own IPF holdings. The Motoinvest case showed that a well-financed group, with whatever intentions and background, could commandeer the Czech economy.

Motoinvest attracted negative attention from the state. Alarmed by the uncertainty surrounding Motoinvest's principals and the source of the company's funds, the Czech Central Bank froze Motoinvest's advertising campaign in November and December of 1995. After Motoinvest joined forces with Agrobanka to create a large independent financial group, the four large banks with large state shareholders (KB, ČS, IPB, and ČSOB) acted simultaneously to withdraw deposits from Agrobanka. Why did state officials react uncharacteristically aggressively to Motoinvest's incursions? After obtaining control of Agrobanka, Motoinvest pursued control of ČS, the huge state bank with 80 percent of Czech deposits. State officials feared, probably correctly, that Motoinvest might loot the bank. Stopping Agrobanka meant stopping Motoinvest.[11] The state-organized conspiracy bankrupted Agrobanka and thereby cut off a large sum of funds to Motoinvest.

In spring 1996, the state prepared a series of laws that would establish greater scrutiny of IPFs. Harvard's Kožený, as usual, was in the vanguard of IPF reaction. He hastily held a "private" shareholders meeting in a tiny town in order to transform Harvard into an industrial holding company to circumvent the coming new legislation. As an industrial holding company, no law forced Harvard to disclose its holdings to shareholders or to state regulators. Consequently, Kožený could manipulate IPF assets without scrutiny or opposition. Seventy nonbank IPFs followed suit quickly.[12] The state sat passively by in the face of this blatant tactic to sidestep state regulation. Nobody doubted that these funds were up to no good. Indeed, the lack of state scrutiny of the holding companies was a prerequisite for the upcoming asset stripping.

The Motoinvest and Harvard cases marked watersheds in the postprivatization stage. Prior to Motoinvest, corruption and collusion went on quietly, orderly. The accumulation of wealth from privatization had been a steady process punctuated by enterprise consolidation and cross-holding. In the background, the economy seemed to be developing well. Bamboozled, the press and academics penned articles about the country's remarkable social peace and the success of Klaus's brand of neoliberalism. However, the financial manipulations of Motoinvest and Harvard vaulted the wealth accumulation process into a feeding frenzy. To the financial and state elite, the audacity of Motoinvest and Harvard proved that anything was possible in the Czech version of the "Wild East." Previously troublesome, irksome, but somehow tolerable, market manipulation and corruption were about to assume a new dimension.

THE FEEDING FRENZY, JANUARY 1996 TO DECEMBER 1997

Public illusions about the Czech system crumbled in 1996, when the Czech public first learned that the funds designed to invest the public vouchers were instead systematically stealing from their own investors. But that's the least of it. The Czech public also learned that dishonest operators were systematically squeezing the assets from many of the country's best companies, its municipalities, and its banks (private and state owned). The locals coined a charming euphemism for the criminals—*tunnelers* (*tuneláři*). The tunnelers achieved wealth with the cooperation, or at the very best the benign neglect, of the state.

Theoretically, the tunneler seeks to transform himself from agent to owner or from joint owner to sole owner. Gaps between ownership and control, undisturbed by state regulation, identify the opportunities. Tunnelers commonly are enterprise managers, IPF managers, and shady financial groups. The victims usually are asset owners (typically, the state and private investors) or lien holders (typically, banks). A high quality of capitalism and democracy is impossible when tunnelers are prominent economic and political actors.

Tunneling suggested that the Czech economy had reached a heightened state of corruption that went beyond "standard" corruption. Tunnelers did not seek to become a mere transaction cost. Rather, they aimed to capture all the assets of a transaction. They sucked assets from the legal owner or escaped the obligations of the legal creditor. They normally deposited those assets in a personal account, preferably overseas, or simply consumed them.

This section focuses on the tunneling activities of IPF managers because they were egregious and because they were public. In practice, nonbank IPF managers were more aggressive tunnelers then bank IPF managers because of bank management supervision. Analysis of IPF tunneling techniques reveals

Table 9.4. Fifteen Tunneling Techniques

1. Interconnect several companies.
2. Incur bogus business fines.
3. Purchase worthless shares.
4. Conclude unfavorable options and futures contracts.
5. Transfer cash advances for security purchase to friendly dealer.
6. Establish long settlement period for securities sold.
7. Loan securities at unfavorable terms.
8. Draw up incomplete agreements for securities transfer.
9. Manipulate securities prices through self-trading.
10. Trade in securities at ridiculous prices.
11. Trade in securities at unfavorable prices.
12. Engage in insider trade against IPF.
13. Concentrate fund assets in hard cash.
14. Do not comply with rules for restricting and spreading risk.
15. Tunnel into individual companies through general shareholders meeting.

just how prevalent and how economically damaging the stealing had become. IPF tunneler-managers usually stole absolutely every Czech *koruna* from enterprises and shareholders. Unimaginable thievery. The Czech Ministry of Finance enumerated fifteen tunneling techniques in a widely distributed report. The ministry report euphemistically refers to these methods as a "failure to comply with zákon č. 248/1992 Sb. [the Law on Investment Funds and Investment Companies plus amendments]" (Czech Ministry of Finance 1997, 4) (see table 9.4). IPF tunneler-managers variously used each of these techniques to move cash assets from IPFs to personal accounts.

- *Tunneling Technique #9—Manipulate securities prices through self-trading.* The IPF tunneler-manager sells shares to one company that then turns around it and sells them to another company, and so forth in a chain that leads ultimately back to the original IPF. The IPF gets the shares back, but it has paid a higher price than it originally sold them for. The middle link companies now hold the trading profit. Of course, these middle company links are associated with the IPF tunneler-manager. Since the public capital market trades only negligible quantities of most securities, it is very easy to manipulate share prices (Czech Ministry of Finance 1997, 6).
- *Tunneling Technique #13—Concentrate fund assets in hard cash.* The IPF tunneler-manager gradually sells the shareholdings, and he keeps the proceeds in cash. When all the fund assets are converted into cash, the IPF tunneler-manager then simply transfers the funds abroad. ČS Fund, one of the largest nonbank IPF funds, used this stunningly straightforward procedure to rip off its shareholders (Czech Ministry of Finance 1997,

7). Ironically, a *Wall Street Journal* article had lauded ČS Fund manager
T. Chrz as a shining example of the new Czech entrepreneur just a few
years earlier. Regrettably, that characterization was precise.

- *Tunneling Technique #15—Tunnel into individual companies through general shareholders meeting.* IPF shareholders band together to obtain a voting majority. The majority shareholders then push through transactions involving company assets at the general shareholders meeting. Usually, these transactions benefit the majority shareholder to the detriment of the enterprise. According to this technique, the main loser is the integrity of the enterprise (including the minority shareholders) and probably the IPF shareholder. The Finance Ministry report calls this technique "frequent" (Czech Ministry of Finance 1997, 7).

Some Western analysts contend that the extent of IPF tunneling was not material to the Czech economy. They argue that tunnelers stole about $100 million and caused $2 billion of indirect damage resulting primarily from the underpricing of enterprise shares and IPF shares. The direct damage according to these statistics amounts to about 0.2 percent of stock market capitalization and about 0.1 percent of GDP; the indirect damage is about 10 percent of stock market capitalization and about 5 percent of GDP.[13]

I believe those figures underestimate the extent and the damage of Czech tunneling. There are three reasons. First, tunneling has devastated the reputation of Czech capital markets to potential investors. Consider that the capital market values IPFs at large discounts, even by the standards of emerging markets—some nonbank IPFs trade at less than 10 percent of net asset value. Consider that foreigner investors withdrew 9.7 bn CZK from Czech capital markets in the first quarter of 1997, a period when foreign investors were generally net buyers of emerging market equities. Consider that Czech enterprises sometimes suffered huge decreases in market value after a controlling block sale involving an IPF. It was rational for potential investors to avoid Czech capital markets when tunnelers lurked, even if the absolute amount of tunneling seemed minor.

Second, IPF tunneling involved more than just the buying and selling of assets on the capital market. It encompassed the wholesale economy-wide stripping of enterprise assets, a process underrated by estimates of tunneling volume on stock markets. Tunnelers sucked assets out of firms by leasing valuable firm assets and by selling enterprise assets at bargain prices to companies they controlled. One of the most insidious of the enterprise tunneling tricks was for the tunneler to take out loans using enterprise assets as collateral and then to default on the loans. The tunneler kept the money or transferred enterprises to a company he wholly owned, while the lien holders were stuck with unwanted assets. This was common practice in enterprises privatized by standard privatization methods. Moreover, as I noted earlier, banks played a variant of the tunneling game by overloading enterprises with needless debt, thereby transferring resources from the enterprise to the bank. Tunneling didn't only cheat investors, it also severely damaged the long-term viability of enterprises.

Third, and most important, tunneling signaled that stealing would go unpunished, and that government participation in illegal and immoral activities was for sale. The problem wasn't so much that the legal framework was inadequate, which it surely was, but that the laws that were on the books were ignored.[14] Prominent Western analysts accurately observed that

> The overriding need is to develop a system for monitoring and enforcing compliance with the governance system the legislation is designed to mandate. In the current system there is a lack of clear penalties and punitive action against those who are out of compliance.... We found in direct comparison with the German and UK models that the Czech legislation is in need of minor additions and redrafting, but is for the most part sound. The primary need in the Czech Republic to improve corporate governance is thorough enforcement of the law, which will lead to a more defined business ethic which currently seems to be lacking. (Coopers & Lybrand and Phare 1997, 1)

The thievery of the tunnelers epitomized the system of corruption that had come to define the new Czech political economy. According to the forthcoming government "Blue Book" on the state of the economy, "Instead of establishing enterprises on the basis of economic rationality and strategic development, Czech privatization ensured that a substantial number of enterprises would permanently face the (tunneling) threat" (Draft of government Blue Book 1999 [forthcoming], 15). The uncontrolled and incompetent state bureaucracy over this period enabled tunneling, and in so doing, it undermined the future of capitalism and democracy.

Feeding the Frenzy: The Regulatory Role of the State

The begging questions from the perverse Czech capital markets and tunneling revolve around the benign neglect of the state. The tunneling of the IPFs exposed the half-heartedness of state capital market regulation. A modern capitalist country would certainly have stopped the wholesale thievery. Why didn't the Czech state protect its citizens and defend its own interests from the tunelers, particularly the IPF tunneler-managers?

The state's hands-off posture stems from neoliberal ideology, personal self-interest, and a weak bureaucratic competence. From an ideological vantage,

Czech leading neoliberals insisted that the state should abstain from markets. The apparent, overwhelming political and economic success of voucher privatization reaffirmed the ideological litany: free markets, good; state, bad.

From a self-interested vantage, IPFs and their capital market allies successfully lobbied state officials against aggressive state regulation. Market participants counseled individual shareholders and IPF investors against restrictive market regulation. The IPFs and capital market allies combined public lobbying with private entreaties to state officials. One Czech capital market participant remarked that the "good old boys" network in Prague, including the old communists in the IPFs and the Finance Ministry, set state capital market policy. To be sure, Finance Ministry officials are reluctant to discuss the market-ministry relationship. For instance, engineer Křivohlávek, then–head of department at the Czech Ministry of Finance, pronounced that an interview between the author and himself was successful "because I told you nothing." The very real possibility that state officials have personally benefited from unregulated capital markets lurks in the background of this black box of information.

At the very least, there was a conflict of interest or an appearance of impropriety between the regulators and regulated. R. Salzmann, the first chairman of the Prague Stock Exchange, was simultaneously the chairman of KB, as well as a luminary in Klaus's ODS political party. Tříska headed the RM-System, one of the two Prague stock exchanges; his relatives are major securities investors. V. Rudlovčák, then the deputy finance minister, served on the board of ČS along with L. Klausová (Klaus's wife). I. Kočárník went from being minister of finance to chair of the supervisory board of Česká pojišťovna (the Czech Insurance Company) immediately after rendering several favorable rulings for the company. Representatives of state institutions regularly sit on enterprise boards, partly owing to the large state ownership stakes. State representatives are invariably attractive allies for aggressive shareholders seeking to manipulate company finances or the stock price.

Self-interest wasn't limited to greedy state bureaucrats. Political parties participated in the feeding frenzy. Klaus's ODS political party (along with coalition partners ODA and KDU-ČSL) was implicated in the patronage system. ODS established cozy relationships with IPFs (including V. Kožený's Harvard Fund), shady businessmen, and the banks. I mentioned earlier the close relations between ODS and KB, but I must also add ODS's (and ODA's) tight relationship with IPB. Furthermore, ODS and its coalition partners solicited political contributions from privatization suitors. A 1998 audit revealed that anonymous depositors had deposited millions of crowns into an ODS Swiss bank account. That same year ODA admitted to having accepted contributions from Philip Morris, Vitkovice, and PPF (a nonbank IPF). The shameless ODS display was the 1994 fund-raising dinner attended by most major state banks and industrial companies. Ruling politicians belonged to the plutocracy, not to the solution.

From a bureaucratic competence standpoint, the Czech state would have been hard-pressed to properly regulate capital markets at the beginning of the postprivatization period, even if state officials had the inclination. There was no trained bureaucracy and no body of coherent regulatory laws available when the capital markets opened for business in the spring of 1993. A defiant tunneler successfully defended his business practices by noting that there was no law against tunneling.[15] A lawyer for a tunneling client similarly concluded that "What is not banned is permitted" (Brož 1997, 7). Moreover, the party of the neoliberals, ODS, put party members at the head of control organizations and state investigative organs and then proceeded to enfeeble them.[16] No person has ever been convicted of bank fraud or tunneling in the Czech Republic, though even the Ministry of Finance admits that these practices are endemic (Czech Ministry of Finance 1997).

The reality that judges and courts in the Czech Republic are tragically overloaded and ignorant of market practices accentuates deficiencies in the letter and enforcement of the law. A police team trained by the FBI, for instance, couldn't guard against market abuses because they were ignorant of basic financial market terms. Private collection-agency firms have emerged to address enforcement issues, but their control and behavior is beyond the law and therefore not under public control in any sense. Not surprisingly, the state has brought no one to justice for the obvious and systemic improprieties. The summary assessment is that the whole notion of a clean business deal in the Czech Republic is as foreign to Czechs as Disneyland.

The enforcement that the state did carry out to protect fair markets was farce, not deterrent. At various times, the government formally charged the top managers of IPB and Motoinvest of various crimes. Some served time in jail, though none actually went to trial. The bizarre Kožený-Wallis affair is the quintessential example of state bumbling. Kožený claimed that V. Wallis, a former secret police agent, was blackmailing him. Wallis counterclaimed that he was demanding payment of Kožený for secret police state files on political officials. A court accepted Wallis's side of the story, but tossed him in prison anyway for violating his duties as a state officer and for disclosing state secrets.[17] Amazingly, the state never charged Kožený with bribery or for possession of Wallis's information, and the state still allows Kožený (or his relatives) to do business in the country. The outcomes of the Kožený-Wallis case and the other major corruption cases demonstrate the arbitrariness of Czech justice and suggest that the state exploits economic laws for political purposes.

The neglect of capital market regulation during privatization precluded fair and enforceable regulation. Ježek wrote that

> In the moment when shares were issued to people and when trading began on the public markets, in that moment there should have been a superstrong regulatory authority which would never slip and which had to be a hundred times sharper than in America and two hundred times sharper than in Poland, because regulation was like a child who needed to be diapered every two hours. It was instead thrown out into the cold, like a wild animal, without supervision. (*RP*, 1998, 1, 4)

Could the Czech state have regulated capital markets systems if it had so chosen given the rapid privatization imperative? My answer to this key question is no. Radical privatization bequeathed comprehensive and complex financial markets and a compromised and incompetent bureaucracy. In addition, rapid privatization was purposefully antagonistic to state interference (including regulation) in the economy. We must conclude that by the time share trading began, the state was incapable of autonomous and strong regulation of capital markets, even if state leaders had so desired. A. Hrbotický, head of the short-lived Interministerial Commission to Fight Economic Crime, concluded that proper regulation of markets was "too complicated" and "even in the U.S. would take years" to implement. The Czech neoliberal rapid privatization approach ensured that the Czech regulators would have no more than months.

Finally, although collusion bears the main responsibility for the perverse results of Czech rapid privatization, the lack of market experience, sheer incompetence, and ideological dogmatism apparent on all levels of the Czech bureaucracy deserve a sizable share of the blame. The feckless state efforts to regulate IPFs; the inability of its courts, investigators, and judges to bring tunnelers to justice; the disarray and inconsistency of its tax system; the government's failure to keep accurate financial records; and its failure to protect assets in enterprises in which it owns controlling share stakes—particularly the banks—are attributable to incompetent state management. Dogmatic free-market state policy exacerbated market inexperience. It was one matter to forbid discussion of "industrial policy," a concept that relates to how the state should intervene in free markets, as the Czech privatizers did. But it was quite another matter to forbid "state regulation," a concept that relates to how the state protects markets from the muscle and cheating of unscrupulous operators, as the Czech privatizers also did. The lack of state capacity—aided by the misdirection of state policy—can undermine market and democratic development every bit as much as the lack of state autonomy.

Bank Privatization

The accumulation of uncollectable loans in Czech banks reflected the neoliberal aversion to operational state enterprise management and the rapid Czech privatization policy. The Czech state relinquished authority to Czech bankers before a bank regulatory policy had been thought out and established. The root problem was that rapid privatization and the neoliberal project behind it diverted state resources from a regulatory focus. Consequently, by the time state decision-makers realized that domestic banks could not direct resources for socially desirable ends (for instance, industrial restructuring), the banks already had squandered billions of CZK in subsidies and were themselves in drastic need of reorganization.

On the surface, the Czech banks seemed to avoid the excesses of voucher privatization. The supposedly neoliberal state conducted bank policy in a decidedly "un-neoliberal" way. The state retained large share packages in the four Czech banks and scions of the communist bank, which together account for 61 percent of loans. Moreover, it remained entwined in Czech banking. The Czech Central Bank retained influence over interest rates, currency policy, bankruptcy policy, bank regulation, and so forth. Furthermore, the Czech government relieved banks of nonperforming loans and recapitalized banks when the bad loan portfolio reached crisis proportions (Schwartz 1997; McDermott 1994). The state remained "the guarantor of last resort." The seemingly involved role of the state in domestic banking seemed to protect the large banks from being tunneled and from acting as tunnelers themselves.

Nonetheless, the state left itself vulnerable to many of the same pathologies occurring in the capital markets and in domestic enterprise by ceding operational supervision to bank management. The state put lending decisions involving to whom to lend, how much to lend, and at what terms to lend in the hands of the bankers. Understanding why this passive management approach—which *is* characteristic of Czech neoliberalism—inevitably led to disaster is essential to an understanding of banking in the Czech Republic of the 1990s.

Czech banks, like most CEEC banks, don't always function in the traditional way. Czech bankers often issue commercial or personal loans with only casual regard to the interest rate and to the risk of a loan default. Part of the reason is that most enterprises were badly in need of restructuring (particularly engineering and chemicals) or development (the unproven start-ups) funds, yet were terrible credit risks. No foreign or domestic bank would willingly finance these domestic companies.[18] The incentives to lend were dampened further by the high market interest rates prevailing in the Czech Republic over this period. Companies would have to earn huge profits to repay loans. If Czech banks based credit decisions on a conventional risk/reward basis, they would retain deposits and rarely lend.

How did Czech banks make lending decisions? One ingredient was *corruption*—knowledgeable Czechs say that loan officers normally charged prospective borrowers as much as 10 percent of the total loan. Politicians were involved; they sometimes arranged loans for large contributors to political parties. Tunnelers were eager borrowers. According to one published estimate, tunneling is responsible for half to two-thirds of bad bank debt (*Respekt*, June 1998). The absolute value, if not the percentage, of actual debt due to tunneling is certain to be far larger, given that most bad debt still remains unclassified as bad debt on bank books.

A second ingredient was *the size of the borrower*. Particularly large debtors whose loan balances numbered in the billions of CZK raised additional money from their bank creditors because they could threaten to default on the loan and thereby risk the bank itself. This "too big to fail" logic kept Czech bankers and Czech industrialists on the same side in negotiations with the government for subsidies and funds for loan forgiveness. Many times state officials joined the alliance of big business and big banking. It was often in their best political interest to keep the big industrial enterprises from failing. On occasion, therefore, state officials directed banks to lend to prospective borrowers. Senior bank officials were willing conspirators; their jobs depended on it.

A third ingredient was *standard privatization* (excluding state shareholding). The state's rapid privatization pressure spread to bankers. They were expected to support standard privatization by loaning money to enterprise managers and investors in order to buy enterprises, and they did. Companies privatized by standard privatization show far greater outstanding bank loan balances (35 percent of capital in 1997) versus companies privatized by other means (the economy-wide average is 24 percent of capital in 1997). Bank officials, however, had no experience in loan evaluation or were corrupt, and in any case lacked the time to properly evaluate collateral. The result is that over half of the privatization loans will never be paid back. Essentially, the neoliberals used state banks to lubricate the new market economy.

A fourth ingredient was *personal connection*. The people who normally made the major credit decisions at the big banks were at the level just below the board of directors. Many were refugees from the communist state ministries or from the Czechoslovak secret police (Stb), or were holdovers from the days when one "monobank" served the entire country. They maintained their old contacts both within the banks and throughout the country's enterprises and the state ministries. In practice, bank officials with old ties represented an obstacle to bank modernization, to bank privatization to foreigners, and to an economically rational loan policy. Getting a loan at favorable terms meant being part of the "old guard."

The predictable and regrettable side effect of a noneconomic rationale for bank lending was a massive buildup of bad loans. The Czech bank loan portfolios in 1997 and 1998 resemble those of the East Asian financial institutions that roiled global capital markets over that same period. In 1997, nonperforming loans accounted for over 25 percent of GDP in the Czech Republic, compared with less than 5 percent of GDP in Hungary and Poland.[19] One senior "Big 4" Czech banker confided at the time that his bank's loan portfolio might have been worth 20 percent of its stated value. The reshuffling of shares and assets in the tattered apron of loose and arbitrarily enforced laws created economic entities that caricatured conventional labels, such as banks.

Incidentally, the situation in private banks was no better than in the four large state banks. Many of the private owners tunneled their banks, leaving depositors angry and the state to pick up the pieces. The cases of Agrobanka and Kreditní banka are notorious. Minimal state oversight of the Big 4 banks and private ownership were equally vulnerable to the excesses of the free market.

The underlying problem of ineffectual state management of its residual bank shareholdings was state unpreparedness (and unwillingness) to regulate the banking sector. This was a function of rapid privatization. The Czech state directed time, talent, money, and legitimacy toward rapid privatization and, at the same time, drained the state of those scarce resources, as this study has emphasized throughout. This pathology also infected the state agencies charged with bank supervision. According to P. Kysilka, acting governor of the Czech National Bank in 1998, the Central Bank's own "inexperience of banking supervision and lack of restriction of the liberal licensing policy between 1990 and 1992" (Lešenarová 1998, 14) caused the state to lose control over money flows. We can also cite the state's reluctance to reform the legal system, especially regarding the realization of creditors' rights. For example, the creditor cannot easily recover assets since banks cannot confiscate real estate used as loan collateral without the approval of the defaulted borrower. According to Kysilka, "well-known financial institutions . . . approached us because they wanted to buy out some of the banks' receivables. But, after they discover the legislative framework, they leave this market" (Lešenarová 1998, 14).

One solution may have been bank privatization to or joint ventures with foreign bankers. That would have broken the political power of the banks' old guard. It also would have curbed state influence on bank policy. The rapid privatization approach delayed bank privatization to foreign investors in the first half of the 1990s. The Czech state's fixation on free markets and its neglect of bank regulation (and its best alternative—bank privatization to foreigners) jeopardized the health of the banks and endangered the economy.

The Chicago Boys—Milton Friedman or Al Capone?

Plutocratic capitalism is government by the rich, for the rich. A plutocracy is a class of elites who use government institutions to secure personal wealth. The label *plutocratic capitalism* applies to the Czech political economy of the 1990s. The Czech plutocrats are bankers, IPF managers, state officials, large enterprise managers, and shady operators. They are enabled by the virtual absence of regulation to separate government and business. A snapshot of the Czech ownership regime circa 1997 illustrates that the evolution of the Czech political economy since privatization developed into plutocratic capitalism, a turn unexpected by neoliberals.

Czech enterprise owners in 1997 were a diverse lot—including local investors seeking to restructure enterprises, individual shareholders, and foreign strategic partners. *Dominant owners* though were banks, bank IPFs, nonbank IPFs, industrial holding companies, industrial conglomerates, and state ministries (particularly the FNP). This set of owners reflected the concentration in economic control that took place in the wake of privatization. The buildup of debt in the banks accompanied the concentration in economic power, which, in turn, enhanced the control of the banks and ultimately the state ("the guarantor of last resort"). Working in cahoots with other owners or agents, the plutocrats frequently extracted wealth from the assets under their stewardship, usually to the detriment of the nominal organization-owner. They showed little inclination or talent to restructure enterprises, though unlike most first owners many plutocrats were sufficiently capitalized.

The evolved *ownership structure* suggests the penetration and methodology of the plutocrats. They established control over assets in complicated ways—futures contracts, management contracts, collateralized loans, and so forth. The purpose of this maze was to ensure that no outsider could monitor and therefore police the interconnections. Under such conditions, ownership may not translate into control. Structure may not reveal process. Extreme complexity is the signature of the Czech plutocracy.

A decline in the importance of the Czech *stock markets* accompanied the emergence of the plutocracy. It partly can be explained without reference to ownership changes and asset movements. As noted earlier, most listed companies were tiny—the average market capitalization of the 1,000 smallest Czech stocks (out of 1,600) was under 7.5 mn CZK ($270,000). Their shares were unlikely to be traded actively on public markets. More important was the capture and corruption of the market by market manipulators and tunnelers. Prospective buyers and sellers couldn't use the market. Czech capital markets were a useless fund-raising venue for the companies themselves. V. Junek, the chairman of Chemapol, a large energy company, declared that for industrial companies the market is "absolutely unusable" (Junek 1998). The Czech capital markets were irrelevant to price discovery, the raison d'être of capital markets in capitalist economies. Instead, transactions involving asset movements occurred as negotiations among the dominant owners, including the state.

Regulation of Czech stock markets, as noted above, was insignificant and, considering the decline in importance of Czech stock markets, increasingly irrelevant. By contrast, broader regulation of the financial system as a whole—encompassing bank regulation, state management of residual shareholdings, and the efficacy of laws, including the police and the court system—was proving to be increasingly relevant. But as privatization and the neoliberal agenda had sabotaged capacity and autonomy of the state, so the plutocrats could co-opt state officials, including many of the country's leading politicians. Lax regulation seems to have been a necessary and sufficient condition for the creation of plutocratic capitalism.

The Czech ownership regime of 1997 diverged from the free-market system that neoliberals had imagined when they conceived their version of rapid privatization (see table 9.5). The combination of first owners incapable of restructuring firms, an ownership structure replete with owner-agent gaps, a stock market illiquid and poorly understood by market players, and most importantly, a state unprepared and hostile to the idea of regulation and government management inevitably and predictably produced the plutocratic capitalism described above. Neoliberals had expected by this time that active owners would be forcing restructuring, passing and enforcing laws to enforce property rights, and pushing to make government transparent. Instead, plutocrats were ignoring restructuring and concentrating instead on accumulating wealth; they were subverting and blocking laws to rationalize property rights; and they were fighting to keep their own dealings and those of the government opaque. Plutocratic capitalism caricatured democracy and capitalism, the aims of neoliberalism.

Table 9.5.   The Czech Ownership Regime, 1997

| | | | Level of State Autonomy and Capacity | |
| | | | Of Capital Market Regulator | Of Financial System |
Owners	Ownership Structure	Financial System		
Plutocrats, State Officials, Managers	Cross-holding, Concentrated at Enterprise Level	Mixed: (1) Public Equity Markets, (2) State Management, (3) Bank/ Finance Capital	Low	Low

The tangible consequences of plutocratic capitalism in the Czech Republic were economic and political. The main economic result was a hollowed-out Czech economy that lags its neighbors Hungary and Poland in capital investment and investments in research and development, but leads in the accumulation of bad debts. Czech macroeconomic balances deteriorate even as Poland and Hungary emerge from the communist economic darkness and the postcommunist recession. The main political result was the popular disillusionment in democratic government and in the stewardship of Klaus and the neoliberals.

In the June 1998 elections, the Social Democrats led by M. Zeman replaced the Czech right-wing coalition. They were trying to restore the population's faith in the integrity of markets and politics. Their success will depend on whether they can break the power of the plutocracy by building an autonomous and capable regulatory apparatus. If they cannot, the Social Democrats will merely replace the neoliberals in the plutocracy, much like one gang seizing the turf of another. The spoils of cooperation are substantial, as is the pain of attempting to dislodge the plutocracy. How the Social Democrats choose will probably determine whether the Czech Republic continues along a path of compromised economics and politics or whether it takes a U-turn toward modern capitalism and democracy.

Economic Outcome: Minimal Restructuring

The low quality of capitalism is evident in the low level of enterprise restructuring. By restructuring, we refer to the degree to which former communist enterprises adapt to the market economy. Communist enterprises require a complete overhaul in function and market orientation. Communist enterprises performed dual roles as production units and as vehicles to satisfy the regime's need to educate, feed, and house people. Communist managers normally directed factories, and also schools, housing complexes, vacation centers, and power plants. Therefore, the postcommunist context demands a multidimensional view of restructuring, encompassing changes in management, organizational structure, number and composition of employment, wage policy, technology, production techniques, marketing, product distribution, pricing, balance sheet accounting, financing, research and development, suppliers, and corporate culture. The level of enterprise restructuring in postcommunist economies points to the future direction of the economy.

If neoliberals are correct, then we would expect that rapid privatization would have led to active owners restructuring companies. If the predictions generated by the ownership regime are correct, then we would expect limited enterprise restructuring. Voucher privatization should show particularly poor enterprise restructuring results since it caused pronounced shareholder–minority shareholder gaps and principal-agent gaps. Though imperfect, the data clearly support the ownership regime theory.

To be sure, enterprise restructuring has been occurring in the transition Czech Republic. First, the aggregate statistics for the Czech Republic show that the share of GDP attributable to manufacturing declined from 49.2 percent in 1992 to 34.6 percent in 1995 (Chvojka 1996, 348). From 1989 to 1995, 500,000 workers had left jobs in industry and another 200,000 had left jobs in agriculture (Chvojka 1997, 516). Second, comparative enterprise-level data from 1995 show that the Czech Republic had the highest or tied for the highest performance in the CEECs in the following categories:

1. Firms with operating cash flow—98 percent;
2. Average operating cash flow as a percentage of revenue—14 percent;
3. Annual growth in labor productivity—7 percent (1992–1995);
4. Annual growth in total factor productivity—5 percent (1992–1995); and,
5. Annual growth in exports in 1995 prices—22 percent (1992–1995). (Pohl, et al. 1997)

Third, comparative trade data involving Czech intraindustry trade to the EU hints at enterprise restructuring. Intraindustry trade is exchange within a supply chain of producers representing diverse packages of wages and technical skills. It may represent evidence of complex international production networks and of enterprise restructuring in CEECs. The Czech Republic shows the highest overall intraindustry trade figures in Central and Eastern Europe. Intraindustry trade is particularly pronounced in the country's traditional heavy manufacturing sector (Zysman and Schwartz 1998b). Fourth, comparative foreign direct investment (FDI) data show that the Czech Republic is a regionally desirable location. From 1989 to 1995, for instance, the Czech Republic ($5.0 bn) trailed only Hungary ($9.9 bn) and Poland ($7.4 bn) as a site for FDI (Schwartz and Haggard 1997, 24). The data indicate that enterprise restructuring in the Czech Republic is ongoing and active. This lends support to the claims of supporters of Czech privatization that the country is suffering more from bad publicity and "negative perceptions" than from bad policy.

Closer examination of the data suggests flaws in that reasoning. First, broad transfers of economic resources from manufacturing to services are common to all CEECs. The extent that the shifts were greater in the Czech Republic probably reflects better starting conditions, as indicated by the low unemployment at the beginning of transition. Second, comparative data does not travel well in CEECs. Cross-national enterprise data may reflect accounting differences. It may also reflect differences in the starting competitive position of different enterprises. Czech industry was by far the most advanced in the region when the communists were toppled. Third, intraindustry trade measures, though suggestive, are not conclusive. For example, although these statistics indicate that the Czech Republic is part of an international vertical division of labor, we still do not know where their specialization lies in the productive process. Intraindustry trade does not identify product mix and pricing. Fourth, geography and national privatization best explain FDI, not the level of enterprise restructuring (Schwartz and Haggard 1997). On the one hand, the data show clearly that the Czech Republic is not a basket case. On the other, they beg for a closer analysis to evaluate the state of enterprise restructuring and the impact of Czech rapid privatization policy.

Convincing evidence suggests that Czech enterprise restructuring stagnates. This evidence comes in several pieces. One piece is the stagnation of macroeconomic indicators (see below). A second piece is the analysis revealing that enterprises have been slow to reduce dependence on the old communist supply networks (McDermott 1994). A third piece is the dearth of enterprise bankruptcies. Unlike its neighbors, particularly Hungary, the Czech banks (prodded by the state, no doubt) have been reluctant to bankrupt nonpaying creditors. The number of proposed bankruptcies is well under 1,000 per year, and the realized number of bankruptcies is under 100 per year. The tiny number of bankruptcies implies that assets are tied up unproductively, when they could otherwise be diverted toward profitable endeavors. A fourth piece is the anecdotal information that enterprise managers participated in dismantling enterprises, rather than in trying to restructure them. A restructuring expert estimated that only 25 percent of top enterprise managers were committed to company restructuring. This evidence might not be critical if enterprise managers had been reinvesting proceeds. Rather, they seem to either use the moneys for consumption or for investment abroad. A fifth piece is the shortage of assets devoted to research and development by Czech firms. Overall, the stock of research and development workers declined from 137,000 in 1989 to 40,200 in 1993 (Czech Statistical Office 1994). Finally, a sixth piece is the buildup of nonperforming bank loans, especially in comparison with Hungary and Poland. Bad loans on bank books indicate that resources are misused.

The decisive evidence that Czech enterprise restructuring could have been more extensive given better regulation is data that break down enterprise performance by privatization method (see table 9.6). Two starting points are necessary to evaluate the data. First, the enterprise performance indicators shown here are good surrogates for enterprise restructuring since they report 1996 and 1997 data, by which time the effects of privatization on enterprise restructuring were well apparent. Second, the data address only *manufacturing enterprises*. The sample encompasses the stereotypical cases of technologically backward

Table 9.6. Economic Results of Industrial Enterprises by Privatization Method

Indicator	Privatization Method	1996	1997
Market Share (%)	Voucher Privatization	27.3	25.3
	State Shareholding	25.4	19.2
	Foreign Privatization	12.0	14.6
	Other Standard Methods	9.2	10.5
	Total	100.0	100.0
Return on Invested Capital (%)	Voucher Privatization	−0.27	−0.16
	State Shareholding	0.65	4.38
	Foreign Privatization	8.02	18.58
	Other Standard Methods	1.80	3.75
	Total	2.60	4.84
Productivity (Added	Voucher Privatization	234.9	277.2
Value/Worker,	State Shareholding	303.7	361.5
Thousands of CZK)	Foreign Privatization	491.7	680.3
	Other Standard Methods	256.4	306.4
	Total	283.5	331.8
Capital Share of Bank Debt (%)	Voucher Privatization	26.8	27.0
	State Shareholding	23.3	23.0
	Foreign Privatization	12.7	10.0
	Other Standard Methods	36.3	35.0
	Total	24.6	24.0

Source: Author calculations based on Ministry of Finance data.
Notes: Missing industries lack clear ownership structures. They comprised 26.1% of total industry share in 1996 and 30.4% in 1997.

Czech industry, such as steel, machinery, transportation, chemicals, and textiles. It excludes service companies, banks, and most energy companies (such as ČEZ, the gas and electricity distribution companies, coal mines, and the oil pipeline company Transgas). The composition of companies in the sample makes the analytic outcomes especially significant. It is precisely these companies that are in desperate need of restructuring.

The data show that companies privatized by vouchers badly lagged companies privatized by other methods on return on invested capital and on worker productivity. In addition, a comparison of 1996 and 1997 indicators shows only a modest improvement in the performance of companies privatized by vouchers and no gains in relative performance. A 1994 survey confirms that "voucher privatized firms are less innovative, they undergo less organizational changes, they have lower productivity and care less about quality" (Zemplínerová and Laštovička 1997, 12). Recent work showing a positive correlation between ownership concentration and enterprise performance, *but only when the concentrated owners are neither bank IPFs nor nonbank IPFs*, supports the proposition that IPF tunnelers de-emphasized restructuring (Weiss and Nikitin 1997). Evidently, concentrated IPF owners were preoccupied in gathering assets, collecting fees, and abusing shareholders rather than restructuring enterprises. That speculation is consistent with the data presented here: manufacturing companies privatized to concentrated owners through (other) standard privatization methods showed relatively better performance than voucher privatized companies.[20] Shockingly, state enterprises performed better than enterprises newly privatized. Evidently, no privatization was better than privatization (to domestic interests). I will explain this unexpected result below.

The best dominant owner in terms of enterprise restructuring is the foreign investor. Enterprises privatized to foreign investors record dramatically greater increases in return on invested capital and productivity. Also, the 1996 and 1997 data show that the relative and absolute economic performance of these enterprises continues to improve.[21] Other studies confirm that foreign investors undertake the deep enterprise restructuring that the transition countries desperately need for further economic development (Zysman and Schwartz 1998a; Zysman and Schwartz 1998b; Zemplínerová and Benáček 1997; Carlin, Van Reenen, and Wolfe 1994).[22] Further, multinational corporate (MNC) ownership is displaying spillover benefits of technology transfer and added demand to domestic suppliers as the mother enterprise becomes a part of an international production network (Zysman and Schwartz 1998a; Zysman and Schwartz 1998b). This is a foreseeable consequence in a highly vertically inte grated economy such as the Czech Republic (Mládek 1997). Although skeptics of the view advocating foreign participation may correctly assert that foreign investors purchased stakes in the enterprises with the best prospects—so-called cherry picking—the dramatic successes of foreign investors relative to most domestic managements suggests that more is at work. Simply, the foreign investors are active owners; they are restructuring Czech enterprises.

The data demonstrate a compelling link between privatization policy and enterprise restructuring. A key factor is an active owner, that is, an owner willing to restructure enterprises. A second-best solution is an owner who protects enterprise assets. Over time, most Czech voucher privatized enterprises acquired a dominant owner, but not necessarily an active owner or an owner who safeguarded enterprise assets. Enterprises privatized by standard privatization methods did acquire an active owner, but one too often burdened by bank debt. This (potentially) active owner was better off by transferring the valuable assets to a self-owned company or selling them. State enterprises performed still better because they (modestly) safeguarded assets, though the state only rarely was an active owner. Naturally, then, foreign investors were the optimal owners because they restructured enterprises and protected enterprise assets. These conclusions demonstrate that Czech rapid privatization failed to set conditions for the transfer of stakes from first owners to active owners, the economic justification for the entire endeavor.

WHY RAPID PRIVATIZATION LEGACIES UNDERMINED
ENTERPRISE RESTRUCTURING

Rapid privatization created an ownership regime inimical to wide-scale enterprise restructuring. That is, the first-ownership regime discouraged first owners from selling enterprise assets to active owners. Disappointing economic restructuring wasn't due to the practical demands of restructuring Czech enterprises (for example, technical backwardness, unemployment, industrial overcapacity, inexperienced management). Czech enterprises typically maintain large cost advantages over most competitors, boast relatively well-trained workforces, and are placed well geographically. One restructuring expert estimated in 1998 that only about 15 percent of Czech enterprises were beyond salvation.[23] The comparatively strong starting positions of Czech enterprises distinguish the restructuring problem from elsewhere in the region, particularly in the former Soviet Republics. Five rapid privatization legacies, each one embodied in that first-ownership regime, are at the root of the lack of restructuring in the Czech Republic:

1. The plutocracy blocks active owners, particularly MNCs.
2. Enterprise ownership structures are convoluted.
3. Enterprises are heavily indebted.
4. Bank lending is economically irrational.
5. Regulatory institutions are incompetent and compromised.

Plutocratic Politics

First owners, the foundation of the Czech plutocracy, have maintained control over enterprises through collusion with state officials. Often, they seek to block active owners. Many first owners would rather regularly call upon the state for subsidies or banks for loans then sell out to active owners. Indeed, that "business" practice has proved even more lucrative than tunneling for some first owners. The determination of first owners to control assets extends to denying competitors active ownership, especially when competitors are foreign multinationals. After all, what would be worse for the plutocrats than an efficient competitor? This describes the situation regarding the privatization case of Big 4 bank ČS. "Domestic" Big 4 bank IPB has lobbied hard to prevent foreign owners from buying the state's controlling ownership share in ČS, though it is common knowledge that many ČS bank officials are incompetent and corrupt, and the loan portfolio is a disaster.[24] Czech plutocrats know that foreign enterprise ownership, though a key to enterprise restructuring, threatens their very existence.

Convoluted Ownership Structure

The rapid privatization policy left companies with a mosaic of different types of first owners, many of whom had tiny amounts of shares. Many enterprises still lack a majority owner despite the substantial amount of ownership concentration that has occurred since the beginning of share trading. Economic restructuring will remain doubtful for these companies until the ownership structure is concentrated. Active ownership nearly always requires one owner with a controlling ownership stake; most active owners demand a majority stake (50 percent). Lacking a majority (or controlling) stake, active owners would risk having minority owners gang up to block enterprise restructuring or to seize enterprise profits. Moreover, in many enterprise cases, the ownership structure is cluttered by outstanding share options and warrants, questions of asset ownership, and, most important, by substantial obligations to creditors. For active ownership to take hold, then, company ownership structures require both concentration and clarification.

Indebtedness

The rapid privatization policy bequeathed outstanding debt burdens to many companies that exceed enterprise capital. No active owner will undertake extensive enterprise restructuring until the debt is cleared from the enterprise balance sheets. Debt restructuring is normally a time-consuming process since creditors tend to be financial institutions with varying interests and capabilities. The debt bottleneck is complicated further by the state's willingness to assume much of the banks' bad loan portfolio. The inevitability of state support has discouraged banks from restructuring part of the bad debt and from taking unnecessary losses on the loan portfolio. Active ownership, the key to enterprise restructuring, cannot occur until the enterprise indebtedness problem is solved.

Economically Irrational Bank Lending

The rapid privatization policy created the underlying condition for irresponsible bank lending policies: state ownership sans state supervision cum state debt forgiveness. Bankers often lent to enterprises that promised personal favors or enterprises that were "too large to fail," given what added up to carte blanche from the state. These borrowers were rarely active owners. Indeed, banks normally charge owners without privileges high interest rates to offset losses from privileged borrowers. Active ownership will require an end to economically irrational bank lending, perhaps through bank privatization to foreign banks.

Lax Regulation

The rapid privatization policy diverted scarce resources in money, time, and expertise from state market regulation. It also undermined the state regulator by trying to delegitimize the state at every turn. Lax market regulation complicated efforts of prospective active owners to buy enterprise stakes on Czech stock markets or through the FNP. Prospective owners must be prepared to pay high acquisition costs in the form of bribes and manipulated price markups. They also must be able to perform due diligence to ensure that the enterprise assets they seek will remain with the enterprise after purchase. The burdens attached to obtaining active ownership have made the Czech Republic an unnaturally unwelcome destination for foreign investors, particularly relative to Hungary and Poland. One international fund manager acknowledged that he would never invest in the Czech Republic, given the country's unreliable regulatory environment. Reflecting this attitude, foreign portfolio investment actually declined by 9.5 bn CZK in the first quarter of 1997.[25] More important, lax regulation limits Czech FDI. The share of foreign investment in Czech industrial enterprises was 12.0 percent in 1996 (see table 9.6). In Hungary, by contrast, the comparable FDI figure was 33.2 percent, though that country's industrial base at the outset of transition was far less developed than in the Czech Republic (Hunya 1997). Hungary used a foreign-friendly privatization strategy, has provided foreign investors financial incentives, and most important, has established relatively firm regulatory policy, particularly concerning stock markets and banks (which are predominantly foreign owned). At its core, lax regulation is the key to the political and economic control of the plutocrats.

Despite the evidence showing that plutocrats have not restructured Czech industry, who is to say that that they won't restructure in the future? The pessimistic indications are that plutocrats have consumed much of their privatization booty or have tended to invest abroad, rather than in the Czech Republic. Czech enterprises are risky investments, market savvy is low, real interest rates are very high, the Czech currency remains overvalued, and the Czech state is unable to protect investors. Economic risk-reward rationality demands that the plutocrats invest abroad rather than restructure enterprises. The logical result was capital flight. The chances of the money returning depend on domestic growth prospects and the Czech ascension to the European Union. The above analysis implies that the Czech economy would be served best if the plutocrats would sell enterprises to foreign MNCs.

Limited enterprise restructuring caused deterioration in basic economic indicators from 1995 to 1997, including GDP growth, the foreign trade balance, the state budget, the currency value, and the unemployment rate. Only the current account balance showed an improvement over this period (see table 9.7).

Table 9.7.   Basic Economic Indicators in the Czech Republic, 1995–1997

Indicator	1995	1996	1997
GDP Growth (%)	4.8	4.4	0.9
Unemployment Rate (%)	2.9	3.5	5.2
Inflation (%)	7.9	8.6	9.8
State Budget Balance	7.2	−1.6	−6.2
Current Acct. Balance	−36.2 or	−116.5 or	−95.0 or
	−2.7% GDP	−7.6% GDP	5.7% GDP
Exchange Rate (CZK/$)	26.6	27.1	35 (Dec.)

Sources: Various national sources and WIIW Handbook of Statistics, 1997.
Note: The state budget balance and the current account balance are presented in billions of CZK.

The dramatic fall in share prices in 1998 reflects the lack of restructuring of Czech-owned companies (see table 9.8). Most devastating to the Czech neoliberal position (and to the Czech psyche) is the robust growth of neighbors and rivals Poland, Hungary, Slovenia, and most galling of all, Slovakia (see table 9.9).

Czechs are painfully aware of the growth of the plutocracy and its economic impact. They rightly attribute plutocratic capitalism partly to the weaknesses of rapid privatization and to voucher privatization. Right or wrong, the population's nagging suspicion was that it "been had" by a rigged lottery. The exposure of fraudulent get-rich-quick schemes in other voucher countries such as Caritas in Albania and MMM in Russia reinforced the growing belief that voucher privatization was a scam to bamboozle decent people. The street sense is that power is in the hands of a select few who manipulate the economy and

Table 9.8.   Share Price Changes of Select Czech-Owned Companies in 1998

	December 30, 1997	December 21, 1998	Percentage Change
Banks			
KB	1305	357	−72.6
ČS	229	101	−55.8
IPB	195	97	−50.2
Energy/Power Companies			
Unipetrol	99	54	−45.7
ČEZ	1135	674	−40.6
Industrial Holding Companies			
ČKD	1150	128	−88.9
Škoda Plzeň	612	178	−70.9

Source: HN, December 23, 1998, 7.

Table 9.9. GDP Growth Rates (Percent) in Central Europe, 1994–1998

	1994	*1995*	*1996*	*1997*	*1998(Est.)*
Czech Republic	**2.6**	**4.8**	**4.4**	**0.9**	**−2.0**
Hungary	2.9	1.5	1.0	3.0	5.2
Poland	5.2	7.0	6.1	5.6	5.8
Slovakia	4.9	7.4	7.0	5.0	3.0
Slovenia	4.9	3.5	3.5	3.5	4.0

Note: The 1998 GDP growth rate estimate for the Czech Republic reflects GDP growth of −2.1% for the first three quarters.

the government for their pleasure. Is it any wonder that many Czechs take an increasingly negative view of the quality of Czech capitalism? (See table 9.10.)

MARKET FAILURE AND CORRUPTION IN THE CZECH REPUBLIC

The fall of Klaus's neoliberal government provoked citizens and politicians to once again reconsider the foundations of Czech society. The prospects for the nation depend on whether it remedies the market excesses of the past and creates new legitimacy for the future. There is a lot of work still ahead. The main job of the next governments will be to restore confidence in the political system and in markets—a difficult, though perhaps not impossible, task in a small country in the heart of Europe.

Encouraging signs that the plutocrats' influence over politics and economics may wane include fewer assets easily available for stealing, gradual marginalization of IPFs, the delisting of companies on the Prague Stock Exchange, the recent formation of a Czech Securities and Exchange Commission, the sale of assets (particularly bank shares) to foreigners, and most important, the slow but steady influx into government of yet another new generation of young people sick of a society's corruption. The optimistic scenario is that Czech rapid privatization cost the country only wealth, time, and innocence, but not its future.

Table 9.10. Q: Are Things Better, Worse, or the Same?

	December 1994	*December 1995*	*December 1996*	*December 1997*
Better	63	58	57	44
Same	20	20	28	35
Worse	15	26	18	21

Source: STEM in *LN*, December 17, 1997.

Discouraging signs that plutocrats may maintain control over politics and economics are budding personal relations between plutocrats and Social Democrats (the political party that replaced Klaus's rightist coalition), appointments of ministers and bureaucrats who have cooperated with plutocrats in the past, indifferent attention to regulatory institutions, and proposed subsidies designed to maintain the managers of unrestructured large industrial companies. The pessimistic scenario is that the time, effort, and money wasted in Czech privatization will perpetuate the structure of corruption and poison the future for the younger generation. The question is whether the privatization-embedded Czech plutocracy can continue to block political and economic reform. The answer, as we will see in the conclusion, surprised most skeptics, and it demonstrates why Central Europe needed to be considered theoretically differently from Russia and the Republics.

The teetering Czech economy of 1997 belatedly awoke many Czechs to the necessity of state supervision of markets. The neoliberals proposed in spring and summer 1997 two economic reform packages—*baličky*—that would increase state market regulation. The packages displayed an apparent government commitment to introduce new banking regulations and new conflict of interest legislation, to establish an American-style Securities and Exchange Commission, and to initiate laws that would diminish the role of IPFs in the economy. The government also began concrete steps toward privatization of the state bank shares. Will the state finally get serious about building a state apparatus that regulates markets?

Skepticism abounds: "Even if new legislation and regulations were to be introduced immediately, it wouldn't change anything, because the people doing the stealing would be left sitting in the same places and would simply find a way around new rules and carry on stealing," said J. Křovák, chief economist at WoodCommerz, a major Prague investment company (*Prague Post*, November 12–18, 1997, C3). "The government is not interested in having capital markets effectively regulated," said J. Müller, a member of the project group responsible for setting up the Prague Securities and Exchange Commission and later its first chairman.[26]

The quality of the legislation surrounding two important issues reinforces the prevailing skepticism. Parliament passed in December 1997 a law authorizing a Czech Securities and Exchange Commission (KCP). The law grants the KCP authorization over the stock exchange, pension funds, and insurance companies. The KCP can freeze shares and pension accounts, review and take away trading licenses, and impose fines up to 100 mn CZK. Honest market participants are concerned that the new KCP will have no teeth. Parliament denies the KCP authority to issue binding regulations, and it has remained in charge of its finances. The risk is that rule breakers will stay ahead of the law by forcing the KCP to go to the Parliament each time there is a potential market infraction not precisely covered by the law. Moreover, the law specifies no investigative powers apart from parliamentary specifications. Regulation skeptics commented that Ministry of Finance bureaucrats will do no more than put the KCP sign on their office doors.

Potentially the most far-reaching legislative agenda targets IPFs. One critical regulation forces the second-wave closed-end IPFs to open if they trade at a 40 percent discount for more than three months; over time the opening discount will move to 25 percent and then to 15 percent. This regulation stipulates that investors opening IPFs may cash out their shareholdings at the net asset value of the share portfolio. The expected result is that most investors will jump at this opportunity, and these IPFs will be forced to gradually reduce their holdings or even liquidate. Another critical regulation forces IPFs to reduce individual holdings from a maximum of 20 percent to 11 percent in three years.

Naturally, the most visible opponents of IPF regulations and a bold independent KCP are IPFs.[27] J. Chroustovský of KB's IKS argues that these regulations will force huge IPF sales and a subsequent plunge in stock prices. Such a decline would ill serve investors, he claims. The only beneficiaries would be foreigners who could then "cherry-pick" the most attractive enterprise shares (Macháček 1997, 2).

IPFs argue a weak hand, in my opinion. First, they demonstrate no interest in maximizing shareholder value. IPFs are first owners who refuse to pass on ownership to the active owners envisioned by neoliberals.[28] They are bottlenecks to the open markets that the country drastically needs. Second, although foreign strategic interests may buy many IPF stakes, I retort that FDI is precisely the elixir for a Czech enterprise sector desperately in need of capital, skill, and regulatory injections. I sympathize with J. Veverka, a former Ministry of Finance Securities office director who asserted that "The creation of investment funds was the biggest mistake of voucher privatization. . . . Now that their historical function has been completed, the time has come to get rid of many of them" (*Prague Post*, November 12–18, 1997, A6).

NOTES

1. The analysis in this chapter excludes IPFs formed with the specific intention to stockpile shares in one specific industry or enterprise. Enterprise managers of large integrated companies—for example, energy company CHEMOPETROL—were often the organizers of these IPFs.

2. Kožený's nonbank IPF Harvard Fund was one exception. The Harvard Fund in the first wave concentrated its holdings in only fifty-one companies.

3. The situation was alleviated somewhat by a May 1996 law mandating supermajorities for important enterprise decisions.

4. Approximately 90 percent of all market transactions by value occur away from the two public stock markets. There was and is no transparency on these extramarket trades. The secrecy and extent of the extraexchange market meant that most stock prices printed in the newspaper were almost meaningless. The state authorities who were discharged to collect proper taxes, the investors in IPFs who might monitor the managers, and the stock exchange authorities who might protect against stock manipulation also had no access to the extraexchange transactions.

5. Using these IPFs that were formed in the first privatization wave. IPFs that were *akciové společnosti* were not unit trust IPFs, which were linked to shareholders by contract and could not be easily replaced.

6. By law, a "Chinese wall" divided a bank and its bank IPF. However, interviews with bank officials suggest that the Chinese wall was meaningless in practice. Managements of the two linked institutions freely interacted.

7. Author interview with IPB IPF managers.

8. It was only sporadically material to asset movements and enterprise corporate governance that IPFs were limited to 20 percent shares in individual enterprises. IPFs sometimes got around the law by recruiting allies to buy shares. At other times, enterprises were governed by informal agreements among IPFs dividing ownership rights and obligations.

9. Who provided the start-up capital for Motoinvest? No one knows.

10. Under Option 1, investors would sell shares in one of seven major funds, with a money-back guarantee in fourteen days. Under Option 2, investors would sell other shares to Plzeňská banka, which would then sell them over the next six months. Under Option 3, investors would invest the shares in a pension fund controlled by Plzeňská banka (Vojenský penzijní fond).

11. Reportedly, the Motoinvest struggle was played out in the government as Klaus versus J. Tošovský, the Central Bank president. Klaus sided with Motoinvest.

12. Only IPB converted its IPFs to holding companies. The other bank IPFs evidently were more concerned about their reputations and legally remained as IPFs.

13. These estimates are lower than most Czech analysts suspect. A normal estimate for tunneling is on the order of 200 bn CZK or nearly $7 bn.

14. For instance, the Prague Stock Exchange operated an electronic trading system using French equipment. Coopers & Lybrand and Phare recommended that transactions taking place outside the stock exchanges, insider trading, and enterprise annual reports should be available on request. Regarding enterprise governance, they recommended strengthening the effectiveness of the supervisory board, improving cooperation between auditors and supervisory boards, strengthening the role of the general meeting, securing property rights of individual shareholders, and provisioning conscientious duties for shareholders (Coopers & Lybrand and Phare 1997, 44–47).

15. Žák cites Paragraph 255 in the criminal code to rebut the tunnelers' claims of legal innocence. Paragraph 255 enables "criminal punishment against someone who breaks according to law or by a formal contract the received obligation to look after or to manage others' property" (Žák 1997, 21). However, as Žák also notes, Paragraph 255 was never used to combat tunnelers.

16. Part of the ODS efforts to limit the powers of the control organizations related to the Nejvyssí kontrolní úřad (NKU), literally the Highest Control Office. ODS ensured that the NKU would be granted a political premium. This means that a political appointment heads the NKU (Reed 1996, 87).

17. In December 1997, a judge who cited the preposterousness of the whole affair released Wallis.

18. Foreign banks normally financed home country MNCs in CEECs. For example, French banks tended to finance French companies doing business in the Czech Republic.

19. Twenty-one percent of loans over 360 days are in arrears, and 36 percent are classified over 30 days (Holle and Pettyfer 1997). Bad loans in Czech banks are totally unrelated to the past, contrary to popular belief in the West.

20. Companies privatized by (other) standard privatization methods lag behind companies with dominant state shareholding. However, these companies are excluded from analysis above because they are dominated by utilities, which show a distinct industry pattern and, in any case, do not meaningfully reflect the impact or approach of the state owner. I must add, however, that enterprises privatized by standard methods might have performed even better had they not been loaded down with bank debt stemming from the original purchase. One solution might have been to sink privatization proceeds back into enterprises. Recall that instead privatization receipts went to the state budget.

21. One study attributes 92 percent of Czech 1996 manufacturing profits to enterprises with foreign equity participation (Zemplínerová [forthcoming]).

22. This is not to say that all FDI is beneficial to the host country (Comisso 1998; Schwartz and Haggard 1997).

23. Based on author interview.

24. The "foreign" privatization of IPB is a fascinating and indicative case. Presumably IPB (as of 1998) was the only Big 4 Czech bank privatized to foreigners. However, the foreign purchaser, Nomura Securities, is widely suspected among Czech insiders of operating according to the direction of the previous management. IPB may have been a case of a privatization by domestic insiders through the use of a foreign "front man." The situation in most other privatization cases involving foreign interests is precisely the reverse.

25. Inflows of foreign portfolio investment into the Czech Republic were 46.7 percent in 1993, 24.6 percent in 1994, 36.1 percent in 1995, and 19.7 percent in 1996 (Czech Ministry of Finance 1997).

26. Based on author interview.

27. Surprisingly, however, opposition also comes from a coterie of left-leaning Parliament members. Z. Jičínský and P. Rychetský, two Social Democratic deputies, argue that the KCP law is "unconstitutional," and M. Ransdorf, a leading Communist deputy,

argues that the KCP is a potential "financial NKVD." Otherwise, distracting issues concerning, for instance, the proper salaries of the KCP officials, divert attention away from the critical regulatory situation. Misdirected debates over the KCP validate the fear of the then twenty-three-year-old advisor to Minister of Finance D. Gladiš that Parliament would choose KCP commissioners on political grounds rather than on understanding of or experience with capital markets (Němeček 1997, 4).

28. This issue has not always been understood in the West. For instance, influential analysts such as Coffee contend that limits on IPFs should be removed (Coffee 1994). I believe that this would be like giving the fox the run of the henhouse.

10

Political and Economic Implications of Czech Rapid Privatization

Andrew Harrison Schwartz and Jiří Havel

Rapid privatization yielded the Czech Republic unexpectedly poor economic performance during the transition decade, especially when compared with fast growing neighbors, Poland and Hungary (see chapter 1). In general, neither the Czech first owners nor the enterprise managers injected time, know-how, and capital into enterprise restructuring. Instead, they devoted resources to obtaining enterprise control, often to strip assets. Dismal economic data coming out of the Czech Republic during that privatization period proved a great disappointment to neoliberals. Yet Czech economic performance revived at the end of the period, after the completion of most privatization.

THE CZECH COMEBACK, 1998–2002

Little has been written in the Western press or in academic publications about Czech economics and politics after 1997, consistent with the country's minor geopolitical importance. Recent scholarship continues to emphasize the disappointing economic results in the Czech Republic (McDermott 2002; Ellerman 2003). But a funny thing happened in the Czech Republic after the world's economic experts left town. The Czech economy recovered briskly. Foreign investors flooded into the Czech Republic.

From an institutional vantage, the broad and unregulated capital markets that had differentiated the postprivatization Czech economy and been the source of intense criticism had been virtually remade. Most shares had been delisted, and only a handful of shares traded actively. Moreover, Czech capital markets were increasingly dominated by bond trading, which carried none of the corrupt baggage associated with equity trading. Even the corrupt IPFs and the tunnelers that had animated critics of Czech voucher privatization had either disappeared or were becoming legitimate. Contrary to the institutionalists, Czech financial institutions had come to resemble those in Poland and in Hungary, and even those in smaller Western countries.

Politically, the Czech recovery came under precisely the Social Democratic government that Western analysts had been telling everyone to dread. The Social Democratic government, with alleged links to former communists, moved to privatize its remaining stakes in Czech companies (including banks), to open the economy to foreign investment, and to reduce corruption in Czech markets—typically over the opposition of the Klaus-led neoliberal reformers. Although the Social Democratic government eventually was buffeted by corruption scandals and penetrated by the mounting influence of industrial lobbies, the Social Democratic Party won reelection in 2002, prompting Klaus's resignation from Parliament. Klaus's government of reformers had sought to stall rather than to drive the development of free markets, and the consequences of the very policies that they had instituted to generate a popular basis of political support proved to be its downfall.[1] Distributional conflicts may reverse the incentives and character of reformers and opponents of reform.

What to make of recent Czech privatization experience: miracle, then mirage, back to miracle? Were the neoliberals right after all? Was institutional experience in the transition fundamentally irrelevant? At the very least, the Czech experience forces analysts to reframe the analysis of neoliberals and institutionalists alike. Our analysis below reconsiders Czech privatization and postprivatization experience and the development of capital markets from an ownership regime prospective.

Conditions in Czech Firms in the Late 1990s

1. *Czech ruling coalitions begin to assert control (but only after several years of dispersed property rights).* As we saw in the prior chapter, Czech property rights were dispersed after privatization. Compared to other privatization programs Czech privatization was extremely rapid but not so quick as to solve the problem of the execution of property rights. Enterprises were in an "ownership vacuum" for many years—second-wave enterprises until at least 1995 (from 1991). Moreover, voucher privatization did not immediately create majority shareholders. The Czech voucher system subdivided ownership by several classes, including individual holders. For many enterprises, an effective coalition of owners occurred in about two years (or longer), meaning that Czech enterprise remained without authoritative leadership well into the late 1990s. In practice, dispersed ownership prompted the hostile behavior of company management toward their enterprises; the volume depended primarily on moral qualities.

In time, majority owners appeared in most Czech enterprises, as most neoliberals had predicted. Typically, the majority owners emanated from various IPFs. Crucial decisions were totally in their hands. Later on, new subjects who bought shares on the secondary market entered this decision-making structure. Among them were company managers, who saw the chance to buy cheap shares and be a partner of the fund pool and eventually the owner. Of course, not all the old managers were booted. Many survived as experts for ruling the technical or commercial processes—but their position was changed. Now it was necessary to convince the new owners that management represents value added. Representatives of the funds in any case changed the original management and the state officers in the company organs such as the supervisory board and the board of directors.

The arrival of a stable, recognizable ownership group prompted companies to start the hands-on process of restructuring. Many times such restructuring was a destructive process. The assets of the companies were many times more interesting for liquidation purposes than the companies as going concerns. An interesting case was ČSNP (Československá námořní plavba, a.s. [Czech Naval Haulage, P.L.C.]), where the owner (V. Kožený's group) sold all its ships and liquidated totally the whole business in the Czech Republic (1998). From the economic point of view it was a quite a good deal (it created for the owner interesting revenue and required liquidity) but the Czech Republic as a country lost the only shipowner company with a long tradition, a company that had also some importance for education and practice of Czech shipmasters.

2. *Stock markets no longer acted as vehicles to strip assets, rather than to raise money.* Stock markets never performed any function for firms. The decision to go to the public markets was not the decision of the firms themselves, but it was a decision of the state. From the firm's point of view, its presence on the public markets was connected only with additional costs and other problems. From the beginning of the new history of Czech financial markets, firms avoided raising money through initial public offerings (IPOs).[2] Firms lacked advantage from the first Czech stock markets, but they had many obligations—to report periodically their results, organize general meetings, and behave in accordance with many other complicated formal rules that they were penalized for violating. Many firms consequently wanted to exit the market, that is, to be delisted. Fortunately, the Czech governments that followed the neoliberals were instituting sweeping changes—delisting, protection of minority shareholder rights, rationalizing of IPFs, deep changes in the penal law and commercial code, and the creation of a Czech SEC—that helped to deter rampant asset stripping.

Table 10.1.   Foreign Direct Investment in the Czech Republic, 1992–2003 (net inflows in US$ mil.)

1992	1993	1994	1995	1996	1997	1998	1999	2000	2001	2002	2003
983	563	749	2,526	1,276	1,275	3,591	6,234	4,943	5,476	9,029	5,000

Source: EBRD 2003.

3. *Assets increasingly ended in hands of final (frequently foreign) own-ers.* The consolidation of a new Czech ownership class along with the ratio-nalization of Czech stock markets signaled that the competition for Czech enterprise assets was largely over.[3] The period of spontaneous stealing was de-emphasized and new values such as reliability, fairness, and positive his-tory increasingly gained importance.

Tunneling is not a process that could be continuously repeated; it's mostly a one-shot weapon. Partners quickly see the game, especially when they lose a huge sum of money. Yet the game could persist in several forms, though the outlines would need to change as conditions dictated. The same people started in 1990–1991 by founding new banks, in 1992 privatization investment funds and broker companies, and later on health insurance companies, pension funds, and eventually banking co-ops (*kampelickas*).[4] Each of these company types gave these asset holders the chance to be present in many firms, which were directly held, indirectly held, or connected by deep financial links. By the late 1990s, with the incoming new government and the public's taste for institutional changes, the self-dealing that had identified Czech equity mar-kets limited the space for "old-style" tunneling. The resulting exit strategy for Czech owners was to sell enterprises to the highest bidders, usually foreign-ers. Ironically, I would argue, Czech owners behaved as the neoliberals had predicted, but a decade late—more and more enterprises entered the hands of final investors, investors who invested for the long run. As had occurred in Hungary years earlier, foreign investors replaced domestic interests who had gradually sold Czech enterprise assets (see table 10.1).

Enter Politics

From an economic perspective, the new ownership regime forced owners with new attributes, a new ownership structure, financial system, and a state regu-lator with a wholly new capacity and, as we shall see below from a political analysis, a degree of autonomy. Rapid privatization should nonetheless not be judged primarily on its economic record. The political outcomes of rapid privatization were just as important as the economic ramifications.

POPULAR DISCONTENT WITH CZECH NEOLIBERALISM

Neoliberals designed rapid privatization to solve a political problem, for political purposes. The political problem was opposition to economic reform by threatened economic interests (workers, mangers, and state bureaucrats, for example) and a population bound to suffer from privatization in the short run. If privatization were rapid, reformers could privatize while threatened interests were in disarray and popular enthusiasm for markets and democracy was robust. From the neoliberal perspective, the political measures of success are the implementation of privatization and popular support for the reformers. The political purpose of privatization—indeed, the main motivation behind economic liberalization—was to break the political stranglehold of the state and replace the state with a system dominated by private owners. The presumption was that private owners would support democratic politics. At its core neoliberalism was a political theory. In conclusion, therefore, we must evaluate rapid privatization mainly based on its political achievements. Having analyzed the evolution of Czech plutocratic capitalism from privatization in the Czech Republic in the prior chapters, the remainder of this chapter moves to a discussion of its political implications.

From a political perspective, rapid privatization in the Czech Republic succeeded on two levels. It created private owners, and it generated popularity for market reformers (at least at first), as neoliberal reformers had expected. The rapid privatization approach also broke the state monopoly on political power, a central objective of privatization. The big surprise was that the private owners generated by rapid privatization worked against civic participation in government. They instead condoned a corrupt political economy—labeled earlier as plutocratic capitalism—that fosters government by the rich, for the rich. The new Czech plutocrats have restricted public access to information and monopolized state decision-making. They are readily identified as bankers, IPF managers, state officials, large enterprise managers, and shady operators. Inadequate financial market regulation as well as corrupt state bureaucrats and politicians characterize Czech plutocratic capitalism. As we saw in the preceding chapters, a main root of Czech plutocratic capitalism is the neoliberal rapid privatization strategy.

Eventually, even a key neoliberal success—public support for market reformers—evaporated in the face of growing evidence of state corruption. Most damaging was proof that implicated neoliberal reformers in scandal. After the discovery of a Swiss bank account at the disposal of his political party in 1997, Klaus resigned as Czech prime minister, thus effectively ending the neoliberal era. The nonviolent fall of Klaus and the neoliberals had clearly demonstrated that popular pressure—the defining trait of a democracy—influenced

Table 10.2. Czech Economic Performance after the Two Privatization Waves (1992–1995) and Klaus Resignation (1996)

		1996	1997	1998	1999	2000	2001	2002
GDP growth	%, real	4.3	−0.8	−1.2	0.5	3.3	3.3	3.0
Industrial production	%, real	2.0	4.5	1.6	−3.1	5.8	6.8	4.0
Construction output	%, real	4.8	−3.9	−7.0	−6.5	5.6	9.6	7.0
Retail sales	%, real	11.4	1.9	−7.2	2.1	4.6	4.3	4.5
Inflation	%, average	8.8	8.5	10.7	2.1	3.9	4.7	4.4
Unemployment rate	%, e. o. p.	3.5	5.2	7.5	9.4	8.8	8.9	8.5

Czech politics. Yet the instigating factors behind Klaus's resignation also suggested that the quality of Czech democracy was quite low, and that the rapid privatization approach advocated by neoliberals had been largely responsible (see table 10.2).

The immediate political outcome of Czech rapid privatization strategy was a plutocracy that flouted the law, monopolized access to policymakers and to information, and contaminated the honesty and competence of the civil service. The worst abuses of the plutocracy involved the new stock markets, standard privatization cases, and tunneling. Each abuse can be linked to the Czech rapid privatization strategy. The main political consequences of those abuses were a decline in popular trust in government institutions and the subsequent fall of the neoliberal Klaus government in December 1997.

Stock market scandals, standard privatization scandals, and tunneling scandals dominated political headlines throughout 1996 and 1997. The government apologized for its failure to prevent such scandals, but the admissions came off as disingenuous. Each day seemed to reveal evidence linking political parties in the governing coalition with contributions from anonymous or untraceable sources, such as dead people. Most of these contributions involved IPFs or standard privatization cases. The revelations of the corrupt business-state partnership caused levels of trust in popularly elected state institutions (the Klaus government and Parliament) to sink below 20 percent (from IVVM, a survey research firm, November 1997). The Czech Republic was, to borrow Havel's faintly vulgar phrase, *v blbé náladě*—"in a crappy mood." Havel vividly and unabashedly tied the *blbá nálada* to Klaus and the neoliberals in a famous speech in December 1997.

[M]any people are convinced—democracy or no democracy—again there are in power untrustworthy people, who are more interested in their own benefit than in the general interest; many people are convinced that honest entrepreneurs have a bad time, as opposed to dishonest rich people who have a green light; the conviction dominates that in this country it pays to lie and to steal, that many politicians and state bureaucrats are bribed and that political parties . . . are secretly manipulating suspicious financial groups.

Many people wonder why after eight years of building the market economy that our economy is so terrible that government must quickly introduce spending packages, why we must suffocate in smog when so much money reportedly is devoted for ecological aims, why prices of everything including rents and energy must grow without regard to the growth of pensions or other social salaries, why we must be afraid to walk at night in the center of our towns, why nobody is building anything other than banks, hotels, villas for the rich, and so forth. Still more people have a distaste for politics, which is understandably and justifiably thought to be responsible for all the bad things; and we are all becoming suspicious of politics if not directly antagonistic. (*HN*, 1997, 6; available at http://old.hrad.cz/president/Havel/speeches/1997/0912_uk.html)

Political dissatisfaction with neoliberal government increased throughout 1996 and 1997. In the 1996 elections, the ODS-led ruling coalition only managed a one-seat majority in the Parliament. In spring 1997, the coalition survived by a one-vote margin a no-confidence vote in Parliament. Popular voting preferences in the right-wing coalition plummeted from March 1997 to October 1997 (see table 10.3). Over 85 percent of the population registered dissatisfaction with the political situation, up from a still high 70 percent in August (*HN*, December 11, 1997, 1).

The death rattle for Klaus and the neoliberal coalition began with the confession of one M. Šrejber, a former world-ranked tennis player. Šrejber confessed that he had anonymously donated 7.5 mn CZK (about $270,000) to ODS. The donation came just prior to a state privatization involving Třinecké železárny, one of the country's largest steelmakers. The state subsequently

Table 10.3. Political Party Preferences, March 1997, October 1997, and January 1998

Party	March 1997 (%)	October 1997 (%)	January 1998 (%)
Coalition Party Total	50	36	31
ODS	29	20	14
KDU-ČSL	9	11	10
ODA	12	5	7
Opposition Party Total	19	29	28
ČSSD	19	29	28
Extremist Party Total	13	15	14
KSČM	8	9	7
SPR-RSČ	5(est.)	6	7

Sources: IVVM in *HN*, November 13, 1997, 7; *LN*, December 17, 1997; ČTK and STEM data from September 1997; FACTUM data *LN*, January 22, 1998, 4.

awarded Šrejber and his associates ownership of the enterprise. It appeared that Šrejber had successfully bribed ODS.

The denouement came when the press learned that ODS had $1.7 mn stashed away in a Swiss bank account. This Swiss bank account had been open for several years. Why ODS had this account and where the money came from is still a mystery, though most analysts presume that the source of the money is illegal.[5] J. Ruml and I. Pilip, two prominent ODS members—Ruml was a famous dissident and former minister of interior and Pilip was then finance minister—called on party leader Klaus to resign. J. Lux, the chief of coalition partner KDU-ČSL, also called for Klaus's head. When Havel criticized the government's contribution to the *blbá nálada*, Klaus mercifully resigned. The neoliberal era was over.

The fall of Klaus's neoliberal government provoked citizens and politicians to once again reconsider the foundations of Czech society. The prospects for the nation depend on whether it remedies the market excesses of the past and creates new legitimacy for the future. The main job of the next governments will be to restore confidence in the political system and in Czech markets. Important indications will be whether the state takes financial market regulation seriously and whether it encourages the participation of a broad spectrum of people, not just those with money and connections.

What Happened to the Czech Plutocrats?

Economically, many Czech plutocrats exited the tunneling games by selling assets to the highest bidder—often a foreign purchaser. Yet Czech plutocrats also self-destructed economically, unlike, say in Russia, where the Russian cognates became a permanent fixture of political and economic life.[6] Politically, the Czech plutocrats were pressured by the popularity of the new Tosovsky and Social Democratic governments and the decline of their neoliberal ally, ODS.

Potential Czech plutocrats, such as Junek, Soudek, Stehlik, Maroušek, and the Ostrava clans (Pětroš, Pastrňák, etc.) started their "entrepreneurial" activities with the strategy "too big to fail," and they were convinced that their losses would be covered by the state or by state banks that lent them huge sums of money. Thus the stage seemingly was set for the analogous state-plutocrat alliances that occurred throughout the region, but would fail under then unique Czech conditions. The dilemma was that the banks were in terrible financial condition, in need of foreign resources and expertise, and in no position to bail out the plutocrats. Ironically, the potential Czech plutocrats invested their ill-gotten gains into their own rotting companies—a classic instance of throwing good money after bad.

Where were lobbyists, the IPFs in this game? Why did these interests lose? What do the new regulatory initiatives say about the fairness and impartiality of the Czech regime? Just before the Czech elections of 1998, nobody wanted to be unpopular, to be against the capital market amendments. The discussion was not about "to be or not to be" (to have regulation or not); it was quite clear to the elite that the situation had to change. Significant momentum came from Tosovsky's government, and especially Ivan Pilip, the ODS finance minister, who wanted to show that he was different from the ODS "reformers." Also, the newly established US (Union of Freedom, a political party spin-off of ODS) accented the role of capital market regulation. Similarly, improvements of capital markets were a serious part of the ČSSD program. Consequently, the ensuing legislative hurricane (*legislativní smršt'*) included many changes in the respective regulatory laws as well as substantial changes in other organs like courts, public attorneys, and special troops of police. Under ČSSD, deep changes occurred in the Czech Commercial Code, Security Act, SEC Act, Investment Fund Act, and many other acts as well as the penal law where many definitions of illegal economic activities were added. These far-reaching political shifts, including the split of ODS, the importance of public opinion in the subsequent elections, the marginalization of interests (and IPFs), and the rationalization of the asset-swapping game, demonstrated that the Czech Republic had a higher underlying quality of democracy and capitalism than either Russia or the Ukraine, much less Romania or Bulgaria.

THE LEFT—NOT THE REFORMIST
RIGHT—RATIONALIZES CZECH MARKETS

How did the broadly based, unregulated Czech stock markets of 1995 become the narrow, (somewhat more) regulated Czech capital markets of today? Institutionalists would expect that the movement would be progressive, perhaps path dependent. Institutional models might not have allowed for such radical change, presuming instead that the fundamental characteristics of the first Czech capital markets would be mimicked in the current one.

Neoliberals, on the other hand, might scoff at the relevance of the question. They might note instead that today's result was preordained; the postprivatization period would lead to the economically natural institution—narrow, relatively tightly regulated financial markets—as had appeared throughout the regime. Little could they have guessed that the impetus for change would emanate from the Left.

In June 1998, the Czech electorate voted in a Social Democratic government in the wake of Klaus's fall from power. In short order, the new government put in place sensible minority shareholder rights, delisted equity shares, emphasized bonds, buttressed the SEC, regulated, privatized the banks to foreigners, and cleaned up the IPFs (including the high discounts). The result was that the Czech equity markets—though hardly perfect—served more of an allocative role than one dominated by stealing.

We address the brief changes of Czech capital markets from an ownership regime viewpoint, the broad notion that the actions of claimants for property shape the function and evolution of institutions. Although ČSSD instituted many market reforms over the late 1990s/early 2000s, we will briefly review four such reforms: minority shareholder rights protection, the IPF cleanup, company delisting, and the formation of Czech regulatory institutions. After the tunnelers finished stripping assets, the equity markets changed abruptly. Institutional change was kinked, not path dependent, contrary to the theoretical formulations advanced by some institutionalists (Stark and Bruszt 1998; Pierson 2000).

Minority Shareholding

Probably the most important reforms were the mandatory offers to minority shareholders in case of a company takeover. When a shareholder reached more than 50 percent of the shares, the shareholder was obliged to make a public offer of a contract for the purchase of this company's other publicly tradable shares.[7] The price of the shares was derived from public market prices (weighted average from the last six-month period). Although hardly ideal, the new minority protection laws did improve the situation, especially as tunneling became less common at the turn of the century.[8]

IPF Cleanup

Another critical question concerned the ensuing Czech market structure. Could the IPFs establish credibility in Czech markets? Without fundamental improvements, the entire industry of collective investment could not survive and would be quickly replaced by competitors from the EU. Fortunately, the IPFs were represented by UNIS (Unie investičních společností a investičních fondů [Union of Investment Companies and Investment Funds]), which started in the second half of the 1990s to build high professional standards.[9] These standards focused mainly on professional ethics. UNIS represents about 95 percent of Czech IPF assets.

The major cleanup issue concerned the discounts IPFs fetched on Czech capital markets. Typical discounts in developed markets do not exceed

20 percent—5 percent to 10 percent is common. In the Czech Republic, discounts in the large funds ran 20 or 30 percent, and as high as 80 percent. The result was that fund shareholders were trapped in the funds; they could only sell assets at deep discounts, that is, bargain-basement prices.

The Social Democratic government solved the problem by transforming the IPFs into open-end funds, that is, funds that would automatically trade at the net asset value of the funds' shares. This maneuver would free the shareholder from the funds' managers, and permit him to sell at a "fair" price. The amendment was passed by Parliament in 1998 (Act. No. 362/2000 Coll.); closed funds were obliged to open at least till the end of 2002.[10] Ultimately, the cleanup of the IPF discounts may help to pave the way for a collective investment industry that may soon rank among the cleanest in the former communist countries.

Share Delisting: The Prague "Bond" Exchange

Perhaps the most dramatic change in Czech stock markets concerned the radical delisting of share issues. Prior to 2001, the delisting decision was fully in the hands of the company management, which normally delisted to circumvent potentially troublesome shareholders.[11] New laws advocated by the

Table 10.4.   Size of Selected Equity Markets, 1995

	Number of Traded Firms
Central Europe	
Czech Republic	**1,635**
Hungary	42
Poland	65
Slovakia	18
Asia	
Malaysia	529
Korea	721
Taiwan	347
Indonesia	238
Latin America	
Argentina	149
Brazil	570
Chile	284
Mexico	185
European Union	
Greece	212
Portugal	169
France	450
Germany	678

Source: Filer and Hanousek 1996, 22.

Table 10.5. Prague Stock Exchange, 2003

	Shares	Bonds	Total
Main market	5	24	29
Secondary market	40	18	58
Free market	31	36	67
New market	0	0	0
Total	76	78	154

Social Democrats obligated the public markets, including the PSE, to downsize the equity markets through delisting.[12] The key requirement was market capitalization: "If the security . . . is a share, the total value of its issue . . . should attain [at least] EUR 1,000,000" (Section 72, subsection 1—English translation "Czech Financial Services Legislation in 2001," Prague, Trade Links).[13]

One consequence of the leftist initiative was that from 1995 to 2003, the number of traded issues on the Prague Stock Exchange (PSE) plummeted over 95 percent, from 1,635 to 76. A mere five traded on the PSE's main market. In just eight years, the left-leaning state transformed the PSE into a size proportional to the size of the Czech market (see tables 10.4 and 10.5).

The second key consequence was that Czech capital markets increasingly became bond markets. The issuers of bonds voluntarily behave in a strong accordance not only with the market rules but also with the conditions of issue. Why? Because firms have a significant benefit from the issuing of bonds and may bear a significant penalty for breaking the rules. The bond market had the same or similar formal rules as the share market had and the same or similar market channels to trade bonds. Bonds finally pushed out the shares from the market in volume terms; at the end of the century, bond trading represented about 80 percent of transactions on the Prague Stock Exchange (see table 10.6).

Table 10.6. Prague Stock Exchange: Trade Value Broken Down by Shares + Units and Bonds

	Total value	Shares + Units value (mil. CZK)	Shares + Units (%)	Bonds value (mil. CZK)	Bonds (%)
1993	9,020.1	7,129.5	79.04	1,890.5	20.96
1994	62,026.2	42,593.9	68.67	19,432.3	31.33
1995	195,406.9	125,642.8	64.30	69,764.1	35.70
1996	393,199.6	249,935.2	63.56	143,264.3	36.44
1997	679,537.5	246,301.9	36.25	433,235.6	63.75
1998	860,191.6	172,594.0	27.06	687,597.6	79.94
1999	1,187,485.7	163,456.7	13.76	1,024,029.0	86.24
2000	1,222,832.8	264,145.3	21.60	958,687.6	78.40
2001	1,987,179.0	128,754.0	6.48	1,858,380.0	93.52

Toward the Creation of an Autonomous and Capable Regulator of Czech Capital Markets (Including the Privatization of Banks to Foreigners)

Serious discussions about the shape of capital market regulation didn't begin until 1995, when tunneling was beginning to become apparent to the Czech finance elite. Some politicians spoke about the necessity of an autonomous body (Ježek, Pilip). Others (Kočárník, Klaus, or Rudlovčák) did not agree. The first side stressed that independence is the first step to efficient regulation; the latter side emphasized that the real powers of the regulatory organ are more important than autonomy. They argued that Czech courts, for instance, are undoubtedly independent, but are not efficient. An independent SEC was founded and it has been functioning since March 1998 (under the Tosovsky government). Perhaps most important, the mere existence of a Czech SEC signaled to potential market participants that the government was serious about solving the problems from the past, and that the country would introduce new ways of regulation with new people and new organs.

Under the Social Democrats,[14] the level of independence of the SEC increased, but remained disputable. The Czech SEC is independent technically from the law, but Parliament approves the budget. On the other hand, there is little chance that the SEC is financed from sources paid by entities trading on the markets. Autonomy is not the crucial problem.

The major problem for Czech regulators lay in their capability to implement laws without perverse impact. The Social Democrats (under Ježek as SEC chairman) implemented many new legal regulations to improve Czech capital markets, but many times these rules had an undesired effect. One dilemma concerned the impact of stricter regulations under the conditions of insufficient enforcement of law. Stricter rules function properly under the conditions of efficient enforcement of laws or under the conditions in which such rules have a high natural authority. In practice, stricter rules relatively worsened the situation of Czech groups that sought to follow rules while helping the "bad" group that ignored the new rules, the theory being: If somebody makes hurdles for my competitor, I am relatively better off. Amendments from 1996, when not followed by the changes in law enforcement, many times had this paradoxical effect. Although this problem abated gradually over time, changes in the law generally were oriented in the right direction. Typically, the Czech problem concerned the quality of the new laws and their minimal accordance with the functioning of other institutions.[15]

Finally, arguably the most important piece of regulation was the privatization of bank shares to foreign interests. Over the frequent objections of domestic interests, including often the impacted banks and the Czech neoliberals, the Social Democrats sold bank shares during their tenure to foreign banks. Those banks, in turn, established a level of stability and internal regulation that substituted for an autonomous and efficient state regulator. The foreign bank behavior demonstrated the key lesson that positive regulation can emanate from a nonstate—indeed, a nondomestic—entity.

The Political Future of Czech Markets

The history of the Social Democratic government and the governments that follow will depend on whether they break the structure of corruption built by the neoliberals and become part of the solution or whether they corrupt the state and become part of the problem. Ultimately, the quality of democratic government will depend on whether plutocratic capitalism implants popular cynicism of public institutions to the point that citizens withdraw completely from political participation, much as they did after the Warsaw Pact invasion of 1968.[16]

We may summarize the chances for a turn away back toward plutocratic capitalism through two scenarios. The optimistic scenario is that Czech rapid privatization cost the country only wealth, time, and innocence, but not its future. This is indicated by fewer assets easily available for stealing, gradual marginalization of IPFs, delisting of companies on the Prague Stock Exchange, formation of a Czech SEC, the sale of assets (particularly bank shares) to foreigners, and most important, the slow but steady influx into government of yet another new generation of young people disgusted with the society's corruption.

The pessimistic scenario is that the time, effort, and money wasted in Czech privatization will perpetuate the structure of corruption and poison the future for the younger generation. This is indicated by budding personal relations between state officials and Social Democrats, appointments of ministers and bureaucrats who have cooperated in the past, indifferent attention to regulatory institutions, and proposed subsidies designed to maintain the posts of managers in unrestructured large industrial companies. The question under this scenario is whether the privatization-embedded Czech corruption can continue to block political and economic reform.

One conclusion is unimpeachable. The neoliberals unnecessarily jeopardized a historic chance to erect an ideological base of right-wing support. Although Klaus constructed a political party with clientelistic tentacles that stretched into many ministries and throughout the regions, he drained citizens of enthusiasm for free-market economics. Klaus resigned in disgrace, a casualty of the inevitable excesses of unbridled markets. The free-market Czech right wing may not return to power in the near future, at least not without abandoning its extreme neoliberal positions. As political policy, rapid privatization ultimately failed. (Ironically, Klaus was elected president and ODS has made a steep comeback as this chapter is being written.)

Finally, Klaus's failure is profoundly a generation's failure. The disappointed generation, those thirty- and forty-year-olds who saw the communists seize much of their youth and who followed the neoliberals into party politics, are being swept from political power, just as Klaus is. The Social Democrats represent a generational alliance between the wizened veterans of 1968 and Prague Spring and a young generation of ambitious twenty-somethings. The legacy of rapid privatization, plutocratic capitalism, is the political economy inherited by this political May-September marriage. The Czech Republic must wait for the new Western-trained postcommunist generation to enter politics and economics if these politicians are not equal to the task. Havel optimistically characterized the challenges ahead:

> If our current crisis forces us again to think seriously about the character of our state, about its ideas, about its identity, and if the result of such thinking permeates our own work, then this crisis wouldn't be at all unnecessary, and all the losses which accrued would be many times given back. (Havel, cited in *HN*, 1997, 6; available at http://old.hrad.cz/president/Havel/speeches/1997/0912_uk.html)

WERE THE NEOLIBERALS RIGHT?

The rapid transformation and rationalization of the Czech ownership regime to one consistent with the original neoliberal expectations begs the question whether the neoliberals were right in the end, at least regarding the Czech case. Analogous to the claims of scholars who claimed that they had predicted the implosion of the USSR decades before it finally happened, the neoliberals claimed to have been right all along in Central Europe, a mere decade after the policies were implanted.

Three subdivisions can categorize the specific problems. We can summarize the main complaint with the observation that the CEECs that followed neoliberal orthodoxy paid far too high a reform tax, frequently paying that tax to outsiders, who in turn returned little in the way of investment. They contributed instead to the corruption of the government and its reformers (see Koženy and Šrejber, for instance). Specifically, contrary to neoliberals,

1. *Assets may change hands via corruption and intimidation during and after privatization, not via business valuation and rationality.* The future of honest government appears limited in the Czech Republic for the time being.
2. *Privatization insensitive to characteristics of the first new owners may result in delayed development* (as measured especially in foreign direct

investment [FDI]—business investment instead went to Poland and Hungary). In practice, delay ruined Czech enterprises, ultimately reducing the prices that the Czech government could reap from privatization. Given the importance of privatization to the Czech state budget, delay's impact was especially pernicious.

3. *Privatization insensitive to the role of state market regulation may embed state corruption, compromising the neutral regulatory (and developmental) potential of the state.* One Czech consequence was that the reform initiatives came from the Left, not the Right. Fortunately, the results seem relatively benign because the game ended. Elsewhere, especially as one travels eastward, the game becomes far nastier and the policy impact potentially more destructive.

The critique of neoliberalism in CEECs points above all to the idea that institutions in one setting may behave differently, perhaps perversely, depending on the political and economic environment. Indeed, the Czech story also raises the question whether too much time was spent on capital markets and on capital market regulation, in particular. Would better regulation have muted corruption? Was it possible to even have better regulation, given Czech conditions? The extent that capital market regulation was important, then, suggests a very small market (as was eventually created), with capital market regulations therefore as an insubstantial part of transition.

If the overall story here is not regulation, but the natural ebbing of the capital market in the context of the gradual rise of a stable political and economic environment, then the institutionalist criticisms of the post–Washington consensus must be called into question or are at least of limited importance. The core dilemma is that institutionalists normally overemphasized formal institutions (and neglected them *in concreto*), while neglecting the role of informal institutions. This leads to our focus on the development of the behavior of entrepreneurs, banks, foreign investment, and especially politics, the core of the ownership regime concept.

In the final section of the book, we now turn to a comprehensive comparison of ownership regime theory, neoliberal, and institutionalist approaches to the study of market transitions.

NOTES

1. See Hellman (1998) for theoretical elaborations of the argument that privatization winners may prevent, rather than initiate, reform. Hellman refers to this phenomenon as a reform trap (Hellman 1998).

2. The only exception was an IPO of software firm T 602.

3. Privatization buccaneers changed quickly into serious salesmen.

4. Now many of them are among the traders with receivables mainly of bankrupted companies. Many times they are buying the bad assets they personally created—no doubt, they know them best.

5. This speculation was supported when police investigators discovered that L. Novák, a former vice-chairman, had access to a Swiss bank account of around 100 mn CZK. No one knows where the money came from or what its uses were. ODS's vice-chairwoman L. Benešová commented that it was "'nice' that this information appeared the week before the election," but she made no effort to contradict the police investigators' claims (*LN*, June 10, 1998, 1).

6. The common term for Russia is "oligarchs," but "plutocrats" is used here due to this group's economic and *political* clout.

7. Czech Commercial Code, Section 183b.

8. This rule is standard in many markets, but in the Czech Republic it opened a space for nonethical behavior. Many of the majority shareholders stopped their purchase of the shares just on the barrier of 49.9 percent of the company because they did not want to cover the costs of a mandatory offer. They argued that they had to invest in the company, not in its shareholders, who bought their shares for a price many times lower than the offering price. Other shareholders made hidden concerted conduct: they really controlled more than 50 percent of the company, but did not report it. For minority shareholders, it was very complicated or sometimes impossible to find some proof for the court decision.

9. It is also a personal question. Successes of UNIS are connected mainly with Jiří Brabec, who was the chairman of this organization for three years (from 1998 to 2000). Jiří Brabec is a general director of ŽB TRUST, an investment company of Živnobanka. In the early 1990s he was a deputy minister of foreign trade. Brabec is a personification of the new fairness of the market.

10. Funds with the discount over 40 percent were obliged to open twelve months after the amendment of fund act was in effect, funds with the discount over 30 percent after twenty-one months, and funds with the discount over 20 percent after thirty months, all of the closed funds till the end of 2002. (See Sections 35k and 35l of Investment Companies and Funds Act No. 248/1992 Coll.)

11. The Czech Commercial Code (under the Tosovsky government; No. 148/1996 Coll.) subsequently changed the locus of decision-making to oblige the company to make a public offer to these shareholders, who were against delisting or were absent from the general meeting. From January 1, 2001 (No 370/2000 Coll.), those shareholders who voted for the abolition of listing (in Czech—*registrace*, a term that replaced former public tradability, *veřejná obchodovatelnost*) were obliged to buy these shares later from the company. (See subsection 186a of the Czech Commercial Code, Act No. 513/1991 in the wording of later amendments.)

12. Act No. 362/2000, which took legal effect on January 1, 2001, amended the Securities Act (Zákon o cenných papírech) No. 591/1992.

13. The second important requirement is a minimal dispersion among the public of 25 percent of the nominal value of all units (or lower, because the size of the

issue ensures problems of free trading). How could shareholders sell shares if they were delisted? It is not possible to sell them on the PSE and through the RM-System, because they both are public markets and these shares do not fill the requirements. Shares could be traded by broker companies or individually. Dematerialized securities have to register the change of owner in the Securities Center. The Securities Center is an official register of dematerialized shares in the Czech Republic.

14. Regulation of Czech financial markets is provided basically by three institutions: Capital market subjects are regulated by the SEC; insurance companies and pension funds are regulated by the Ministry of Finance; and banks are regulated by the Czech National Bank. Still, it is not the whole system. For example, a special bureau regulates small banking co-ops (*kampeličky*).

15. Ironically, and somewhat tongue in cheek, new critiques of the SEC and generally of the new regulation under the Social Democrats appeared, arguing that the equity market is now overregulated, and administrative requirements are so strict that it represents a bottleneck. In 2002, for instance, only three subjects submitted new applications for a license for brokerage.

16. The bounce-back of ODS in the June 1998 elections and in opinion polls later in the year are discouraging signs. Other discouraging signs are the evident influence of plutocrats in the new Zeman government regarding bank privatization policy and enterprise subsidy policy.

Part IV

CONCLUSIONS—OWNERSHIP REGIME
THEORY IN COMPARATIVE PERSPECTIVE

11

Plutocracy Escaped, Plutocracy Avoided, Plutocracy Embedded

Andrew Harrison Schwartz and Jordan Gans-Morse

THE PUZZLE REVISITED: EXPLAINING TRANSITION OUTCOMES

With the dissolution of the Soviet empire, it seemed that market capitalism had triumphed and that democracy would replace totalitarian regimes. Instead, a wide range of political and economic systems have appeared in the postcommunist region, only a handful of which approximate liberal democracy. This surprising variation among the transition paths of postcommunist countries has reopened basic questions about the nature of markets, the role of governments in building capitalism, and the relationships between market economies and democracy. How can we account for this variation?

This book has explored three distinct explanations, each with a unique logic regarding the process of transition. The *neoliberal explanation* (see chapter 1) reduces transition outcomes to a question of economic policy. Throughout the first postcommunist decade, neoliberals argued that those countries that implemented programs of price liberalization, macroeconomic stabilization, and, most of all, rapid privatization would have the best chance of creating capitalism (Åslund 2002; World Bank 1996; EBRD 1999). Capitalism, in turn, would produce a new class of private owners who would lobby for the rule of law in a quest to protect their property rights; these private owners would replicate the historic role of the bourgeoisie in building democracy in the West (Boycko, Shleifer, and Vishny 1995; Shleifer and Vishny 1998). The main challenge to the neoliberal position has come from scholars who have emphasized the importance of market-supporting institutions. This *institutionalist explanation* (see chapter 2) asserts that economic reform policies that fail to devote sufficient attention to the formation of legal and regulatory institutions breed corruption and criminality, leading to economic stagnation (Cohen and Schwartz 1993; Roland 2000; Stiglitz 1999, 2002). Consequently, rapid neoliberal privatization unaccompanied by institution building fosters a politics of greed, not a politics of democracy.

As an alternative to neoliberal and institutionalist approaches, this book has presented a third explanatory framework: *ownership regime theory*. This alternative explanation emphasizes that during transition periods, it is not institutions that structure politics but politics that shape the design of institutions. In particular, ownership regime theory conceptualizes transition as a series of political struggles among powerful interest groups seeking to control and profit from privatized assets unleashed from state hands during the process of economic and political reforms. It is these political struggles that shape the prospects for institution building in each postcommunist country. In countries that conducted *neoliberal rapid privatization*, unregulated and hasty divestment of state assets produced a set of inefficient ownership, corporate governance, and regulatory structures—what we refer to as an *ownership regime*. Inefficient ownership regimes created strong incentives for new private owners to asset strip instead of invest in newly acquired enterprises. As a consequence, neoliberal rapid privatization strategies fostered a Wild East brand of capitalism featuring dominant interest groups that aimed to subvert the rule of law, which would have reduced their illegal or semilegal opportunities to continue enriching themselves. By contrast, in countries that chose *gradualist regulated privatization*, more efficient ownership and corporate governance structures emerged that created incentives for new private owners to invest instead of steal. These incentives stimulated the formation of dominant interest groups that sought to secure property rights; these groups thus became powerful political forces in favor of institutional consolidation.

Ownership regime theory's framework for linking privatization strategies, interest group formation, and the political struggles that underlie the process of institution building addresses many shortcomings of the neoliberal and institutionalist approaches. As discussed in greater detail below, the preceding chapters have shown that when applied to the Czech Republic, ownership regime theory provides insights into the behavior of new private owners and the prospects for institution building where neoliberal and institutionalist theories have proven inadequate. But how generalizable is the logic of ownership regime theory? Can it provide similar insights into the evolution of other postcommunist transitions? Is it applicable to market transitions more broadly?

This concluding chapter explores these questions. In the second section, we compare the Czech ownership regime that resulted from *neoliberal rapid privatization* with the ownership regimes that emerged from *gradualist regulated privatization* in Hungary and Poland. We examine how each of these ownership regimes molded the political struggles that would determine the prospects of institution building in these three cases. For each case, we test the utility of ownership regime theory by asking: Given each country's privatization strategy, what political and economic outcomes would ownership regime theory predict? How well do these predictions match the empirical evidence? And how do these predictions fare against the prognoses of neoliberal and institutionalist theories? As will be shown, ownership regime theory offers a more comprehensive and compelling explanation of the twists and turns of the transition experience in Central-East European countries than competing theories.

This focus on these three Visegrád countries allows us to control for some of the factors other than privatization strategies that influenced the prospects of democracy and capitalism in postcommunist countries. All three cases enjoyed close proximity to a democratic and prosperous Western Europe, faced equally strong incentives to join the EU, and experienced relatively similar historical exposure to political and economic liberalism (at least as compared to postcommunist countries in southeastern Europe or the former Soviet Union). To be clear, we do not claim that privatization strategies were the sole or determinative cause of transition outcomes. But we do believe, as demonstrated in the preceding chapters and in the case studies that follow, that it is possible to trace the significant impact of privatization strategies on a host of variables essential to the formation of democracy and capitalism. In particular, reformers' choices of privatization strategies influenced the prospects for enterprise restructuring and economic growth, levels of corruption, and the consolidation of legal and regulatory institutions essential to the rule of law in CEECs. Moreover, battles for control of privatized assets often spilled out of the marketplace and became entangled with the process of building political institutions such as state bureaucracies, parliaments, and political parties. In short, privatization strategies directly and definitively shaped the institutional configuration of newly emerging national varieties of capitalism, with significant consequences for the quality of market economies and democracy in the CEECs.

Having explored the applicability of ownership regime theory to the CEEC region, we further test the limits of ownership regime theory's generalizability through a brief analysis of privatization strategies in the former Soviet Union (FSU) in the final section. In contrast to the clearly identifiable relationship between privatization strategies and ownership regime formation in CEECs, *distinct* privatization strategies in Russia and Ukraine produced *similar* ownership regimes, contrary to ownership regime theory's predictions. Russia conducted neoliberal privatization while Ukraine's privatization program remained stalled well into the first decade of transition. Yet in both countries a political economy best described as *plutocratic capitalism* emerged, a system marred by collusion between business and political elites, unequal distribution of wealth, widespread asset stripping, and the absence of the rule of law. This analysis indicates that reformers in FSU countries (with the exception of the Baltic states) and, perhaps, in countries such as Bulgaria and Romania faced very different conditions than reformers in CEECs. The weakness—and in some cases outright collapse—of state institutions, the greater number of failing enterprises inherited from the communist era, the minimal prospects for foreign direct investment (FDI), and the absence of a guiding concept such as a "return to Europe" meant that the Hungarian path of gradualist regulated privatization most likely did not exist for the successor states of the Soviet Union. FSU reformers seemingly faced the grim choice between the inefficient ownership regimes of neoliberal rapid privatization and the equally devastating descent into plutocratic capitalism that resulted from delayed or aborted privatization programs.

This comparison of the FSU and CEECs' privatization experiences serves to identify some of the *preliminary conditions* that must be present for ownership regime theory's predictions regarding privatization strategies' impact on transition outcomes to hold true, such as the existence of a functioning state. It does not, however, negate ownership regime theory's insight that interest group competition for control of privatized assets shapes the process of institution building. As such, ownership regime theory offers insights into the prospects of institutional consolidation even beyond the CEEC region.

Finally, in the conclusion we turn to some of the policy implications of ownership regime theory and present some preliminary proposals for future research. Before turning to the case studies, however, we reacquaint the reader with the basic tenets of ownership regime theory so as to highlight the logic behind the comparison of neoliberal rapid privatization with gradualist regulated privatization strategies in CEECs.

THE LOGIC OF OWNERSHIP REGIME THEORY

Beyond Neoliberalism and Institutionalism

Ownership regime theory builds on the insights of neoliberalism and institutionalism to develop a more comprehensive framework for analysis of key questions that have been inadequately treated in neoliberal and institutionalist approaches: Under what conditions do new private owners support the rule of law? Under what conditions do institutions such as laws, norms, and regulatory organizations come to constrain most actors most of the time, a process that we refer to as institutional consolidation?

From an ownership regime theory perspective, we wholeheartedly concur with the institutionalist premise that well-established market institutions are what separate crony capitalism from growth-producing market economies. However, we argue that institutionalist approaches often fail to recognize that during the instability of transition, institution building may be difficult or even impossible. Instead of shaping the "rules of the game" as they do in stable political economies, institutions such as laws and regulatory bodies remain pawns in the game itself as powerful interest groups compete for the spoils of political and economic reforms. Institutions, in other words, cannot simply be designed and built. They are the outcome of vicious political struggles.

Neoliberals have provided a reasonable starting point for analysis of these political battles. They argue that market-supporting institutions will naturally evolve once state assets are transferred to private hands, for new private owners will become a forceful lobby in favor of the development of secure property rights. However, while ownership regime theory accepts the neoliberal premise that the political lobby of new private owners is essential to the formation of market-supporting institutions, it rejects neoliberals' faulty assumption that it is *inherently* in the interest of private owners to support institutional consolidation *regardless of the national privatization strategy adopted.*

Neoliberals believed that all forms of privatization ultimately lead to similar market conditions, providing similar incentive structures for new private owners. This conviction was based on the Coase Theorem (Coase 1960), which neoliberals interpreted to suggest that once assets were in private hands, market forces would soon lead to a redistribution of property resulting in an efficient allocation of assets (Boycko, Shleifer, and Vishny 1995, chap. 3). Faith in the Coase Theorem additionally legitimated neoliberals' claim that state-owned enterprises should be privatized *rapidly* so as to take advantage of the window of political opportunity that followed the collapse of the Soviet system and to remove enterprises from the interference of corruptible state bureaucrats (Boycko, Shleifer, and Vishny 1995; Kaufman and Siegelbaum 1996; Sachs 1990a; Sachs 1990b). Even if rapid privatization initially created inefficient ownership structures governed by inexperienced owners, market forces would soon reallocate property rights, leading to a welfare-maximizing outcome.

Ownership regime theory's critique of neoliberals' inattention to the *form* and *pace* of privatization stems from the observation that, contrary to neoliberals' predictions, privatization strategies have had an *enduring* impact on numerous aspects of economic and political development in postcommunist countries. To demonstrate this impact, we first explore the connection between privatization strategies and the formation of ownership regimes. We then investigate the ways in which ownership regimes continue to structure

Table 11.1. Privatization Methods

Nonstandard Privatization Methods (Mass Voucher Privatization)	Standard Privatization Methods (Case-by-Case Privatization)
1. Voucher Privatization with Investor Choice • Without Investment Funds • With Privately Owned Investment Funds 2. Voucher Privatization without Investor Choice • State-Owned Investment Funds	1. Insider Privatization • Manager Preference • Worker Preference 2. Market Privatization • Public Sale, Domestic Buyers • Public Sale, Foreign Buyers • Public Sale, Open 3. Tender Privatization 4. Reprivatization 5. State Residual Shareholding 6. Other Methods

political and economic developments in transition countries even after privatization comes to an end.

State officials in postcommunist countries faced two major decisions with regard to how to privatize. The first concerned *rapid versus gradual* privatization, as defined by the amount of enterprise assets privatized over a given time period. The second was whether to use a *standard versus nonstandard* approach to privatization. By *standard methods* we mean methods used previously in the West or the developing world, including auctions, tenders, and manager or employee buyouts. By *nonstandard methods* of privatization we mean the various forms of voucher privatization, which were based on mass giveaways of enterprise shares via distribution of vouchers to citizens or enterprise employees.[1] (The forms of possible privatization methods are listed in table 11.1.) Numerous factors influenced the speed of the privatization process and reformers' choice of standard versus nonstandard methods. These factors have been explored in greater detail in chapters 3 and 5 of this study. Suffice it to note here that neoliberals' emphasis on the political necessity of rapid reform and their belief that the type of initial owners and ownership structures did not matter led them in many cases to support rapid voucher privatization.

Greatly simplifying the complex process of privatization in order to illustrate the logic of ownership regime theory, we can thus identify two privatization paths: *neoliberal rapid voucher privatization strategies* and *gradualist standard privatization strategies.*[2] Each privatization strategy leads to a unique *initial ownership regime.* Ownership regimes consist of four components. The first component describes the *attributes of owners*, such as their skill sets, resources, cultural backgrounds, business experiences, and contacts with the West. The second component pertains to *systems of corporate governance.*

Systems of corporate governance represent the mechanisms by which owners oversee managers in enterprises marked by separation of ownership and control. They can be described by the distribution of ownership stakes within enterprises; the networks of cross-holding among owners from different firms, banks, and institutional investors; and the encompassing system of laws and regulation governing ownership structures, such as the tax system, bankruptcy procedures, intellectual property laws, and auditing requirements. Systems of corporate governance develop in the context of *capital and financial markets*, the third component of ownership regimes. Capital and financial markets provide an additional constraint on the behavior of managers, both by transmitting information about firms' performance to current and potential investors as well as by using capital allocation to reward and discipline firms in accordance with performance. Financial markets are described by the role, efficiency, and transparency of stock exchanges, debt markets, banks, investment funds, and brokerage firms in the financing of enterprises. The final component of an ownership regime is the *state regulatory framework*, especially with regard to financial markets and systems of corporate governance. The state regulatory framework in turn has two major aspects: its autonomy, as described by its independence from both private interests and politicians, and its capacity, as described by the state's ability to enforce regulations.

Examination of the types of ownership regimes that emerge from distinct privatization strategies demonstrates the logic behind ownership regime theory's predictions regarding privatization strategies and transition outcomes. As illustrated in the case studies that follow, we expect that *neoliberal rapid voucher privatization* creates ownership regimes characterized by inexperienced citizen owners without the resources and skills to restructure privatized firms; dispersed patterns of ownership that hinder government oversight and provide perverse incentives for asset stripping; large and unwieldy capital markets that fail to discipline poorly performing firms and reward profitable enterprises; and an underdeveloped state regulatory apparatus. This ownership regime is conducive to the formation of interest groups with the incentives to subvert the rule of law and impede the consolidation of institutions governing the market. Conversely, *gradualist standard privatization* strategies increase the likelihood of privatization to strategic investors with the incentives and resources to conduct restructuring; concentrated ownership structures that provide for effective corporate governance; well-regulated and relatively efficient capital markets and banking systems that monitor enterprise performance; and state regulatory frameworks that have developed in stride with privatization rather than trying to catch up after corruption has already been unleashed by premature privatization programs. Figure 11.1 depicts these relationships between privatization strategies and initial ownership regimes.

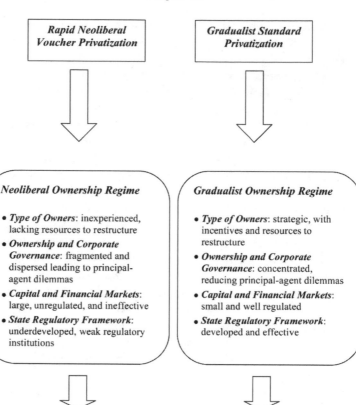

Figure 11.1.   Privatization Strategies and Ownership Regimes.

Thus, the logic of ownership theory unfolds as follows: Privatization strategies create unique ownership regimes. Ownership regimes influence interest group formation and the incentive structures faced by new private owners. What remains is to investigate how interest group and incentive structures shape the political struggles that underlie the process of building institutions.

Ownership Regime Evolution: Transition as Asset Competition and Institutional Consolidation

Transition as viewed through the lens of ownership regime theory is a struggle between major interest groups for control and ownership of privatized assets. During the privatization process, these battles are as much political as economic. The rules of the game that will underlie the emerging market system are being written as property rights are established, laws drafted, and state regulatory agencies formed. We refer to these ongoing battles for control and ownership of privatized assets—struggles which may turn into violent criminal battles—as *asset competition.* As privatization comes to an end, initial ownership regimes may evolve according to one of two logics of asset competition. At one end of the spectrum is the *neo-Coasian economic logic* predicted by neoliberals; at the other there is a *non-Coasian political logic.* Ownership regime theory helps to explain when neoliberal predictions come true—and when they do not.

Ownership regime evolution in accordance with a neo-Coasian economic logic occurs if, at the end of privatization, an ownership regime emerges that provides incentives for powerful interest groups to protect their property rights rather than asset strip. For instance, if privatization has transferred assets to strategic owners and created sound corporate governance structures, these new private owners will find it profitable to support the establishment of institutions that ensure predictable and equitable market interactions that maximize the value of privatized assets. Struggles for these assets continue, but they become primarily economic in nature, involving sales, takeovers, mergers, and a variety of other market mechanisms that take place within an established arena of laws, norms, and regulations. As the process of institutional consolidation continues, the criminality and asset stripping that characterized the privatization period decline. This is the path of ownership regime evolution that we would expect from gradualist regulated privatization.

Ownership regime evolution according to a non-Coasian political logic occurs if the new ownership regime impedes the establishment of clearly defined property rights and facilitates asset stripping. For example, if ownership is highly dispersed and state regulations weak, then intense and possibly violent competition over the consolidation of ownership rights of privatized enterprises may ensue—even after the process of privatization has come to a close. In this case, the very legal, political, and market institutions that are supposed to form the rules of the game themselves remain tools in the battle for control of assets. Struggles for privatized assets continue in an environment that lacks stable regulations and legal frameworks, and lasting institutional consolidation cannot occur until the major players are satisfied with the outcome of these conflicts. As a consequence, new private owners do not seek to deploy privatized assets in order to maximize profits through production for the market but instead devote themselves to asset stripping, obtaining state subsidies, acquiring additional state assets, and developing political patrons who can provide protection against other major economic actors as battles for privatized assets continue. This is the path of ownership regime evolution that we expect to emerge from neoliberal rapid privatization, but as discussed in chapter 10, the Czech case indicates that it is possible to escape this path as asset competition declines.

The following section tests this logic of ownership regime theory against the empirical evidence from concrete country cases. We maintain that by exploring the relationships between privatization strategies, ownership regimes, and interest group formation, ownership regime theory provides a superior *analytical framework* for understanding *when* and *why* private owners restructure instead of asset strip and *when* and *why* institution building succeeds as compared to the alternative frameworks of neoliberalism and institutionalism. We highlight the differences between these three perspectives in table 11.2.

OWNERSHIP REGIMES IN CENTRAL AND EASTERN EUROPE

This section explores the formation and evolution of ownership regimes in three CEECs: the Czech Republic, Hungary, and Poland. These countries are widely considered to be the postcommunist leaders in political and economic reforms (World Bank 2002b; EBRD 1999). However, the common grouping of these cases as the vanguard of reformers obscures significant differences in the reform strategies, emerging institutional configurations, and paths of political and economic development in each of these countries.

As shown below in table 11.3, the choice of three distinct privatization strategies in these three countries provides the opportunity to explore the logic of ownership regime theory and to study the emerging varieties of national capitalisms and democracies in the CEEC region. In the Czech Republic, *neoliberal rapid voucher privatization* created powerful interest groups with an incentive to subvert the rule of law in order to continue asset stripping. This instigated a period of economic crisis and political scandal in the latter half of the 1990s, leading to comparisons with the plutocratic capitalism of Russia (Barnes 2000, 542). Only as competition for privatized assets subsided did the Czech ownership regime come to evolve according to a neo-Coasian economic logic. In contrast to the Czech path, the *gradualist standard privatization* strategy employed in Hungary created an initial ownership structure and regulatory bodies that minimized asset stripping and provided incentives for the new class of private owners to support institutional consolidation. Poland, meanwhile,

Table 11.2.   Ownership Regime Theory versus Alternative Theories

Neoliberalism	Ownership Regime Theory
• Type of first owners irrelevant; Coase Theorem dictates that assets will change hands via market transactions until most efficient allocation of assets occurs. • The greatest threat of corruption and inefficiency emanates from state officials and bureaucrats. • Speed is essential to depoliticize ownership of enterprises and prevent government interference in the privatization process. • Institutions form organically as the result of private entrepreneurs reacting to economic incentives.	• The type of owners and ownership structures that emerge from privatization determine whether future competition over privatized assets will take place according to market transactions or via violence and political connections. • Unregulated private entrepreneurship is an equally grave threat in terms of corruption and economic inefficiency as state bureaucrats. • Rapid privatization produces ineffective corporate governance and regulatory systems. • Institutions form as the result of political struggle; they cannot consolidate while major interest groups have a stake in opposing institution building.
Institutionalism	Ownership Regime Theory
• Institutions should be developed before or during the privatization process. • Institutions viewed as a policy design problem, and institutions a decade into reforms reflect institution building efforts at reform's outset. • Transition may be perceived as path dependent, shaped by the institutional remnants of the former regime or by the institutions created early in the transition period.	• Institutions may be impossible to develop during the flux of transition and period of competition over privatized assets. • Institutions a decade into reform do not reflect policy design efforts but the unpredictable and jagged path of political struggles between interest groups and the state.

experienced intense political struggles over the design of its privatization programs. As a result, reformers' initial attempts to conduct neoliberal rapid privatization were thwarted. The resulting delays in privatization inadvertently allowed Poland to escape the pitfalls of hasty and unregulated privatization and provided vital time for regulatory institutions to develop. Poland's privatization path, which we believe is best described as *gradual privatization by accident*, thus falls closer to the Hungarian experience than the Czech privatization route.

For each of these cases, we trace the impact of privatization strategies on such outcomes as economic growth, levels of corruption, and the prospects for institution building (see table 11.4). This analysis allows us to test the

Table 11.3. Ownership Regimes in Central and Eastern Europe

Country	New Owners and Corporate Governance System	Financial System	State Regulatory Regime
Czech Republic— Neoliberal Rapid Privatization	Ownership structure fragmented between voucher holders, IPFs, banks, and state. Lack of owners with controlling stake and convoluted cross-ownership leads to tunneling and asset stripping.	Large and unregulated stock market leads to lack of trading, delisting of public companies. Unreformed and unprivatized banking sector causes politicization of loans and prevents hard-budget restraints needed for enterprise restructuring.	Neoliberal aversion to regulations fosters corruption of stock market, political party finance, state regulatory agencies, and the privatization process.
Hungary— Gradualist Regulated Privatization	Concentrated ownership including many strategic foreign investors encourages enterprise restructuring and limits asset stripping.	Absence of voucher privatization leads to small, well-regulated stock market. Banks privatized to foreigners and well regulated.	Regulation a major focus of reforms. Limits on spontaneous *nomenklatura* privatization and asset stripping enforced.
Poland— Gradual Privatization by Accident	High levels of continued state ownership, but even state-owned enterprises undergo restructuring. Mass privatization program conducted under state supervision leading to investment funds that serve as active owners. Privatization through liquidation puts assets in hands of insiders, but strong worker councils prevent asset stripping by managers.	Mass privatization program small enough and well regulated enough to ensure functioning stock market. Successful loans consolidation program links reform of the banking system to enterprise restructuring.	Delays in privatization provide time for development of regulatory apparatus. Neoliberals' control over reforms limited by political turnover, providing incentives for all parties to institutionalize the rules of the game before losing office to the opposition.

Table 11.4. Selected Indicators for CEECs

Annual Real GDP Growth, 1992–2003 (in %)

	1992	1993	1994	1995	1996	1997	1998	1999	2000	2001	2002	2003
Czech Rep.	-0.5	0.1	2.2	5.9	4.3	-0.8	-1.0	.05	3.3	3.1	2.0	3.0
Hungary	-3.1	-0.6	2.9	1.5	1.3	4.6	4.9	4.2	5.2	3.7	3.3	3.0
Poland	2.6	3.8	5.2	7.0	6.0	5.8	4.8	4.1	4.0	1.0	1.4	3.0

Private Sector as Share of GDP, 1991–2002 (% of GDP)

	1991	1992	1993	1994	1995	1996	1997	1998	1999	2000	2001	2002
Czech Rep.	15	30	45	65	70	75	75	75	80	80	80	80
Hungary	30	40	50	55	60	70	75	75	85	80	80	80
Poland	40	45	50	55	60	60	65	65	65	70	70	75

Foreign Direct Investment, 1992–2003 (net inflows in US$ mil.)

	1992	1993	1994	1995	1996	1997	1998	1999	2000	2001	2002	2003
Czech Rep.	983	563	749	2,526	1,276	1,275	3,591	6,234	4,943	5,476	9,029	5,000
Hungary	1,471	2,328	1,097	4,410	2,279	1,741	1,555	1,720	1,123	2,255	598	1,341
Poland	284	580	542	1,134	2,741	3,041	4,966	6,348	8,171	6,928	3,700	4,000

Transparency International Corruption Perceptions Index, 1995–2004 (10 = low corruption, 1 = high corruption)

	1993	1994	1995	1996	1997	1998	1999	2000	2001	2002	2003	2004
Czech Rep.	–	–	–	5.37	5.20	4.8	4.6	4.3	3.9	3.7	3.9	4.2
Hungary	–	–	4.12	4.86	5.18	5.0	5.2	5.2	5.3	4.9	4.8	4.8
Poland	–	–	–	–	5.08	4.6	4.2	4.1	4.0	4.0	3.6	3.5

Sources: Data for GDP growth and foreign direct investment are from EBRD (2003) (2003 data are EBRD projections); data for private sector as share of GDP are from EBRD (2000) for the years 1991–2000 and EBRD (2003) for the years 2001–2002; data for the corruption perceptions index can be found at www.transparency.org.
Note on Corruption Index: As a point of reference, Finland, the least corrupt country in the 2004 TI Corruption Perceptions Index, scored a 9.7. The United States received a 7.5. Hungary's 4.8 put it between Costa Rica and Italy, the Czech Republic's 4.2 fell between Suriname and El Salvador, and Poland's 3.5 placed it between Peru and Sri Lanka.

predictions of ownership regime theory presented in the preceding section vis-à-vis the explanations of transition outcomes offered by neoliberal and institutionalist frameworks.

Neoliberal Privatization: The Czech Republic's Flirtation with Plutocratic Capitalism

Until the late 1990s, the Czech privatization program represented the neoliberals' "best practice" case. Czech reformers' mass voucher privatization led to the most rapid creation of a private sector in the postcommunist region and was touted at World Bank seminars as a major success (Nellis 2002). As demonstrated in the preceding chapters, the Czech case thus presents an ideal opportunity to test the tenets of neoliberalism against ownership regime theory: if rapid privatization is essential for the creation of capitalism and democracy, as neoliberals claim, then a market economy bolstered by the rule of law should have quickly developed in the Czech Republic. Here we briefly summarize the findings of the preceding chapters to facilitate direct comparison with the subsequent analyses of the gradual privatization approaches adopted in Hungary and Poland.

The Czech rapid voucher privatization program reflected all of the neoliberal tenets—inattention to ownership structures, loathing of state regulations, and emphasis on speed—discussed in the preceding section of this chapter. By the end of 1994, 1,664 enterprises, or 48.2 percent of joint-stock enterprises slated for privatization, had been privatized via the voucher method, the largest voucher auction in the region (Fund of National Property 1995, 10–11). Even when the Czech reformers utilized standard privatization methods, they placed a premium on the pace of privatization, forcing harried Ministry of Privatization officials to adjudicate between thousands of competing privatization proposals in a rushed two months prior to the first wave of privatization in 1992 so as to not delay the state's divestiture of assets (Czech Ministry of Privatization 1993).

If the neoliberal perspective was that rapid privatization *of any type* would create the foundations for capitalism and democracy, then the Czech Republic's privatization plan should have proved a remarkable success. By the end of 1996, 75 percent of GDP was produced by the private sector, among the highest percentage in the postcommunist region and a huge leap given the country's nearly nonexistent private sector in 1990 (see table 11.4). However, as ownership regime theory would predict, the rapid unregulated privatization process promoted by neoliberals had created an ownership regime that facilitated asset stripping and corruption. The voucher program placed assets in the possession of inexperienced owners who lacked capital; meanwhile, corporate governance mechanisms characterized by dispersed patterns of shareholding effectively left enterprise managers without overseers. The investment privatization funds (IPFs) that reformers had sanctioned in order to address these corporate governance problems themselves became entangled in labyrinthine chains of ownership that exacerbated principal-agent dilemmas (Rona-Tas 1997), especially when IPFs came under the control of the still unreformed and largely state-owned banking sector (Cull, Matesova, and Shirley 2001). Rapid voucher privatization also created highly illiquid capital markets epitomized by the Prague Stock Exchange, which boasted over sixteen hundred share issues by 1996 (a few hundred or less was typical for emerging markets), with nearly eight million individual shareholders and over four hundred IPFs (Filer and Hanousek 1996). No SEC or similar regulatory agency existed until 1997, and neoliberals in government and Parliament fought attempts to create one until crisis had already erupted. Given their condition, the Czech capital markets clearly could not fulfill their corporate governance role of rewarding high-performing firms with capital and disciplining low-performing firms with bankruptcy.

In accordance with ownership regime theory's predictions, the Czech neoliberal ownership regime bred political and economic crisis. Until 1996, the Klaus government managed to portray outbreaks of corruption as isolated incidents, and few observers challenged this position.[3] But as voucher privatization came to a close, the frenzied battles over privatized assets unleashed by the fractured ownership structure and weak regulatory framework produced a series of scandals that could no longer be ignored. Minority owners sought to consolidate their holdings using any means possible, while enterprise and IPF directors, lacking oversight from active owners and government regulators, turned company assets into personal treasure troves. In many cases, IPF fund managers, banking executives, enterprise directors, and state officials colluded to acquire control or ownership of companies in order strip their assets, a process that soon became known as "tunneling" in reference to the hollowing out of a firm's value from the inside (Czech Ministry of Finance 1997). The most infamous tunneling scandal involved a shady group called Motoinvest, which acquired an estimated $3 bn worth of assets in IPFs and banks, much of which it stripped and moved offshore (Rona-Tas 1997).

By 1997, party financing scandals tied to illicit privatization deals had toppled the neoliberal Civic Democratic Party (ODS), while financial crises in the unreformed banking sector and widespread asset stripping had plunged the country into recession (see table 11.4). In accordance with ownership regime theory's expectations, neoliberal rapid privatization had created an ownership regime in which nearly all major interest groups in society—the ruling political parties, enterprise directors, and bank and IPF managers—possessed serious incentives to impede the development of the rule of law, effective regulatory agencies, and transparent corporate governance, capital markets, and banking systems, all of which would put an end to their lucrative sources of illicit wealth.

Thus, the neoliberal expectation that new private owners would become a powerful lobby for the rule of law and a market economy clearly proved false in the Czech Republic, at least in the years during and immediately following privatization. But institutionalist perspectives also fall short in their analysis of capitalism's and democracy's formation in the Czech Republic. Given the ownership regime that emerged and powerful interest groups that possessed strong incentives to oppose the rule of law, it is not clear that institutional consolidation would have been possible in the early reform period, even if it was undeniably desirable. Additionally, institutionalist perspectives assume that unregulated privatization sets a country down the path to crony capitalism, but they provide few insights into how a country might escape this fate.

Ownership regime theory, on the other hand, predicts that ownership structures and regulatory institutions will evolve as battles for privatized assets subside. By the end of the decade, ownership in the Czech Republic had become increasingly concentrated and the flurry to control privatized assets diminished (Blaszczyk et al. 2003). Tunnelers had stolen what they could, leaving few opportunities for additional asset stripping. Viable enterprises had been sold to strategic investors, in many cases foreigners, as was evident in a notable increase in FDI that began in the late 1990s (see table 11.4). The state's shares in the major banks had been privatized, leading to the depoliticization of the loaning process. Voters finally tossed out the ODS in 1998, bringing the Czech Social Democratic Party (ČSSD) to power. The Social Democrats implemented an anticorruption program and supported a newly formed SEC to improve capital market regulation. As unviable companies were delisted from the stock market, liquidity increased. By 2000, the Czech Republic had emerged from its recession and returned to growth.

This is not to say that a fully institutionalized market economy has developed. The anticorruption program has received mixed reviews (Appel 2002, 544–545). The regulatory environment continues to be weak, and consequently even foreign owners of enterprises and banks have proven susceptible to scandal, as witnessed in the illegal dealings committed by the Japanese Nomura business group after it acquired shares in the Czech Investment Postal Bank (Barnes 2000, 553). It remains to be seen whether the Czech ownership regime has begun to evolve according to a neo-Coasian economic logic. But it is evident that as battles for control over privatized assets come to a close, ownership structures may evolve, creating new incentives for powerful interest groups to support instead of subvert institutional consolidation. In such cases, ownership regimes can escape the non-Coasian political path of evolution.

Even if private owners in the Czech Republic have now begun to act in accordance with neoliberal predictions, this behavior emerged only after a decade of intense political and economic battles over privatized assets. As we have seen, the ups and downs of this turbulent decade could not have been predicted by either neoliberal or institutionalist frameworks. By contrast, ownership regime theory's focus on how interest groups' battles for control of privatized assets shape the political course and economic well-being of each country provides a compelling framework for understanding the Czech transition.

Gradualist Standard Privatization: Institutional Consolidation in Hungary and Poland

We have demonstrated throughout this study that the predictions of both neoliberal and institutionalist approaches fail to fully explain the behavior of new private owners or the process of institutional consolidation in the Czech Republic, the CEEC that most fully implemented rapid neoliberal privatization. But how well do the prognoses of these competing frameworks compare to ownership regime theory's insights when applied to countries that avoided the neoliberal privatization path?

We now turn to exploration of this question through analysis of the Hungarian and the Polish privatization experiences. Hungary's gradualist standard privatization strategy represents the clearest alternative to the Czech neoliberal rapid voucher privatization program. It is the best example in the postcommunist region of a pragmatic, regulated approach to privatization aimed at placing enterprises in the hands of owners possessed with the incentives and means to restructure privatized companies (Simonetti 1993). Hungary also stands out as one of the few postcommunist countries that did not implement any version of voucher-based mass privatization.[4] Poland's reformers, meanwhile, initially sought to implement a rapid neoliberal voucher privatization program. Political conflict, however, slowed the pace of privatization and limited the number of enterprises privatized by voucher methods. Poland, we argue, thus inadvertently adopted a gradualist approach to privatization that fostered an ownership regime that avoided many of the political and economic pitfalls experienced by the Czechs.

Hungary: Gradualist Regulated Privatization

In contrast to the Czech reformers' ideologically driven privatization strategy based on faith in market forces, Hungarian reformers adopted a pragmatic privatization strategy tailored to legacies inherited from communist-era reforms. When the communist regime collapsed, the private sector in Hungary already accounted for 30 percent of GDP (as opposed to 5 percent in Czechoslovakia) (EBRD 2000). Previous price liberalization had attenuated macroeconomic imbalances, diminishing the need for a shock-therapy approach to reforms (Bartlett 1997, 142). But the communist regime had also bequeathed the Hungarian reformers with significant problems. Decentralization of enterprise control had ignited a flurry of "spontaneous privatization," whereby managers sought personal gain by transferring assets from state-owned enterprises into private joint ventures or newly created subsidiaries under their control (Hanley 2000; Voszka 1999). The previous regime's efforts to improve consumption levels by borrowing from abroad had saddled Hungary with a massive debt, a setback not faced by Czech reformers (Canning and Hare 1996). As in all postcommunist regimes, Hungarian enterprises were in need of radical restructuring, but low levels of domestic savings meant that investment in restructuring was unlikely to come from the population at large.

The Hungarian strategy of gradualist and regulated privatization reflected these concerns. The goal was to reign in spontaneous privatization, maximize revenue to repay the debt, and identify strategic investors with the incentives and resources to invest in enterprise restructuring. To these ends, Hungarian reformers reasserted state control over the privatization process via the newly created State Privatization Agency (SPA), which closely managed the approval process of privatization initiatives submitted by investors or enterprises (Barnes 2000, 547). Hungarian reformers continued the former regime's policy of special tax incentives for foreign direct investment aimed at overcoming low levels of domestic savings and attracting foreign management expertise, which they hoped would additionally limit asset stripping by enterprise directors (Hanley 2000). (This strategy made Hungary the leader in the CEEC region with regard to FDI inflows until the mid-1990s, as seen in table 11.4.) To pay down the debt, they favored a combination of competitive auctions and insider buyouts over voucher giveaways, which would provide minimal revenue for the state budget.

Conducting well-regulated, competitive auctions was of course not without technical and political difficulties. Determining the value of enterprise assets was problematic in an economy where the market was still being created; nationalist pressures forced the government at times to level restrictions on foreign investment and increase the percentage of shares that employees and managers could purchase at preferential rates (Canning and Hare 1996, 7; Hanley, King, and Istvan Toth 2002; Simonetti 1993, 82–84); and Hungary drew criticism from international financial institutions for the slow pace of its privatization approach, especially when incidents of privatization scandals and asset stripping flared up in the early 1990s (Bartlett 1997; Meagher 2000). But in 1995 and 1996, contrary to neoliberal fears regarding leftist political parties, a coalition led by the Socialist Party pushed through not only the privatization of the majority of assets still in the hands of government privatization agencies but also of banks and companies in strategic sectors that had been excluded from earlier privatization rounds. The new government additionally removed all limits on foreign investment, opening the way for the highest levels of foreign ownership in the postcommunist region (Hanley, King, and Istvan Toth 2002). By 1998, 1,188 of 1,858 enterprises in the SPA's portfolio had been privatized (Voszka 1999), and overall levels of private sector output of GDP reached 80 percent, higher than those found in the Czech Republic that year (see table 11.4).

As ownership regime theory would predict, gradualist standard privatization in Hungary created an ownership regime characterized by concentrated ownership that has led to restructuring of privatized enterprises, a functioning capital market, a privatized and reformed banking system, and a well-developed state regulatory apparatus. Competitive, transparent auctions and tenders placed privatized enterprises in the hands of strategic owners, especially foreign multinationals, who sought to turn them into profitable ventures. Estimates show that a majority of privatized firms have three owners or less and that approximately 80 percent of all firms have a single majority shareholder (Voszka 1999, 16; also see Hanley, King, and Istvan Toth 2002). These owners possessed the financial incentives and resources to monitor managers' behavior, reducing the principal-agent problems that plagued the Czech Republic in the first years following privatization.[5]

Also in accordance with ownership regime theory's predictions, the Hungarians' measured approach to privatization provided time for their capital and financial markets to develop, leading to the formation of a financial sector capable of fulfilling its corporate governance role of disciplining and rewarding enterprises according to their performance. Most notably, the absence of a voucher privatization program meant that Hungary never developed a large, unregulated stock market. The smaller number of listed firms combined with better quality regulations boosted liquidity and allowed Hungarian firms to raise more funds than their Czech counterparts operating on the Prague Exchange (Glaeser, Johnson, and Shleifer 1999, 35–37). Meanwhile, Hungary became the region's leader with regard to bank privatization. By 1997, only 21 percent of banks were state owned, with foreigners holding a 60 percent stake in the banking sector (Majnoni, Shankar, and Varhegyi 2003). This is not to say that banking sector reform was without challenges. The banking sector experienced a massive shock in the early 1990s as liberalization of prices put formidable pressures on state-owned enterprises leading to a mountain of unpaid bank loans. The government carried out an unsuccessful loan-consolidation program between 1992 and 1993 (Bonin 1993) and subsequently was forced to bail out the banks several times in the early 1990s before bank privatization finally created hard-budget constraints that forced banks to clean out their loan portfolios (Meagher 2000). But through several rounds of bank recapitalization, the state created new regulations for the banking sector and raised the standard for accounting practices. The banks never captured the state, and the lending process never became politicized to the extent that it did in Russia and the Czech Republic (Barnes 2000, 550).

Finally, as an ownership regime theory perspective would expect from gradualist regulated privatization, Hungarian reformers successfully maintained state oversight of the reform process. From the early 1990s to the present, the creation of a sound legal and regulatory framework for their market economy was one of the central goals of Hungarian reformers (Barnes 2000, 540; Simonetti 1993). Some even refer to Hungary's legal reforms and financial sector restructuring as "legislative shock therapy" (Meagher 2000, 30). Its careful monitoring and regulation of the privatization process again provides a striking contrast to the Czech neoliberals' hands-off approach. For example, while Czech reformers considered all bureaucracies to be impediments to privatization, the Hungarian SPA's staff grew from forty officials at its founding to two thousand officials by 1992. It was subordinated directly to the prime minister, rather than the fragmented Parliament, and played the overseer role throughout the privatization process that was nonexistent in Czech neoliberal privatization (Barnes 2000, 548–549).

From the neoliberal vantage, Hungary's gradual privatization approach should have stalled the development of a market economy and hindered the emergence of a class of private owners with a stake in promoting the rule of law. However, contrary to neoliberal expectations, and in vivid contrast to the Czech case, the winding down of the Hungarian privatization process did not unleash a flurry of battles to consolidate ownership stakes in privatized enterprises. Consequently, political parties and state officials were able to avoid becoming embroiled in the murky transactions of plutocratic capitalism that provide infertile ground for the institutionalization of market-based transactions. Banks established arm's-length relationships with business customers, and the cozy collusion between bankers, enterprise directors, and state officials that characterized the Czech political economy in the late 1990s declined. Corruption in both the political and business realms has consistently been lower than in the Czech Republic from the late 1990s onward (see table 11.4). While significant political conflicts persist, as evidenced by the head-to-head competition in the 2002 parliamentary elections that led to a Socialist Party victory by one seat, these disputes focus less on political economy issues and more on issues of nationalism (Racz 2003).

By the turn of the decade, Hungary had silenced neoliberal critics with a dramatic turnaround and become widely recognized as one of the least corrupt postcommunist countries (*Nations in Transit* 2004). Organizations such as the World Bank and USAID attributed this outcome to successful efforts to develop market institutions, especially the creation of a well-governed financial system (Meagher 2000; World Bank 2002a). If the Czech Republic had been the darling of the neoliberals in the mid-1990s, Hungary appears to be emerging as international financial organizations' new favorite, lending credence to institutionalists' claims that institution building must accompany or precede privatization.

The institutionalist perspective, however, cannot fully explain why early efforts to develop institutions failed whereas efforts in the late 1990s succeeded; it attributes the different levels of institutional consolidation in the Czech Republic and Hungary to the ideology and political will of reformers, which is only part of the story. Ownership regime theory, on the other hand, offers a more comprehensive account of the Hungarian transition experience. Gradualist regulated privatization created ownership structures and regulatory bodies that fought to limit asset stripping early on in the transition. Hungary thus succeeded at preventing the emergence of interest groups with the incentives to subvert the rule of law in order to protect their sources of illicit wealth. This did not mean that successful institution building occurred without challenges or on the first try, but over time Hungary's ownership regime fostered interest groups with a stake in the rule of law, allowing momentum in favor of institutional consolidation to build. By the end of the 1990s, Hungary's political economy was evolving according to a neo-Coasian logic, contrary to neoliberals' expectations—*and* it had avoided the Czech Republic's flirtation with plutocratic capitalism.

Poland: Gradual Privatization by Accident

The Hungarian case provides support for ownership regime theory's contention that gradualist regulated privatization strategies produce ownership regimes that foster enterprise restructuring, economic growth, and, consequently, the formation of interest groups with a stake in the rule of law. But how do ownership regime theory's predictions fare in other CEECs that avoided neoliberal rapid privatization? Poland presents an additional opportunity to compare a gradual approach to privatization with the Czech neoliberal strategy. Although Poland was the first postcommunist country to carry out the rapid price liberalization and strict macroeconomic stabilization programs known as "shock therapy," its neoliberal reformers devised but were unable to implement a rapid, large-scale voucher privatization program. Political struggles delayed privatization for much of the first half of the 1990s, leading, as with Hungary, to opprobrium from advocates of the Washington consensus. Poland's privatization path could thus aptly be described as *gradual privatization by accident*.

Poland's unintended privatization strategy reflected the intense political challenges faced by neoliberal finance minister Leszek Balcerowicz. Unlike Czech finance minister Václav Klaus, he faced a well-developed civil society built around trade unions and enterprise workers' councils that had grown increasingly powerful during Poland's two decades of partial political and economic reforms (Mizsei 1992, 289). In contrast to the Czech neoliberals' clear electoral victory, an intense political struggle that some have labeled the "war of privatization blueprints" erupted in Poland (see Orenstein 2001, 117). The July 1990 Act on the Privatization of State-Owned Enterprises was a compromise bill that endorsed a multitrack approach to privatization, including a mass voucher program; employee buyouts, auctions, and direct sales; and investment fund and bank-led privatization. The law, however, provided no concrete mechanism for voucher privatization. Political turmoil delayed the establishment of the legislative framework for voucher privatization until April 1993, and the center-left coalition that came to power in the same year further impeded its implementation until the end of 1995 (Hashi 2000, 92; Rondinelli and Yurkiewicz 1996).

This political turbulence dislodged Poland from a neoliberal privatization path and altered the privatization process in ways that would have important ramifications for the ownership regime that would emerge. First, the political stalemate of the early 1990s inadvertently fostered the widespread use of a leasing variant of privatization, a method largely unique to Poland (McDermott 2004). In many cases, this leasing option meant that, while politicians bickered about how to formally proceed with divestment of state assets, managers and workers took advantage of provisions in the legislative framework governing economic reforms that allowed them to create new corporate entities that then leased—with the eventual option to purchase—assets from state enterprises. Over time, these state enterprises were thus slowly transformed into new, private companies. Neoliberals had loathed this insider approach to privatization, believing that worker-owners in particular would fail to restructure firms (Boycko, Shleifer, and Vishny 1995, chap. 3), but more recent appraisals have viewed leasing variants as the missed opportunity that might have provided a plausible and effective alternative to mass privatization (Ellerman 2003).

Second, political conflict dramatically diluted Poland's voucher privatization program. In the end, only 512 enterprises were selected for this form of privatization (Orenstein 2001, 121–122), not even a third of the number that participated in the Czech program. More importantly, the Polish reformers made a serious effort to mitigate the effects of dispersed ownership and weak regulatory environments that had incited economic disaster following the Czech voucher privatization. The state itself created fifteen national investment funds (NIFs), each with a government supervisory board, rather than leaving this to market forces, which in the Czech Republic allowed funds to proliferate by the hundreds. Shareholders could exchange their vouchers only for NIF shares, not for enterprise shares, which further encouraged concentration of ownership. In 1997 the NIFs themselves were then privatized by floating their shares on the Warsaw Stock Exchange (Hashi 2000; Pistor and Spicer 1996).

Throughout the privatization process, these leasing and voucher programs were supplemented by case-by-case auctions and direct sales, but continued political conflict and administrative hassles ensured that these programs proceeded slowly. Thus, as the first postcommunist decade came to a close, Poland continued to exhibit high levels of state ownership. In 1997 it still had 6,000 state-owned enterprises, only 2,500 less than it had in 1990 (Orenstein 2001, 111; Slay 2000, 60), and even by the end of the decade Poland's private sector accounted for only 65 percent of GDP, compared with 80 percent in the Czech Republic and Hungary (see table 11.4).

If neoliberal expectations had proven true, Poland would have been a political and economic disaster due to the absence of a new class of capitalists devoted to economic and democratic reforms. But Poland's gradual, windy privatization path inadvertently created an ownership regime that avoided some of the pitfalls exhibited by the Czech approach. In particular, Poland's smaller, better-regulated voucher privatization program reduced tunneling, asset stripping, and other corporate governance problems by concentrating ownership and ensuring that NIFs would become active agents of restructuring (Hashi 2000, 104–115, 125). The leasing option also ended up creating mechanisms that limited asset stripping, as protracted negotiations between potential owners and stakeholders improved actors' access to information and ability to effectively monitor each other's behavior (McDermott 2004). Finally, the 1993 electoral backlash against neoliberalism installed a government with a more pragmatic approach to managing assets that remained in state hands. Unlike Czech neoliberals who maintained a hands-off approach to state management of enterprise assets on ideological grounds, Poland has been a leader in restructuring state enterprises prior to privatization and creating hard-budget restraints for those enterprises that remain under state ownership, reducing their drag on the economy (Slay 2000, 60; 1993, 245).

The Polish case also conforms with ownership regime theory's prediction that gradual, standard privatization improves the prospects for developing a financial sector capable of contributing to the sound corporate governance of privatized enterprises. Poland's smaller voucher program combined with reformers' attention to the importance of market regulations facilitated the development of functioning capital markets, as compared with the stillborn Prague Exchange. Limited voucher privatization reduced the number of listed companies on the Warsaw Exchange, making monitoring and regulation feasible for the infant regulatory institutions and inexperienced state regulators common to transition economies. The Poles developed an independent Securities Commission in 1991, seven years before the Czechs, and the Warsaw Stock Exchange subjected individual brokers and brokerage firms to strict licensing requirements and high-quality regulations (Glaeser, Johnson, and Shleifer 1999, 21–24). The Polish reformers conducted similarly successful banking reforms, in particular, a loan consolidation program from 1993 to 1994 that forced banks to cut off politicized loans to state-owned enterprises (Slay 2000, 63; Bonin 1993, 109). As in Hungary, debt work-out programs took place under careful government supervision, which again stood in contrast to the laissez-faire approach of the Czech reformers (McDermott 2004, 206–207).

Finally, the evidence suggests that delays in privatization fostered the development of a sound legal and regulatory framework in much the same way that ownership regime theory would predict from an intentionally gradual privatization approach. Delays provided additional time for state officials to acquire the skills and knowledge needed to regulate a market economy, which increased the prospects of future institutional consolidation. In most surveys, the efficacy of Poland's corporate and securities laws tops even Hungary. And while Poland has not been immune from corporate governance and financial sector scandals, when they have occurred they have been exposed and punished, a rare occurrence in the Czech Republic (Glaeser, Johnson, and Shleifer 1999, 28). As in Hungary, efficient ownership structures and effective corporate government mechanisms have served to limit asset stripping and prevent the emergence of interest groups that aim to obstruct the rule of law.

However, while the twists and turns of Polish politics in the 1990s that delayed privatization may have helped Poland avoid the vicious ownership conflicts inflicted on the Czech Republic, they had their own costs, including continued delays in privatization. The implementation of hard-budget constraints on state-owned enterprises and the rapid development of new businesses initially spurred some of the highest growth rates in the region despite the slow pace of privatization (Slay 1993, 2000). But in recent years Poland's growth has slowed, suggesting that it may have exhausted its growth potential without further ownership transformation (Nellis 2002). Moreover, as Poland works to complete the process of transferring state assets to private hands, it remains to be seen whether new and ongoing battles for control of assets will continue to provoke competition among interest groups and complicate the process of institutional consolidation. Indeed, levels of corruption in Poland have remained high throughout the transition, and in recent years Poland has even fallen behind the Czech Republic, which has experienced a gradual turnaround since the end of the 1990s (see table 11.4).

The Polish case thus provides further reason to question the neoliberal proposition that rapid privatization is essential to the formation of a market economy and the rule of law. Contrary to neoliberal expectations, repeated delays in privatization did not prevent the emergence of a class of new private owners, nor did they squelch economic growth. The institutionalist perspective, meanwhile, seems in many ways validated; Polish reformers' attention to legal reforms and regulatory practices limited asset stripping, especially as compared to the Czech Republic. However, institutionalist theories have difficulty accounting for persistent and rising levels of corruption in Poland, nor, once again, do they sufficiently address the issue of when and why institutional consolidation is feasible.

The logic of ownership regime theory, we argue, is more consonant with the Polish privatization experience than either the neoliberal or institutionalist stories. Asset stripping in Poland was minimized not only because reformers focused on the development of legal and regulatory frameworks but also because the pace and forms of privatization that they implemented contributed to the creation of efficient ownership and corporate governance structures. The emerging ownership regime has thus hindered the formation of interest groups with an interest in fighting the rule of law. That said, the privatization process in Poland has dragged on for longer than in the Czech Republic and Hungary. If the logic of ownership regime theory is correct, continued competition between interest groups over privatized assets could present obstacles for institution building until the privatization process comes to a close, which perhaps provides insights into the rising levels of corruption in Poland. Overall, it appears that Poland's delayed privatization allowed it to escape the Czech Republic's near brush with plutocratic capitalism, but gradual privatization by accident is an imperfect substitute for the more coherent gradualist strategy adopted by Hungarian reformers.

THE LIMITS AND APPLICATIONS OF OWNERSHIP REGIME THEORY BEYOND THE CEECs

We have seen that privatization strategies have greatly influenced the institutional configuration of the national varieties of capitalism forming in three CEECs, with significant implications for the prospects of economic growth, levels of corruption, and development of the rule of law in these countries.

Ownership regime theory's framework provides insights into the behavior of new private owners and the timing of institutional consolidation in transition countries where neoliberal and institutionalist frameworks have proved inadequate. But how applicable is ownership regime theory as we move further east? Why, contrary to ownership regime theory's predictions, did *neoliberal rapid privatization* in Russia and *delayed privatization* in Ukraine result in *similar* ownership regimes that both fostered plutocratic capitalism?

In this section, we compare the Russian and Ukrainian privatization experiences to the CEEC cases examined in the preceding section in order to investigate the conditions that must pertain for ownership regime theory's predictions concerning privatization strategies to hold true. In particular, we return to the classic social science dilemma of structure and agency and examine the influence of reformers' choices versus external factors beyond human control, such as state capacity and the initial condition of enterprises slated for privatization. The more significant structural pressures present in countries such as Russia and Ukraine, we argue, account for the difference in transition outcomes between the CEEC and FSU cases; states cannot accomplish more than they are institutionally capable of accomplishing, regardless of reformers' strategies.[6] We then turn to some of the insights that ownership regime theory's focus on interest group competition offers with regard to the prospects for capitalism and democracy in FSU countries.

TWO PATHS TO PLUTOCRATIC CAPITALISM: OBSTACLES TO MARKET REFORM IN THE FSU

The difference between the Russian and Ukrainian approaches to privatization could hardly have been more extreme. Russia's neoliberal reform team succeeded in privatizing nearly 18,000 of Russia's approximately 25,000 large- and medium-sized enterprises in the short span between the end of 1992 and June 1994; many of these enterprises were privatized via voucher methods, albeit in a different form than the Czech case[7] (Blasi, Kroumova, and Kruse 1997, table 1, 189). At the end of the 1990s, 70 percent of enterprise assets were in private hands (see table 11.5 below). By contrast, key factions of the Ukrainian elite, who had broken with the Soviet Union with the hope of insulating themselves from the tide of glasnost and perestroika (Prizel 2002), proved adept at blocking privatization efforts. At decade's end the private sector still only accounted for just over half of GDP (see table 11.5).

Neoliberal frameworks would predict that Russia's rapid privatization should improve its prospects for democracy and capitalism. Institutionalists and proponents of ownership regime theory would forecast that Russia's rapid

Table 11.5. Selected Indicators for FSU Countries

Annual Real GDP Growth, 1992–2003 (in %)

	1992	1993	1994	1995	1996	1997	1998	1999	2000	2001	2002	2003
Russia	−14.8	−8.7	−12.7	−4.0	−3.6	1.4	−5.3	6.4	10.0	5.0	4.3	6.2
Ukraine	−9.7	−14.2	−22.9	−12.2	−10.0	−3.0	−1.9	−0.2	5.9	9.2	4.8	5.5

Private Sector as Share of GDP, 1991–2002 (% of GDP)

	1991	1992	1993	1994	1995	1996	1997	1998	1999	2000	2001	2002
Russia	5	25	40	50	55	60	70	70	70	70	70	70
Ukraine	10	10	15	40	45	50	55	55	55	60	65	65

Foreign Direct Investment, 1992–2003 (net inflows in US$ mil.)

	1992	1993	1994	1995	1996	1997	1998	1999	2000	2001	2002	2003
Russia	–	–	409	1,460	1,657	1,679	1,496	1,103	−463	−64	−328	2,500
Ukraine	–	–	151	257	516	581	747	489	594	769	698	850

Transparency International Corruption Perceptions Index, 1995–2004 (10 = low corruption, 1 = high corruption)

	1993	1994	1995	1996	1997	1998	1999	2000	2001	2002	2003	2004
Russia	–	–	–	2.58	2.27	2.4	2.4	2.1	2.3	2.7	2.7	2.8
Ukraine	–	–	–	–	–	2.8	2.6	1.5	2.1	2.4	2.3	2.2

Sources: Data for GDP growth and foreign direct investment are from EBRD (2003) (2003 data are EBRD projections); data for private sector as share of GDP are from EBRD (2000) for the years 1991–2000 and EBRD (2003) for the years 2001–2002; da a for the corruption perceptions index can be found at www.transparency.org.
Note on Corruption Index: As a point of reference, Finland, the least corrupt country in the 2004 TI Corruption Perceptions Index, scored a 9.7. The United States received a 7.5. Russia's 2.8 put it between Nepal and Tanzania, while Ukraine's 2.2 placed it between Sudan and Cameroon.

privatization should create unsound ownership structures, hindering the development of the rule of law and impeding economic growth, whereas gradual privatization should avoid these fates. However, contrary to all these predictions, the distinct Russian and Ukrainian approaches to privatization *both* led to political economies marked by significant concentration of wealth, collusion between business and political elites, high levels of corruption, slow economic growth, and weakly institutionalized market institutions that encouraged asset stripping, as shown in table 11.5. In Russia, rapid, unregulated privatization allowed financial magnates to acquire inordinate assets, especially in the second phase of cash privatization and the infamous loans-for-shares deal. Some analysts estimated that prior to the 1998 financial crisis, the ten largest Russian financial-industrial groups (FIGs) controlled an estimated 25 to 30 percent of the economy (Johnson 1997). In Ukraine, the lack of leadership changeover in the first years of postcommunism allowed communist-era elites to transform political power into personal wealth, leading to the emergence of powerful regional clans, especially in the coal-mining region of Donetsk, the metallurgy and military-industrial complex based in Dnepropetrovsk, and the capital city of Kiev (Åslund 2000).

Although the Russian economy's long-awaited return to growth in 1997 was greeted optimistically by the Western business and journalistic communities, spurring sizable foreign portfolio investment that led to a stock market boom (Frye 2000), these rosy economic reports masked key features of Russia's emerging political economy that distinguished it from the market economies and liberal democracies of the West. In the absence of legal and regulatory institutions to protect property rights, market relations were marked by threats of violence and coercion (Volkov 2002); informal economies based on barter and cash surrogates (Gaddy and Ickes 1998; Woodruff 1999); and the haphazard political intervention of elected and state officials in disputes between market actors (Hendley 1997). The sheen covering the Russian economy fell away when the Russian government defaulted on its loans and broke its promises to prevent devaluation of the ruble in August 1998. In the span of a few weeks, the international community reclassified Russia from promising emerging market economy to the latest example of crony capitalism. Ukraine, exhibiting similar features of plutocratic capitalism, remained mired in an unbroken economic depression until the year 2000.

Why did different privatization strategies in FSU countries not lead to the formation of distinct ownership regimes as in CEECs? We argue that reformers and the new private owners who emerged from privatization faced fundamentally different challenges in countries such as Russia and Ukraine than in the Czech Republic, Hungary, and Poland. In the CEEC region, state institutions did not collapse with the advent of transition as occurred in much of the FSU

(Holmes 1997), which meant that regulation of the privatization process was *possible*, although, as the Czech case indicates, CEEC reformers did not always utilize this state capacity. Moreover, in the CEEC region the challenge of restructuring enterprises, although significant, paled in comparison to the task of reforming the tens of thousands of FSU enterprises inherited from the distorted "hyper-militarized" (Gaddy 1996) economy of the Soviet Union. Finally, new private owners in FSU countries faced much dimmer prospects for attracting FDI than their CEEC counterparts, and they did not have the likely scenario of EU membership to improve the outlook of future business ventures. In these circumstances, ownership regimes characterized by owners who lacked capital, ineffective corporate governance structures, inefficient capital markets, and weak regulatory institutions were likely to emerge *regardless* of the privatization strategies chosen by reformers.

It follows from this analysis that the feasibility of a gradualist regulated privatization approach depends on the state's institutional capacity vis-à-vis the economic challenges it confronts. In the FSU the economic challenges were far greater and the state significantly weaker than in the CEEC region. Consequently, the alternative to hasty and unregulated neoliberal divestment of state assets was most likely the muddled Ukrainian path of semi-reforms, not the Hungarian or Polish privatization strategies. This is not to say, however, that the *logic* of ownership theory lacks relevance for FSU countries, even if ownership regime theory's predictions regarding privatization strategies and transition outcomes do not hold as we move east. Analysis of ownership regimes offers important insights into the prospects of institutional consolidation in countries such as Russia and Ukraine. Just as the flux of transition continued in the Czech Republic until major interest groups were satisfied with the division of privatization's spoils, ownership regime theory would predict that the new business class in FSU countries will not become a force for the rule of law until competition for privatized assets comes to a close. When will this occur in Russia and Ukraine?

A detailed analysis of the FSU is beyond the scope of this study, but we do not agree with the argument that high growth rates and increased industrial investment in Russia after the 1998 financial crisis and in Ukraine since 2000 indicate that these countries have already turned the corner (see Åslund and Boone 2002; Shleifer and Treisman 2003). The 1998 crisis undeniably ushered in a new phase in Russia's and Ukraine's political and economic development, but these countries' ownership regimes continue to evolve according to a non-Coasian, political logic, albeit a different one than before the crisis. Many of the pre-crisis rents that originated in market distortions resulting from differentials between domestic and world prices, hyperinflation, and unequal access to government subsidies have indeed dried up. Still, battles for control of privatized assets by no means occur within an institutionalized framework of rules and regulations, as vividly demonstrated by the Putin government's seizure and auction of Yukos oil company assets in 2004. To position themselves for further asset competition, Russian business interests have increasingly sought to install their representatives in the State Duma (*Moscow Times*, November 13, 2003), a longstanding practice in Ukrainian politics (Åslund 2000). And when acquiring assets, business leaders continue, in many cases, to think less about cost-benefit analyses than about the *political* leverage that a position in strategic markets will offer for the future acquisition of assets (Barnes 2003).

As ownership regime theory would predict given this ongoing competition for assets, Russian business interests continue to view legal and regulatory institutions as political pawns, not the defining rules of the game. While some institutional reforms, such as tax reform, have recently occurred (Jones Luong and Weinthal 2004), it appears that Russia's new private owners support the institutional reforms that are to their advantage and fight against the rest; a strategy favored by oligarchs is to promote regulations and taxes that apply to competitors, but not themselves (Åslund 2000, 270). Thus, if the tenets of ownership regime theory hold true, we do not expect the institutions of liberal democracy and a modern, regulated market economy to take root in Russia and Ukraine until dominant interest groups turn their attention from winning additional assets to securing the rights to the property they already have acquired. Only then might Russia and Ukraine escape the grasp of plutocratic capitalism.

CONCLUSION

These analyses of the formation and evolution of ownership regimes in five postcommunist countries point to the need to build upon the neoliberal and institutionalist approaches to the study of political and economic transformation and institution building. The neoliberal assumption that private owners inherently have an interest in lobbying for the rule of law has proven false. As the preceding study of Czech *rapid neoliberal voucher privatization* illustrates, business elites who emerge from privatization only have a stake in the rule of law when the profits they can earn from securing their property rights and competing in a transparent market economy are greater than the profits to be made from market distortions, political connections, and theft of enterprise assets. Institutionalists, meanwhile, are correct in their observation that a market economy without legal and regulatory frameworks breeds political and economic crisis, but institutionalism provides few insights into how the rule of law might develop when powerful interest groups have a stake in preventing its emergence. In contrast to these approaches, ownership regime theory integrates the study of privatization strategies, interest group formation, and institution building, thus providing a framework for the analysis of institutional consolidation—as demonstrated by our case studies of *gradualist regulated privatization* in Hungary and Poland.

This framework has implications for both policymakers and analysts. On the policy side, it suggests that the neoliberal vilification of government and glorification of private owners is overly simplistic. All effective modern political economies, including liberal market economies such as the United States and United Kingdom, are highly regulated; the only question is what form this regulation will take (Vogel 1996). The goal of economic policymaking in times of transformation from planned to market economies must be to dismantle overly intrusive bureaucracies that foster inefficiency and corruption while remaining wary of unleashing the unregulated forces of entrepreneurial greed that lead to theft rather than investment in production. Given that regulatory institutions are unlikely to consolidate during the flux of transition, an additional aim of economic reform—and of privatization in particular—must be to develop sound ownership structures that create owners with the incentives to lobby for the rule of law, as opposed to owners who become powerful interest groups seeking to block institution building.

On the academic side, ownership regime theory points to the need for further research on the interaction between the new postcommunist business elites and the state. This study has developed a general framework for explaining how privatization strategies affect the development of ownership regimes and how ownership regimes structure political and economic development. The story of Czech privatization in particular makes clear that choices about privatization can impact the formation not only of the legal and regulatory institutions most directly related to the market but also the development of political parties, state bureaucracies, law enforcement agencies, and the other political institutions essential to the functioning of democratic regimes. However, there are many ways that state capture by powerful business interests can occur. Business elites can form or finance parties, bribe bureaucrats, place their own representatives on party rosters, run for office themselves, blackmail state officials, or lobby legally for legislation that is in their interest. Which strategies they choose—and how this choice is related to particular ownership regimes—presumably has implications for the prospects of market formation and the rule of law.

Researching these subterranean relationships between interest groups and the state will not be easy; in many cases in the postcommunist region it may be downright dangerous. But it is essential to understanding the origins of the institutions vital to the performance of market economies.

NOTES

1. Reformers in postcommunist countries undertook privatization on a scale never attempted in the West. To facilitate a rapid transition, overcome the administrative challenge of simultaneously privatizing tens of thousands of enterprises, address the problem of low domestic savings, and encourage popular support for the privatization process, neoliberal reformers in countries ranging from the Czech Republic to Russia to Kyrgyzstan developed a plan based on mass giveaways of enterprise shares via distribution of vouchers to citizens or enterprise employees. Voucher privatization had several variants that differed according to whether citizens exchanged their vouchers directly for enterprise shares or allowed institutional investors such as privatization investment funds to mediate their investments (Pistor and Spicer 1996), but we collectively refer to these variants as *nonstandard privatization*.

2. It warrants emphasis that these privatization paths are stylized ideal types, and in reality each actual country case exhibits a *mixed privatization strategy*, although some cases, such as the Czech Republic's neoliberal privatization and Hungary's gradualist privatization, closely resemble the ideal types. Additionally, while these were the two *intentional* privatization strategies adopted by CEEC reformers, the de facto privatization program of many countries in the FSU and southeastern Europe, as discussed above, was neither a rapid neoliberal privatization nor a gradualist regulated approach. Rather, corruption and state capture in many cases facilitated privatization to enterprise insiders or other groups with close connections to privatization officials. This path, as surely as neoliberal rapid privatization, facilitated the emergence of plutocratic capitalism.

3. Note the lag in the decline of the Czech Republic's scores on the Transparency International Corruption Index (see table 11.4), which are based on the perceptions of business people. The scores do not begin to fall until 1998, once the business community realized that the apparent Czech miracle was a mirage. They then drop precipitously thereafter and have only begun to slowly rise again since 2002.

4. The only other serious reformers that rejected voucher privatization in its entirety were Estonia and East Germany. Belarus, Azerbaijan, Turkmenistan, Uzbekistan, and Tajikistan also did not implement voucher privatization, but this reflects a lack of privatization reforms in general rather than an alternative privatization strategy (EBRD 1997, 90). It should be noted that Hungary's 1992 Small Investor Share Purchase Program did propose the use of some minimal voucher privatization methods, but the program was terminated before it was implemented (Canning and Hare 1996, 7; Takla 1999, 363).

5. Although early studies (Stark 1992, 1996) drew attention to the convoluted ownership structures resulting from spontaneous privatization, more recent studies show

that these observations focused on a few major conglomerates, some of which have since evolved (Barnes 2000, 539; Hanley, King, and Istvan Toth 2002).

6. To a significant degree, we believe that this argument also applies to countries such as Romania and Bulgaria, which avoided neoliberal rapid privatization but fell prey to ineffective and delayed insider privatization.

7. The Russian voucher program gave enterprise insiders—employees and managers—privileged access to company shares, unlike the Czech program that allowed all eligible citizens to participate in enterprise auctions on equal footing.

References

Acemoglu, Daron. 2003. "Why Not a Political Coase Theorem? Social Conflict, Commitment, and Politics." *Journal of Comparative Economics* 31, no. 4: 620–652.

Akerlof, George. 1970. "The Market for 'Lemons': Qualitative Uncertainty and the Market Mechanism." *Quarterly Journal of Economics* 84, no. 3: 488–500.

Allison, Graham, and Grigory Yavlinsky. 1991. Window of Opportunity. Paper prepared for the Joint Program for Western Cooperation in the Soviet Transformation to Democracy and the Market Economy. Mimeo.

Amsden, Alice H., Jacek Kochanowicz, and Lance Taylor. 1994. *The Market Meets Its Match: Restructuring the Economies of Eastern Europe.* Cambridge, MA: Harvard University Press.

Appel, Hilary. 2002. "Corruption and the Collapse of the Czech Transition Miracle." *East European Politics and Societies* 15, no. 3: 528–553.

Arbess, Dan. 1992. "One-Stop Shopping in Czech Privatisation." *Financial Times*, September 15.

Arthur, Brian W. 1989. "Competing Technologies, Increasing Returns, and Lock-in by Historical Events." *Economic Journal* 99: 116–131.

Åslund, Anders. 1995. *How Russia Became a Market Economy.* Washington, DC: Brookings Institute.

———. 2000. "Why Has Ukraine Failed to Achieve Economic Growth?" In *Economic Reform in Ukraine: The Unfinished Agenda,* edited by Anders Åslund and George de Menil, 255–278. London: M. E. Sharpe.

———. 2002. *Building Capitalism: The Transformation of the Former Soviet Bloc.* Cambridge: Cambridge University Press.

Åslund, Anders, and Peter Boone. 2002. "Russia's Surprise Economic Success." *Financial Times* (October 9): 19.

Baránek, Rudolf. 1994. *Soukromníci.* Czech Republic: Kotis.

Barnes, Andrew. 2000. "Comparative Theft: Context and Choice in the Hungarian, Czech, and Russian Transformations, 1989–2000." *East European Politics and Societies* 17, no. 3: 533–565.

———. 2003. "Russia's New Business Groups and State Power." *Post-Soviet Affairs* 19, no. 2: 154–186.

Bartlett, David L. 1997. *The Political Economy of Dual Transformations: Market Reform and Democratization in Hungary.* Ann Arbor: University of Michigan Press.

Bauman, Zygmunt. 1988. "Poland—On Its Own." *Telos* 77: 47–68.

Bentley, Arthur F. 1949. *The Process of Government*. Evanston: Principia Press of Illinois. Third Reissue.

Berle, A., and G. Means. 1932. *The Modern Corporation and Private Property*. New York: Macmillan.

Black, Bernard, Reiner Kraakman, and Anna Tarassova. 2000. "Russian Privatization and Corporate Governance: What Went Wong?" *Stanford Law Review* 52: 1731–1804.

Bláha, Zdeněk, Oldřich Kýn, Michal Mejstřík, and Jan Mládek. 1992. "Tři uzly na kupónové privatizace." *Respekt*, no. 5.

Blanchard, Oliver, Rudiger Dornbusch, Paul Krugman, Richard Layard, and Lawrence Summers. 1991. *Reform in Eastern Europe*. Cambridge, MA: MIT Press.

Blasi, Joseph R., Maya Kroumova, and Douglas Kruse. 1997. *Kremlin Capitalism: Privatizing the Russian Economy*. Ithaca, NY: Cornell University Press.

Blaszczyk, Barbara, Iraj Hashi, Alexander Radygin, and Richard Woodward. 2003. "Corporate Governance and Ownership Structure in the Transition: The Current State of Knowledge and Where to Go from Here." Warsaw: Center for Social and Economic Research.

Boguszak, Marek, and Vladimír Rak. 1990. *Československo-květen*. Prague: AISA— Skupina pro nezávislou sociální analýzu, July.

Bonin, John P. 1993. "On the Way to Privatizing Commercial Banks: Poland and Hungary Take Different Roads." *Comparative Economic Studies* 35, no. 4: 103–119.

Boycko, Maxim, Andrei Shleifer, and Robert Vishny. 1995. *Privatizing Russia*. Cambridge, MA: MIT Press.

Brož, Jiří. 1997. "Královopolské Brno Chief Accused of Tunneling." *Lidové noviny* (November 27): 7.

Buchtíková, Alena, and Aleš Čapek. 1993. "Časový rozměr privatizace." *Ekonom* 17: 21–22.

Campbell, John L., and Ove K. Pedersen. 1995. "The Evolutionary Nature of Revolutionary Change in Postcommunist Europe." Copenhagen: Center for Offentlig Organization Og Styring.

Canning, Anna, and Paul Hare. 1996. "Political Economy of Privatization in Hungary: A Progress Report." Edinburgh: Centre for Economic Reform and Transformation.

Carlin, Wendy, John Van Reenen, and Toby Wolfe. 1994. "Enterprise Restructuring in the Transition: An Analytical Survey of Case Study Evidence from Central and Eastern Europe." EBRD.

Centrum kuponové privatizace (CKP). 1995. "Kupónová privatizace ve faktech a cislech."

Charap, Joshua, and Alena Zemplínerová. 1993. Management Buyouts in the Privatisation Programme of the Czech Republic. Paper presented at the Management and Employee Buyouts in the Process of Privatisation, Budapest, March 31 to April 2.

Chvojka, Petr. 1996. "The Role of Commercial Banks in the Czech Economy Transformation Process." *Prague Economic Papers* 4: 334–354.

———. 1997. "Banking Sector's Role in Restructuring Central and Eastern European Countries' Economies (Case Study of the Czech Republic)." *Ekonomický časopis* 45, no. 6–7: 511–545.

Coase, Ronald H. 1960. "The Problem of Social Cost." *Journal of Law and Economics* 3, no. 1: 1–44.

Coffee, John C. 1994. "Investment Privatization Funds: The Czech Experience." Policy Research Department Working Paper. Washington, DC: World Bank.

Cohen, Stephen, and Andrew Schwartz. 1993. "Privatization in Eastern Europe: The Tunnel at the End of the Light." *American Prospect* 4, no. 13 (March): 99–108.

Cohen, Stephen, Andrew Schwartz, and John Zysman. 1998. *The Tunnel at the End of the Light.* Berkeley: International and Area Studies, University of California, Berkeley.

Collier, David, and Ruth Berins Collier. 1991. *Shaping the Political Arena: Critical Junctures, the Labor Movement, and Regime Dynamics in Latin America.* Princeton, NJ: Princeton University Press.

Collier, Ruth Berins, and James Mahoney. 1995. "Labor and Democratization: Comparing the First and Third Waves in Europe and Latin America." Berkeley, CA: Institute of Industrial Relations.

Comisso, Ellen. 1998. "Implicit Development Strategies in Central East Europe and Cross-National Production Networks." In *Enlarging Europe: The Industrial Foundation for a New Political Reality*, edited by John Zysman and Andrew Schwartz, 380–423. Berkeley: University of California, Berkeley.

Coopers & Lybrand and Phare. 1997. "Corporate Governance and Financial Control in the Czech Republic: Legislative Analysis." Prague.

Cull, Robert, Jana Matesova, and Mary Shirley. 2001. *Ownership Structure and the Temptation to Loot: Evidence from Privatized Firms in the Czech Republic.* Washington, DC: World Bank.

Czech Ministry of Finance. 1997. *Current Aspects of the Czech Capital Market.* Prague: Ministry of Finance, Mimeo.

Czech Ministry of Privatization. 1993. *Report on the Privatization Process for the Years 1989 to 1992.* Prague: Ministry for the Administration of the National Property and Its Privatization.

Czech Statistical Office. 1994. *Statistical Yearbook of the Czech Republic 1994.* Prague: Czech Statistical Office.

ČSFR Federal Parliament. 1992. *Zpráva vlády ČSFR pro Federální shromáždění ČSFR o dosavadním průběhu kupónové privatizace.* Prague: ČSFR Federal Parliament.

Dabrowski, Marek, Stanislaw Gomulka, and Jacek Rostowski. 2000. "Whence Reform? A Critique of the Stiglitz Perspective." Centre for Economic Performance Discussion Paper. London School of Economics and Political Science, September.

Dahl, Robert A. 1971. *Polyarchy: Participation and Opposition.* New Haven, CT: Yale University Press.

Dahrendorf, Ralf. 1990. *Reflections on the Revolution in Europe: In a Letter Intended to Have Been Sent to a Gentleman in Warsaw.* New York: Random House.

Desai, Raj M., and Vladěna Plocková. 1997. "The Czech Republic." In *Between State and Market: Mass Privatization in Transition Economies*, edited by Ira W. Lieberman, Stilpon S. Nestor, and Raj. M. Desai, 190–196. Washington, DC: World Bank.

Dhar, Sanjay. 1992. "Public Enterprise Restructuring: Achilles' Heel of the Reform Process." *Transition* 3, no. 3: 6–8.

Diamond, Larry. 2002. "Thinking about Hybrid Regimes." *Journal of Democracy* 13, no. 2: 21–35.

Dlouhý, Vladimír, and Václav Klaus. 1990. "Strategie radikální ekonomické reformy, Přiloha II." Proposal to the Czechoslovak Government, spring.

Donahue, John D. 1989. *The Privatization Decision: Public Ends, Private Means.* USA: Basic Books.

Dvořák, Ladislav, and František Vlasák. 1990. "Strategie postupného přechodu k tržní ekonomice v ČSFR (druhá varianta radikální ekonomické reformy), Přiloha I and II." Proposal to the Czechoslovak Government, Prague, April 27.

Earle, John S., and Saul Estrin. 1994. Worker Ownership in Transition. Paper prepared for the World Bank conference Corporate Governance in Central Europe and Russia, Washington, DC, December 15–16.

Earle, John S., Scott G. Gehlbach, Zuzana Saková, and Jiří Večerník. 1997. "Mass Privatization, Distributive Politics, and Popular Support for Reform in the Czech Republic." Working Paper No. 97: Institute of Sociology, Academy of Sciences of the Czech Republic: 13.

EBRD. 1997. *Transition Report: Enterprise Performance and Growth.* London: EBRD.

———. 1999. *Transition Report: Ten Years of Transition.* London: EBRD.

———. 2002. *Transition Report: Employment, Skills, and Transition.* London: EBRD.

———. 2003. *Transition Report: Integration and Regional Cooperation.* London: EBRD.

Ekiert, Grzegorz. 1997. "Rebellious Poles: Political Crises and Popular Protest under State Socialism, 1945–89." *East European Politics and Societies* 11, no. 2: 299–338.

Ellerman, David. 2003. "On the Russian Privatization Debate." *Challenge* 46, no. 3: 6–28.

Elster, Jon, Claus Offe, and Ulrich K. Preuss. 1998. *Institutional Design in Postcommunist Societies.* Cambridge: Cambridge University Press.

Estrin, Saul, and Robert Stone. 1996. "A Taxonomy of Mass Privatization." *Transition* 7, no. 11–12: 8–9.

———. 1997. "A Taxonomy of Mass Privatization." In *Between State and Market: Mass Privatization in Transition Economies*, edited by Ira W. Lieberman, Stilpon S. Nestor, and Raj. M. Desai, 173–176. Washington, DC: World Bank.

Falbr, Richard. 1994. "Jsou odbory protidemokratické?" *Rudé právo*, December 12.

Filer, Randall K., and Jan Hanousek. 1996. *The Extent of Efficiency in Central European Equity Markets.* Prague: CERGE-EL.

Flek, Vladislav. 1996. "Wage and Employment Restructuring in the Czech Republic." Working Paper No. 60: Česká Národní Banka, Institut Ekonomie, Prague.

Fond národního majetku [Fund of National Property]. 1995. *Annual Report, 1995.* Prague: Fond národního majetku.

Freeland, Chrystia. 2000. *Sale of the Century: Russia's Wild Ride from Communism to Capitalism.* New York: Random House.

Friedman, Milton. 1962/1982. *Capitalism and Freedom*. Chicago: University of Chicago Press.

Friedman, Milton, and Rose Friedman. 1979. *Free to Choose: A Personal Statement*. New York: First Harvest/HBJ.

Frydman, Roman, and Andrzej Rapaczynski. 1991. "Markets and Institutions in Large-Scale Privatization: An Approach to Economic and Social Transformation in Eastern Europe." In *Reforming Central and Eastern European Economies: Initial Results and Challenges*, edited by Vittorio Corbo, Fabrizio Coricelli, and Jan Bossak, 253–274. Mimeo.

———. 1994. *Privatization in Eastern Europe: Is the State Withering Away?* London: Central European University Press.

Frydman, Roman, Andrzej Rapaczynski, and John S. Earle. N.d. "Preface" and "Part I: The Czech Republic." Mimeos (drafts): 10–36 and 36–180.

Frye, Timothy. 2000. *Brokers and Bureaucrats: Building Market Institutions in Russia*. Ann Arbor: University of Michigan Press.

Fukuyama, Francis. 1992. *The End of History and the Last Man*. New York: Avon Books.

Gaddy, Clifford. 1996. *The Price of the Past: Russia's Struggle with the Legacy of a Hypermilitarized Economy*. Washington, DC: Brookings Institute.

Gaddy, Clifford G., and Barry W. Ickes. 1998. "Russia's Virtual Economy." *Foreign Affairs* 77, no. 5: 53–67.

Gál, Fedor. 1991. *Z prvey ruky*. Bratislava: Archa. (in Slovak)

Glaeser, Edward, Simon Johnson, and Andrei Shleifer. 1999. "Coase versus the Coasians." National Bureau of Economic Research Working Paper 7447.

Granovetter, Mark. 1978. "Threshold Models of Collective Behavior."*American Journal of Sociology* 83, no. 6: 1420–1443.

Gray, Cheryl, et al. 1993. *Evolving Legal Frameworks for Private Sector Development in Central and Eastern Europe*. Washington, DC: World Bank.

Greenfeld, Liah. 1992. *Nationalism: Five Roads to Modernity*. Cambridge, MA: Harvard University Press.

Grégr, Miroslav, Zoltán Berghauer, and Jan Hrabě. 1990. "Iniciativní material ke koncepci deetatizace a privatizace." Proposal by Svaz průmyslu ČR, Svaz průmyslu SR, Svaz státních podniků a akciových společností, Prague. Mimeo.

Grossman, Gregory. 1994. "What Was—Is, Will Be—the Command Economy?" *Moct-Most* 4: 5–22.

Grzymala-Busse, Anna. 1998. "Reform Efforts in the Czech and Slovak Communist Parties and Their Successors, 1988–1993." *East European Politics and Societies* 6, no. 3 (Fall).

———. 2003. "Political Competition and the Politicization of the State in East Central Europe." *Comparative Political Studies* 36, no. 10: 1123–1147.

Haggard, Stephan, Robert Kaufman, and Methew Shugart. 1998. *Politics, Institutions, and Macroeconomic Adjustment: Hungarian Financial Policy-Making in Comparative Perspective*. Budapest: Collegium Budapest.

Hall, Peter A., and David Soskice. 2001. *Varieties of Capitalism: The Instit' Foundations of Comparative Advantage*. Oxford: Oxford University Pres'

Hanley, Eric. 2000. "Cadre Capitalism in Hungary and Poland: Property Accumulation Among Communist-Era Elites." *East European Politics and Societies* 14, no. 1: 143–178.

Hanley, Eric, Lawrence King, and János Istvan Toth. 2002. "The State, International Agencies, and Property Transformation in Postcommunist Hungary." *American Journal of Sociology* 108, no. 1: 129–168.

Hartl, Jan. 1991. "Perceptions of Social Safety in the Czech and Slovak Republics, Hungary, and Poland." Mimeo.

Hashi, Iraj. 2000. "The Polish National Investment Fund Programme: Mass Privatization with a Difference." *Comparative Economic Studies* 62, no. 1: 87–134.

Hausner, Jerzy, Ove K. Pedersen, and Karsten Ronit. 1995. *Evolution of Interest Representation and Development of the Labour Market in Post-Socialist Countries.* Cracow: Cracow Academy of Sciences.

Havel, Václav. 1993. Interview, "I trh musí mít morálku." *Ekonom* 5: 15–16.

———. 1997. "Z projevu prezidenta Václava Havla k poslancům a senátorům v Rudolfinu." *Hospodářské noviny* (December 10): 6.

Havlík, Petr. 1990. "Můj názor." Mimeo.

Havlík, Petr, and Marek Stoniš. 1998. *Klaus & ti druzí.* Prague: Pallata.

Hayek, F. A. 1944/1994. *The Road to Serfdom.* Chicago: University of Chicago Press.

Hellman, Joel S. 1998. "Winners Take All: The Politics of Partial Reform in Post-Communist Transitions." *World Politics* 50, no. 2: 203–254.

Henderson, J., R. Whitley, G. Lengyel, and L. Czaban. 1995. "Contention and Confusion in Industrial Transformation: Dilemmas of State Economic Management." In *Industrial Transformation in Europe*, edited by E. Dittrich, G. Schmidt, and R. Whitley. London: Sage.

Hendley, Kathryn Ann. 1993. "Trying to Make Law Matter: Legal Reform and Labor Law in the Soviet Union." PhD diss., Department of Political Science, University of California, Berkeley.

———. 1997. "Legal Development in Post-Soviet Russia." *Post-Soviet Affairs* 13, no. 3: 228–251.

Hirschman, Albert O. 1977. *The Passions and the Interests: Political Arguments for Capitalism before Its Triumph.* Princeton, NJ: Princeton University Press.

Hoff, Karla, and Joseph E. Stiglitz. 2002. "After the Big Bang? Obstacles to the Emergence of the Rule of Law in Post-Communist Societies." Policy Research Working Paper Series 2934. Washington, DC: World Bank.

Holle, Denise Vergot, and Stephen Pettyfer. 1997. "Czech Banks: Weighted Down by Debt." New York: Merrill Lynch, Pierce Fenner & Smith, February.

Holmes, Stephen. 1997. "What Russia Teaches Us Now: How Weak States Threaten Freedom." *The American Prospect* 8, no. 33 (July–August).

Holub, Petr. 1994–1995. "České odbory mezi pravým a levým extrémem." *Respekt* (December 12–January 1).

———. 1997. "V obkličém byrokratů." *Respekt* 32.

Holub, Petr, Jan Macháček, and Vladimír Mlynář. 1997. "Proč končí Klausova éra." *Respekt* 26: 9–11.

Honajzer, Jiří. 1996. *Občanské fórum: vznik, vývoj a rozpad.* Prague: Orbis.

Huntington, Samuel P. 1968. *Political Order in Changing Societies.* New Haven, CT: Yale University Press.

Hunya, Gábor. 1997. "Foreign Direct Investment and Economic Modernization in CEECs." Vienna: WIIW.

Husák, Petr. 1997. *Budování kapitalismu v Čechách: Rozhovory s Tomášém Ježkem.* Prague: Volvox Globator.

Institute for EastWest Studies, Policy Brief. 1994. "Policy Recommendations on Banks, Capital Markets, and Enterprise Restructuring." Sponsored by EBRD, World Bank, UN Development Program.

James, William. 1907/1991. *Pragmatism.* Buffalo, NY: Prometheus Books.

Janáček, Kamil, and Eva Zamrazilová. 2002. "Czech Economy at the Beginning of 2002." *Prague Economic Papers* 9, no. 2.

Jermakowicz, Wladyslaw W. 1995. "Privatization and Foreign Investment in Poland, 1990–1993: Results, Problems, and Lessons." In *Privatization and Foreign Investments in Eastern Europe*, edited by Iliana Zloch-Christy, 65–93. Westport, CT: Praeger.

Ježek, Tomáš. 1998. "Svobodný trh byl někdy zástěrkou pro zloděyny." *Rudé právo* (January 6): 1, 4.

Jičínský, Zdeněk. 1993. *Československý parlament v polistopadovém vývoji.* Prague: Nadas-Afgh.

Jičínský, Zdeněk, and Jan Škaloud. 1996. "Transformace politického systému k democracii." In *Transformace české společnosti (1989–1995)*, edited by Vlasta Šafaríková, 50–113. Brno, Czech Republic: Doplněk.

Johnson, Juliet. 1997. "Russia's Emerging Financial-Industrial Groups." *Post-Soviet Affairs* 13, no. 4: 333–365.

Jones Luong, Pauline, and Erika Weinthal. 2004. "Contra Coercion: Russian Tax Reform, Exogenous Shocks, and Negotiated Institutional Change." *American Political Science Review* 98, no. 1: 139–152.

Junek, Václav. 1998. "Budujeme kapitalismus bez kapitálu." *Ekonom*: 10–12.

Juraj, Hon. 1994. "Odbory v měnící se společnosti." Ostrava, Czech Republic: Regionálni komora odborových svazů severní Moravy, Marketingová laboratoř, Ostrava.

Kagan, Robert. 1978. *Regulatory Justice: Implementing a Wage-Price Freeze.* New York: Russell Sage Foundation.

Kaufmann, Daniel, and Paul Siegelbaum. 1996. "Privatization and Corruption in Transition Economies." *Journal of International Affairs* 50, no. 2: 419–458.

Kayal, Michele. 1994. Report on the Czechoslovak Press (inexact title). Prague. Mimeo.

Keefer, Philip, and Mary Shirley. 1997. "Privatization in Transition Economies: Politics as Usual?" Discussion Paper. *The Center for International Private Enterprise*, July.

Kirschbaum, Stanislav J. 1995. *A History of Slovakia.* New York: St. Martin's Press.

Kiss, Yudit. 1994. "Privatization Paradoxes in East Central Europe." *East Europ Politics and Societies* 8, no. 1: 122–152.

Kitschelt, Herbert. 1992. "The Formation of Party Systems in East Central Europe." *Politics and Society* 20, no. 1: 7–50.

Klaus, Václav. 1991a. *Ekonomická věda a ekonomická reforma.* Prague: Gennex & Top Agency.

———. 1991b. "Main Obstacles to Rapid Economic Transformation of Eastern Europe: The Czechoslovak View." In *A Road to Market Economy: Selected Articles, Speeches and Lectures Held Abroad,* edited by Václav Klaus, 34–38. Prague: Top Agency.

———. 1994. *Česká cesta.* Prague: Profile.

———. 1995a. *Ekonomická teorie a realita transformačních procesů.* Prague: Management Press.

———. 1995b. *Dopočítávání do jedné.* Prague: Management Press.

———. 1995c. "Snahy o hled'aní třetí cesty stále nekončí." In *Naše současné spory o liberalismus,* edited by Milan Znoj, 91–93. Prague: Aleko a Centrum Liberálních Studií.

———. 1997. "Ludwig Erhard a jeho odkaz dnešní Evropě." In *Obhajoba zapomenutých myšlenek,* edited by Václav Klaus, 44–47. Prague: Academia.

Klvačová, Eva. 1991. "Czechoslovak Privatization and Foreign Investors." *Privatization Newsletter of Czechoslovakia,* no. 1: 1.

———. 1992. "Velká privatizace a její pravidla." *Ekonom* 34: 19.

Kolodko, Grzegorz W., and D. Mario Nuti. 1997. "The Polish Alternative. Old Myths, Hard Facts and New Strategies in the Successful Transformation of the Polish Economy." Research for Action, 33. Helsinki: United Nations University, World Institute for Development Economics Research (WIDER).

Komárek, Valter a kolektiv. 1990. *Prognóza a program.* Prague: Vydala Academia.

Kornai, János. 1980. *Economics of Shortage.* Amsterdam: North-Holland.

———. 1992. *The Socialist System: The Political Economy of Communism.* Princeton, NJ: Princeton University Press.

Kotrba, Josef. 1994. "Czech Privatization: Players and Winners." Cerge Working Paper #58: Prague, April.

———. 1995. "Czech Financial Market and Financial Intermediaries: Regulatory Institutions." Paper presented at the Workshop on Regulatory and Institutional Reform in the Transitional Economies, Warsaw, Poland, November 7–9.

Kotrba, Josef, and Jan Švejnar. N.d. "Rapid and Multifaceted Privatization: Experience of the Czech and Slovak Republics." Research Paper Series Enterprise Behavior and Economic Reforms: A Comparative Study in Central and Eastern Europe and Industrial Reform and Productivity in Chinese Enterprises, no. 19, World Bank.

Krejčí, Oskar. 1994. *Kniha o volbach.* Prague: Victoria Publishing.

Leff, Carol Skalnik. 1997. *The Czech and Slovak Republics: Nation versus State.* Boulder, CO: Westview Press.

Lešenarová, Hana. 1998. "Central Bank Head Blasts Imprudent Lending, Supervision." *Prague Business Journal* (June 29–July 5): 14.

Lešenarová, Hana, and Quentin Reed. 1997. "Negligence Is No Crime." *Prague Business Journal*: 17.

Levitsky, Steven, and Lucan A. Way. 2002. "The Rise of Competitive Authoritarianism." *Journal of Democracy* 13, no. 2: 51–63.

Lewandowski, Janusz, and Jan Szomburg. 1989. "Property Reform as a Basis for Social and Economic Reform." *Communist Economics* 1, no. 3: 257–268.

Lieberman, Ira. 1997. *Between State and Market: Mass Privatization in Transition Economies.* Washington, DC: World Bank.

Linne, Thomas. 1996. "Akteinmärkte in Mittel-und Osteuropa: Anlegereuphorie trotz institutioneller Hemnisse." *Wirtschaft im Wandela,* Institute für Wirtschaftsforschung, Halle, no. 1: 11–15.

Lízal, Lubomír, Miroslav Singer, and Jan Švejnar. 1995. "Manager Interests, Breakups and Performance of State Enterprises in Transition." In *The Czech Republic and Economic Transition in Eastern Europe,* edited by Jan Švejnar, 211–232. San Diego: Academic Press.

Macháček, Jan. 1992. "Ekonomická moc je ve Lnářích." *Respekt*: 5–6.

———. 1997. "Kdyz potrefené husy kejhají." *Respekt* 47: 2.

———. 1998. "Velká slova, malé skutky." *Respekt* 9: 3.

Majnoni, Giovanni, Rashmi Shankar, and Eva Varhegyi. 2003. "The Dynamics of Foreign Bank Ownership: Evidence from Hungary." World Bank Policy Research Working Paper 3114.

Malá československá encyclopedia: Š–Ž, Vol. VI. 1987. Prague: Encyklopedický institut ČSAV, 867

Mansfeldová, Zdenka. 1993. "The Emerging New Czech Political Elite." Paper prepared for presentation at European Consortium for Political Research, Madrid, Spain, April 17–22.

Marek, Vladimír. 1991. "Bilióny bez hranic." *Obrana Lidu* 42: 3.

Matějka, Milan. 1992. *Spor o reformu.* Prague: Alternativy.

McDermott, Gerald A. 1994. "Renegotiating the Ties That Bind: The Limits of Privatization in the Czech Republic." Berlin: WZB.

———. 2002. *Embedded Politics: Industrial Networks and Institutional Change in Postcommunism.* Ann Arbor: University of Michigan Press.

———. 2004. "Institutional Change and Firm Creation in East-Central Europe: An Embedded Politics Approach." *Comparative Political Studies* 37, no. 2: 188–217.

Meagher, Patrick. 2000. "Changing Hands: A Case Study of Financial Sector Governance in Hungary's Market Transition." Baltimore, MD: Center for Institutional Reform and the Informal Sector.

Mejstřík, Michal. 1997a. "The Emergence of Institutional Owners: The Role of Banks and Nonbanking Financial Institutions in the Privatization of the Economy and the Banks." In *The Privatization Process in East-Central Europe: Evolutionary Process of Czech Privatization,* edited by Michal Mejstřík, 145–170. Dordrecht, Netherlands: Kluwer Academic.

———, ed. 1997b. *The Privatization Process in East-Central Europe.* Vol. 36 of *International Studies in Economics and Econometrics.* Dordrecht: Kluwer Academic Publishers.

Mihályi, Peter. 1996. "Policies and Constraints for Divesting Residual Stakes through Trade Sale: The Experience in Hungary." Paper presented at the Conference on the Management and Sale of Residual State Shareholdings, Berlin.

Milanovic, Branko. 1989. "Privatization Options and Procedures." In *The Transition from Socialism in Eastern Europe*, edited by Arye L. Hillman and Branko Milanovic, 41–82. Washington, DC: World Bank.

Mizsei, Kalman. 1992. "Privatization in Eastern Europe: A Comparative Study of Poland and Hungary." *Soviet Studies* 44, no. 2: 283–296.

Mládek, Jan. 1992. "The Different Paths of Privatization: Czechoslovakia, 1990–?" Prague. Mimeo.

———. 1994. "Voucher Privatization in Czechia and Slovakia." Draft paper presented at the conference on Mass Privatisation: A First Assessment of the Results, sponsored by the OECD Advisory Group on Privatisation, Fifth Plenary Session, Paris, March 2–4.

———. 1996. "Privatization and 'Third Wave' in the Czech Republic." Prague: Czech Institute of Applied Economics.

———. 1997. "Is Czech Privatization a Success? No: A Too Costly Social Engineering Project." *Transitions* 4, no. 4: 92–95.

Mlčoch, Lubomír. 1992. *The Behavior of the Czechoslovak Enterprise Sphere: A Survey of Microeconomic Works of 1968–1989*. Prague: Economic Institute, Czechoslovak Academy of Sciences.

———. 1993. "The Dynamics of Changes in Behavior within the Czech Enterprise Sphere." Released by Institute of Sociology, Academy of Sciences of the Czech Republic, for the project East Central Europe 2000, Prague, May. Mimeo.

Moore, Barrington. 1966. *Social Origins of Dictatorship and Democracy: Lord and Peasant in the Making of the Modern World*. Boston: Beacon Press.

Müller, Jiří. 1994. "Odvrácená tvář privatizace." *Hospadářslé noviny* (July 12): 11.

Myant, Martin. 1993. "Czech and Slovak Trade Unions." *Journal of Communist Studies* 9, no. 4, 59–84.

Nařizení vlády ČSFR o vydávání a použití investíčních kuponů. N.d. Proposal.

Nations in Transit. 2004. New York: Freedom House.

Nellis, John. 1996. *Privatization in Transition Economies: An Update*. Washington, DC: World Bank.

———. 1999. "Time to Rethink Privatization in Transition Economies?" International Finance Corporation Discussion Paper Number 38. Washington, DC: World Bank.

———. 2002. "The World Bank, Privatization, and Enterprise Reform in Transition Economies." *Transition Newsletter* 13, no. 1: 17–21.

Němeček, Tomáš. 1997. "Všechnu moc parlamentu." *Respekt* 47: 4.

North, Douglass C. 1981. *Structure and Change in Economic History*. New York: W. W. Norton.

———. 1990. "*Institutions, Institutional Change and Economic Performance*." In *The Political Economy of Institutions and Decisions*, edited by James Alt and Douglass North. Cambridge: Cambridge University Press.

Oberman, Jan. 1991. "Two Landmark Bills on Privatization Approved." *Report on East Europe* (March 15): 12–15.

O'Donnell, Guillermo. 1994. "Delegative Democracy." *Journal of Democracy* 5, no. 1: 55–69.

Orenstein, Mitchell. 1996. "Out of the Red: Building Capitalism and Democracy in Post-Communist Europe." PhD diss., Department of Political Science, Yale University.

———. 2001. *Out of the Red: Building Capitalism and Democracy in Post-Communist Europe.* Ann Arbor: University of Michigan Press.

Ost, David, and Marc Weinstein. 1999. "Unionists against Unions: Toward Hierarchical Management in Post-Communist Poland." *East European Politics and Societies* 13, no. 1: 1–33.

Palouš, Martin. 1997. "Projevy 'českého syndromu'." *Lidové noviny* (November 26): 17.

Páral, Pavel. 1990. "Kosmetické úpravy nestačí." *Rudé právo* (February 8): 7.

Pierson, Paul. 2000. "Increasing Returns, Path Dependence, and the Study of Politics." *American Political Science Review* 94, no. 2: 251.

Pistor, Katharina, and Andrew Spicer. 1996. "Investment Funds in Mass Privatization and Beyond: Evidence from the Czech Republic and Russia." Harvard Institute for International Development Discussion Paper #565.

PlanEcon Report. 1992–1993. "Results of Czechoslovak Voucher Privatization: World's Largest 1991 IPO Successfully Completed." Part I Nos. 50, 51, 52, December 31, 1992 (delayed release on January 25, 1993); Part II Nos. 3, 4, February 16, 1993.

Pleskot, Igor. 1990. Speech presented at the International Labour Conference, Geneva, June.

———. 1994. "Czech and Slovak Trade Union Movement in the Period of Transformation to a Civil Democratic Society." Czech-Moravian Chamber of Trade Unions.

Pohl, Gerald, Robert F. Anderson, Stijn Claessens, and Simeon Djankov. 1997. "Privatization and Restructuring in Central and Eastern Europe." Technical Paper No. 368: World Bank.

Polanyi, Karl. 1944. *The Great Transformation.* Boston: Beacon Press.

Prism. 1992. *Private Privatization: The Czech Experience.* Interview with Minister of Industry Jan Vrba. Arthur D. Little: 50–59.

Prizel, Ilya. 2002. "Ukraine's Hollow Decade." *East European Politics and Societies* 16, no. 2: 363–385.

Průcha, Václav. 1995. "Economic Development and Relations, 1918–89." In *The End of Czechoslovakia,* edited by Jiří Musil, 40–76. Budapest: Central European University Press.

Przeworski, Adam. 1991. *Democracy and the Market.* Cambridge: Cambridge University Press.

Racz, Barnabas. 2003. "The Left in Hungary and the 2002 Parliamentary Elections." *Europe-Asia Studies* 55, no. 5: 747–769.

Rak, Vladimír. 1992. "Kandidáti do parlamentních voleb v Československu v červnu 1990." *Sociologický časopis* 28, no. 2: 200–221.

Reed, Quentin. 1996. "Political Corruption, Privatisation and Control in the Czech Republic: A Case Study of Problems in Multiple Transition." PhD diss., Oriel College (Oxford).

Reschová, Jana. 1992. "Nová politika s novýmí l'ud'mi." *Sociologický časopis* 28: 222–236 (in Slovak).

Riordan, William L. 1963. *Plunkitt of Tammany Hall.* Toronto: Clarke and Irwin.

Roe, Mark J. 1994. *Strong Managers, Weak Owners: The Political Roots of American Corporate Finance.* Princeton, NJ: Princeton University Press.

Roland, Gerard. 2000. *Transition and Economics: Politics, Markets, and Firms.* Cambridge, MA: MIT Press.

Rona-Tas, Akos. 1997. "The Czech Third Wave: Privatization and the New Role of the State in the Czech Republic." *Problems of Post-Communism* 44, no. 6: 53–62.

Rondinelli, Dennis A., and Jay Yurkiewicz. 1996. "Privatization and Economic Restructuring in Poland: An Assessment of Transition Policies." *American Journal of Economics and Sociology* 55, no. 2: 145–161.

Rupnik, Jacques. 1989. *The Other Europe.* New York: Pantheon Books.

Rutland, Peter. 1993. "Workers' Responses to the Market Transition." Middletown, CT: Wesleyan University. Mimeo.

Rychetský, Pavel. 1993. "Zákony pro Fond národního majetku neplatí?" *Lidové noviny* (October 22).

Sabel, Charles F. 1982. *Work and Politics: The Division of Labor in Industry.* Cambridge: Cambridge University Press.

Sabela, Radomir, Terézia Hrnčiřová, and Josef Vais. 1995. "Proces privatizace v oblasti průmyslu a obchodu ČR." Prague: Charles University.

Sachs, Jeffrey. 1990a. "Accelerating Privatization in Eastern Europe: The Case of Poland." World Bank annual conference on Development Economics, April 25–26.

———. 1990b. "What Is to Be Done?" *Economist* (January 19): 61.

———. 1993. *Poland's Jump to the Market Economy.* Cambridge, MA: MIT Press.

Scénář ekonomické reformy (Scenario of Economic Reform). 1990. Prague.

Schumpeter, Joseph. 1942/1975. *Capitalism, Socialism, and Democracy.* New York: Harper & Row.

Schwartz, Andrew. 1997. "The Czech Approach to Residual Share Management." In *Between State and Market: Mass Privatization in Transition Economies*, edited by Ira W. Lieberman, Stilpon S. Nestor, and Raj. M. Desai, 70–79. Washington, DC: World Bank.

Schwartz, Andrew, and Stephan Haggard. 1997. "Privatization, Foreign Direct Investment, and the Possibility of Cross-National Production Networks in Europe." Paper prepared for the conference "Will There Be a Unified European Economy? International Production Networks, Foreign Direct Investment, and Trade in Eastern Europe," Vienna, June 5–6.

Shefter, Martin. 1977. "Patronage and Its Opponents: A Theory and Some European Cases." Western Societies Program Occasional Papers, no. 8: Center for International Studies. Ithaca, NY: Cornell.

Shleifer, Andrei, and Daniel Treisman. 2000. *Without a Map: Political Tactics and Economic Reform in Russia.* Cambridge, MA: MIT Press.

———. 2003. Russia: A Normal Country? National Bureau of Economic Research Working Paper 10057.

Shleifer, Andrei, and Robert W. Vishny. 1998. *The Grabbing Hand: Government Pathologies and Their Cures.* Cambridge, MA: Harvard University Press.

Shonfield, Andrew. 1969. *Modern Capitalism: The Changing Balance of Public and Private Power.* London: University of Oxford Press.

Silberman, Bernard S. 1993. *Cages of Reason: The Rise of the Rational State in France, Japan, the United States, and Great Britain.* Chicago: University of Chicago Press.

Simon, Herbert. 1991. "Organizations and Markets." *Journal of Economic Perspectives* 5, no. 2 (spring): 42.

Simonetti, Marko. 1993. "A Comparative Review of Privatization Strategies in Four Former Socialist Countries." *Europe-Asia Studies* 45, no. 1: 79–102.

Simonian, Aram. 1992. "Jak se stát ministrem." *Ekonom* 12: 29–32.

Siváková, Danica. 1992. "Slovenská národná rada." *Sociologický časopis* 28: 247–263.

Slay, Ben. 1993. "The Dilemmas of Economic Liberalism in Poland." *Europe-Asia Studies* 45, no. 2: 237–257.

———. 2000. "The Polish Economic Transition: Outcome and Lessons." *Communist and Post-Communist Studies* 33: 49–70.

Spencer, Peter D. 2000. *The Structure and Regulation of Financial Markets.* Oxford: Oxford University Press.

Spicer, Andrew, Gerald A. McDermott, and Bruce Kogut. 2000. "Entrepreneurship and Privatization in Central Europe: The Tenuous Balance between Destruction and Creation." *Academy of Management Review* 25, no. 3.

Stark, David. 1992. "Path Dependency and Privatization Strategies in East-Central Europe." *East European Politics and Societies* 6, no. 1: 17–51.

———. 1996. "Recombinant Property in East European Capitalism." *American Journal of Sociology* 101, no. 4: 993–1027.

Stark, David, and László Bruszt. 1998. *Postsocialist Pathways: Transforming Politics and Property in East Central Europe.* Cambridge: Cambridge University Press.

Stiglitz, Joseph E. 1994. *Whither Socialism.* Cambridge, MA: MIT Press.

———. 1999. *Whither Reform? Ten Years of the Transition.* Paper prepared for the annual Bank Conference on Development Economics, Washington, DC, April 28–30.

———. 2002. *Globalization and Its Discontents.* New York: W. W. Norton.

Syllová, Jindřiška. 1992. "Česká národní rada v roce 1990." *Sociologický časopis* 28: 237–246.

Szacki, Jerzy. 1994. *Liberalism after Communism.* Trans. by Chester A. Kisiel. Budapest: Central European University Press.

Szirmai, Emil. 1993. "Neviditelní ruka ekonomických informací." *Respekt* 33.

Šafařík, Josef. 1992. *Cestou & poslednímu*. Brno, Czech Republic: Atlantis.

Šik, Ota. 1991a. "Socialism—Theory and Practice." In *Socialism Today?* edited by Ota Šik, 1–29. New York: St. Martin's Press.

———. 1991b. "O 'třetí cestě' a ekonomické diskusi." *Hospoddářské noviny* (January 24).

Šulc, Zdislav. 1993. "Měla reforma alternativu?" *Listy* 23, no. 5: 33–39.

Švejnar, Jan. 1989. "A Framework for the Economic Transformation of Czechoslovakia." *PlanEcon Report* V, no. 52: 1–18.

———, ed. 1995. *The Czech Republic and Economic Transition in Eastern Europe*. San Diego: Academic Press.

Takla, Lina. 1999. "Privatization: A Comparative Experiment—Poland, the Czech Republic, and Hungary." In *Capital Markets in Central and Eastern Europe*, edited by C. Helmenstein. Northampton, MA: Edward Elgar.

Tocqueville, Alexis de. 1955. *The Old Régime and the French Revolution*. Trans. by Stuart Gilbert. New York: Doubleday.

Transition: The Newsletter about Reforming Economies. 1997. 8, no. 6.

Tříska, Dušan. 1994. "Post-Privatisation Securities Markets in the Czech Republic." Paper presented at the conference Mass Privatisation: A First Assessment of the Results, sponsored by the OECD Advisory Group on Privatisation, Fifth Plenary Session, Paris, March 2–4.

Tucker, Aviezer. 1990. "Havel's Heideggeranism." *Telos* 85 (fall).

Tůma, Oldřich. 1994. *Zítra zase tady!* Prague: Maxdorf.

Tůma, Zdeněk, and Jeffrey E. Dotson. 1995. "Privatization By-products: Firms with Changed Property and Liquidations." In *The Privatization Newsletter of the Czech Republic and Slovakia*, no. 30 (January): 1–3.

UNCTAD. 1996. *World Investment Report 1996: Investment, Trade, and International Policy Arrangements*.

Unger, Roberto Mangabeira. 1976. *Law in Modern Society: Toward a Criticism of Social Theory*. New York: Free Press.

Valeš, Václav, Petr Pithart, and Milan Číč. 1990. "Zajištění strategie deetatizace a privatizace národního jmění." Proposal presented to Úřad předsednictva vlády ČSFR, no. 4 388/90-12, April.

Vanek, Jaroslav. 1990. "Beware of the Yeast of the Pharisees." *Economic Analysis and Workers' Management* 24, no. 1: 113–124.

Vaněk, Miroslav. 1994. *Veřejné mínění o socialismu před 17. Listopadem 1989*. Prague: Maxdorf.

Vejvodová, Anna. 1990. "Je těžké být odborářem." *Rudé právo* (May 6).

Vickers, John, and George Yarrow. 1988. *Privatization: An Economic Analysis*. Cambridge, MA: MIT Press.

Vogel, Steven. 1996. *Freer Markets, More Rules: Regulatory Reform in Advanced Industrial Societies*. Ithaca, NY: Cornell University Press.

Volkov, Vadim. 2002. *Violent Entrepreneurs: The Use of Force in the Making of Russian Capitalism*. Ithaca, NY: Cornell University Press.

Voszka, Eva. 1999. "Privatization in Hungary: Results and Open Issues." *Center for International Private Enterprise*, Economic Reform Today (CIPE) no. 2, at www.cipe.org/publications/fs/ert/e32/e32_5.pdf.

Weber, Max. 1978. *Economy and Society: An Outline of Interpretive Sociology.* Edited by Guenther Roth and Claus Wittich. Berkeley: University of California Press.

Weiss, Andrew, and Georgiy Nikitin. 1997. *Performance of Czech Companies by Ownership Structure.* Boston: Boston University.

Wheaton, Bernard, and Zdeněk Kavan. 1992. *The Velvet Revolution: Czechoslovakia, 1988–1991.* Boulder, CO: Westview Press.

WIIW (Vienna Institute for Comparative Economic Studies). 1997. *WIIW Handbook of Statistics.* Vienna: WIIW.

Wolchik, Sharon. 1991. *Czechoslovakia in Transition: Politics, Economics and Society.* London: Pinter.

Woodruff, David. 1999. *Money Unmade: Barter and the Fate of Russian Capitalism.* Ithaca, NY: Cornell University Press.

World Bank. 1996. *World Development Report 1996: From Plan to Market.* New York: Oxford University Press.

———. 1997. *World Development Report 1997: The State in a Changing World.* New York: Oxford University Press.

———. 2002a. *World Development Report 2002: Building Institutions for Markets.* New York: Oxford University Press.

———. 2002b. *Transition: The First Ten Years.* Washington, DC: World Bank.

Zagrodzka, Danuta. 1993. "Jak to lie robi w Pradze." *Gazeta Wyborcza* (June 19–20): 4–5.

Zemplínerová, Alena. Forthcoming. "Die Rolle der auslaendischen Direktinvestitionen in Restrukturierungsprocess der tschechischen Wirtschaft." *Leipziger Beitraege zu Wirtschaft und Gesellschaft.* Leipzig: Band 8.

Zemplínerová, Alena, and V. Benáček. 1997. *Foreign Direct Investment in the Czech Republic—Environment, Structure, and Efficiency in the Manufacturing Sector.* Prague. Mimeo.

Zemplínerová, Alena, and Radek Laštovička. 1997. "Enterprises Restructuring during and after Privatization." In *The Privatization Process in East-Central Europe: Evolutionary Process of Czech Privatization,* edited by Michal Mejstřík, 203–214. Dordrecht: Kluwer Academic.

Zemplínerová, Alena, and Josef Stíbal. 1997. "Monopoly in the Context of the Privatization Process." In *The Privatization Process in East-Central Europe: Evolutionary Process of Czech Privatization,* edited by Michal Mejstřík, 226–238. Dordrecht: Kluwer Academic.

Zieleniec, Jósef (a kolektiv). 1990. *Československo na rozcestí.* Vol. 1 (svazek edice Archy). Prague: *Lidové noviny.*

Zysman, John, and Andrew Schwartz, eds. 1998a. *Enlarging Europe: The Industrial Foundation for a New Political Reality.* Berkeley: University of California, Berkeley.

Zysman, John, and Andrew Schwartz. 1998b. "Reunifying Europe in an Emerging World Economy: Economic Heterogeneity, New Industrial Options, and Political Choices." *Journal of Common Market Studies* 36, no. 3 (September): 405–429.
Žák, Václav. 1997. "Křižovatky privatizace." *Listy* 27, no. 3: 15–22.

OTHER REFERENCED ARTICLES

"Business Will Have a Big Voice in Duma." *Moscow Times*, November 13, 2003.
"East Europe for Sale." *Economist*, April 14–20, 1990.
"Kde drhne reforma?" *Svobodné slovo*, August 24, 1990.
"Majetku bude dost." *Hospodářské noviny*, September 24, 1991: 12.
"Počítače, peníze i know-how." *Hospodářské noviny*, November 10, 1992: 1, 3.
"Představuje Svaz průmyslu skutečně průmysl?" *Hospodářské noviny*, September 24, 1991: 18.
"Soukromníci chtějí do velké privatizace." *Rudé právo*, 1991: 1–2.
"Umění být v popředí a zároveň v ústraní." *Respekt*, 1993: 8–9.
"Vyšetřovatelé odhalili peněžní kanál Švýcarsko-ODS." *Lidové noviny*, June 10, 1998: 1.
"Ze zákulisí privatizace." *Respekt* 11/39, no. 7 (1991): 6.

PERIODICALS, NEWSPAPERS, AND OTHER NEWS SOURCES

Czech:
Český deník (became *Český týdeník* January 1995) *(ČD)*
ČTK (Czech News Agency)
Ekonomické očekavaní
Hospodářské noviny (*HN*)
Lidové noviny (*LN*)
Mladá fronta dnes (*MFD*)
Mladý svět
Práce
Prague Business Weekly
Prague Post
Privatization Newsletter of Czechoslovakia (later *Privatization Newsletter of the Czech Republic and Slovakia*)
Přitomnost
Respekt
Rudé právo (renamed *Právo* in October 1995) *(RP)*
STEM (a highly regarded survey research firm in the Czech Republic, Jan Hartl, director)

Svobodné slovo (SS)
Trendy
Týden

Foreign:
Business Eastern Europe
Business Wire
Economist (Great Britain)
Financial Times (Great Britain)
Gazeta Wyborcza (Poland)
Moscow Times (Russia)
New York Times (United States)

Index

About the Authors

Andrew Harrison Schwartz (1957–2004) was research associate at the Berkeley Roundtable on the International Economy (BRIE).

John Zysman is codirector of the Berkeley Roundtable on the International Economy (BRIE).